One of the times I'm glad I'm all grown up is when I sneak out for that cup of coffee. Maybe it tastes better because I'm sneaking, but in that moment, I feel truly alive. ...I think I'm getting old. Heh.

– Yoshiyuki Nishi

Yoshiyuki Nishi was born in Tokyo. Two of his favorite manga series are *Dragon Ball* and the robot-cat comedy *Doraemon*. His latest series, *Muhyo & Roji's Bureau of Supernatural Investigat*ion, debuted in Japan's *Akamaru Jump* magazine in 2004 and went on to be serialized in *Weekly Shonen Jump*.

MUHYO & ROJI'S
BUREAU OF SUPERNATURAL INVESTIGATION

VOL. 5
The SHONEN JUMP Manga Edition

STORY AND ART BY
YOSHIYUKI NISHI

Translation & Adaptation/Alexander O. Smith
Touch-up Art & Lettering/Brian Bilter
Design/Izumi Hirayama
Editor/Amy Yu

Editor in Chief, Books/Alvin Lu
Editor in Chief, Magazines/Marc Weidenbaum
VP of Publishing Licensing/Rika Inouye
VP of Sales/Gonzalo Ferreyra
Sr. VP of Marketing/Liza Coppola
Publisher/Hyoe Narita

Printed in the U.S.A.

Published by VIZ Media, LLC
P.O. Box 77010
San Francisco, CA 94107

SHONEN JUMP Manga Edition
10 9 8 7 6 5 4 3 2 1
First printing, June 2008

www.viz.com

SHONEN JUMP MANGA EDITION

Muhyo & Roji's Bureau of Supernatural Investigation

BSI

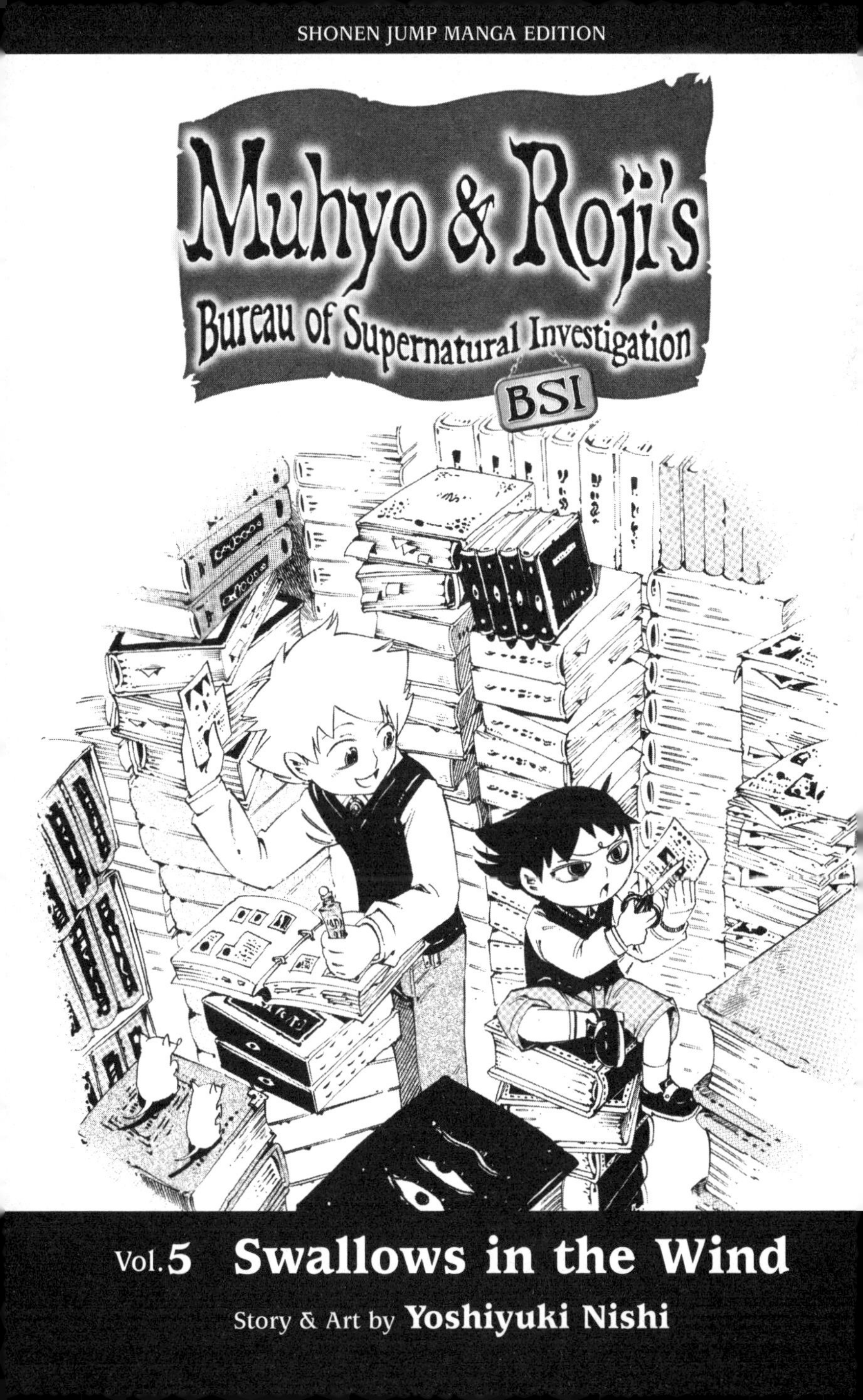

Vol.5 Swallows in the Wind

Story & Art by **Yoshiyuki Nishi**

Dramatis Personae

Toru Muhyo (Muhyo)

Genius elite practitioner of magic law, one of the youngest to achieve the highest rank of "Executor." Always calm and collected (though sometimes considered cold due to his tendency to make harsh comments), Muhyo possesses a strong sense of justice and has even been known to show kindness at times. Sleeps a lot to recover from the exhaustion caused by his practice. Likes: *Jabin* (a manga). Dislikes: interruptions while sleeping.

Jiro Kusano (Roji)

Assistant at Muhyo's office and a "Second Clerk," the lowest of the five ranks of practitioners of magic law. Roji cries easily, is meek and gentle, and has been known to freak out in the presence of spirits. Irritated at his own inability to help Muhyo, Roji has devoted himself to studying magic law. Likes: tea and cakes. Dislikes: scary ghosts and scary Muhyo.

Soratsugu Madoka (Enchu)

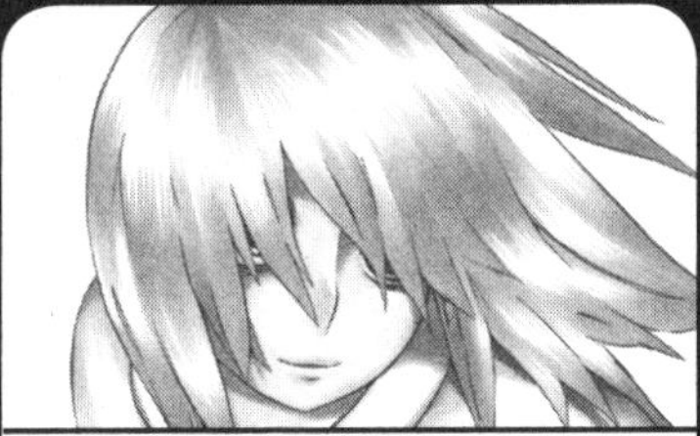

Muhyo's old classmate. Many thought he was destined to become an executor, but one event turned him traitor to the Magic Law Association.

Yoichi Himukai (Yoichi)

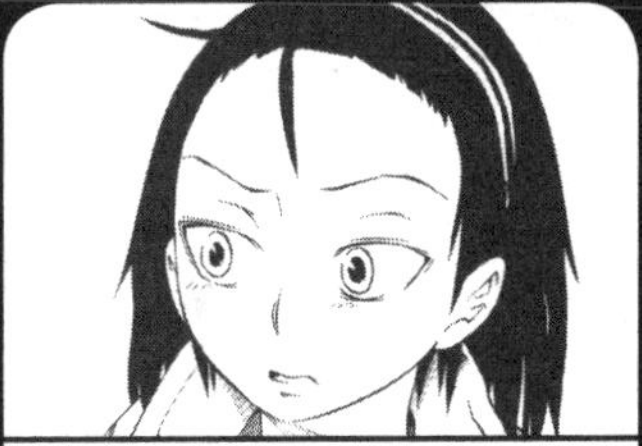

Judge and Muhyo's former classmate. Expert practitioner of all magic law except execution.

The Story

Magic law is a newly established practice for judging and punishing the increasing crimes committed by spirits; those who use it are called "practitioners." Malevolent ghost Face-Ripper Sophie escapes from the bottom-most level of the prison Arcanum but is defeated by Muhyo and friends. All seems well until Biko's beloved teacher Rio suddenly turns against them! The burden of a painful past had grown too heavy, pushing her to become in league with the traitor Enchu. Realizing her imminent betrayal, Yoichi races to warn Muhyo, but it isn't enough to turn the tide. Now Muhyo is exhausted, and the only hope for the gang is Biko's secret elixir…if it works!

Yu Abiko (Biko)

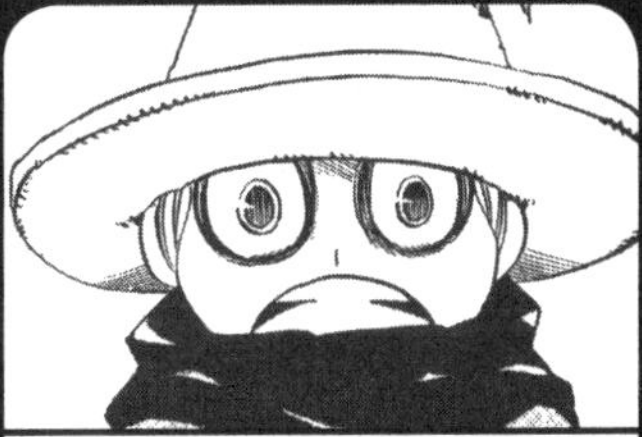

Muhyo's classmate and an artificer. Makes seals, pens, magic law books, and other accoutrements of magic law.

Rio Kurotori (Rio)

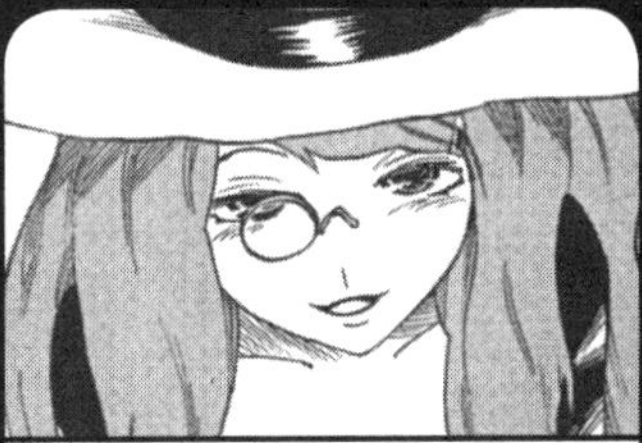

Biko's teacher and a renowned artificer. While artificers can make the tools of the magic law trade, they cannot use them.

Muhyo & Roji's
Bureau of Supernatural Investigation
BSI

CONTENTS

5

ARTICLE 33
ALL OR NOTHING

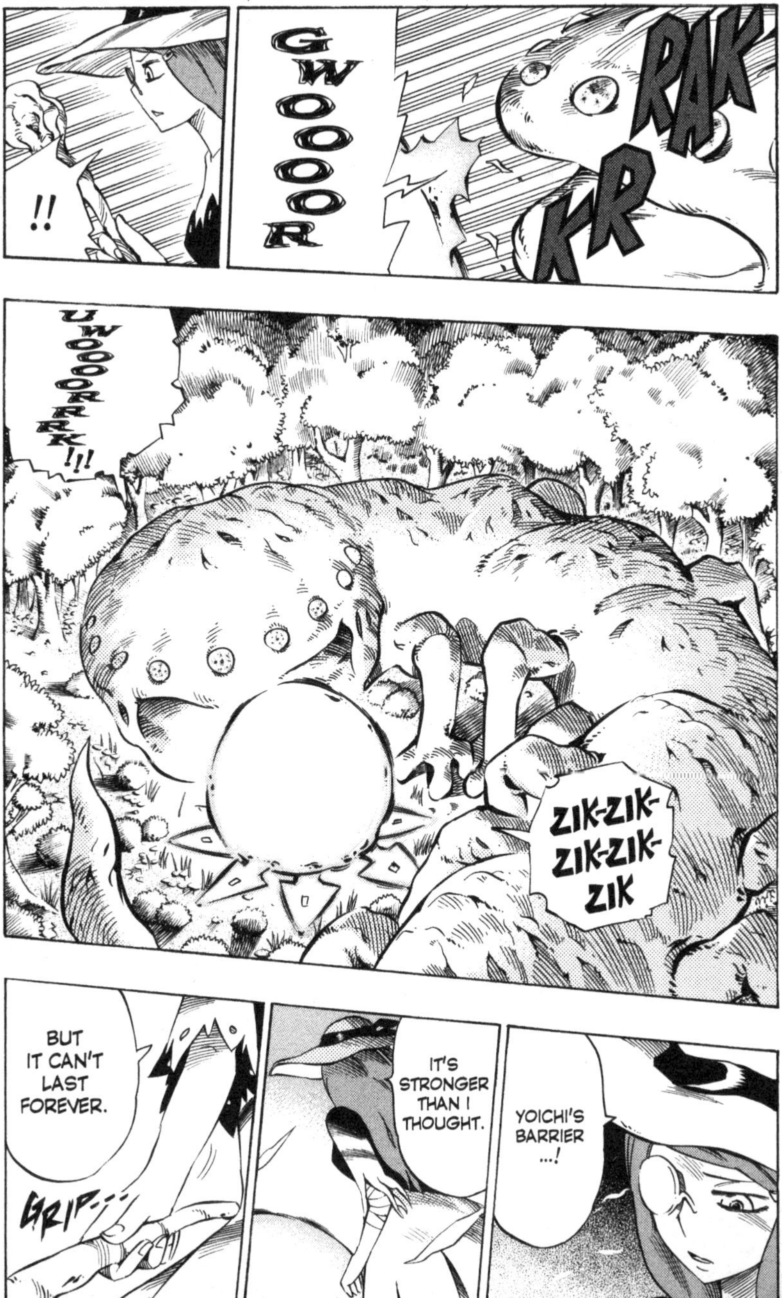
GWOOOOR
KRRAK
!!
UWOOOORRRK!!!
ZIK-ZIK-ZIK-ZIK-ZIK
YOICHI'S BARRIER ...!
IT'S STRONGER THAN I THOUGHT.
BUT IT CAN'T LAST FOREVER.
GRIP...

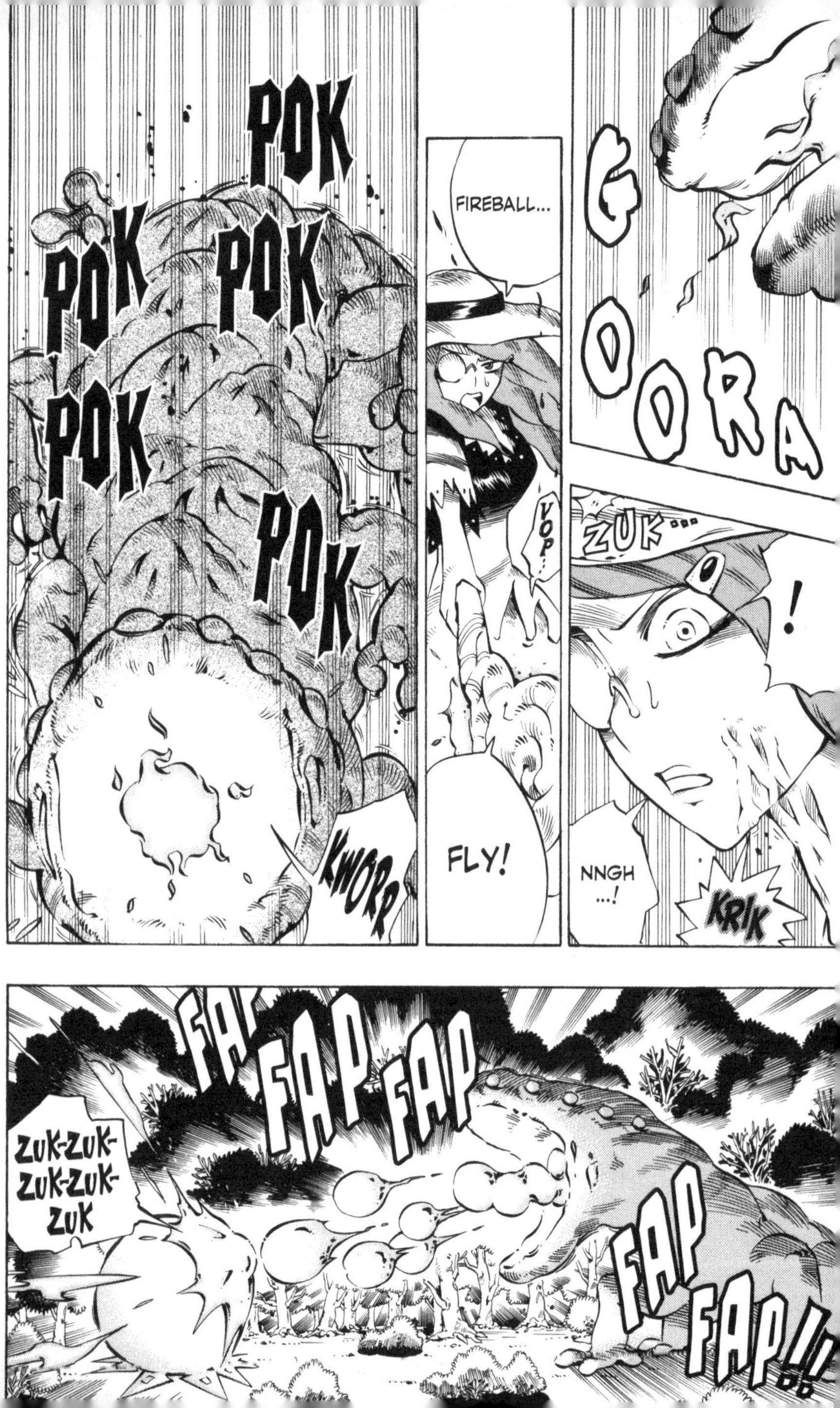
GOORA
ZUK...
!
NNGH ...!
KRIK
FIREBALL...
VOP...
FLY!
POK
POK
POK
POK
POK
KWORR
FAP FAP FAP
FAP FAP!!
ZUK-ZUK-ZUK-ZUK-ZUK

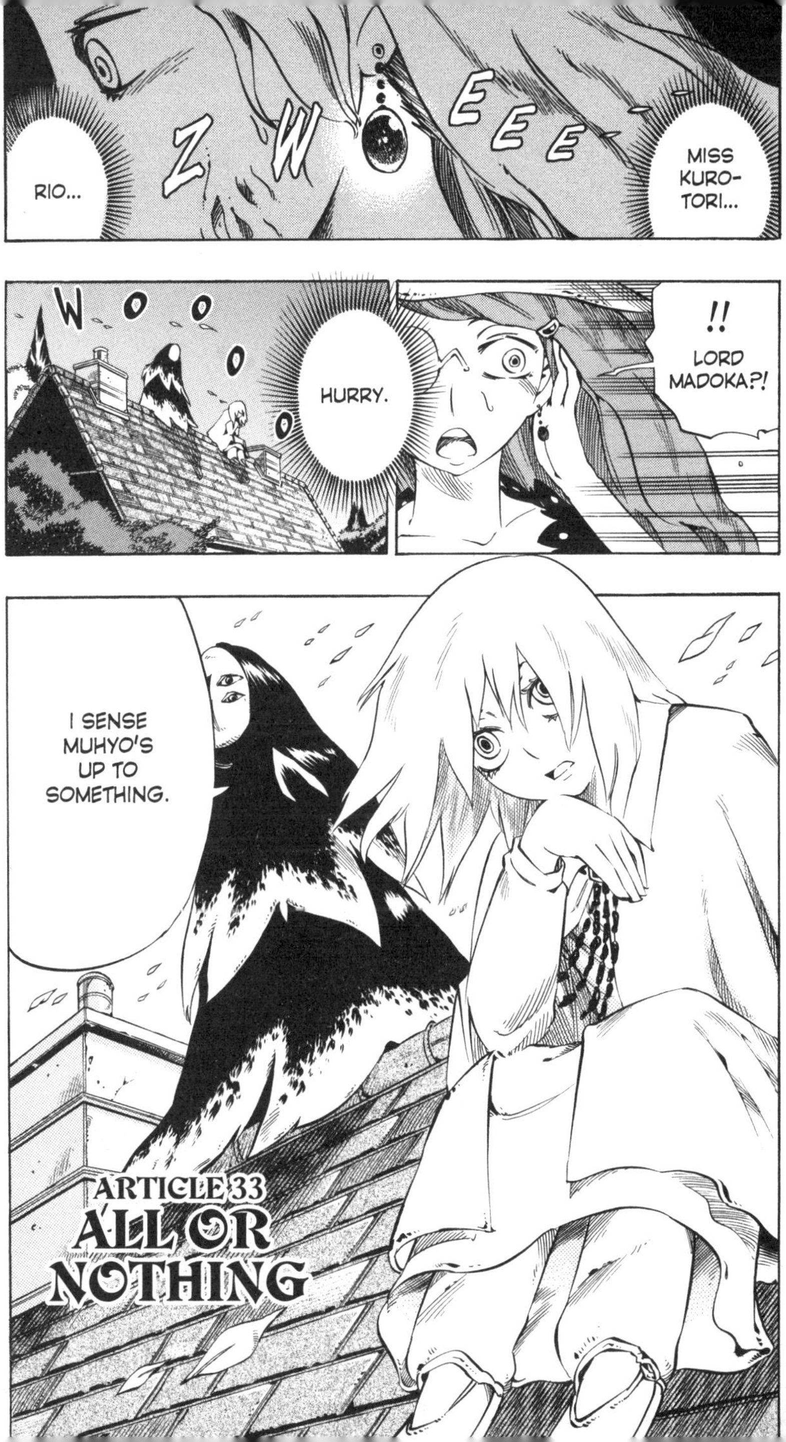
MISS KURO-TORI...
ZWEEEE
RIO...
!!
LORD MADOKA?!
HURRY.
WOOOOO
I SENSE MUHYO'S UP TO SOMETHING.
ARTICLE 33
ALL OR NOTHING

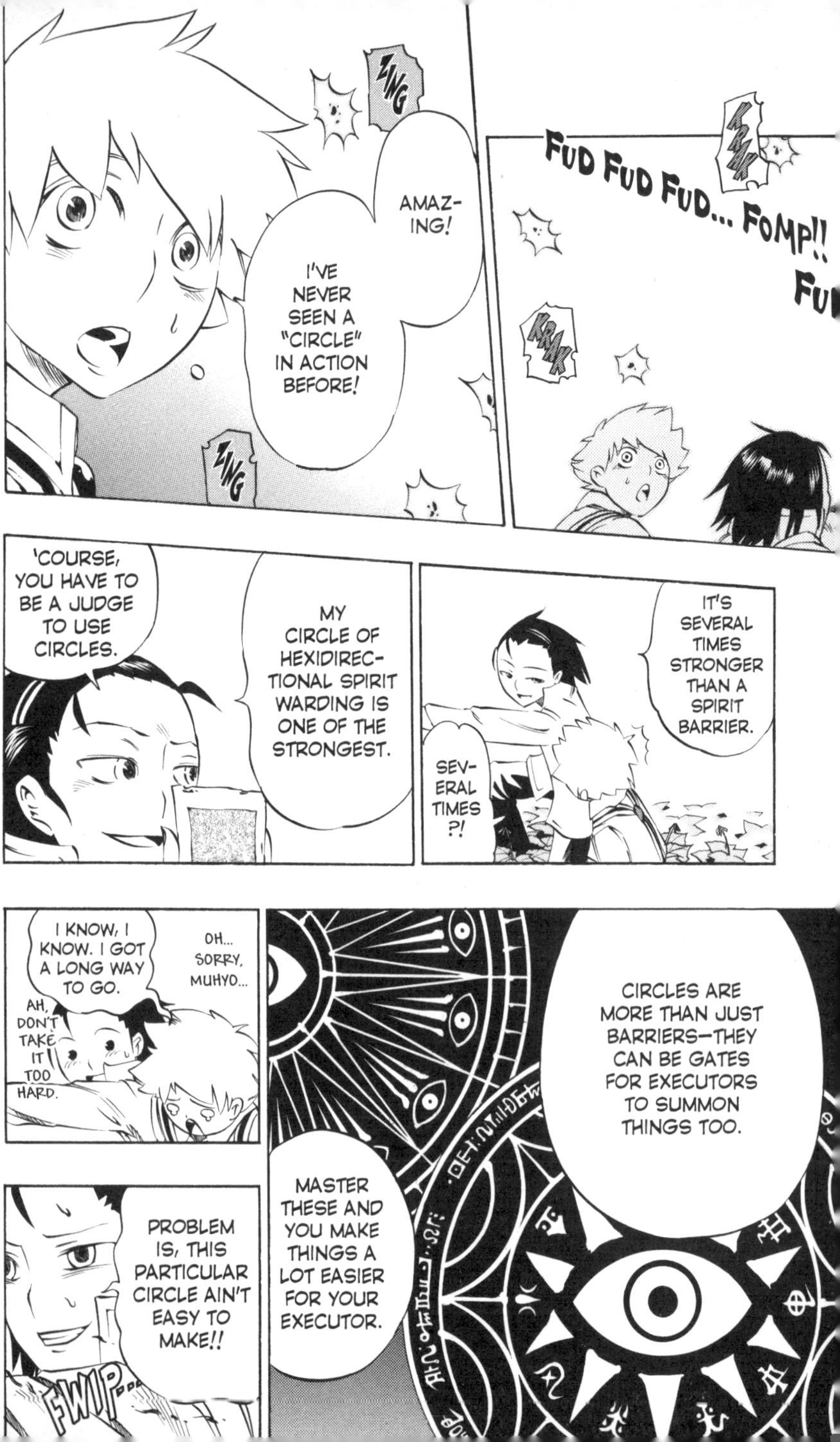
FUD FUD FUD... FOMP!! FU
KRAK
KRAK
ZING
AMAZ-ING!
I'VE NEVER SEEN A "CIRCLE" IN ACTION BEFORE!
ZING
IT'S SEVERAL TIMES STRONGER THAN A SPIRIT BARRIER.
SEV-ERAL TIMES ?!
MY CIRCLE OF HEXIDIREC-TIONAL SPIRIT WARDING IS ONE OF THE STRONGEST.
'COURSE, YOU HAVE TO BE A JUDGE TO USE CIRCLES.
CIRCLES ARE MORE THAN JUST BARRIERS—THEY CAN BE GATES FOR EXECUTORS TO SUMMON THINGS TOO.
MASTER THESE AND YOU MAKE THINGS A LOT EASIER FOR YOUR EXECUTOR.
OH... SORRY, MUHYO...
I KNOW, I KNOW. I GOT A LONG WAY TO GO.
AH, DON'T TAKE IT TOO HARD.
PROBLEM IS, THIS PARTICULAR CIRCLE AIN'T EASY TO MAKE!!
FWIP

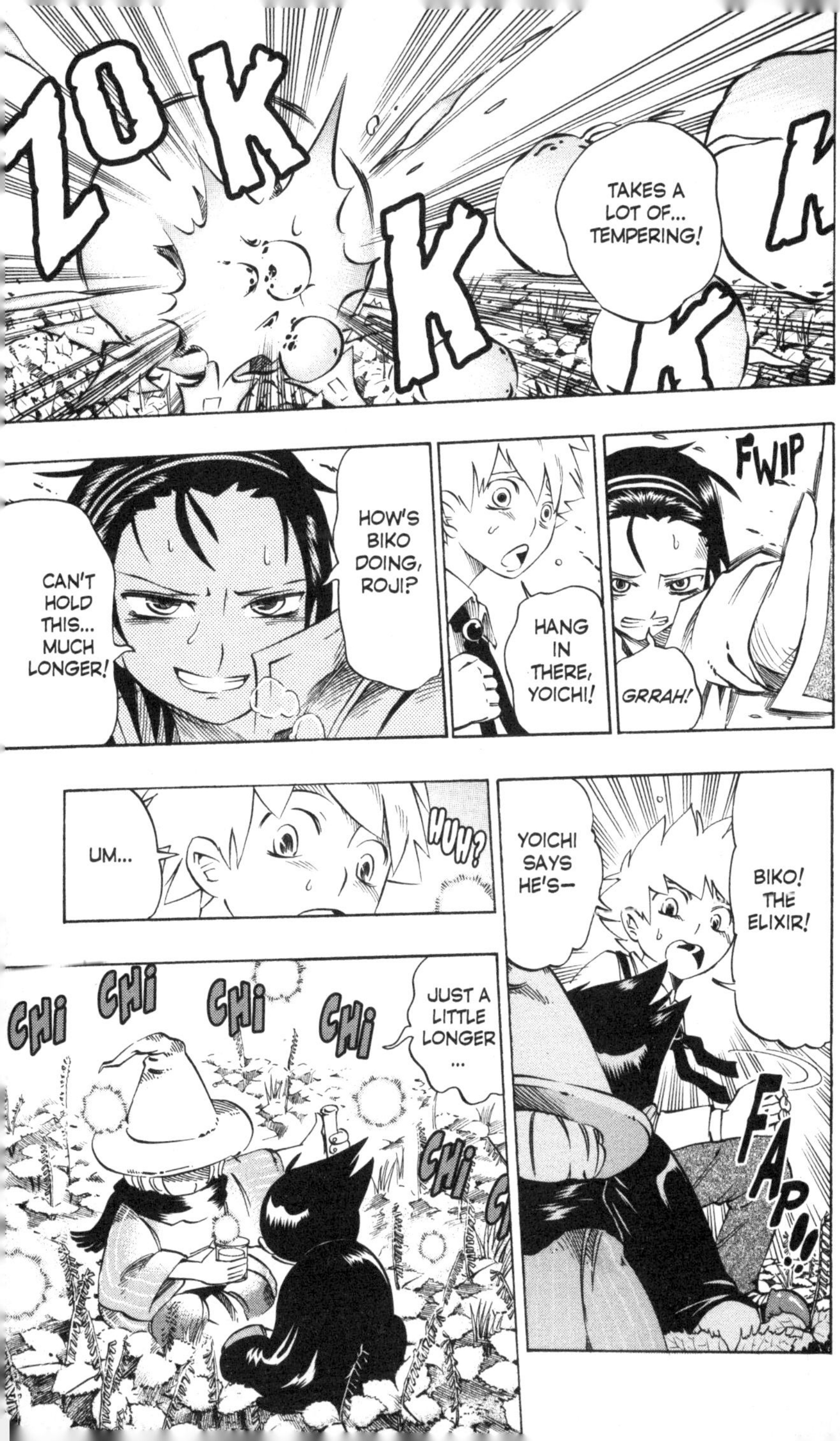
K
TAKES A LOT OF... TEMPERING!
K
ZOK
FWIP
GRRAH!
HANG IN THERE, YOICHI!
HOW'S BIKO DOING, ROJI?
CAN'T HOLD THIS... MUCH LONGER!
BIKO! THE ELIXIR!
YOICHI SAYS HE'S—
FAP!!
HUH?
UM...
JUST A LITTLE LONGER ...
CHI CHI CHI CHI CHI

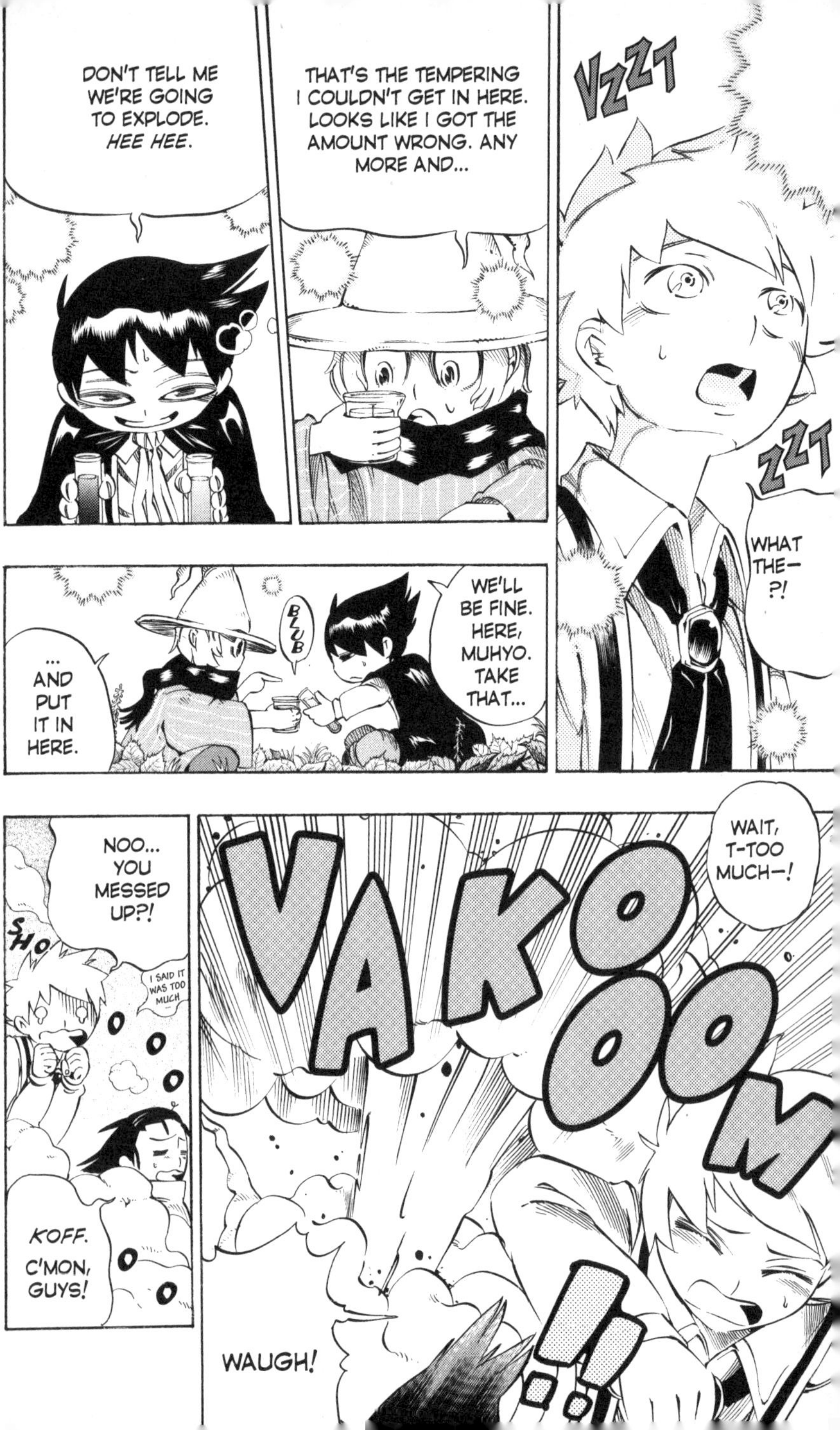
VZZZT
ZZZT
WHAT THE—?!
THAT'S THE TEMPERING I COULDN'T GET IN HERE. LOOKS LIKE I GOT THE AMOUNT WRONG. ANY MORE AND...
DON'T TELL ME WE'RE GOING TO EXPLODE. *HEE HEE*.
WE'LL BE FINE. HERE, MUHYO. TAKE THAT...
BLUB
... AND PUT IT IN HERE.
WAIT, T-TOO MUCH—!
VAKOOOM
!!!
WAUGH!
NOO... YOU MESSED UP?!
SHO
I SAID IT WAS TOO MUCH
KOFF. C'MON, GUYS!

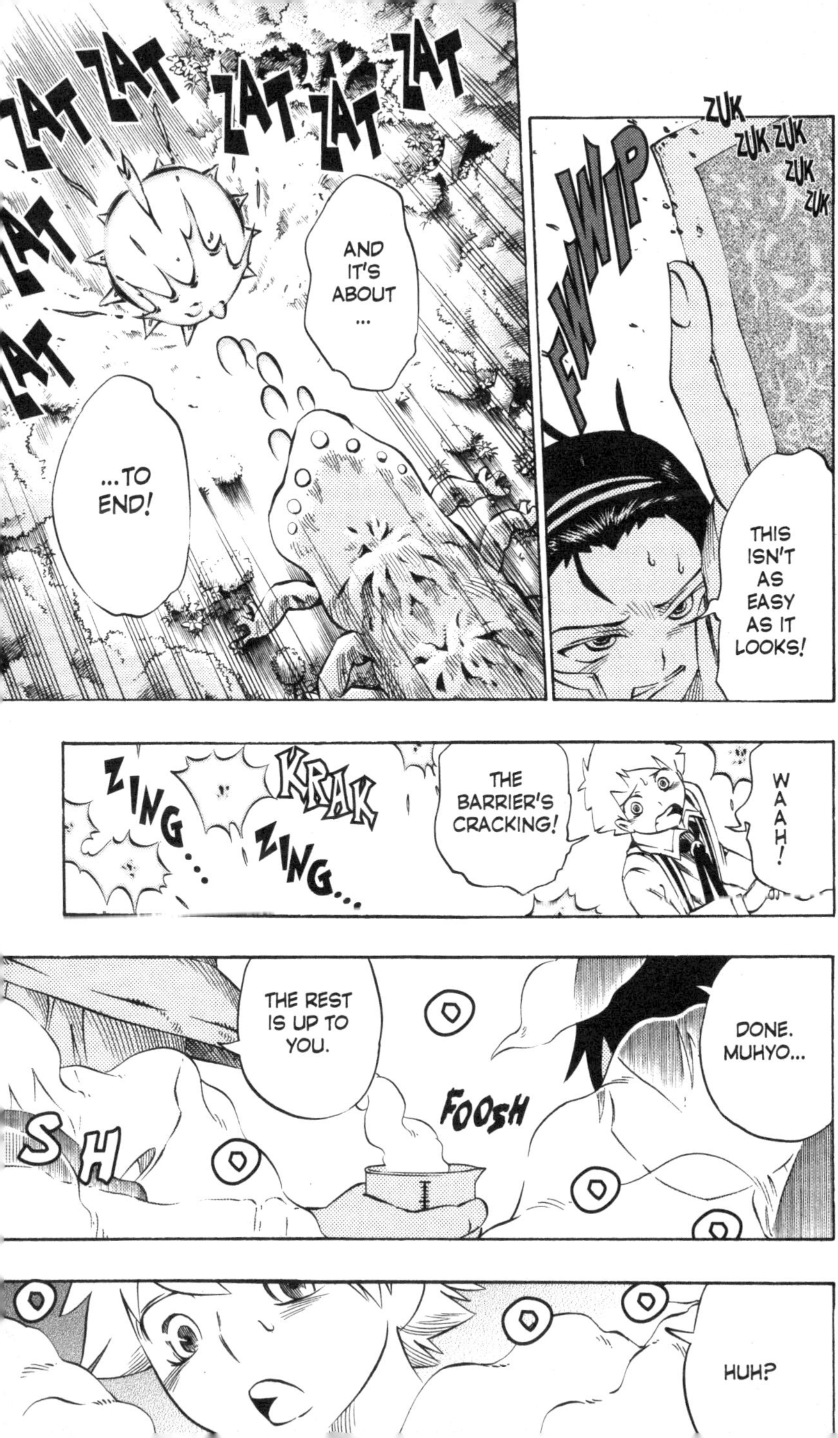

FWWIP
ZUK ZUK ZUK ZUK ZUK
THIS ISN'T AS EASY AS IT LOOKS!
ZAT ZAT ZAT ZAT ZAT ZAT ZAT ZAT
AND IT'S ABOUT ...
...TO END!
WAAAH!
THE BARRIER'S CRACKING!
KRAK
ZING...
ZING...
DONE. MUHYO...
FOOSH
THE REST IS UP TO YOU.
SH
HUH?

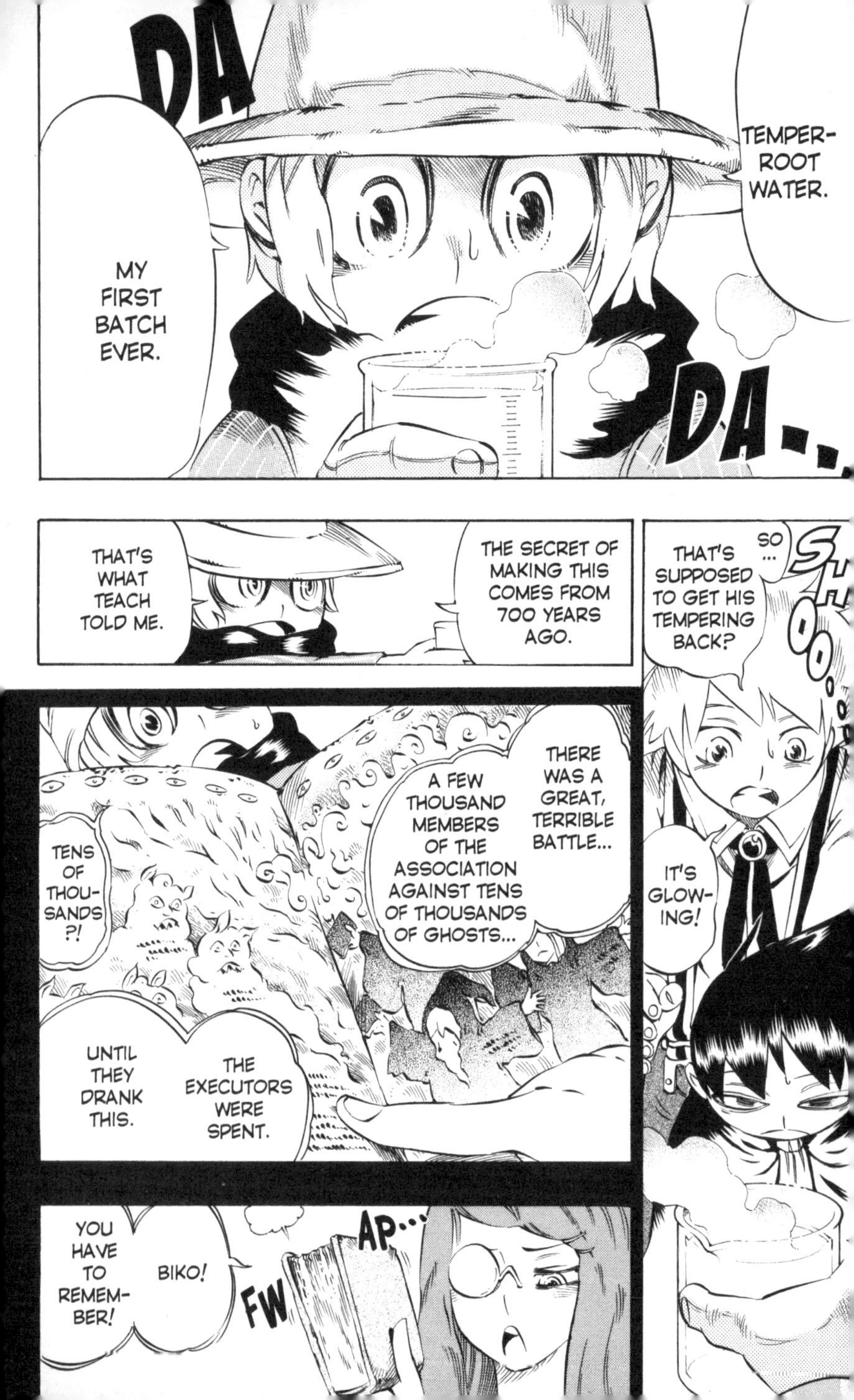
TEMPER-ROOT WATER.
DA
MY FIRST BATCH EVER.
DA...
SO...
SHOOOO...
THAT'S SUPPOSED TO GET HIS TEMPERING BACK?
IT'S GLOWING!
THE SECRET OF MAKING THIS COMES FROM 700 YEARS AGO.
THAT'S WHAT TEACH TOLD ME.
THERE WAS A GREAT, TERRIBLE BATTLE...
A FEW THOUSAND MEMBERS OF THE ASSOCIATION AGAINST TENS OF THOUSANDS OF GHOSTS...
TENS OF THOUSANDS?!
THE EXECUTORS WERE SPENT.
UNTIL THEY DRANK THIS.
BIKO!
AP...
FW
YOU HAVE TO REMEMBER!

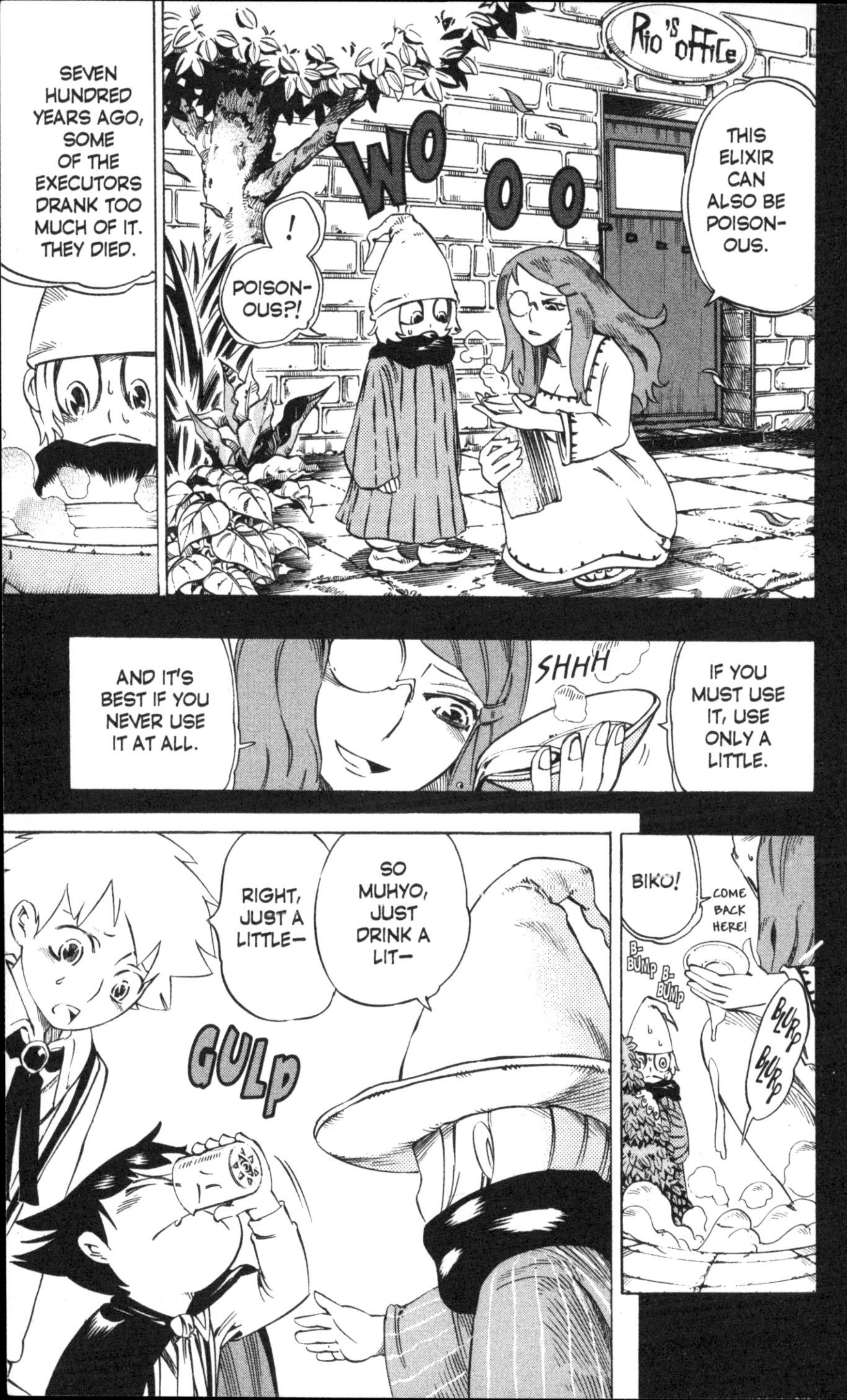
RIO'S OFFICE
THIS ELIXIR CAN ALSO BE POISONOUS.
WOOO
!
POISONOUS?!
SEVEN HUNDRED YEARS AGO, SOME OF THE EXECUTORS DRANK TOO MUCH OF IT. THEY DIED.
IF YOU MUST USE IT, USE ONLY A LITTLE.
SHHH
AND IT'S BEST IF YOU NEVER USE IT AT ALL.
BIKO!
COME BACK HERE!
B-BUMP B-BUMP
BLURP BLURP
SO MUHYO, JUST DRINK A LIT—
RIGHT, JUST A LITTLE—
GULP

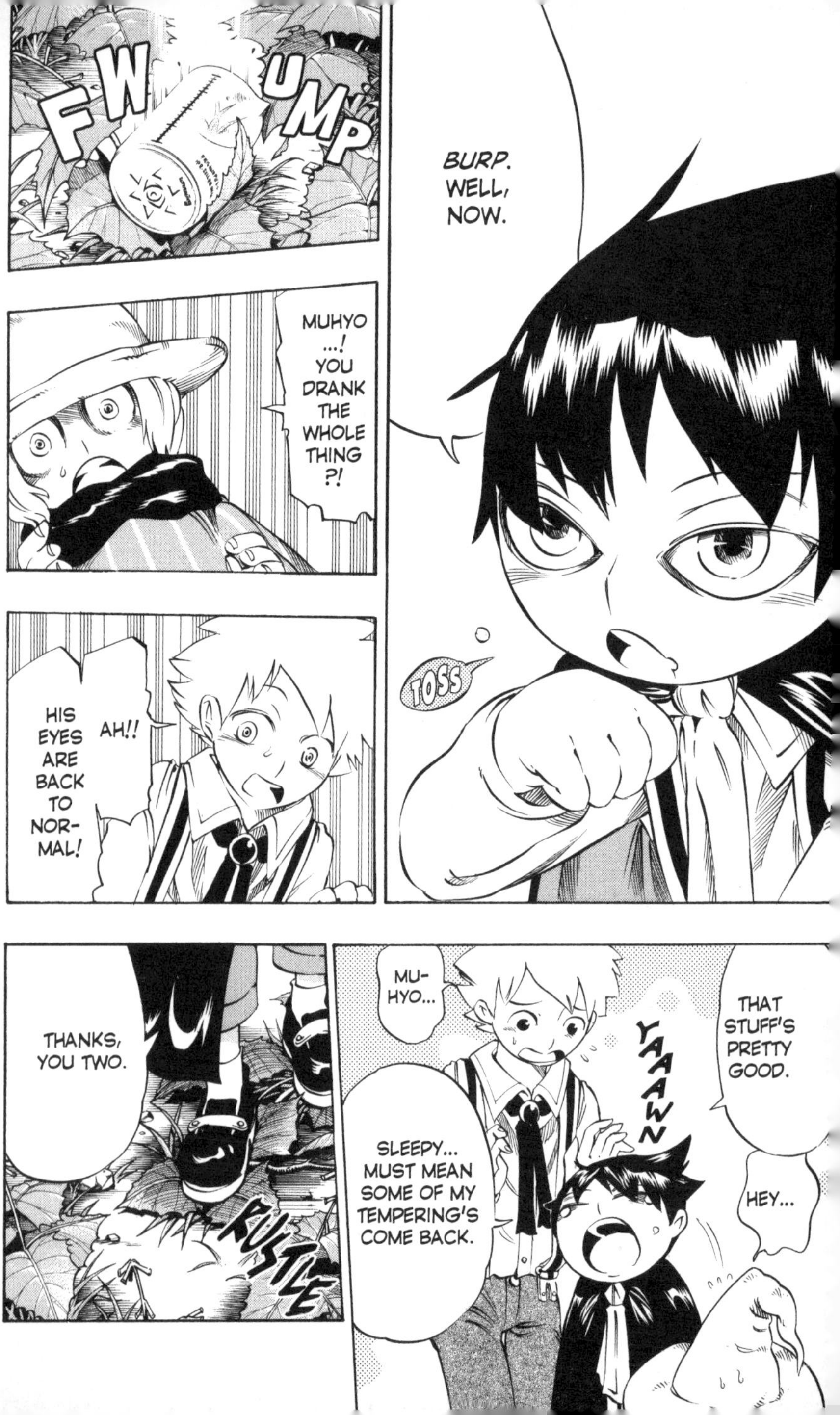
BURP. WELL, NOW.
TOSS
FWUMP
MUHYO...! YOU DRANK THE WHOLE THING?!
AH!!
HIS EYES ARE BACK TO NOR-MAL!
THAT STUFF'S PRETTY GOOD.
HEY...
YAAAWN
MU-HYO...
SLEEPY... MUST MEAN SOME OF MY TEMPERING'S COME BACK.
THANKS, YOU TWO.
RUSTLE

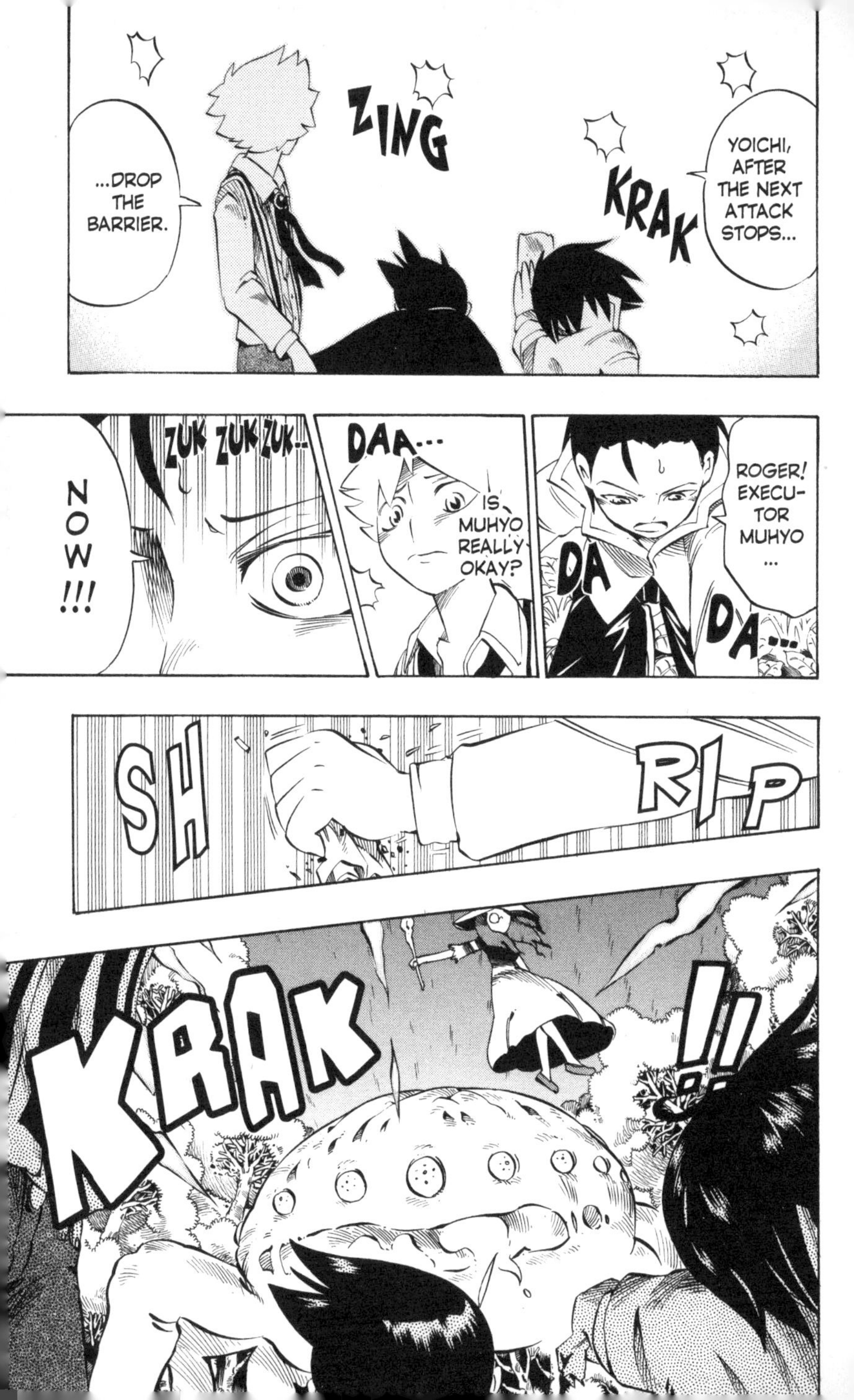
YOICHI, AFTER THE NEXT ATTACK STOPS...
KRAK
ZING
...DROP THE BARRIER.
ROGER! EXECUTOR MUHYO...
DA DA...
DAA...
IS MUHYO REALLY OKAY?
ZUK ZUK ZUK...
NOW!!!
SH RIP
KRAK!!

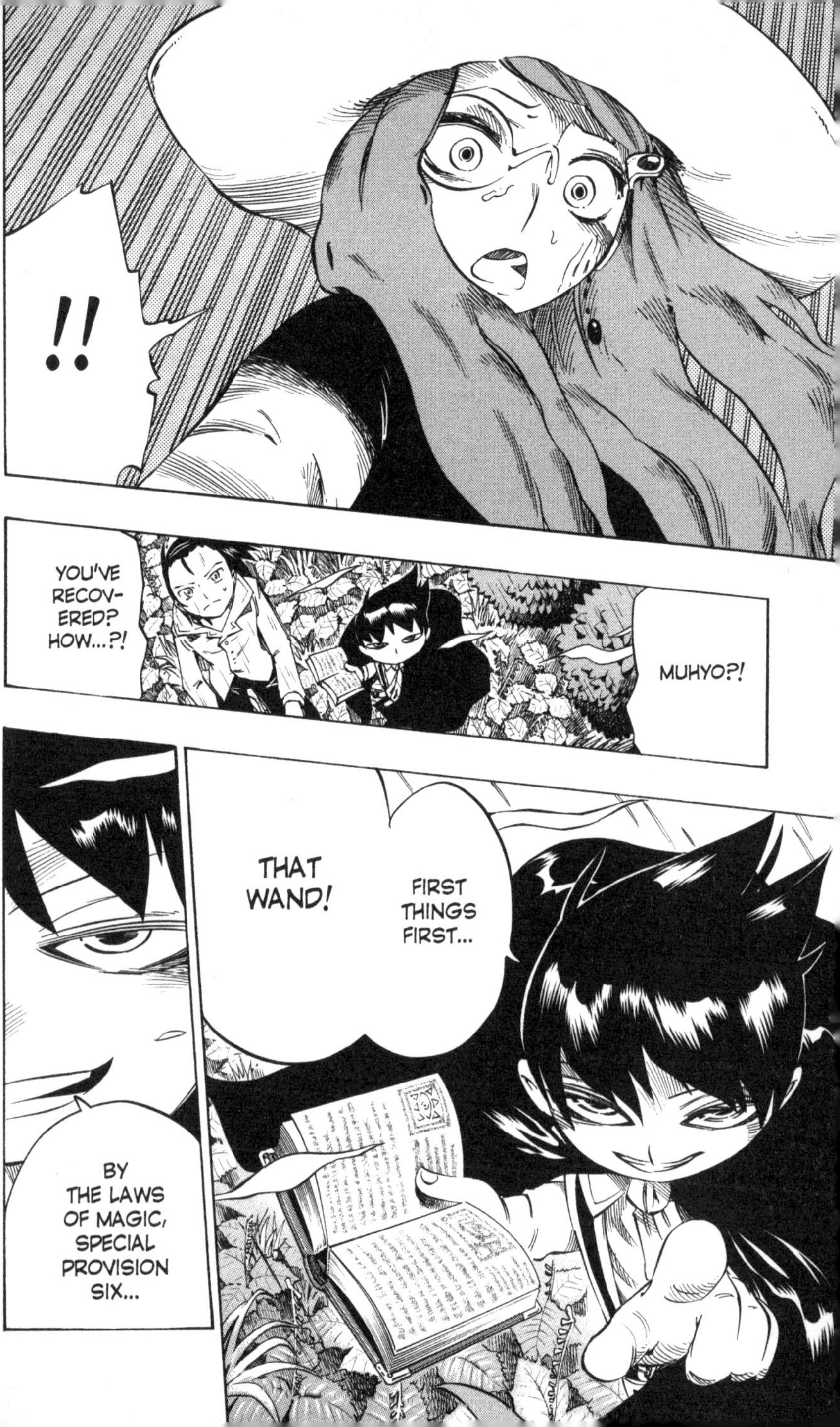
!!
MUHYO?!
YOU'VE RECOVERED? HOW...?!
FIRST THINGS FIRST...
THAT WAND!
BY THE LAWS OF MAGIC, SPECIAL PROVISION SIX...

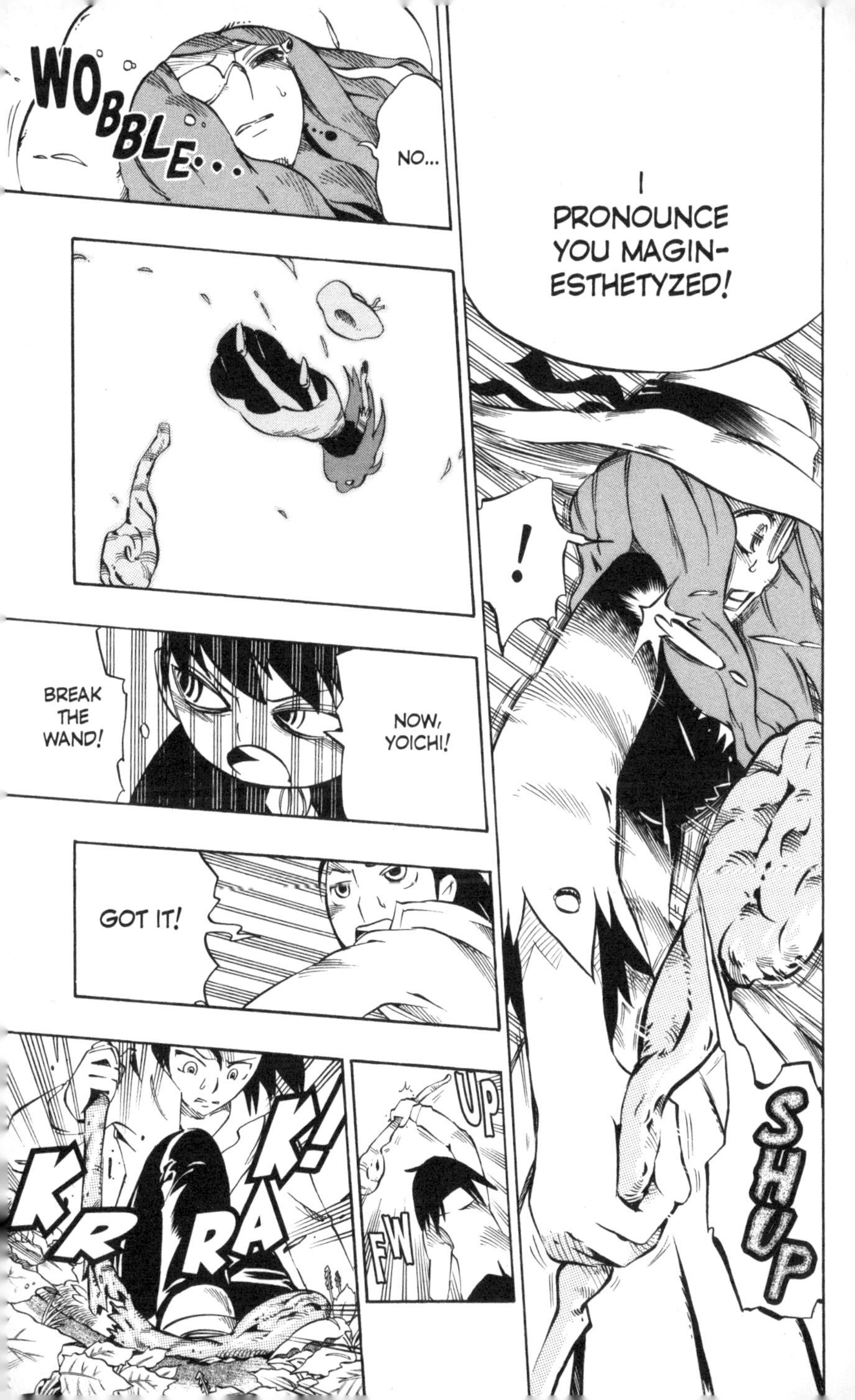

I PRONOUNCE YOU MAGIN-ESTHETYZED!
!
SHUP
NO...
WOBBLE...
NOW, YOICHI!
BREAK THE WAND!
GOT IT!
UP
FW
KRRAK!

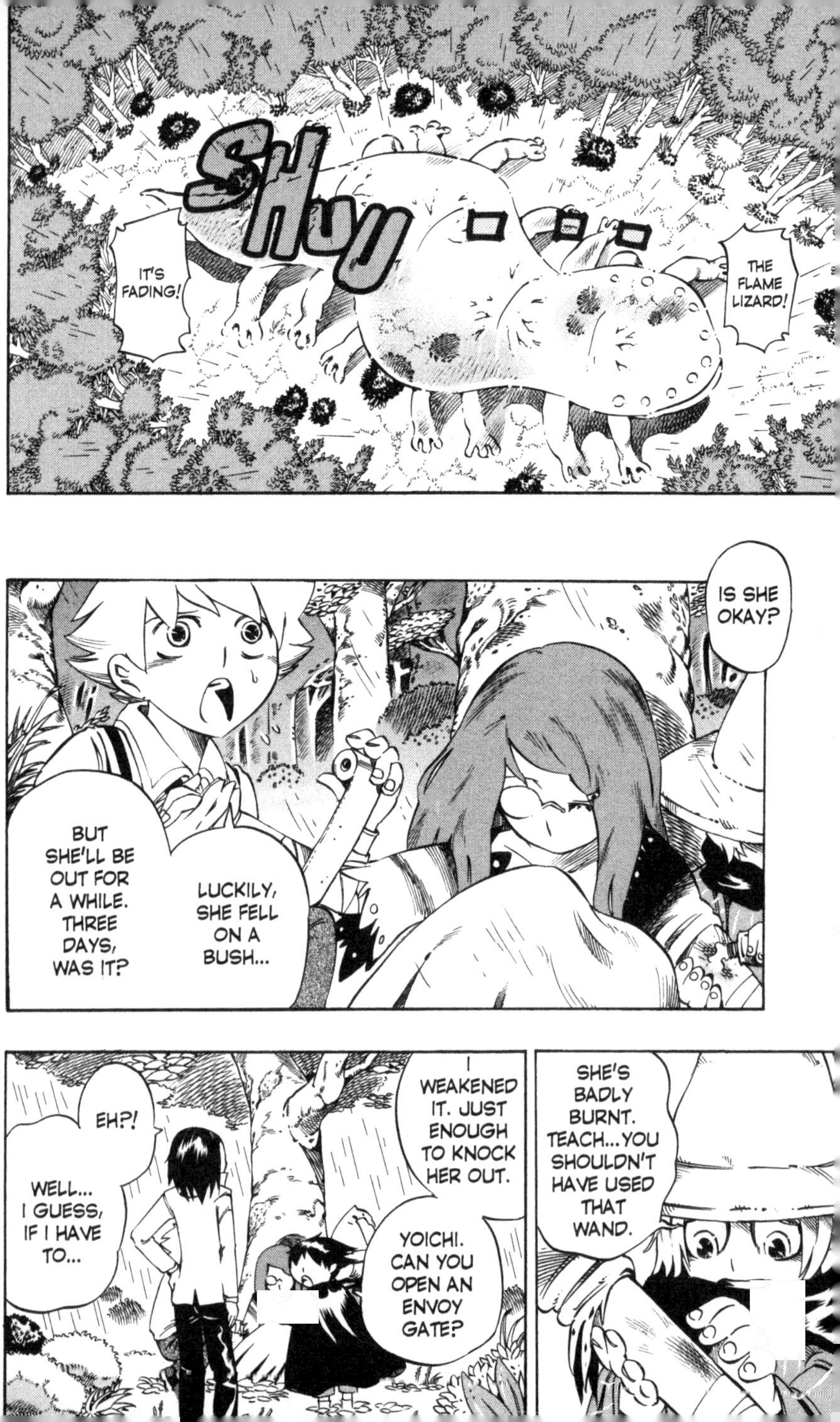
SHUU
THE FLAME LIZARD!
IT'S FADING!
IS SHE OKAY?
LUCKILY, SHE FELL ON A BUSH...
BUT SHE'LL BE OUT FOR A WHILE. THREE DAYS, WAS IT?
SHE'S BADLY BURNT. TEACH...YOU SHOULDN'T HAVE USED THAT WAND.
I WEAKENED IT. JUST ENOUGH TO KNOCK HER OUT.
YOICHI. CAN YOU OPEN AN ENVOY GATE?
EH?!
WELL... I GUESS, IF I HAVE TO...

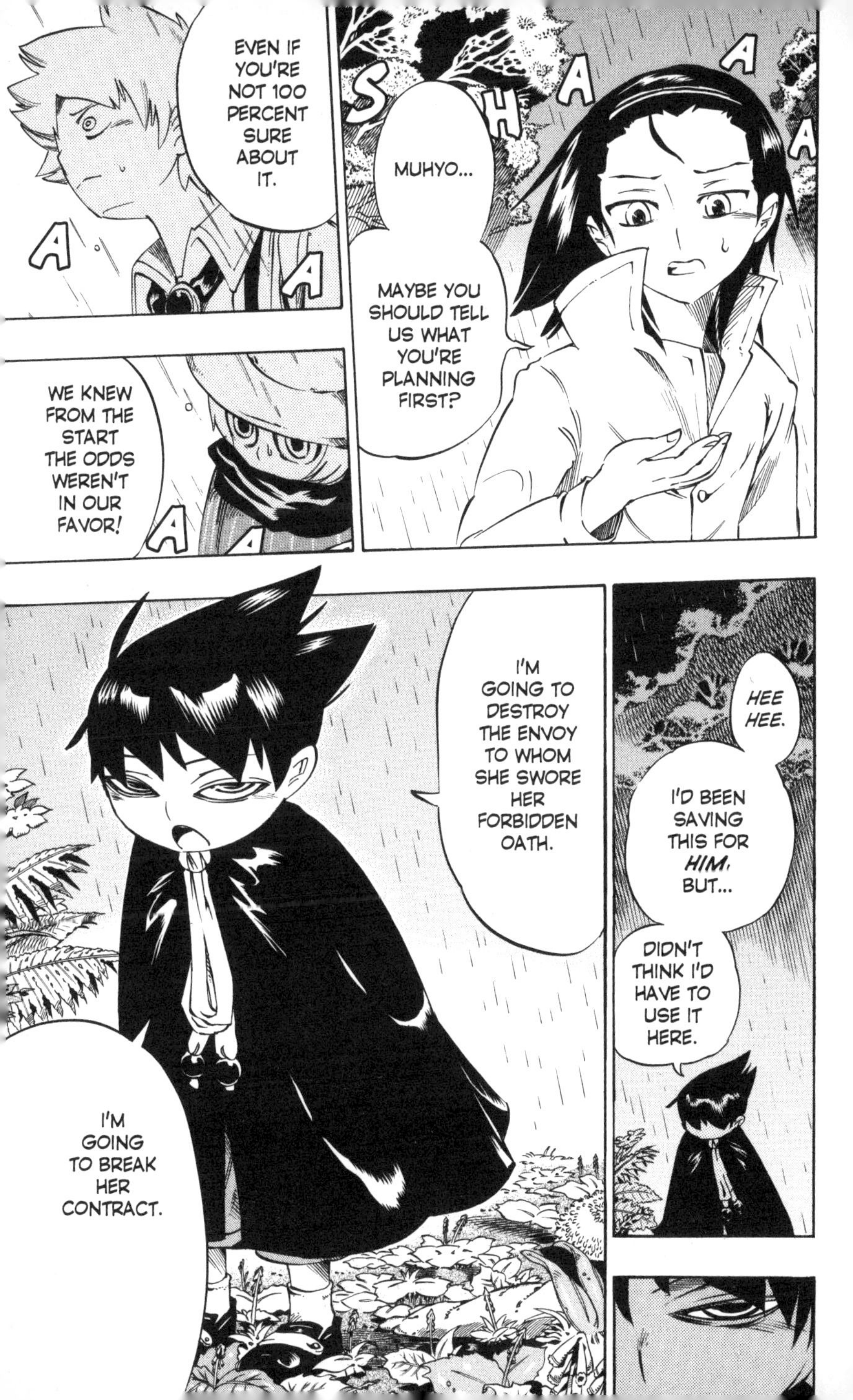
SHAAAA
MUHYO...
MAYBE YOU SHOULD TELL US WHAT YOU'RE PLANNING FIRST?
EVEN IF YOU'RE NOT 100 PERCENT SURE ABOUT IT.
AA
WE KNEW FROM THE START THE ODDS WEREN'T IN OUR FAVOR!
HEE HEE.
I'D BEEN SAVING THIS FOR *HIM*, BUT...
DIDN'T THINK I'D HAVE TO USE IT HERE.
I'M GOING TO DESTROY THE ENVOY TO WHOM SHE SWORE HER FORBIDDEN OATH.
I'M GOING TO BREAK HER CONTRACT.

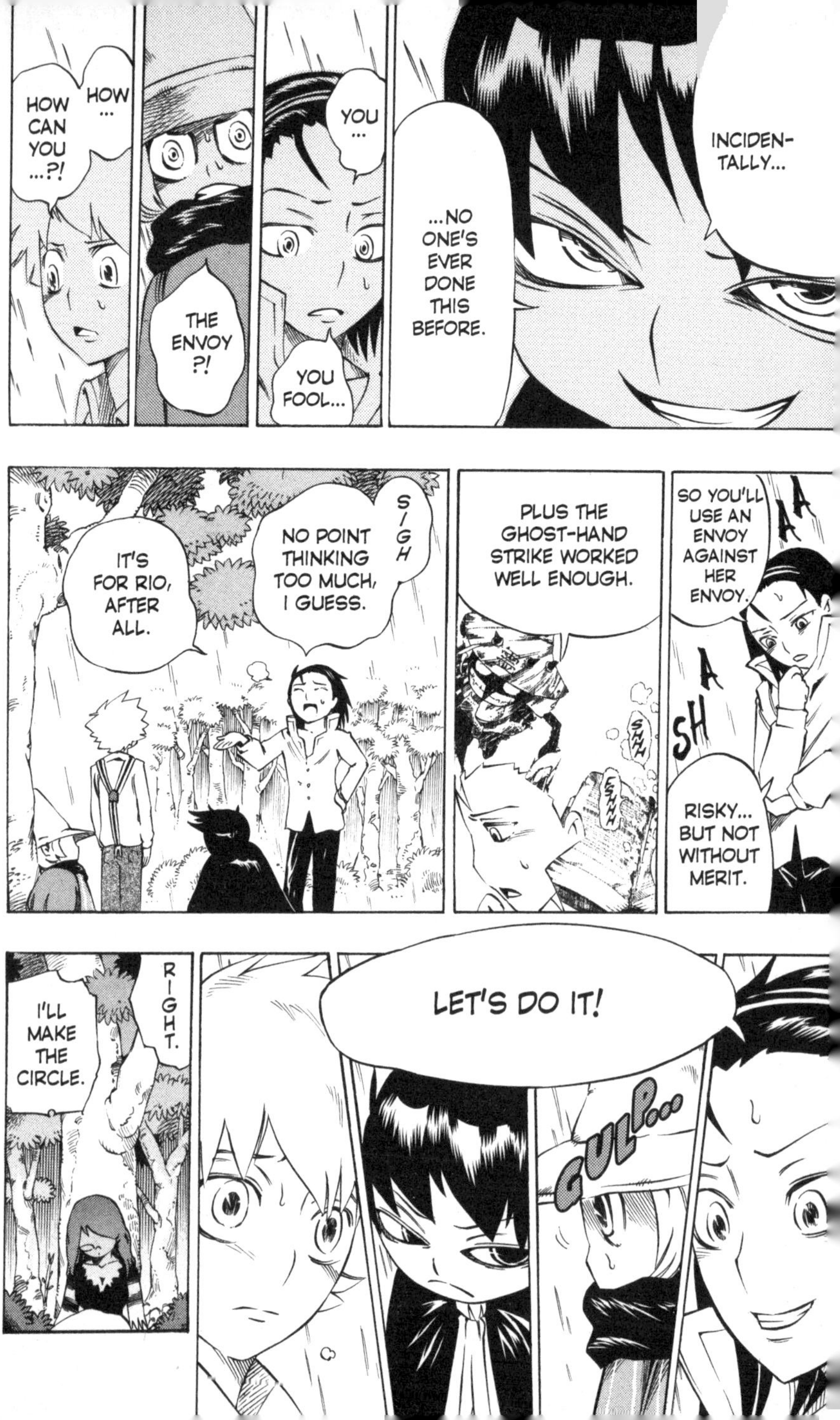
INCIDEN-TALLY...
...NO ONE'S EVER DONE THIS BEFORE.
YOU ...
YOU FOOL...
THE ENVOY ?!
HOW ...
HOW CAN YOU ...?!
SO YOU'LL USE AN ENVOY AGAINST HER ENVOY.
RISKY... BUT NOT WITHOUT MERIT.
PLUS THE GHOST-HAND STRIKE WORKED WELL ENOUGH.
SHHH
SHHH
SIGH
NO POINT THINKING TOO MUCH, I GUESS.
IT'S FOR RIO, AFTER ALL.
LET'S DO IT!
GULP...
RIGHT.
I'LL MAKE THE CIRCLE.

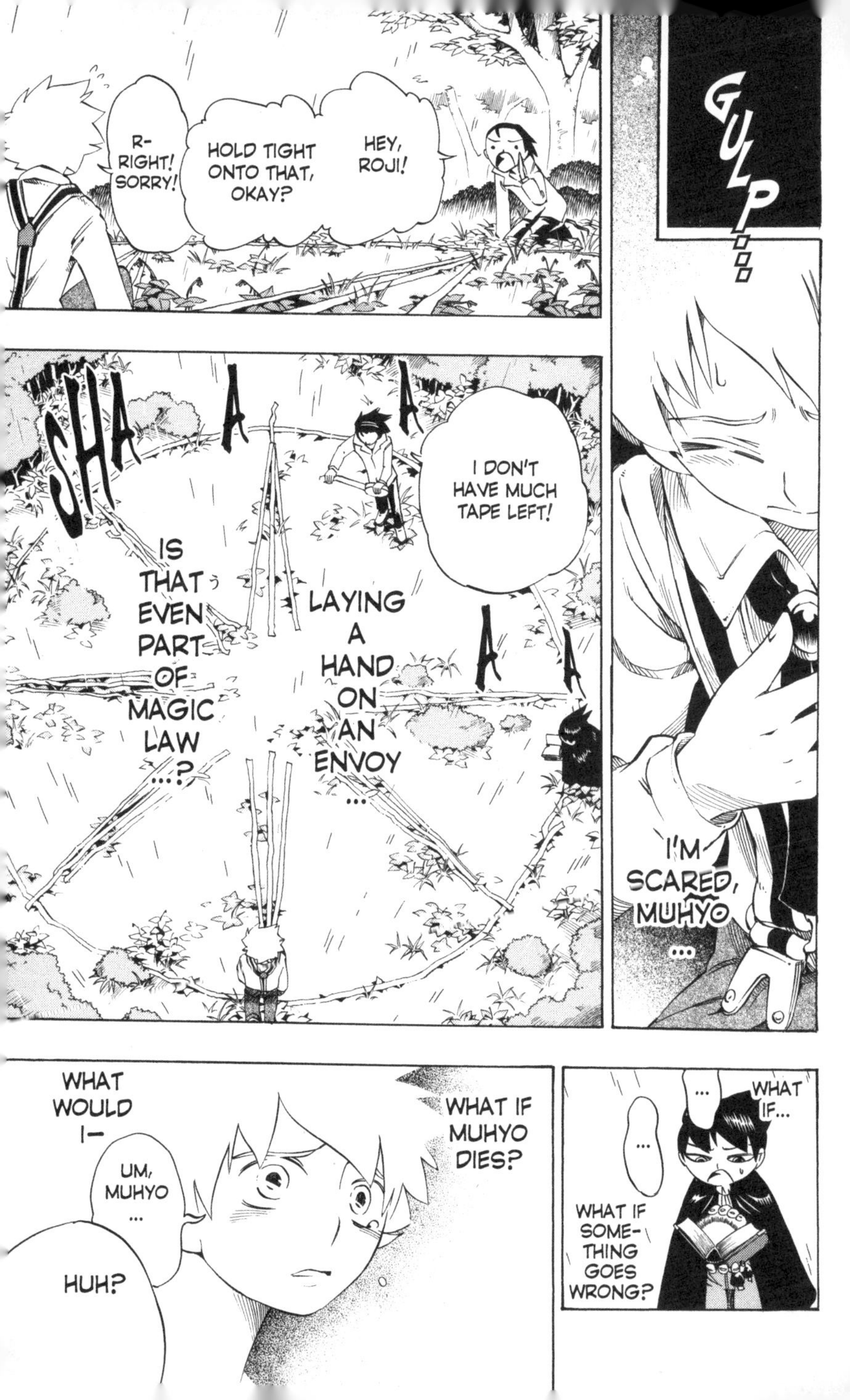
GULP
I'M SCARED, MUHYO...
HEY, ROJI!
HOLD TIGHT ONTO THAT, OKAY?
R-RIGHT! SORRY!
I DON'T HAVE MUCH TAPE LEFT!
SHAAAA
LAYING A HAND ON AN ENVOY...
IS THAT EVEN PART OF MAGIC LAW...?
WHAT IF...
...
...
WHAT IF SOMETHING GOES WRONG?
WHAT IF MUHYO DIES?
WHAT WOULD I—
UM, MUHYO...
HUH?

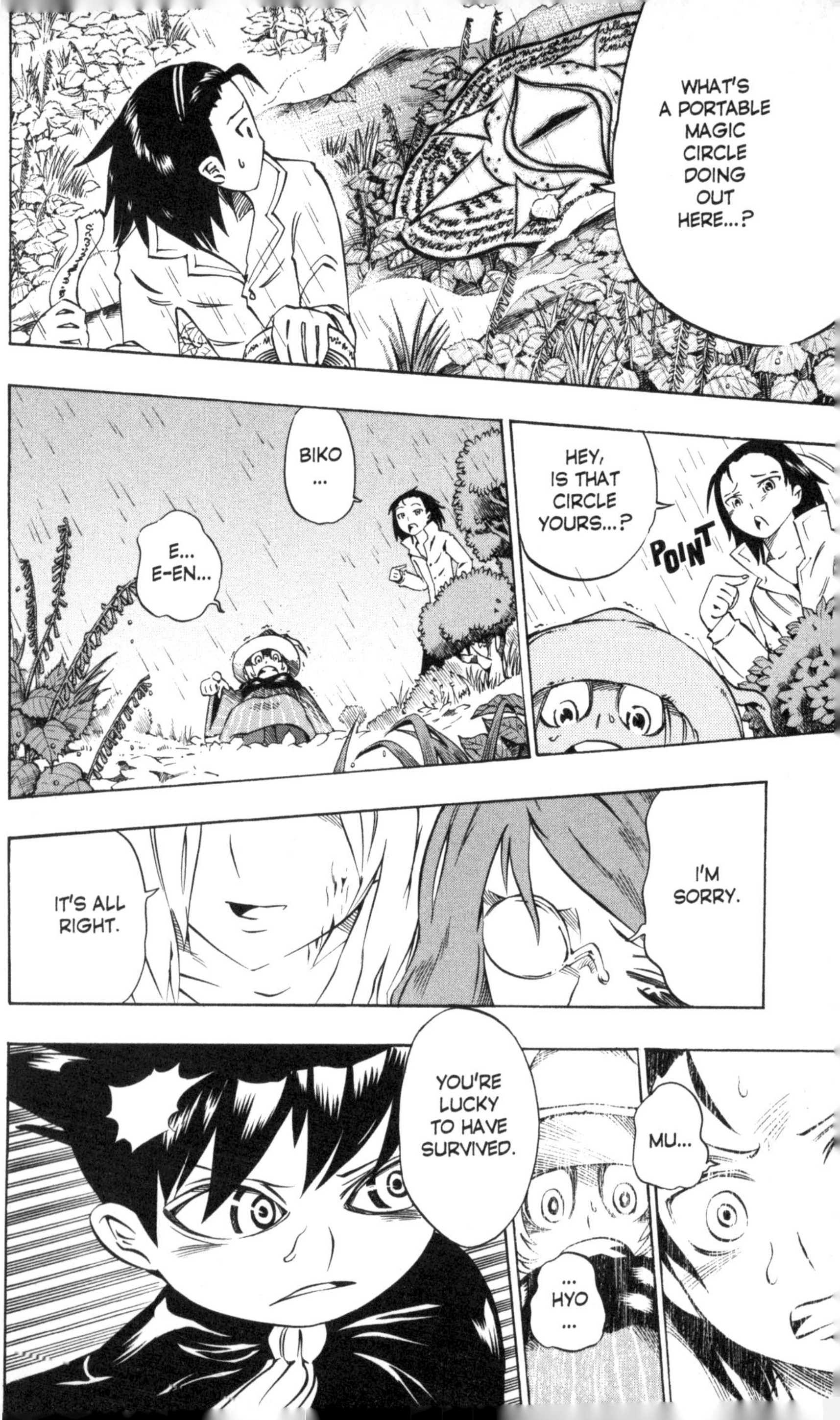
WHAT'S A PORTABLE MAGIC CIRCLE DOING OUT HERE...?
HEY, IS THAT CIRCLE YOURS...?
POINT
BIKO ...
E... E-EN...
I'M SORRY.
IT'S ALL RIGHT.
MU...
YOU'RE LUCKY TO HAVE SURVIVED.
... HYO ...

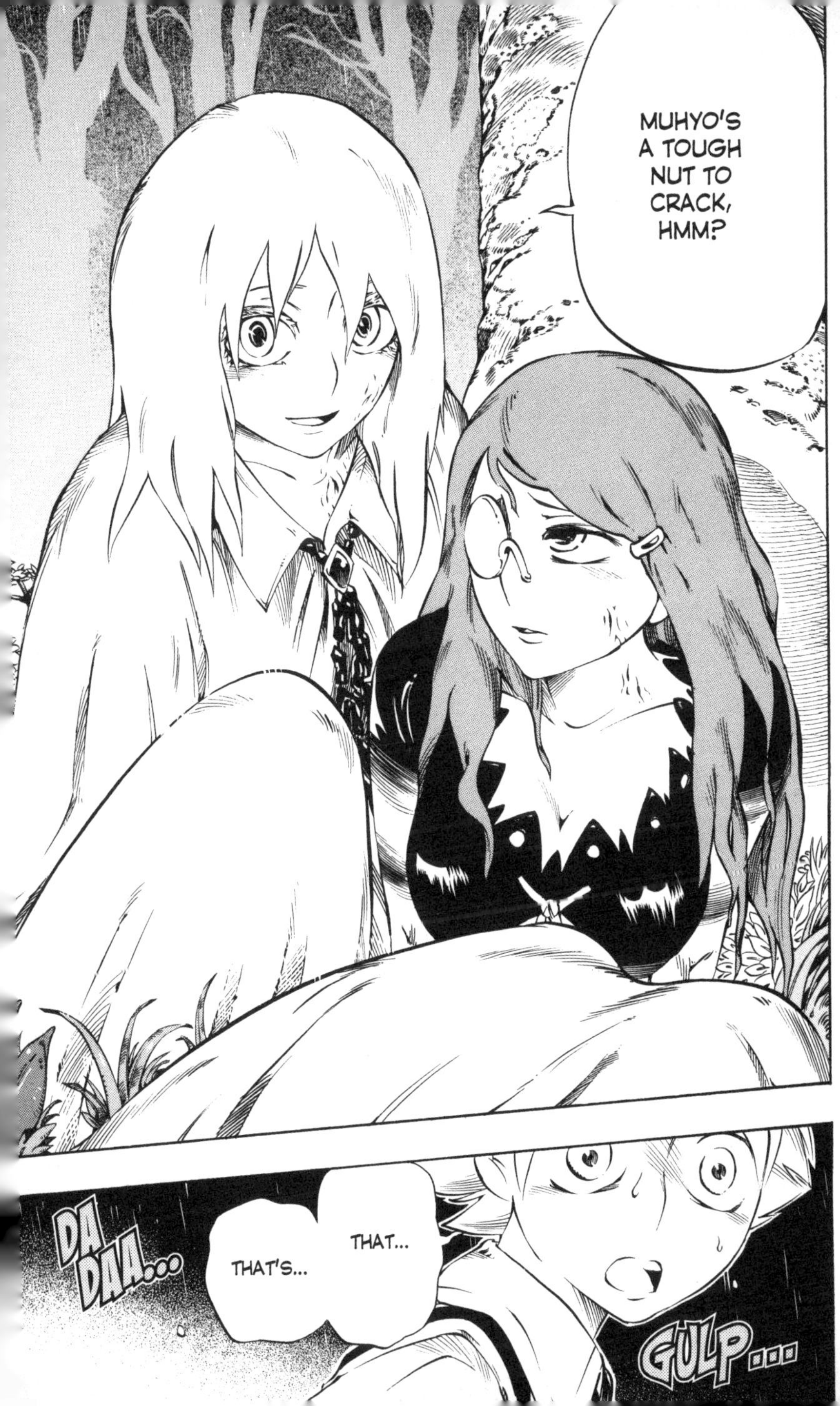
MUHYO'S A TOUGH NUT TO CRACK, HMM?
THAT...
THAT'S...
DA DAA...
GULP...

Q: WILL YOICHI EVER GRAB ANY BOOBS OTHER THAN NANA'S? INQUIRING MINDS WANT TO KNOW.

—H.I., TOKYO

A: ...I GET ASKED THIS A LOT, AMAZINGLY ENOUGH. LET'S SEND HIM A FAX AND ASK, SHALL WE?

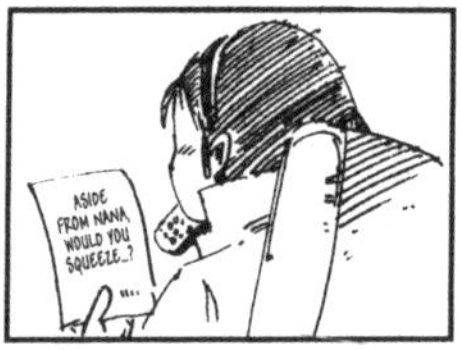
ASIDE FROM NANA, WOULD YOU SQUEEZE...?
...

(YOICHI) "...CAN I?"

(AUTHOR) "...WELL, YOU COULD IF YOU—WAIT, OF COURSE YOU CAN'T GO AROUND GRABBING BOOBS! GEEZ!"

(YOICHI) "I KNOW, I KNOW. I JUST CAN'T HELP IT... HEH HEH..."

(AUTHOR) "OH, REALLY NOW..."

(YOICHI) "YOU GONNA PRINT THIS?"

(AUTHOR) "HAH. NO, I SUPPOSE NOT. HA HA HA."

THERE YOU HAVE IT.

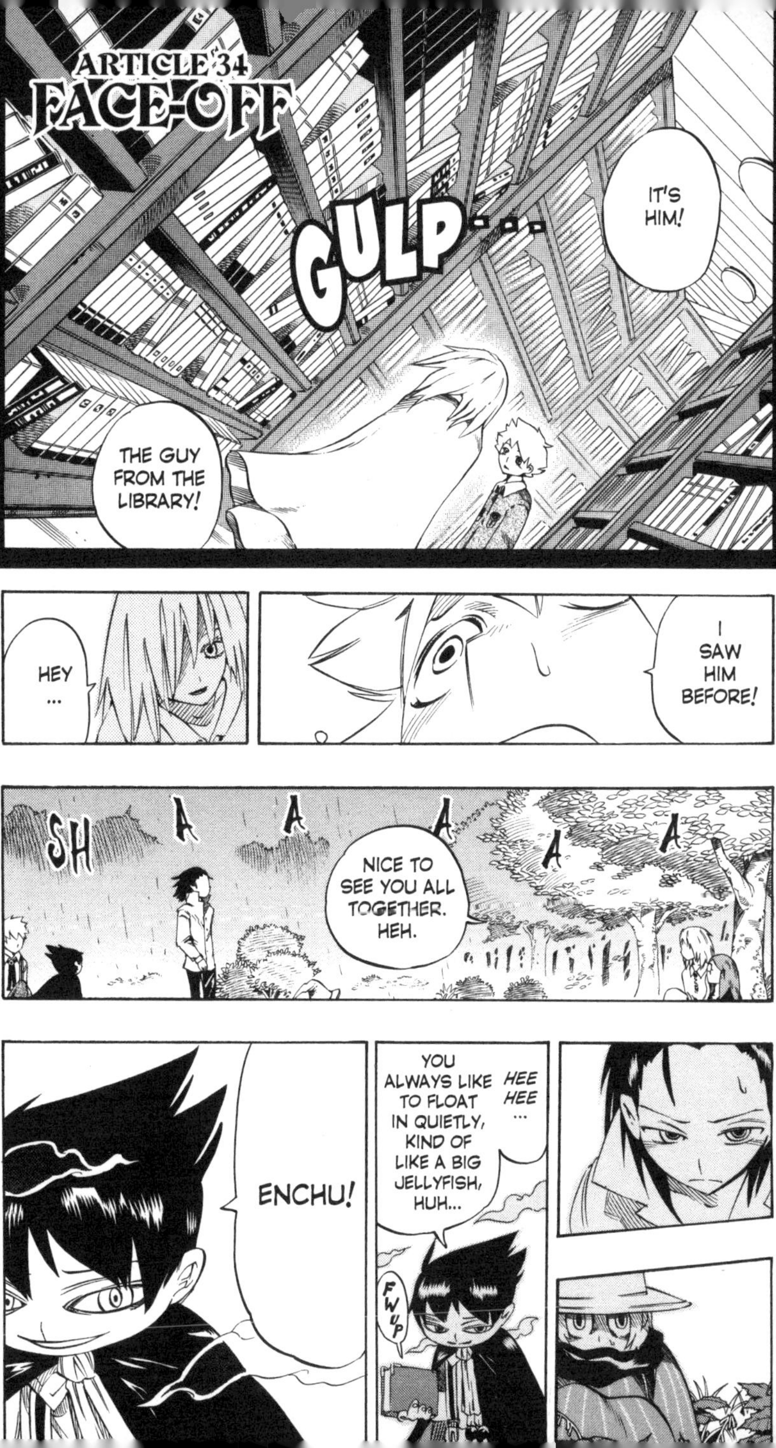
ARTICLE 34
FACE-OFF
IT'S HIM!
GULP...
THE GUY FROM THE LIBRARY!
I SAW HIM BEFORE!
HEY ...
SHAAAA
NICE TO SEE YOU ALL TOGETHER. HEH.
HEE HEE ...
YOU ALWAYS LIKE TO FLOAT IN QUIETLY, KIND OF LIKE A BIG JELLYFISH, HUH...
FWUP
ENCHU!

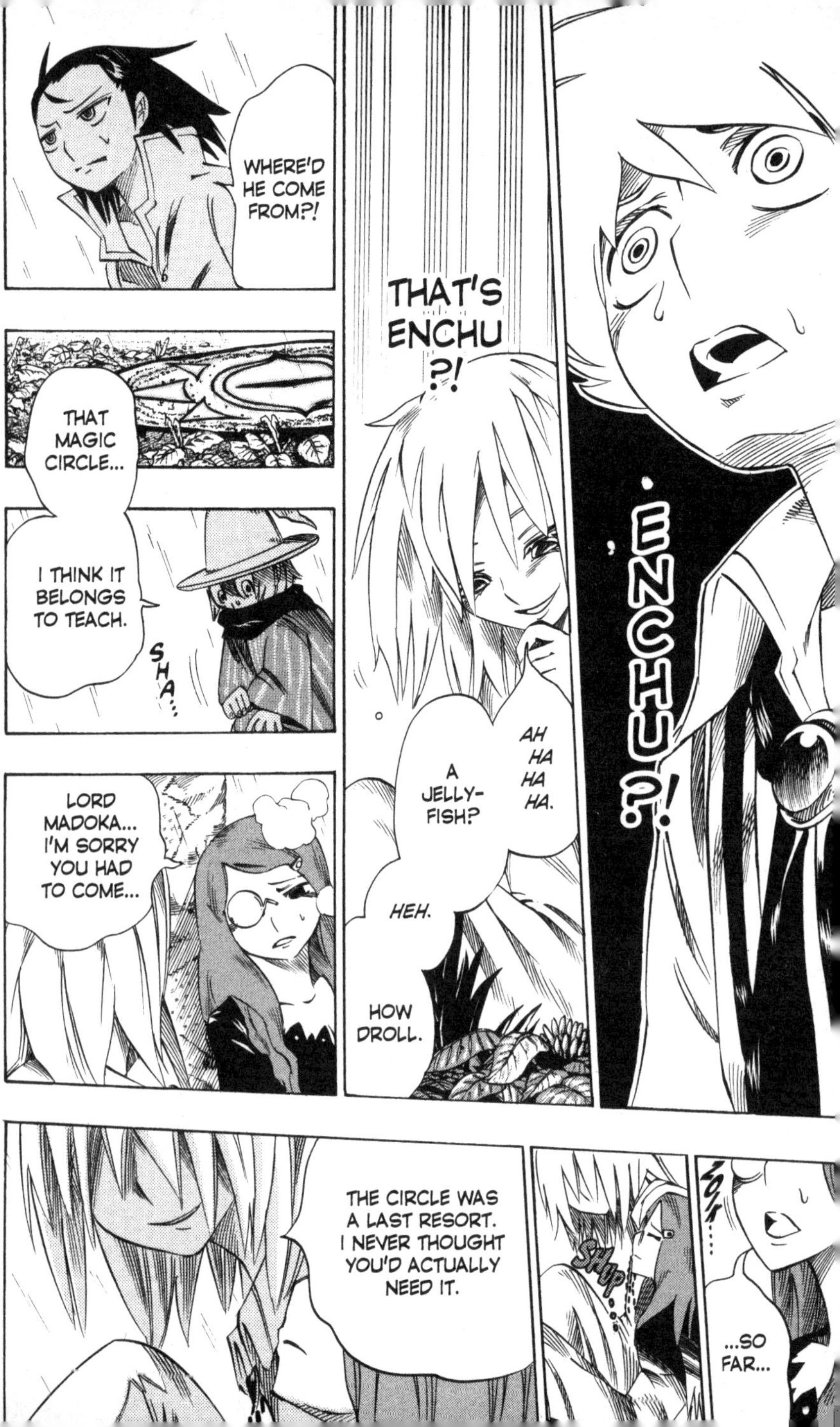
ENCHU?!
THAT'S ENCHU?!
A JELLY-FISH?
AH HA HA HA.
HEH.
HOW DROLL.
WHERE'D HE COME FROM?!
THAT MAGIC CIRCLE...
I THINK IT BELONGS TO TEACH.
SHA...
LORD MADOKA... I'M SORRY YOU HAD TO COME...
ZOT...
...SO FAR...
SHAP
THE CIRCLE WAS A LAST RESORT. I NEVER THOUGHT YOU'D ACTUALLY NEED IT.

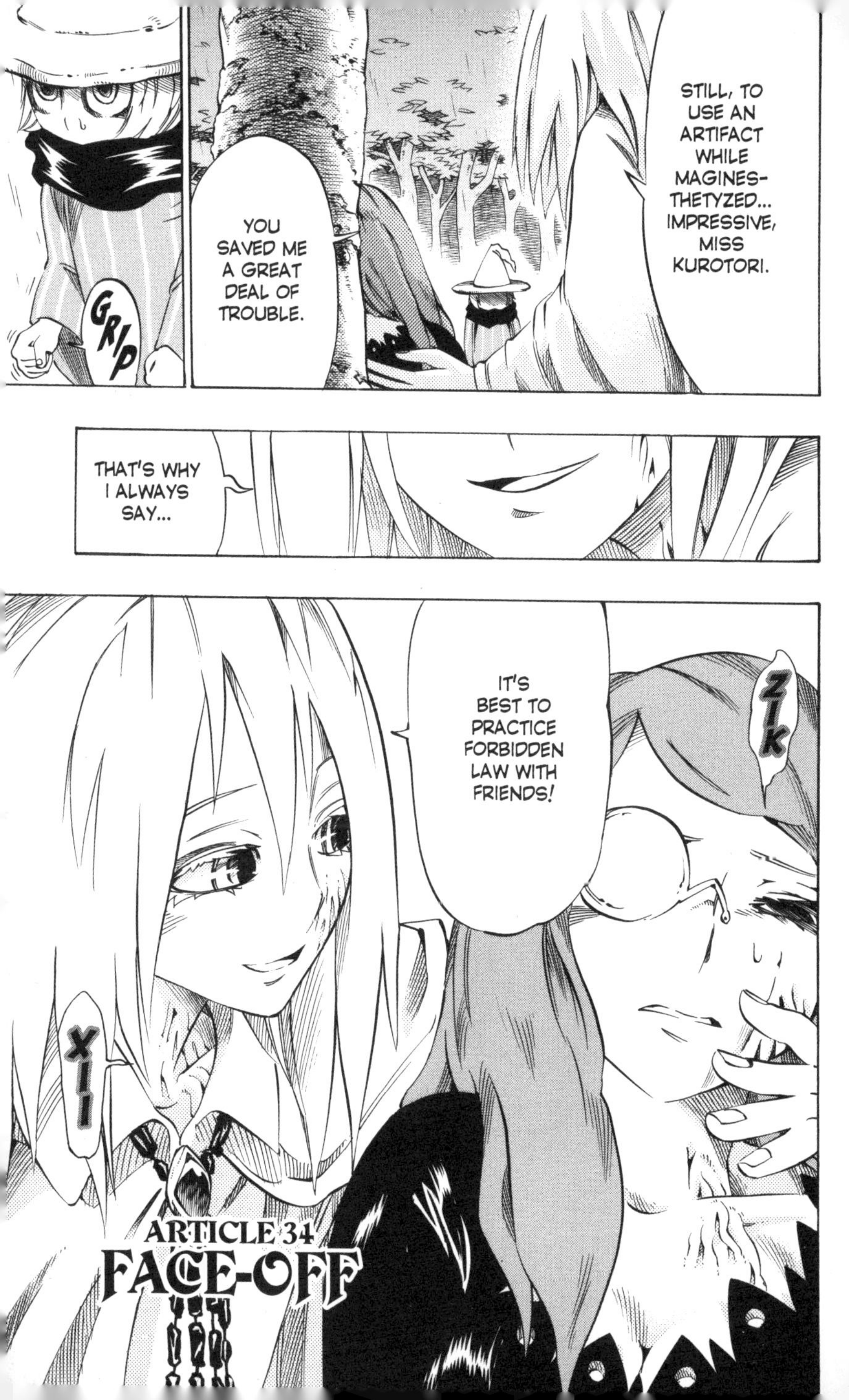
STILL, TO USE AN ARTIFACT WHILE MAGINES-THETYZED... IMPRESSIVE, MISS KUROTORI.
YOU SAVED ME A GREAT DEAL OF TROUBLE.
GRIP
THAT'S WHY I ALWAYS SAY...
ZIK
IT'S BEST TO PRACTICE FORBIDDEN LAW WITH FRIENDS!
ARTICLE 34
FACE-OFF

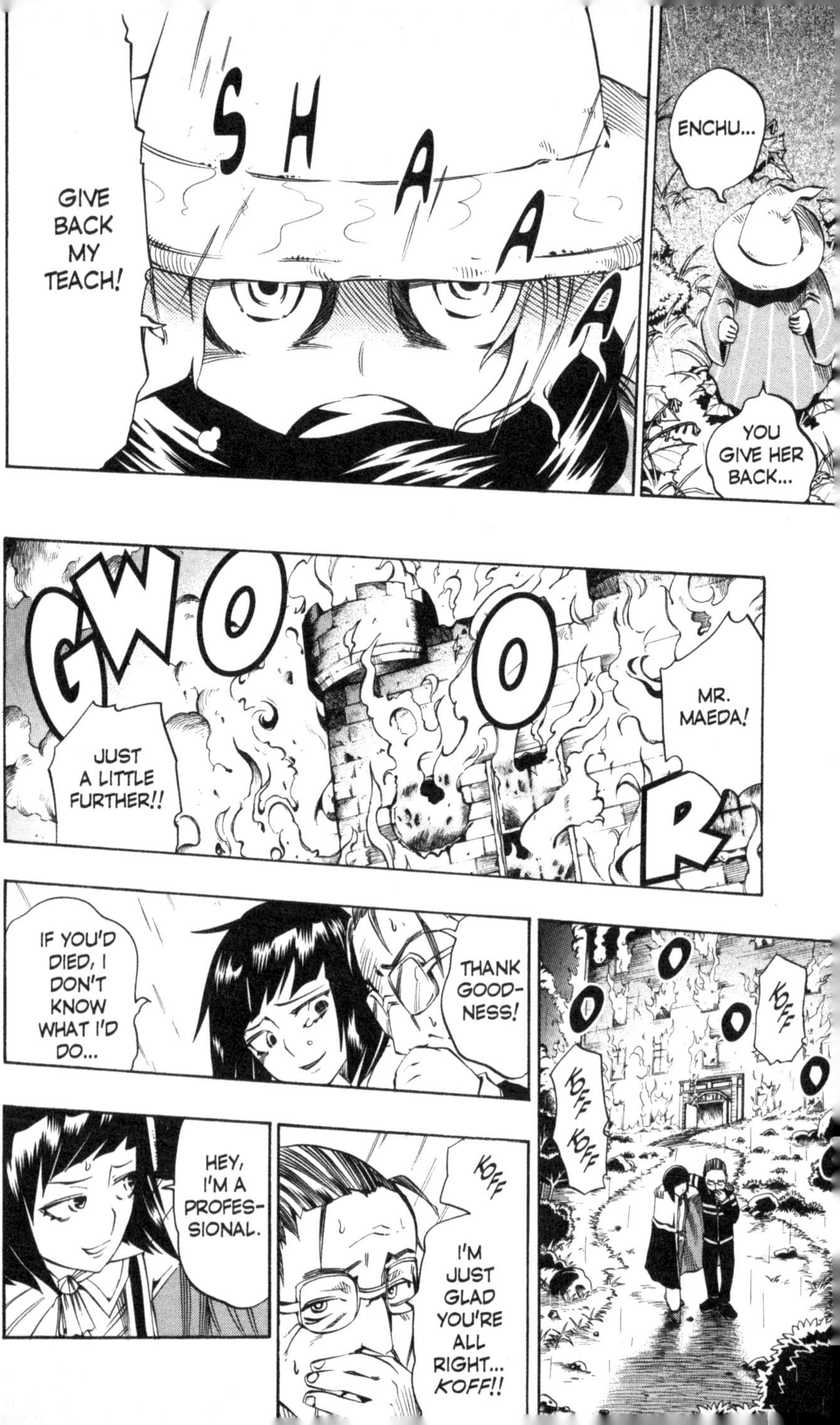
ENCHU...
YOU GIVE HER BACK...
SHAAAA
GIVE BACK MY TEACH!
GWOOOR
MR. MAEDA!
JUST A LITTLE FURTHER!!
OOOO
KOFF
KOFF KOFF
THANK GOODNESS!
IF YOU'D DIED, I DON'T KNOW WHAT I'D DO...
KOFF
I'M JUST GLAD YOU'RE ALL RIGHT... KOFF!!
HEY, I'M A PROFESSIONAL.

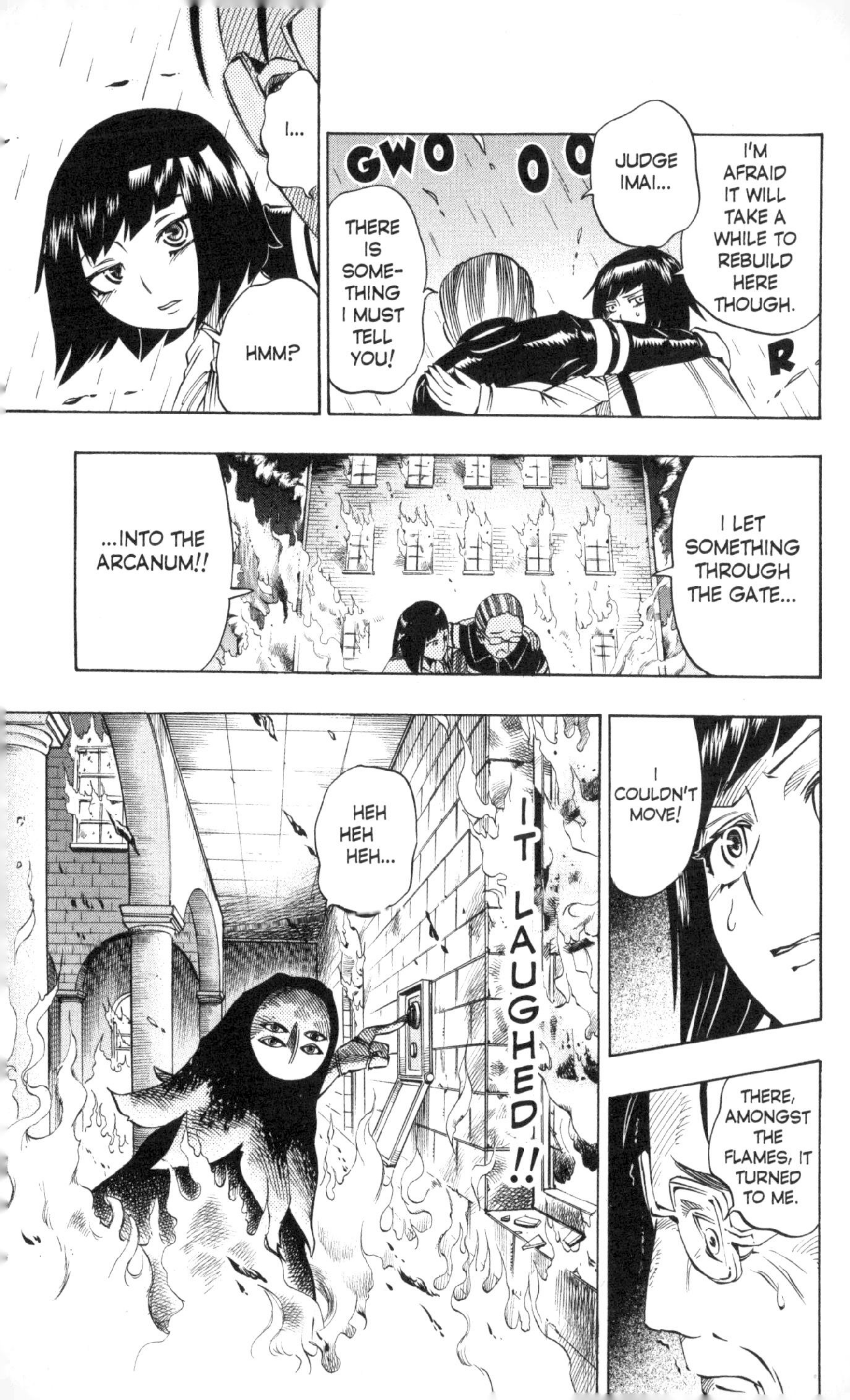
I'M AFRAID IT WILL TAKE A WHILE TO REBUILD HERE THOUGH.
JUDGE IMAI...
GWO O O R
THERE IS SOME-THING I MUST TELL YOU!
I...
HMM?
I LET SOMETHING THROUGH THE GATE...
...INTO THE ARCANUM!!
I COULDN'T MOVE!
THERE, AMONGST THE FLAMES, IT TURNED TO ME.
IT LAUGHED!!
HEH HEH HEH...

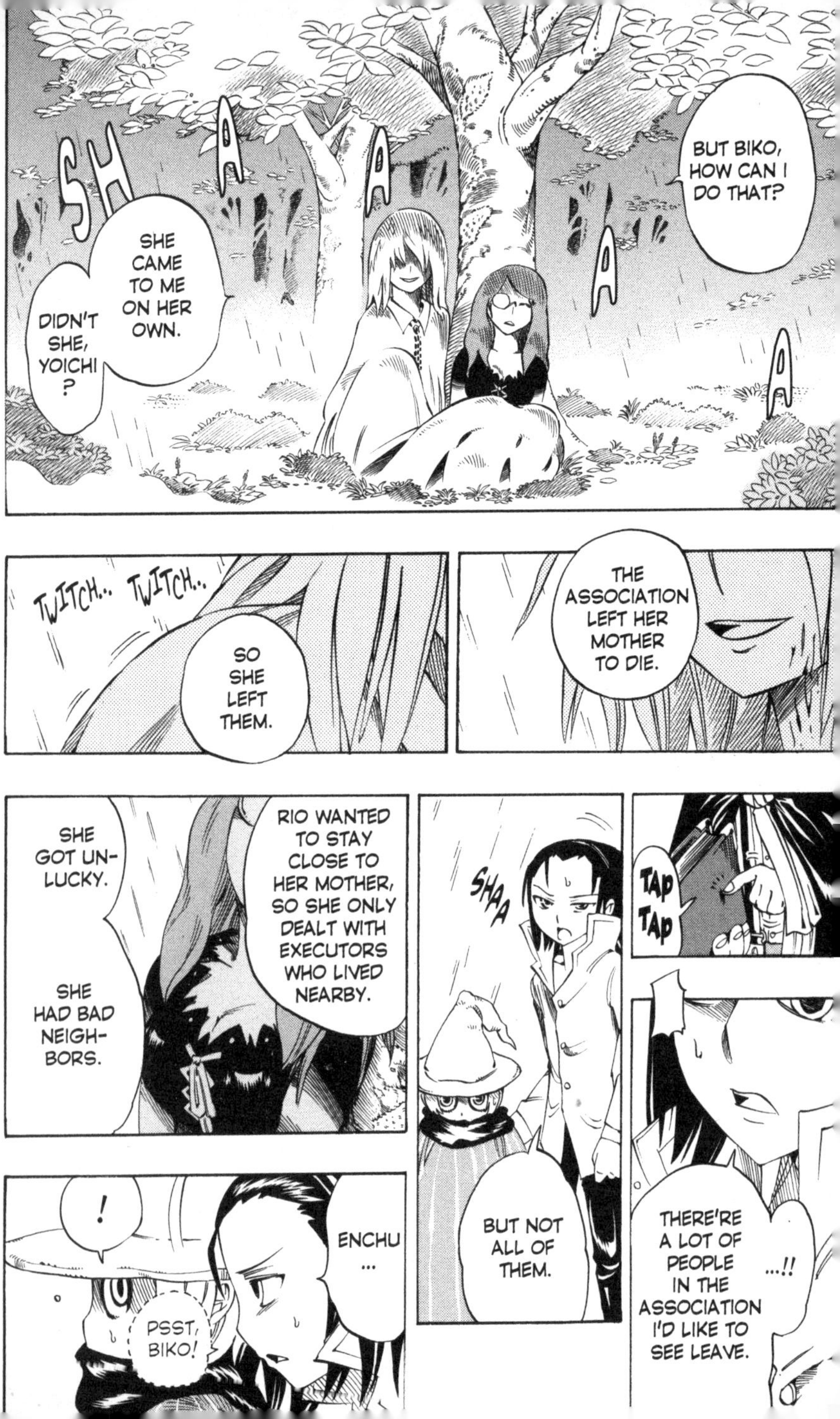
BUT BIKO, HOW CAN I DO THAT?
SHAAAA
SHE CAME TO ME ON HER OWN.
DIDN'T SHE, YOICHI?
THE ASSOCIATION LEFT HER MOTHER TO DIE.
SO SHE LEFT THEM.
TWITCH... TWITCH...
TAP TAP
THERE'RE A LOT OF PEOPLE IN THE ASSOCIATION I'D LIKE TO SEE LEAVE.
...!!
SHAA
BUT NOT ALL OF THEM.
RIO WANTED TO STAY CLOSE TO HER MOTHER, SO SHE ONLY DEALT WITH EXECUTORS WHO LIVED NEARBY.
SHE GOT UN-LUCKY.
SHE HAD BAD NEIGH-BORS.
ENCHU...
!
PSST, BIKO!

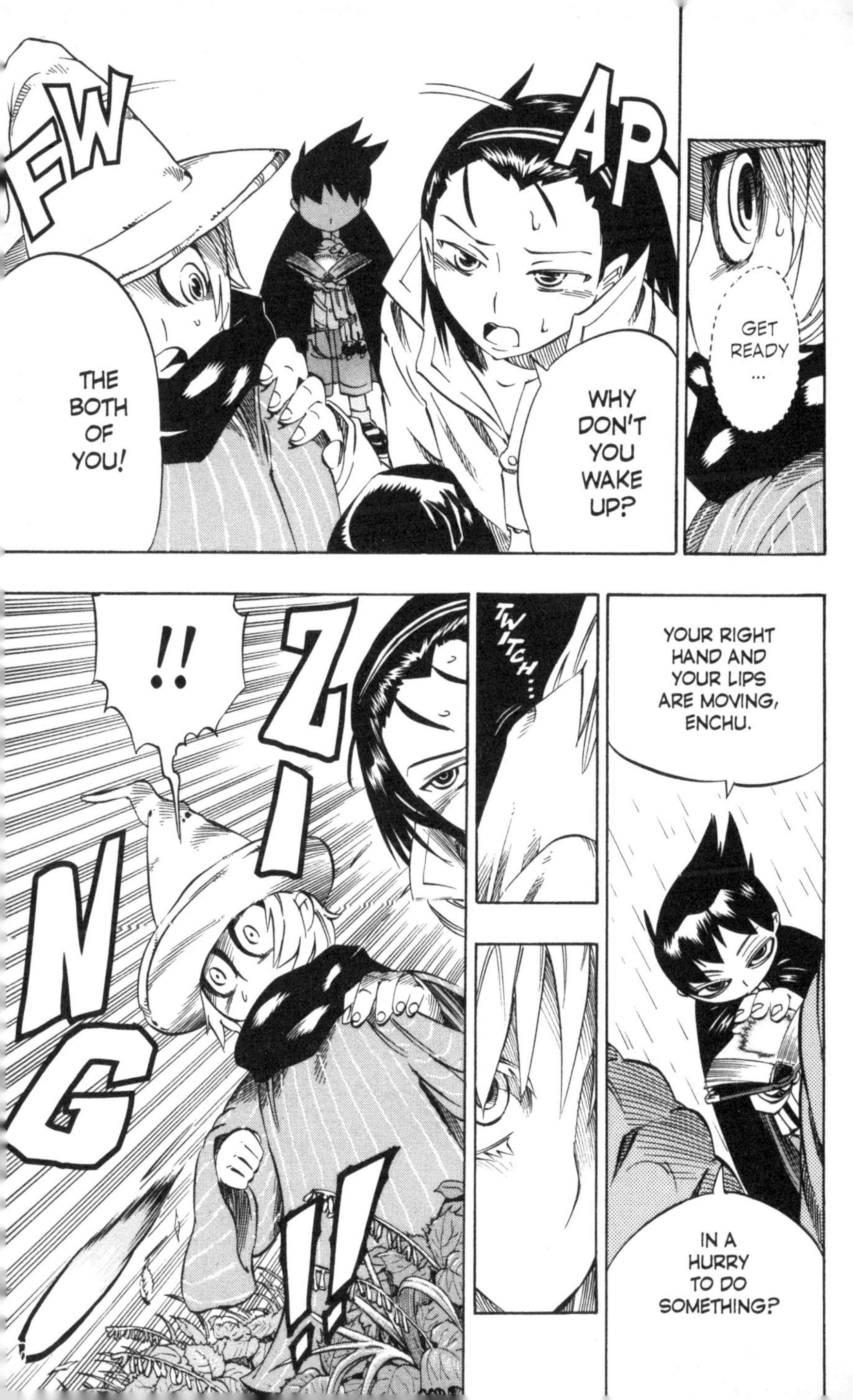
GET READY ...
AP
WHY DON'T YOU WAKE UP?
FW
THE BOTH OF YOU!
YOUR RIGHT HAND AND YOUR LIPS ARE MOVING, ENCHU.
IN A HURRY TO DO SOMETHING?
TWITCH...
!!
ZING
!

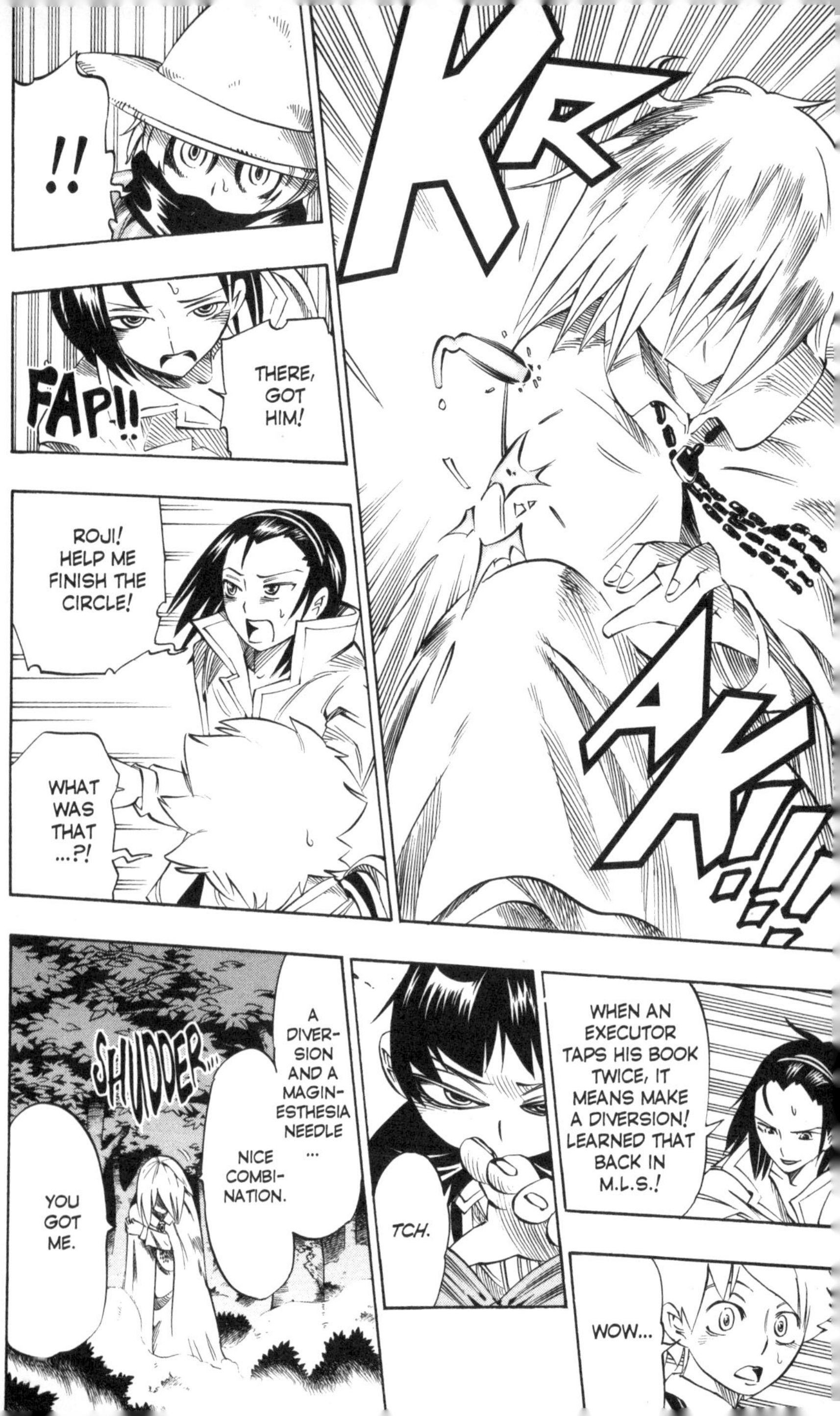
KRAK!!
!!
FAP!!
THERE, GOT HIM!
ROJI! HELP ME FINISH THE CIRCLE!
WHAT WAS THAT ...?!
WHEN AN EXECUTOR TAPS HIS BOOK TWICE, IT MEANS MAKE A DIVERSION! LEARNED THAT BACK IN M.L.S.!
WOW...
TCH.
A DIVERSION AND A MAGINESTHESIA NEEDLE ...
NICE COMBINATION.
SHUDDER...
YOU GOT ME.

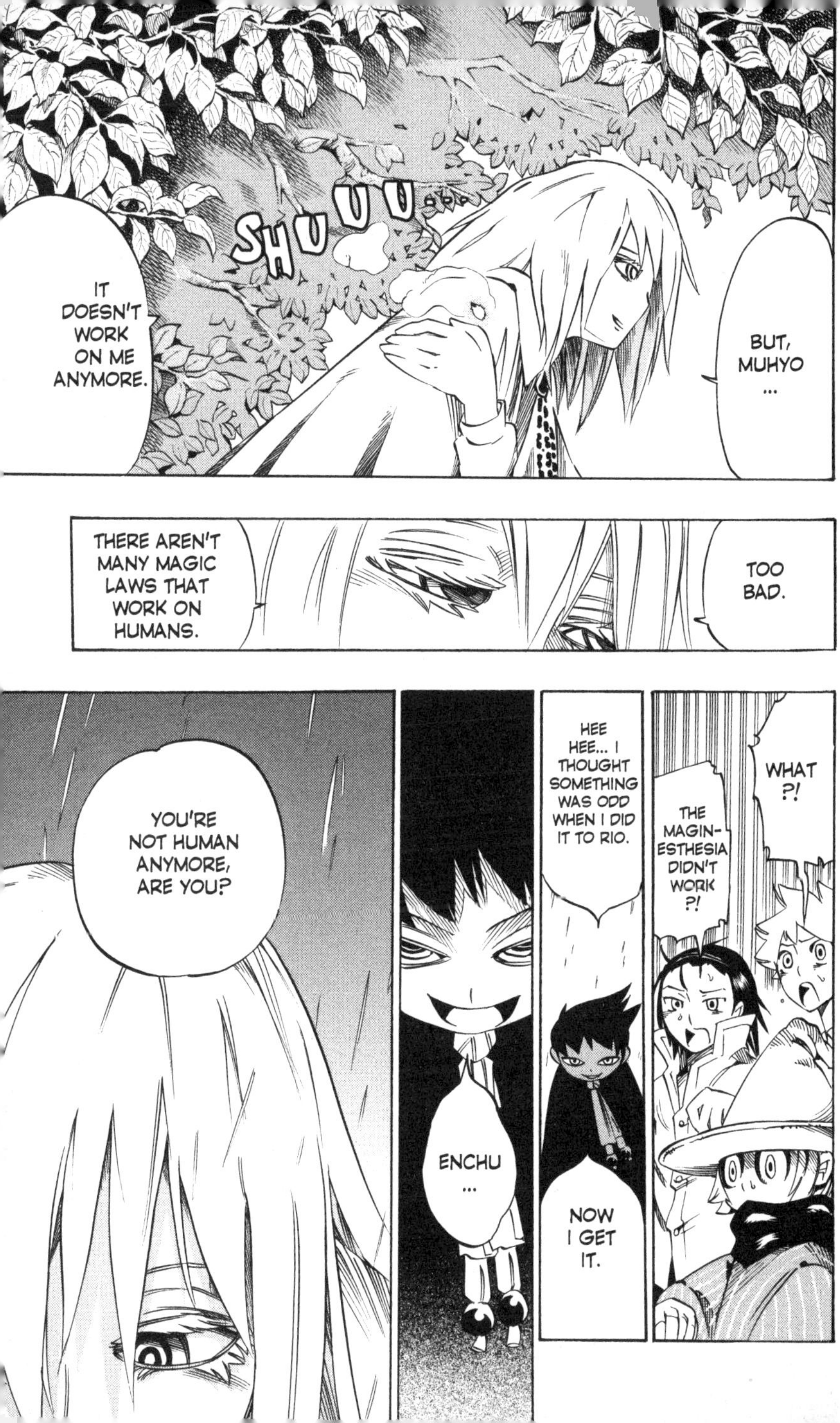
SHUUU...
BUT, MUHYO ...
IT DOESN'T WORK ON ME ANYMORE.
TOO BAD.
THERE AREN'T MANY MAGIC LAWS THAT WORK ON HUMANS.
WHAT ?!
THE MAGIN-ESTHESIA DIDN'T WORK ?!
HEE HEE... I THOUGHT SOMETHING WAS ODD WHEN I DID IT TO RIO.
NOW I GET IT.
ENCHU ...
YOU'RE NOT HUMAN ANYMORE, ARE YOU?

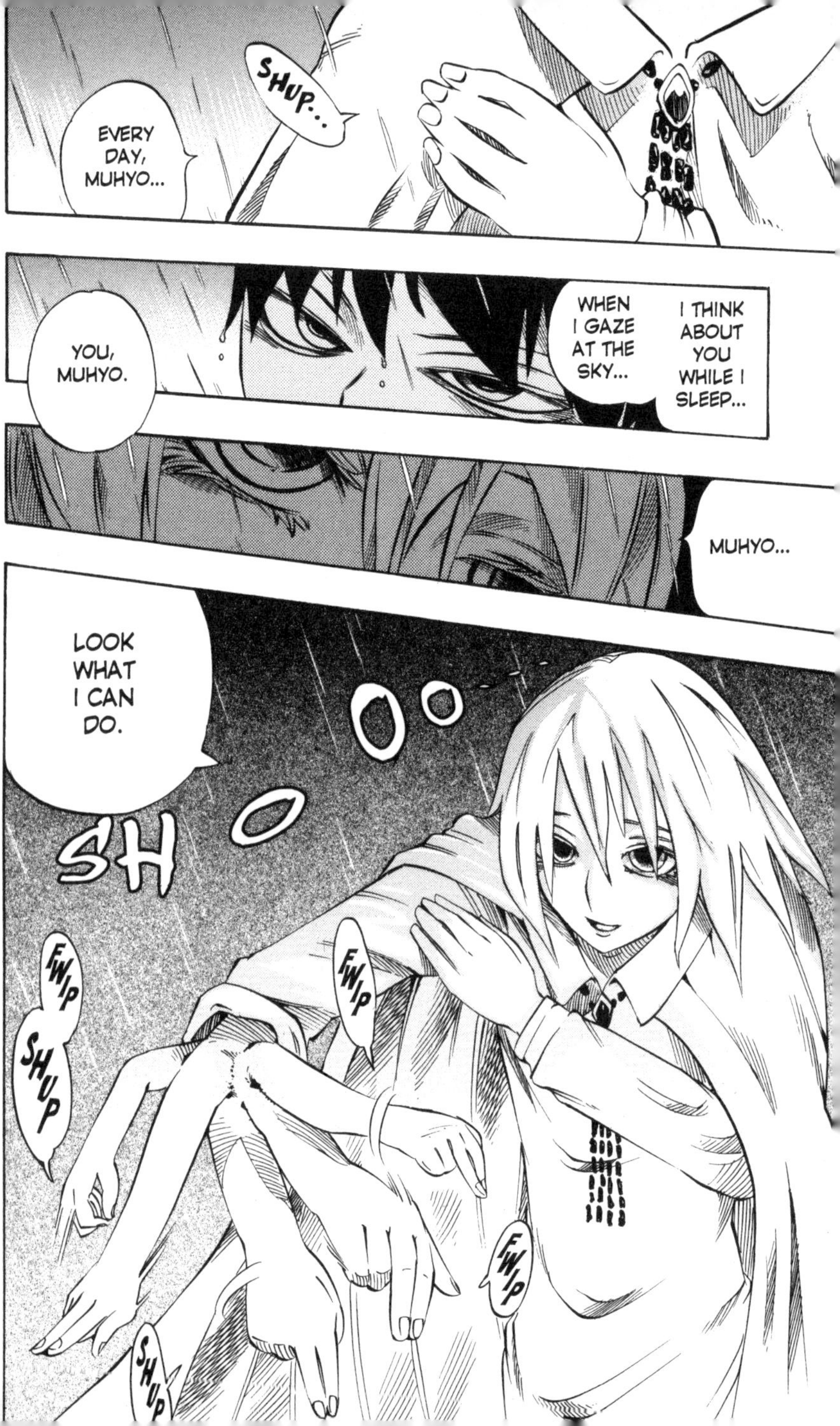
SHUP...
EVERY DAY, MUHYO...
I THINK ABOUT YOU WHILE I SLEEP...
WHEN I GAZE AT THE SKY...
YOU, MUHYO.
MUHYO...
SHOOO...
LOOK WHAT I CAN DO.
FWIP
FWIP
FWIP
SHUP
SHUP

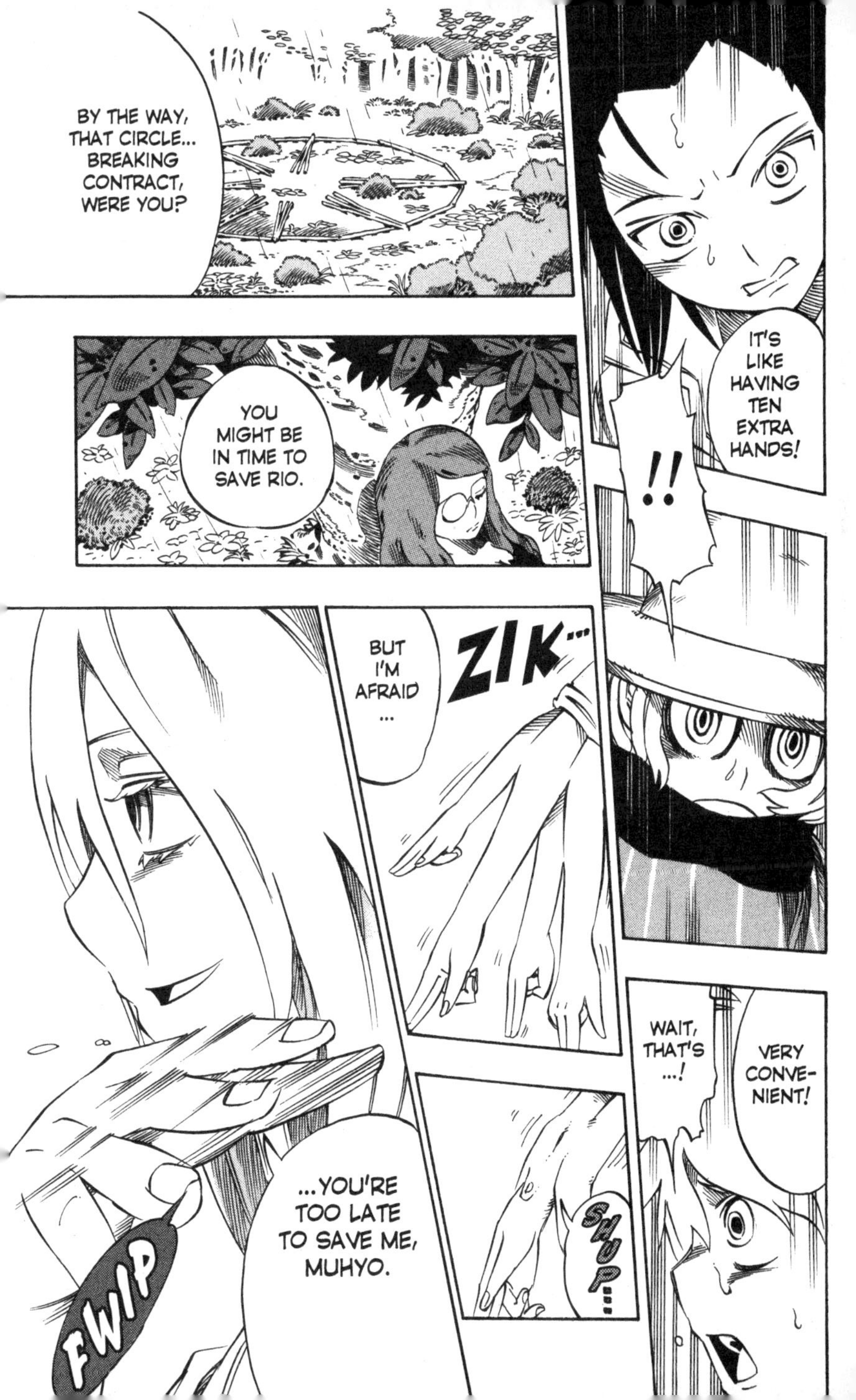
IT'S LIKE HAVING TEN EXTRA HANDS!
BY THE WAY, THAT CIRCLE... BREAKING CONTRACT, WERE YOU?
YOU MIGHT BE IN TIME TO SAVE RIO.
!!
BUT I'M AFRAID...
ZIK...
VERY CONVE-NIENT!
WAIT, THAT'S...!
SHUP...
...YOU'RE TOO LATE TO SAVE ME, MUHYO.
FWIP

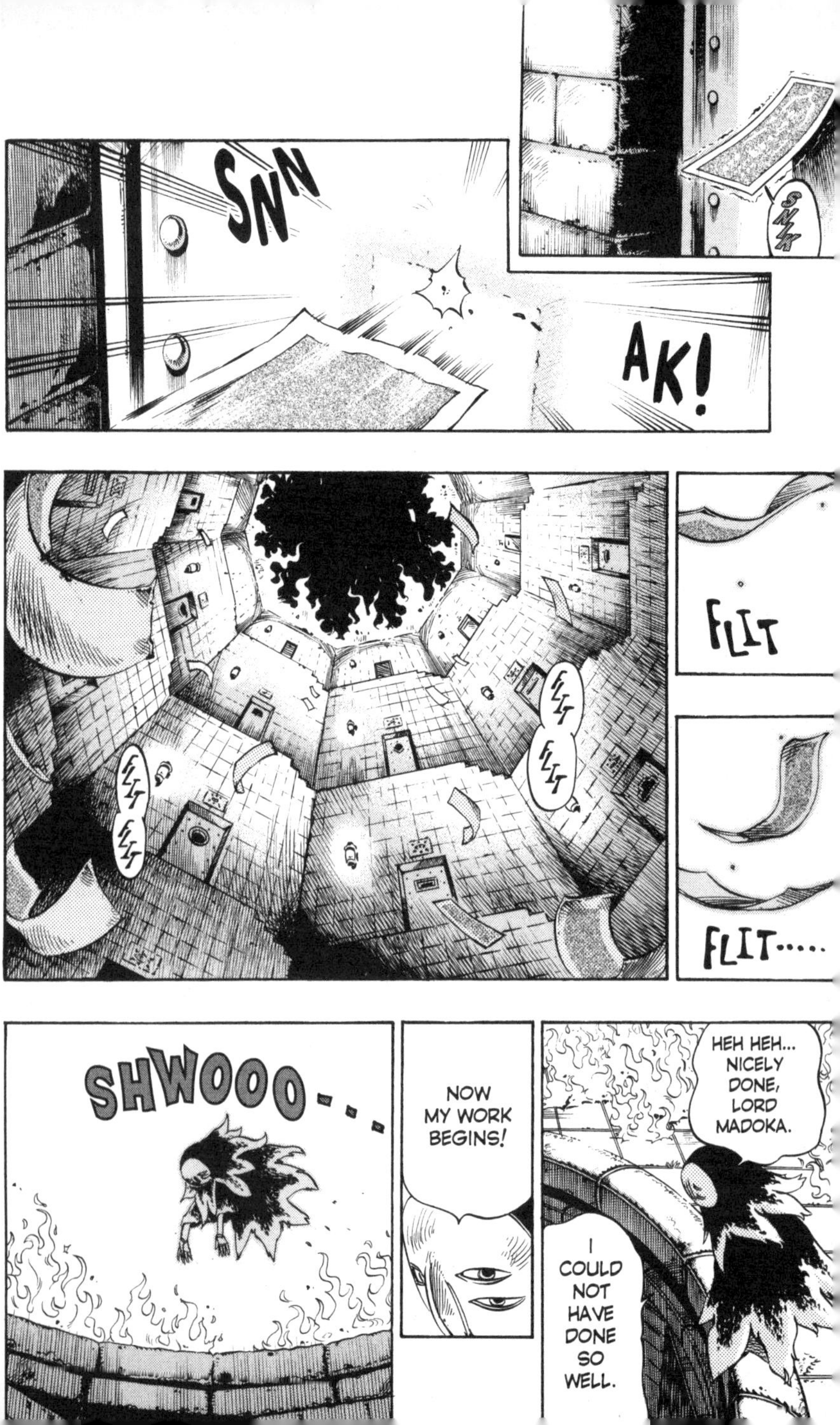
SNIK
SNN
AK!
FLIT
FLIT.....
FLIT
FLIT
FLIT
FLIT
HEH HEH... NICELY DONE, LORD MADOKA.
I COULD NOT HAVE DONE SO WELL.
NOW MY WORK BEGINS!
SHWOOO...

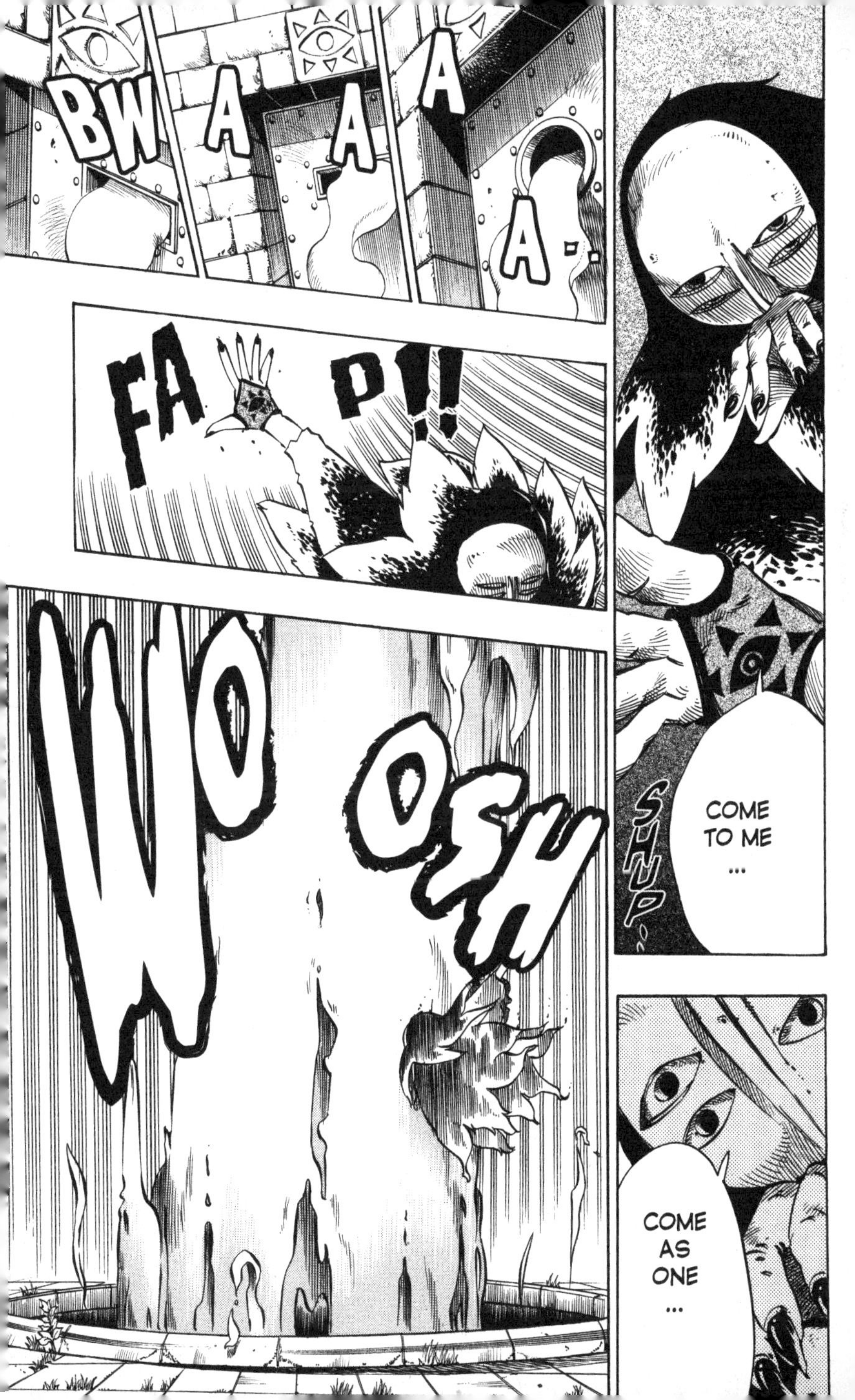
BWAAAA..
FAP!!
COME TO ME ...
SHUP..
WOOSH
COME AS ONE ...

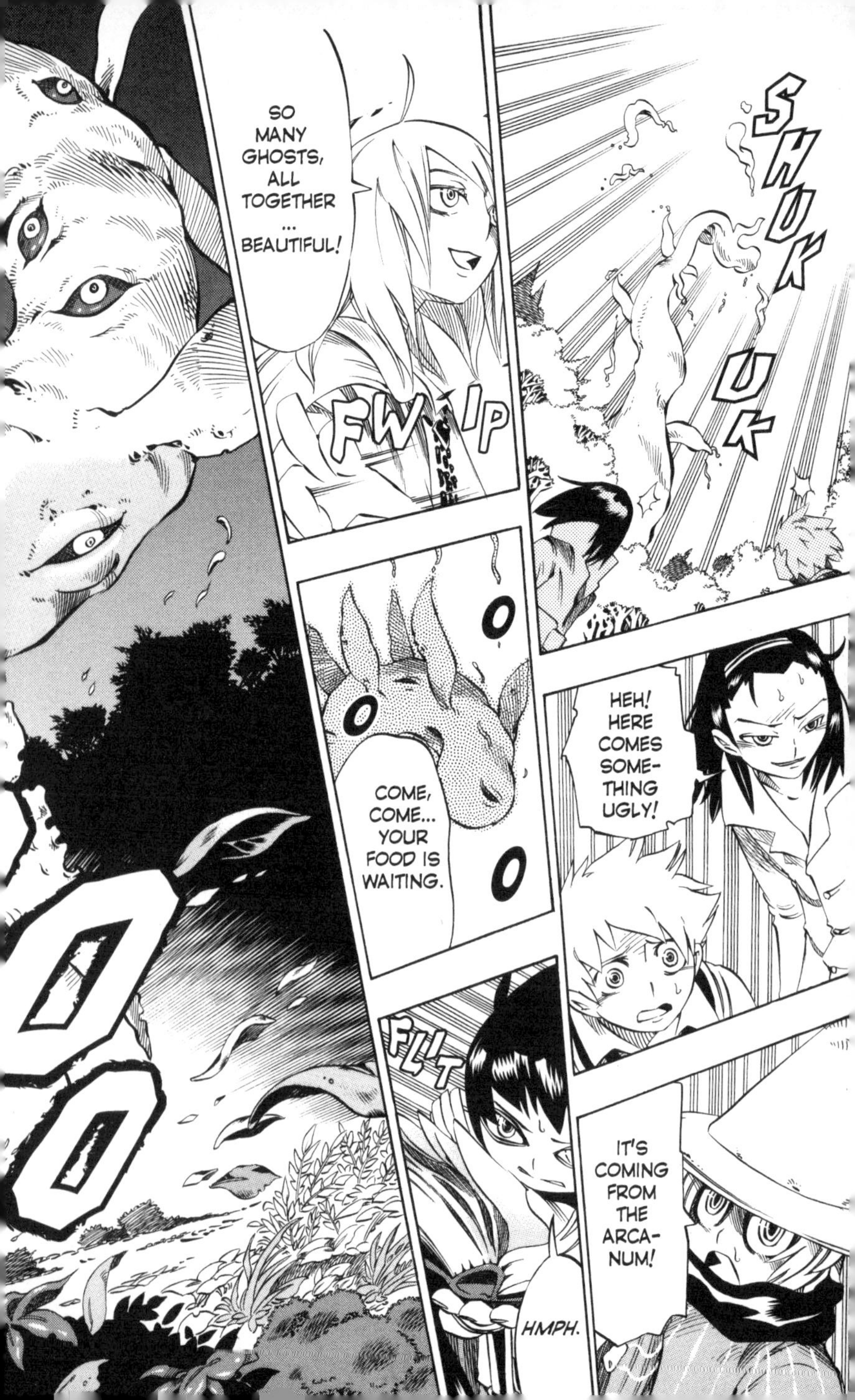
SHUKUK
SO MANY GHOSTS, ALL TOGETHER ... BEAUTIFUL!
FWIP
HEH! HERE COMES SOME-THING UGLY!
OOO
COME, COME... YOUR FOOD IS WAITING.
IT'S COMING FROM THE ARCA-NUM!
FLIT
HMPH.

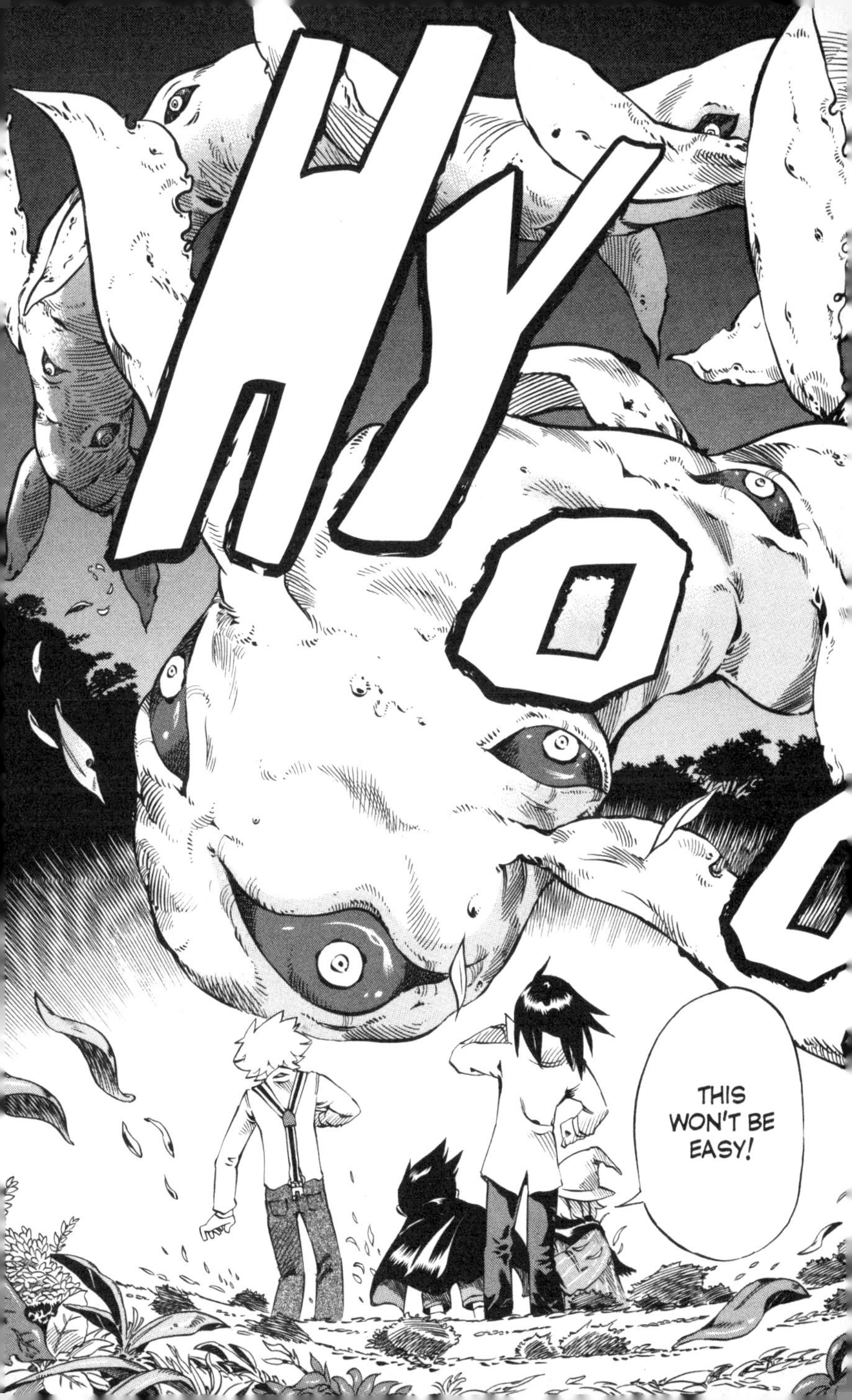
HYOO
THIS WON'T BE EASY!

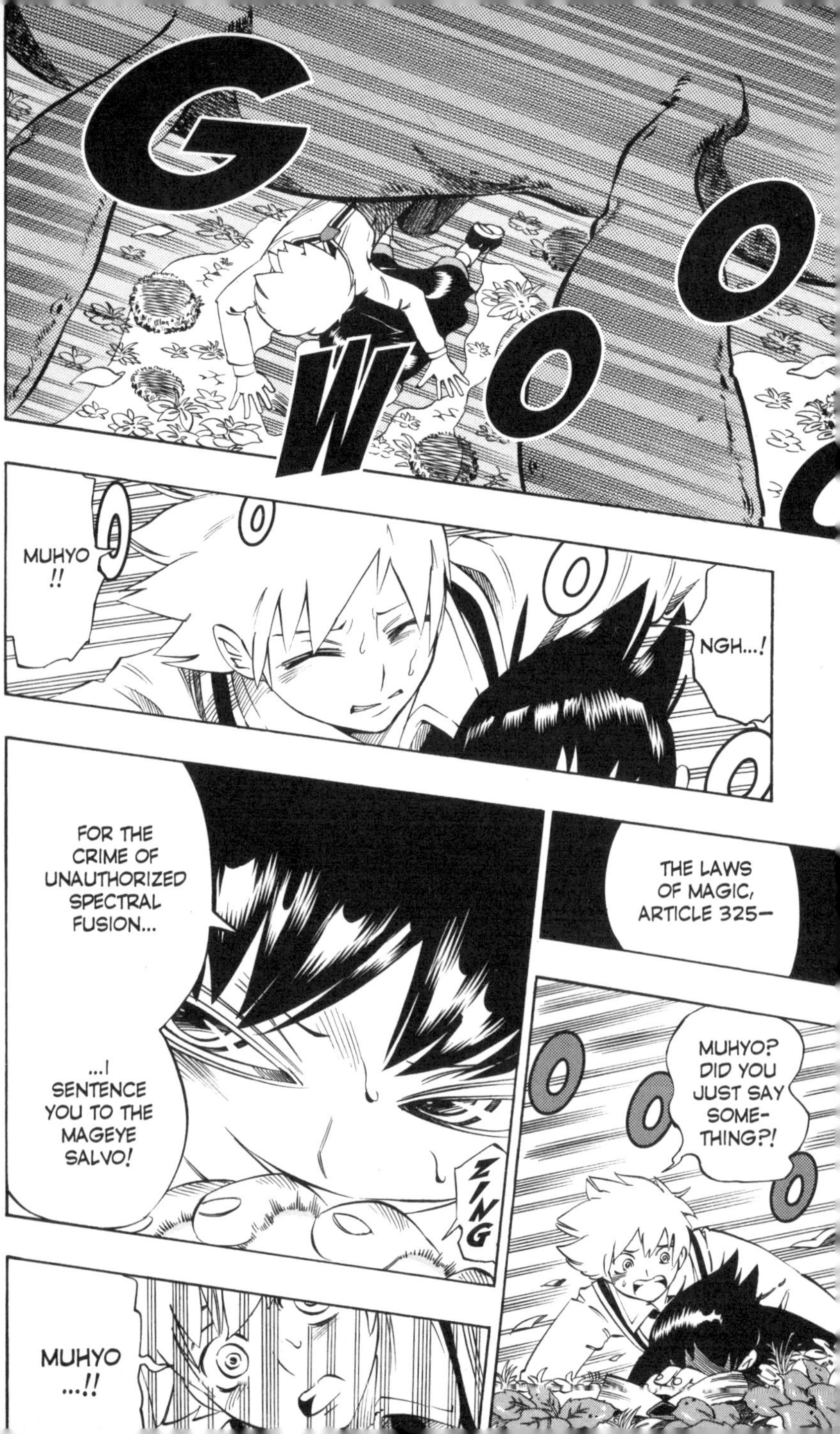
GWOOO
NGH...!
MUHYO !!
THE LAWS OF MAGIC, ARTICLE 325—
FOR THE CRIME OF UNAUTHORIZED SPECTRAL FUSION...
...I SENTENCE YOU TO THE MAGEYE SALVO!
ZING
MUHYO? DID YOU JUST SAY SOME-THING?!
MUHYO ...!!

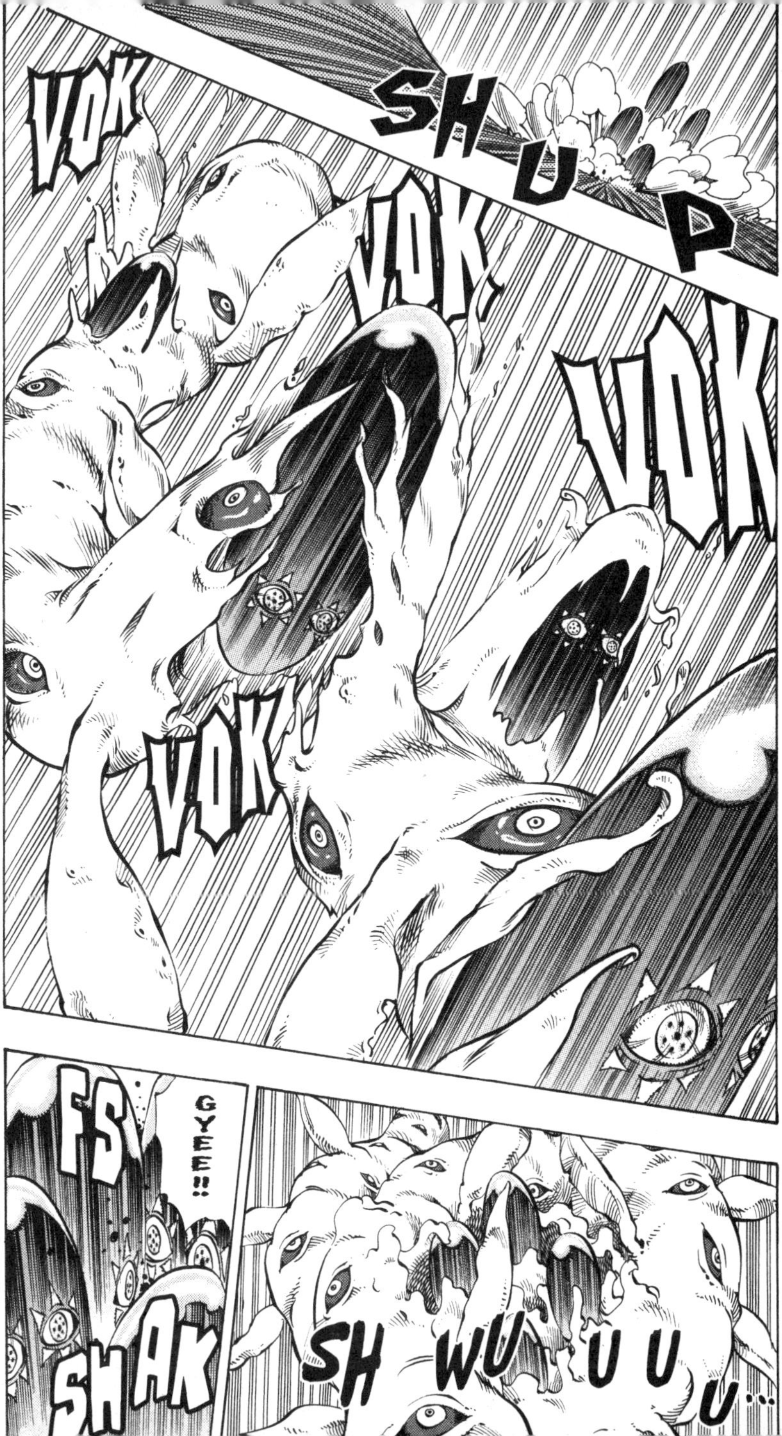
SHUP
VOK
VOK
VOK
VOK
SHWUUUU...
FS
GYEE!!
SHAK

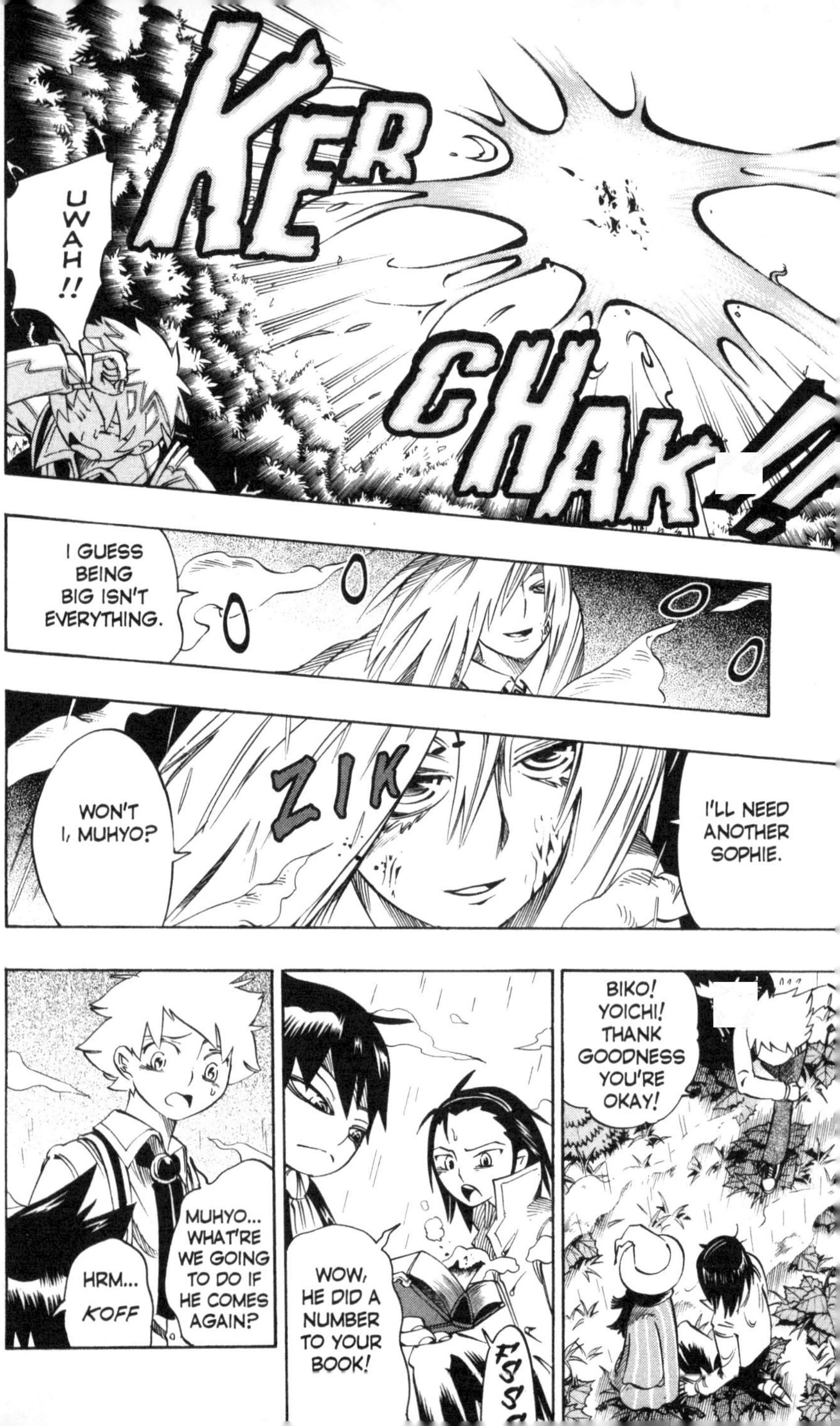
KER
CHAK
UWAH!!
I GUESS BEING BIG ISN'T EVERYTHING.
I'LL NEED ANOTHER SOPHIE.
ZIK
WON'T I, MUHYO?
BIKO! YOICHI! THANK GOODNESS YOU'RE OKAY!
WOW, HE DID A NUMBER TO YOUR BOOK!
FSS
MUHYO... WHAT'RE WE GOING TO DO IF HE COMES AGAIN?
HRM... KOFF

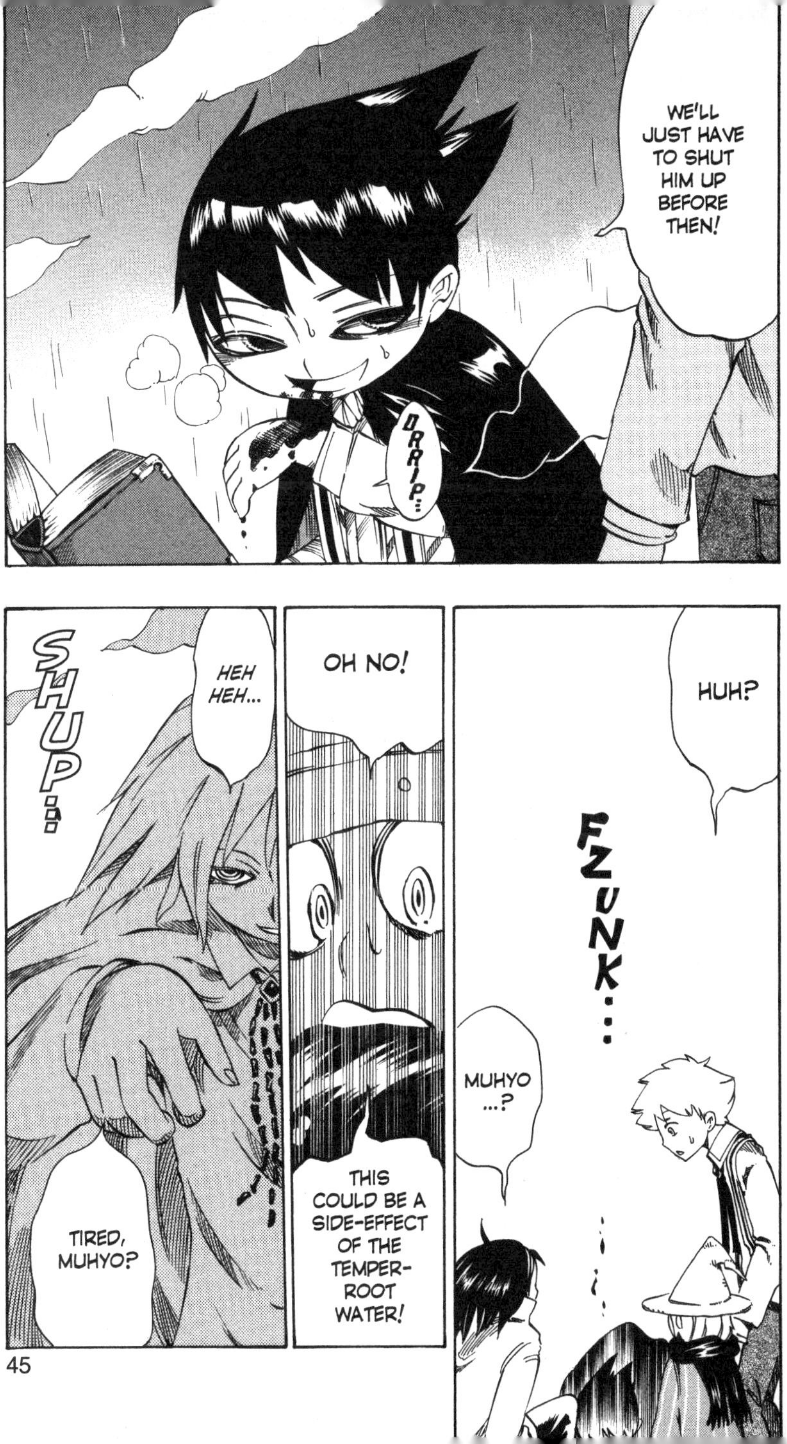
WE'LL JUST HAVE TO SHUT HIM UP BEFORE THEN!
DRRIP...
HUH?
FZUNK...
MUHYO ...?
OH NO!
THIS COULD BE A SIDE-EFFECT OF THE TEMPER-ROOT WATER!
HEH HEH...
SHUP...
TIRED, MUHYO?

I THOUGHT I'D ANSWER LAST VOLUME'S "HOW DID YOU COME UP WITH MAGIC LAW?" QUESTION HERE IN MANGA FORMAT:

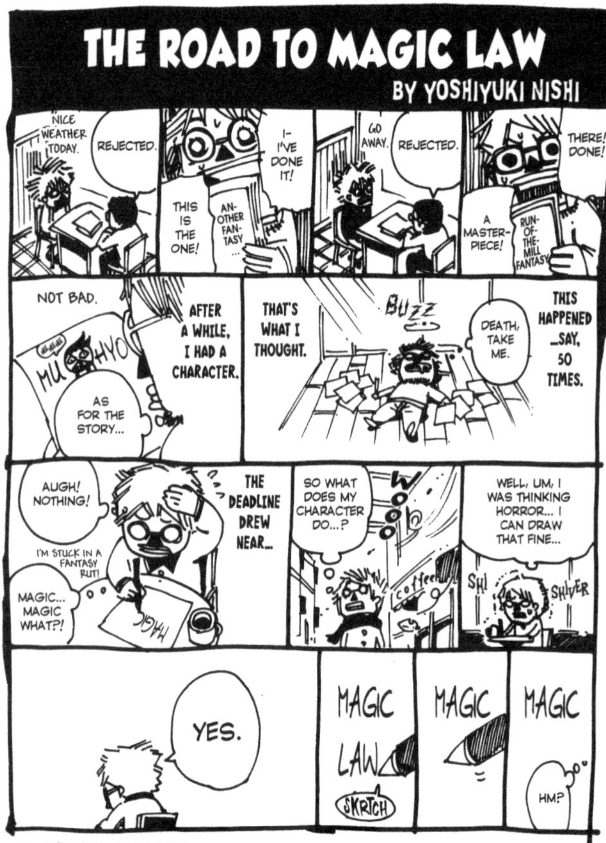
THE ROAD TO MAGIC LAW
BY YOSHIYUKI NISHI
THERE! DONE!
RUN-OF-THE-MILL FANTASY
A MASTERPIECE!
GO AWAY.
REJECTED.
I-I'VE DONE IT!
AN-OTHER FANTASY...
THIS IS THE ONE!
NICE WEATHER TODAY.
REJECTED.
THIS HAPPENED ...SAY, 50 TIMES.
DEATH, TAKE ME.
BUZZ
THAT'S WHAT I THOUGHT.
AFTER A WHILE, I HAD A CHARACTER.
NOT BAD.
MUHYO
AS FOR THE STORY...
WELL, UM, I WAS THINKING HORROR... I CAN DRAW THAT FINE...
SHI
SHIVER
WOOO
SO WHAT DOES MY CHARACTER DO...?
coffee
THE DEADLINE DREW NEAR...
AUGH! NOTHING!
I'M STUCK IN A FANTASY RUT!
MAGIC... MAGIC WHAT?!
MAGIC
MAGIC
HM?
MAGIC
MAGIC LAW
SKRTCH
YES.

A TRUE STORY

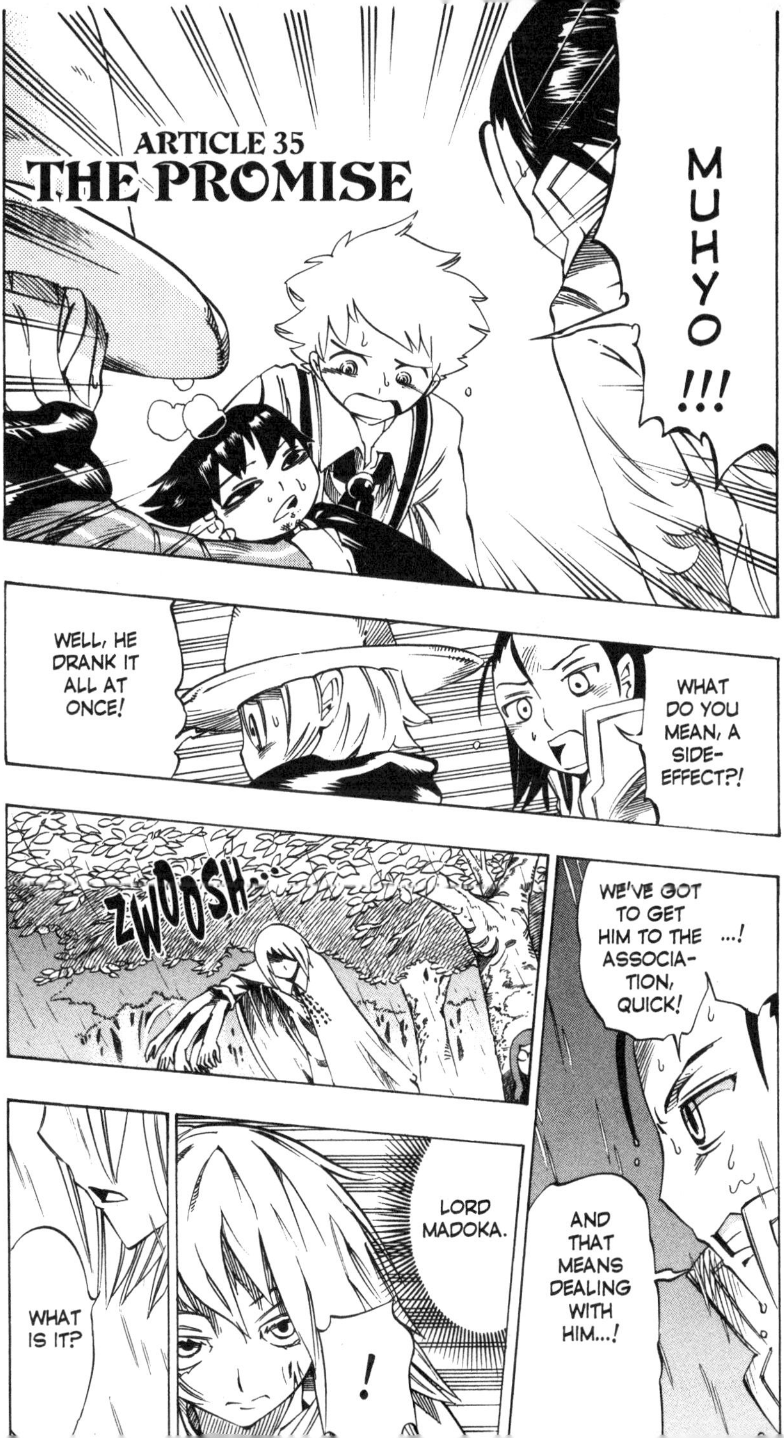
ARTICLE 35
THE PROMISE
MUHYO!!!
WHAT DO YOU MEAN, A SIDE-EFFECT?!
WELL, HE DRANK IT ALL AT ONCE!
WE'VE GOT TO GET HIM TO THE ASSOCIATION, QUICK!
...!
AND THAT MEANS DEALING WITH HIM...!
ZWOOSH...
LORD MADOKA.
!
WHAT IS IT?

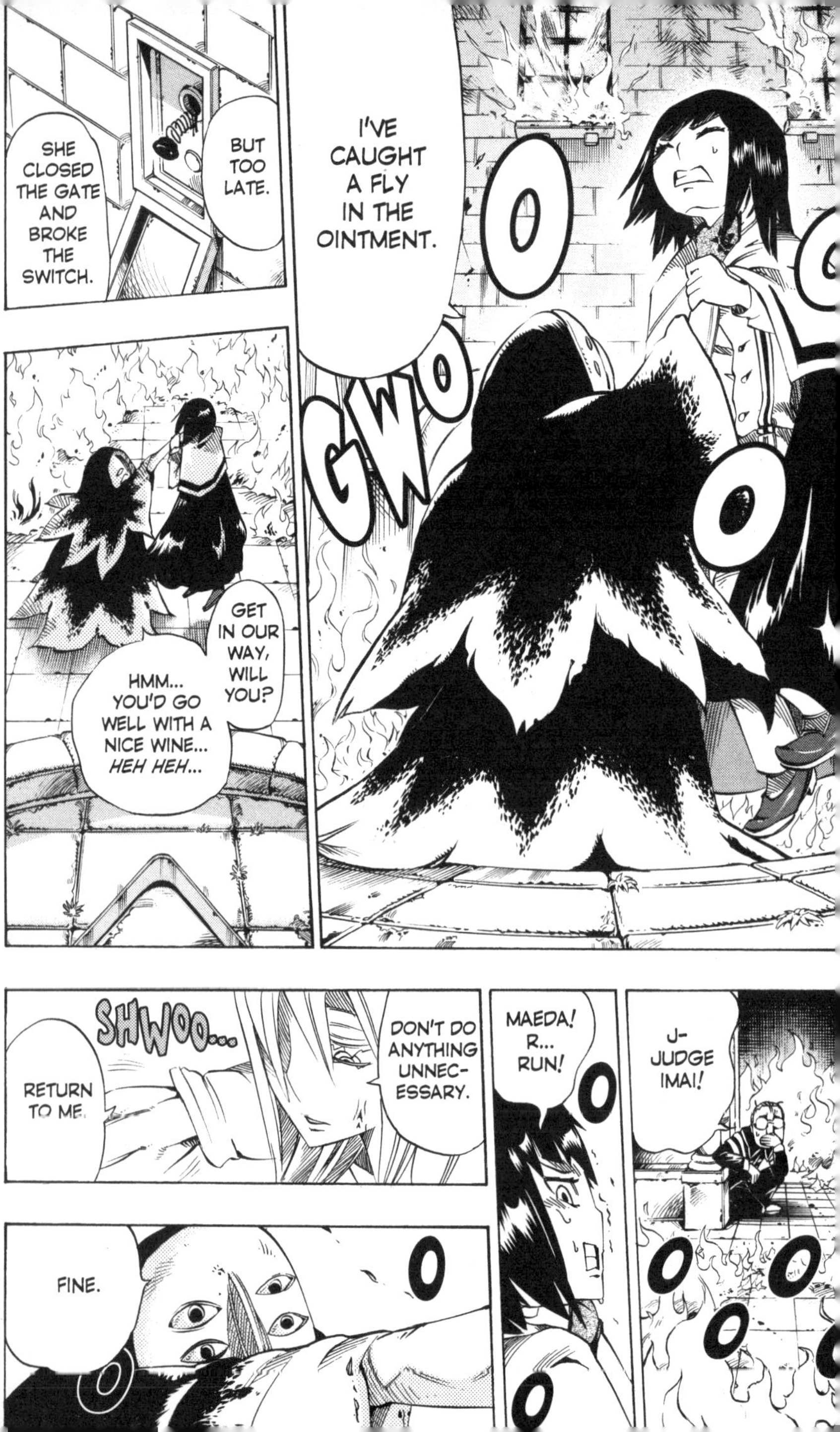
I'VE CAUGHT A FLY IN THE OINTMENT.
GWOOOO
BUT TOO LATE.
SHE CLOSED THE GATE AND BROKE THE SWITCH.
GET IN OUR WAY, WILL YOU?
HMM... YOU'D GO WELL WITH A NICE WINE... *HEH HEH*...
J-JUDGE IMAI!
MAEDA! R... RUN!
DON'T DO ANYTHING UNNECESSARY.
SHWOO...
RETURN TO ME.
FINE.

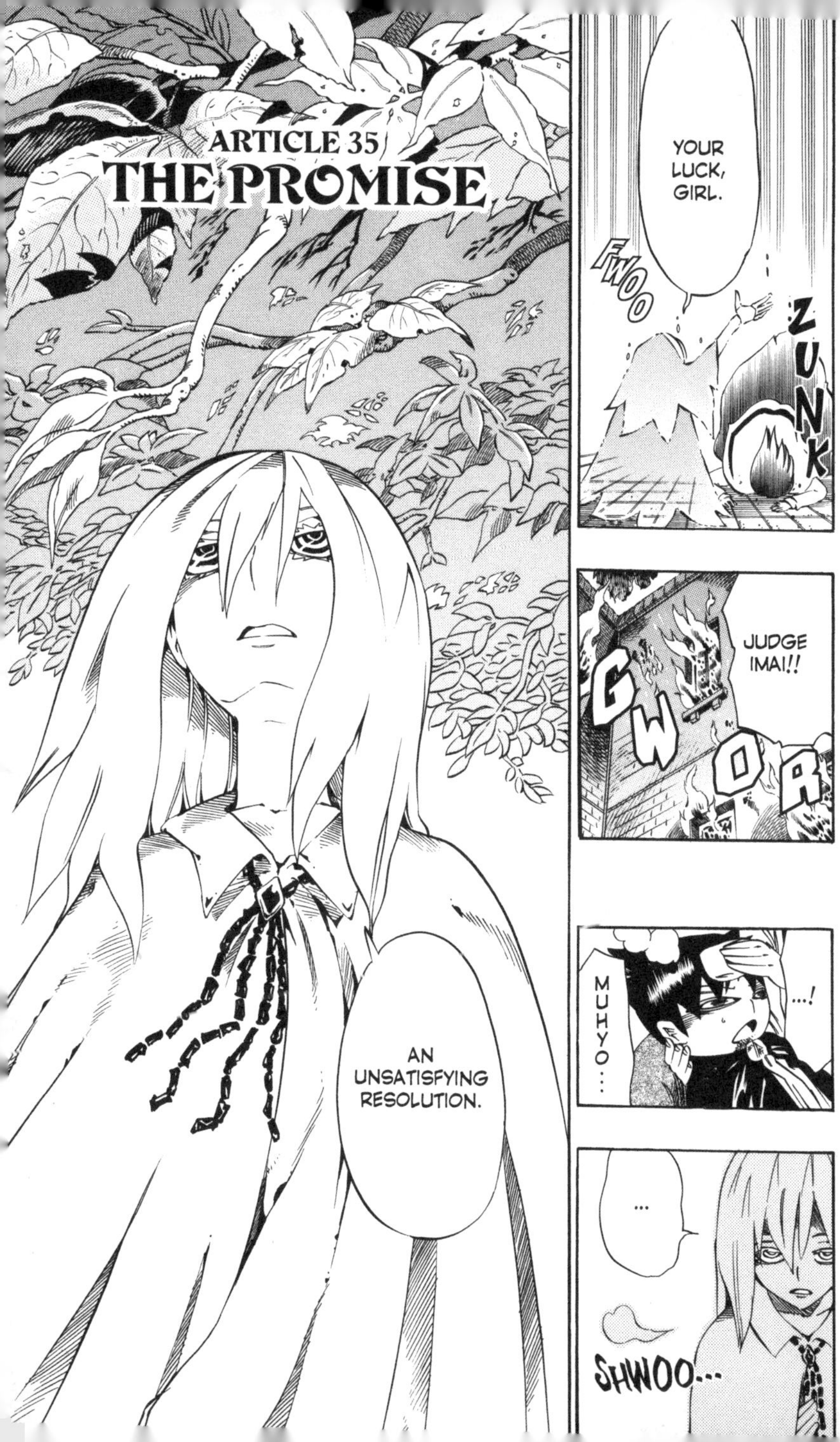
YOUR LUCK, GIRL.
FWOO
ZUNK
JUDGE IMAI!!
GWOR
MUHYO...
...!
...
SHWOO...
ARTICLE 35
THE PROMISE
AN UNSATISFYING RESOLUTION.

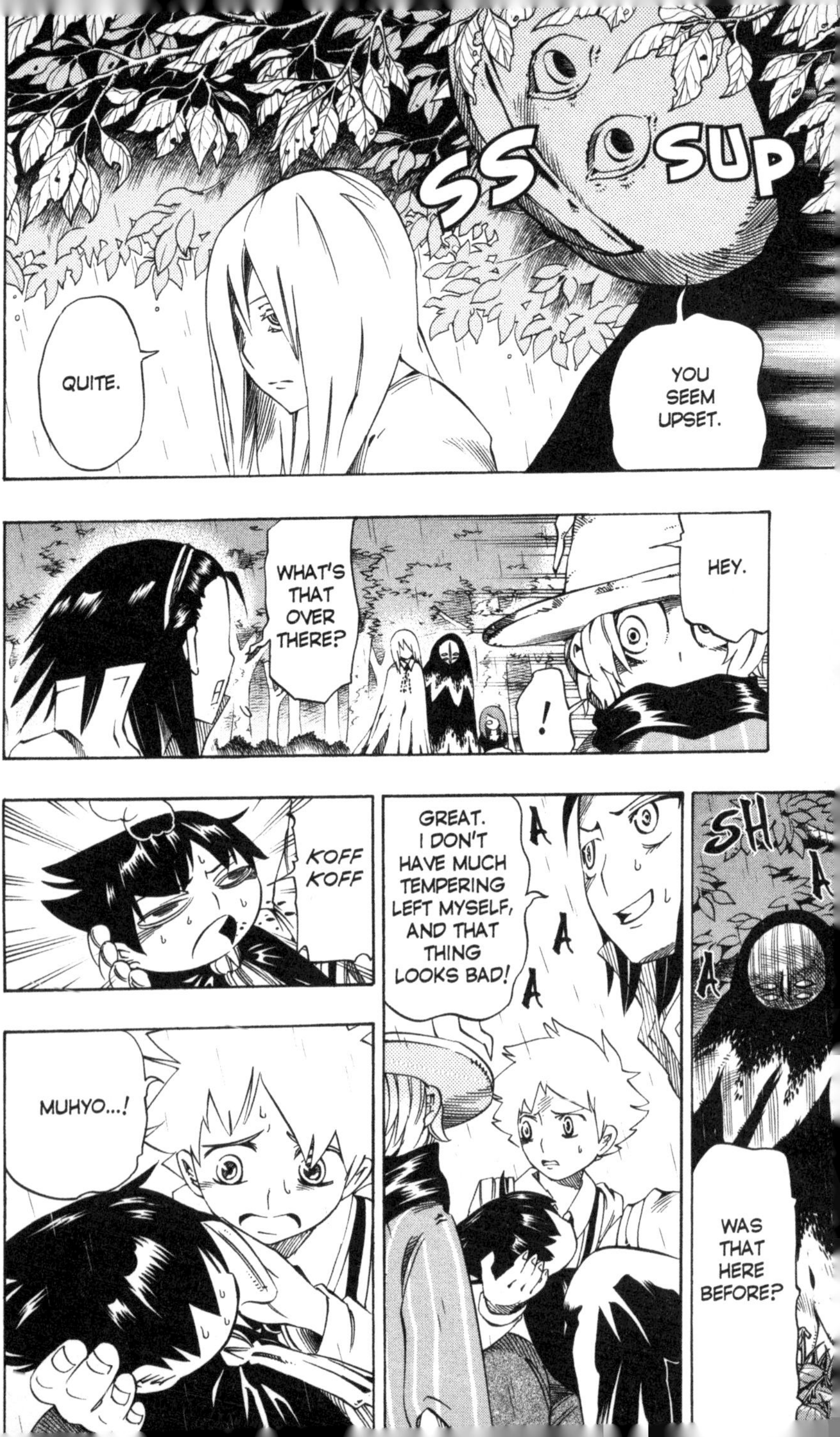
SSSUP
YOU SEEM UPSET.
QUITE.
HEY.
!
WHAT'S THAT OVER THERE?
SHAA
WAS THAT HERE BEFORE?
AAAA
GREAT. I DON'T HAVE MUCH TEMPERING LEFT MYSELF, AND THAT THING LOOKS BAD!
KOFF KOFF
MUHYO...!

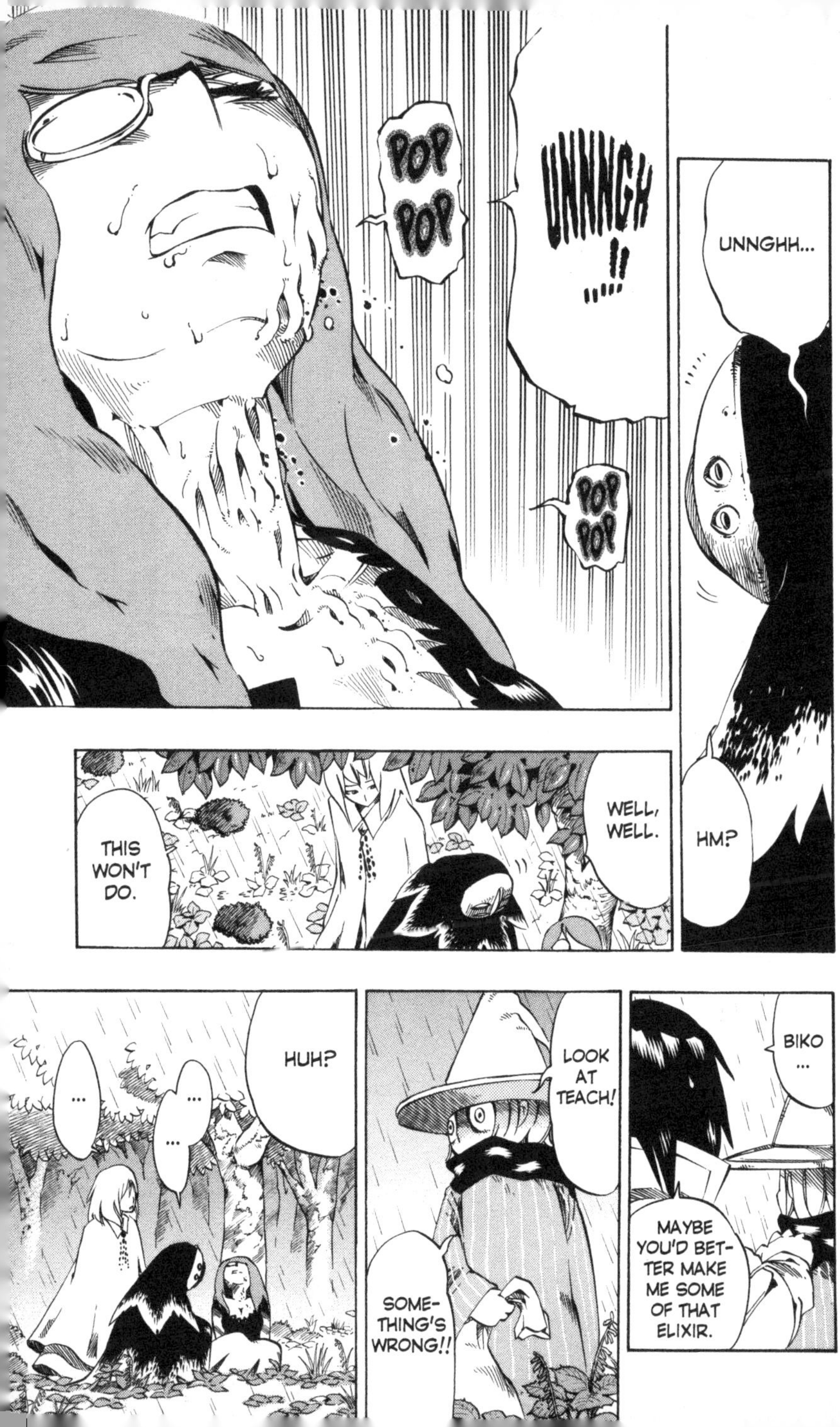
UNNGHH...
HM?
POP POP
UNNNGH ...!!
POP POP
WELL, WELL.
THIS WON'T DO.
BIKO ...
MAYBE YOU'D BET-TER MAKE ME SOME OF THAT ELIXIR.
LOOK AT TEACH!
SOME-THING'S WRONG!!
HUH?
...
...
...

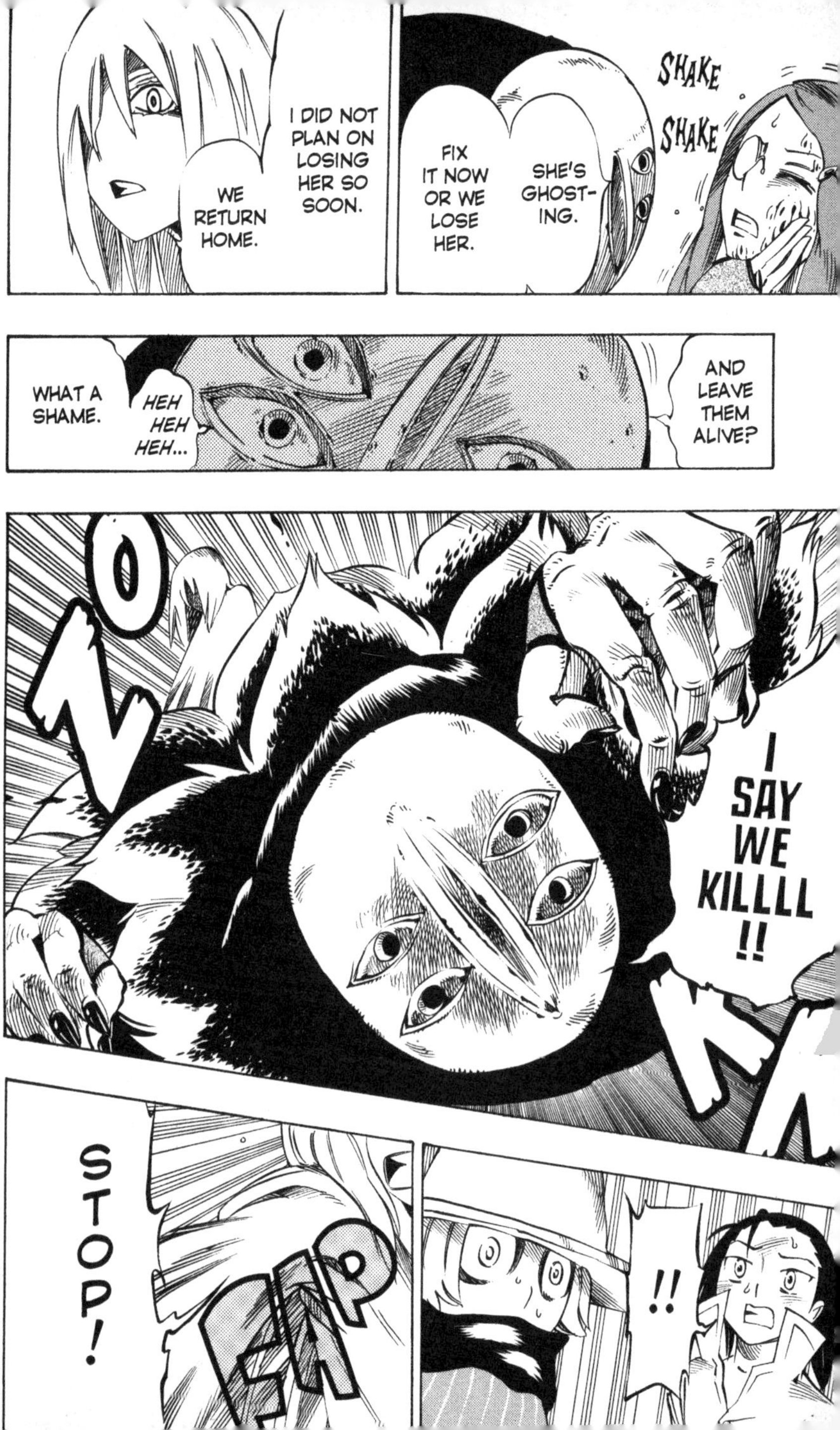
SHAKE
SHAKE
SHE'S GHOSTING.
FIX IT NOW OR WE LOSE HER.
I DID NOT PLAN ON LOSING HER SO SOON.
WE RETURN HOME.
AND LEAVE THEM ALIVE?
HEH HEH HEH...
WHAT A SHAME.
I SAY WE KILLLL !!
!!
STOP!

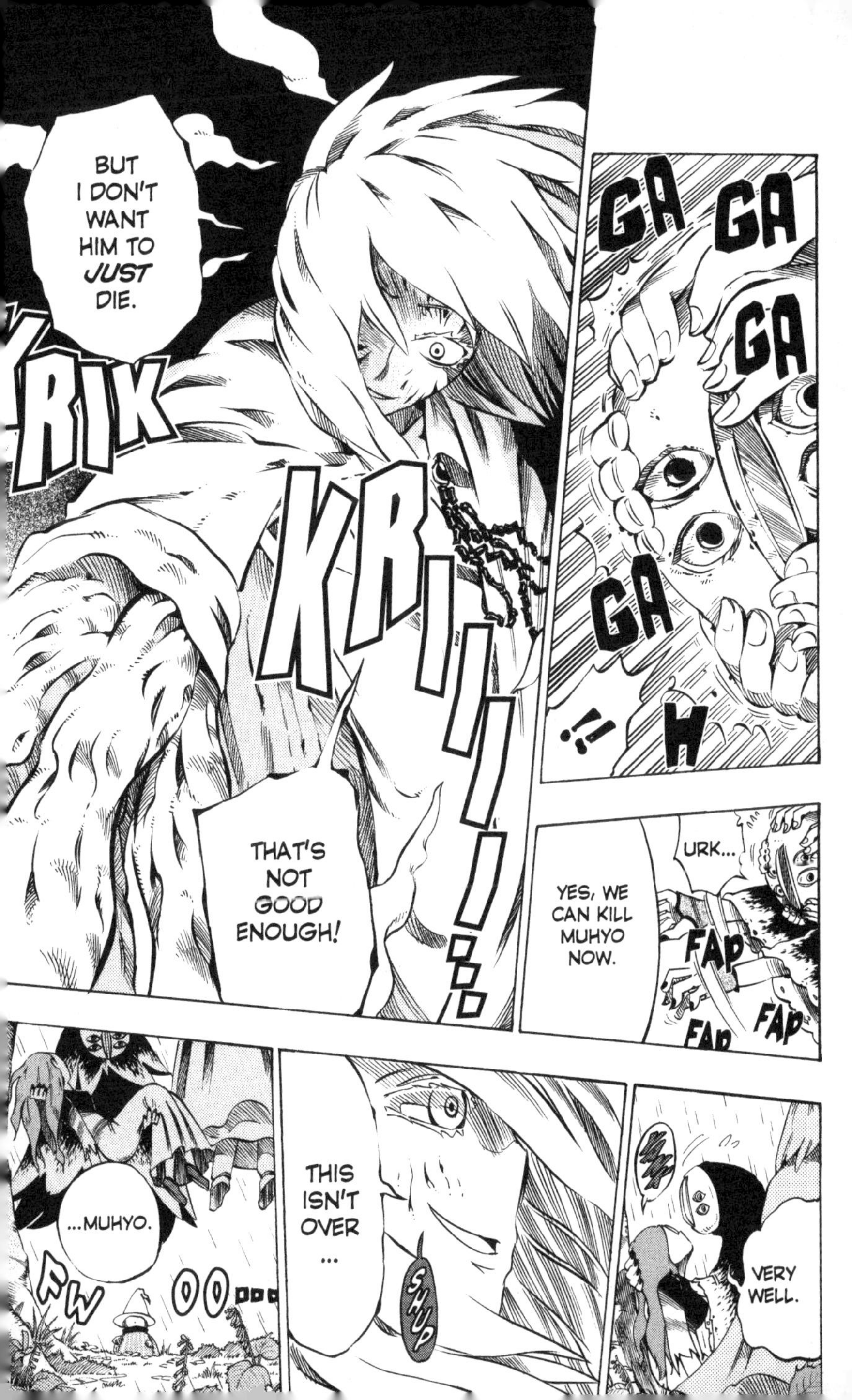
GA GA
GA
GA
H
!!
URK...
YES, WE CAN KILL MUHYO NOW.
FAP
FAP
FAP
BUT I DON'T WANT HIM TO *JUST* DIE.
KRIK
KRIIIIII...
THAT'S NOT GOOD ENOUGH!
VERY WELL.
THIS ISN'T OVER ...
SHUP
...MUHYO.
FWOO...

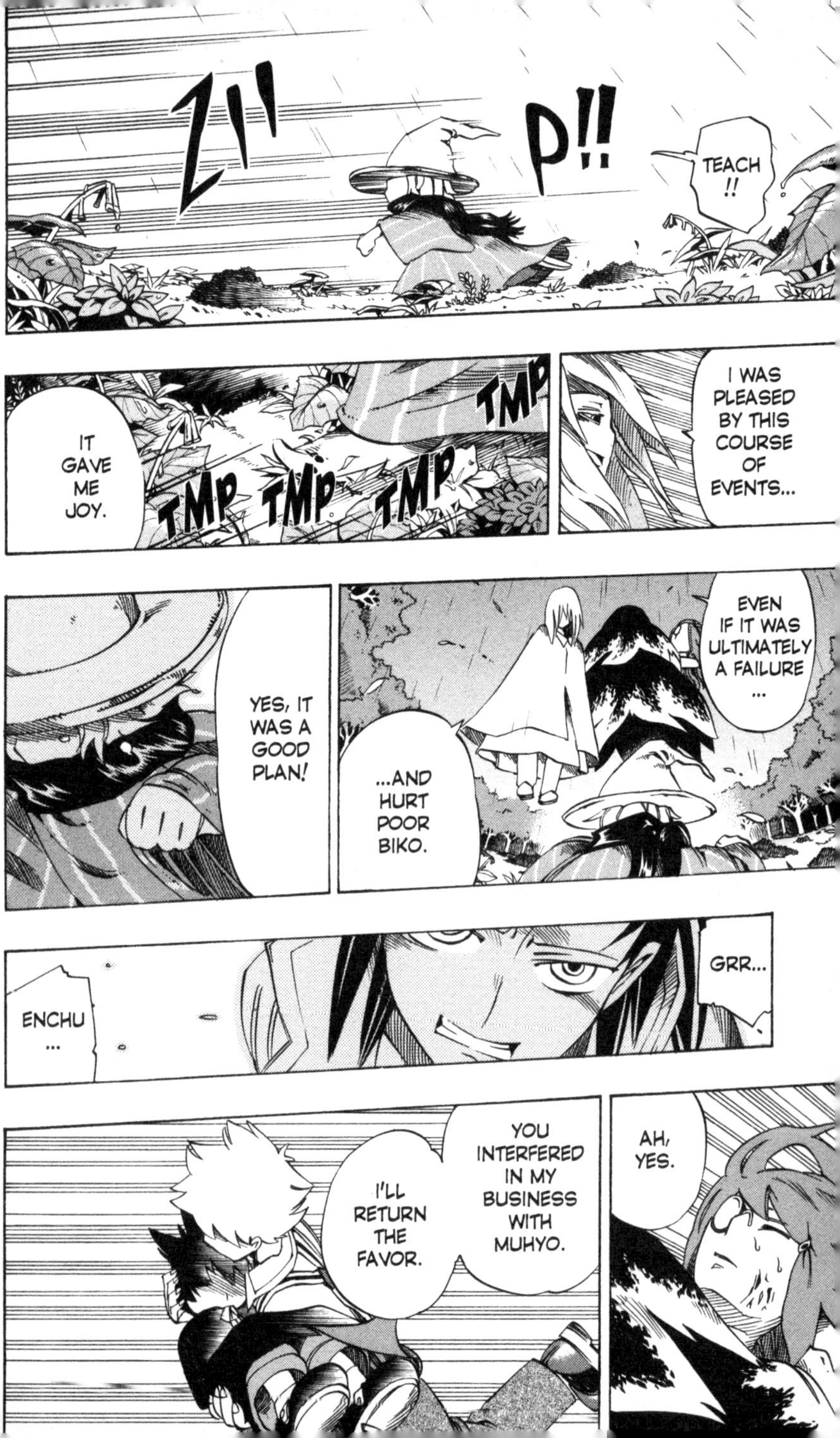
TEACH !!
ZI P!!
I WAS PLEASED BY THIS COURSE OF EVENTS...
TMP
TMP TMP TMP
IT GAVE ME JOY.
EVEN IF IT WAS ULTIMATELY A FAILURE ...
...AND HURT POOR BIKO.
YES, IT WAS A GOOD PLAN!
GRR...
ENCHU ...
AH, YES.
YOU INTERFERED IN MY BUSINESS WITH MUHYO.
I'LL RETURN THE FAVOR.

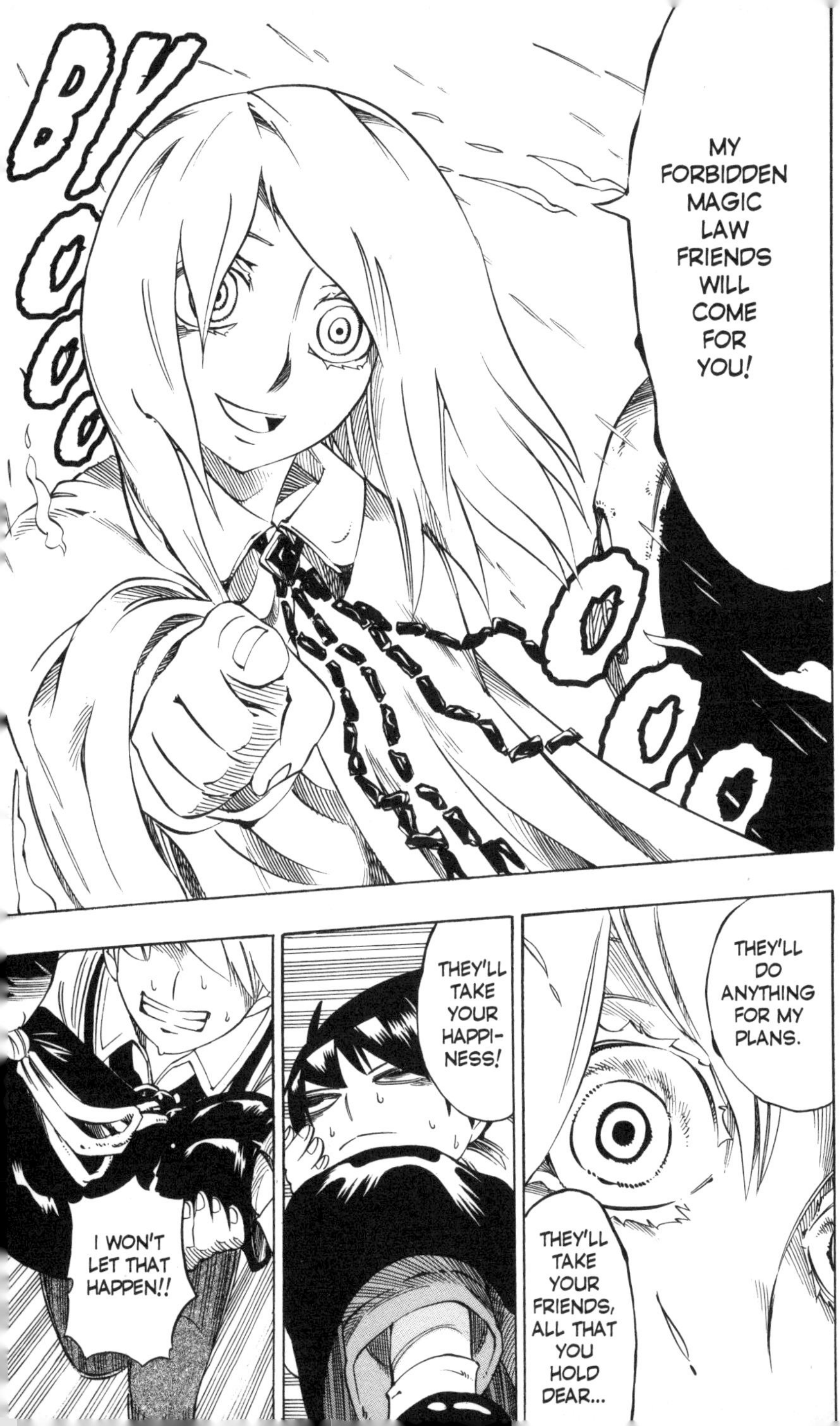
BYOOOO
MY FORBIDDEN MAGIC LAW FRIENDS WILL COME FOR YOU!
THEY'LL DO ANYTHING FOR MY PLANS.
THEY'LL TAKE YOUR FRIENDS, ALL THAT YOU HOLD DEAR...
THEY'LL TAKE YOUR HAPPI-NESS!
I WON'T LET THAT HAPPEN!!

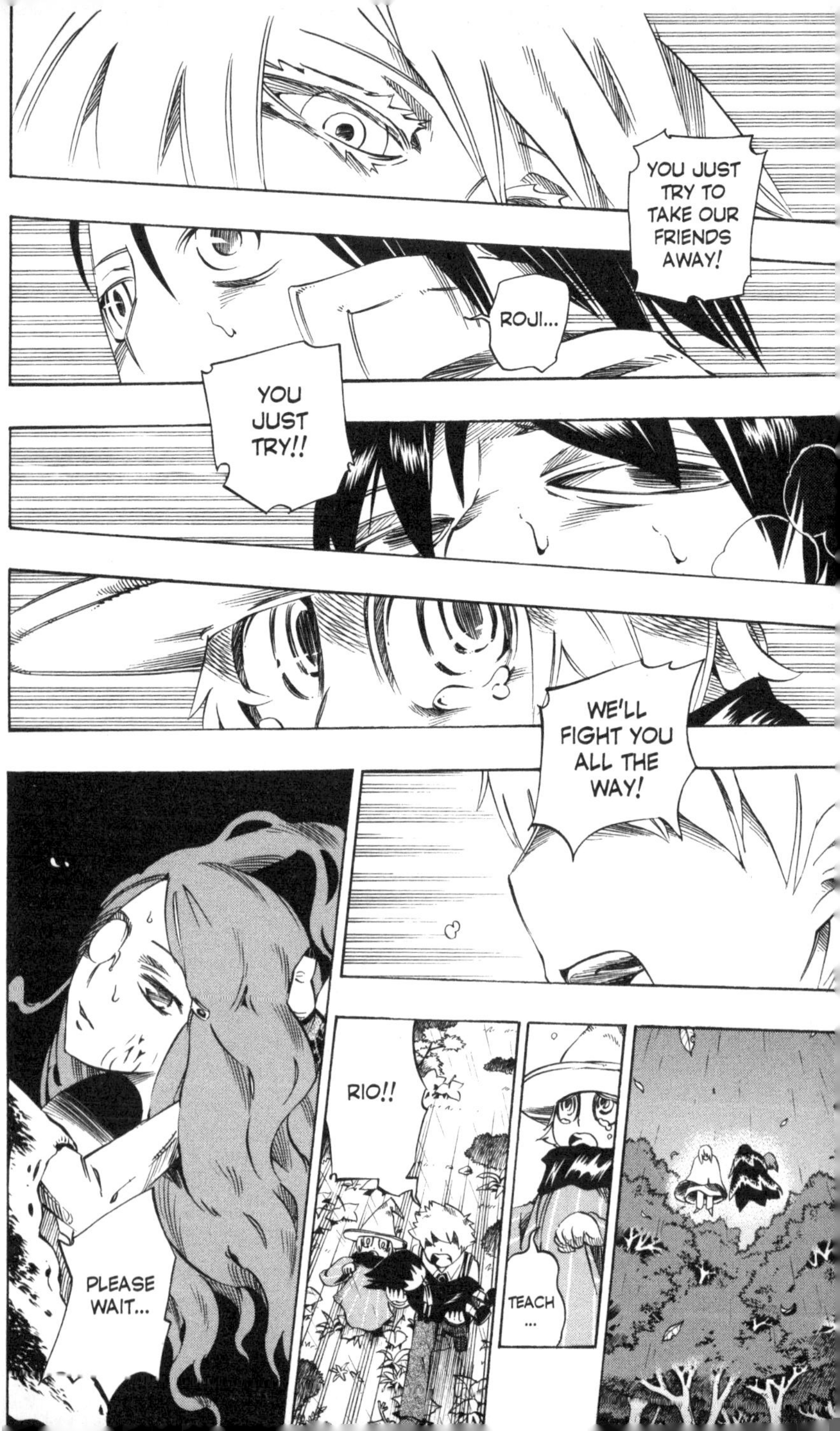
YOU JUST TRY TO TAKE OUR FRIENDS AWAY!
ROJI...
YOU JUST TRY!!
WE'LL FIGHT YOU ALL THE WAY!
TEACH ...
RIO!!
PLEASE WAIT...

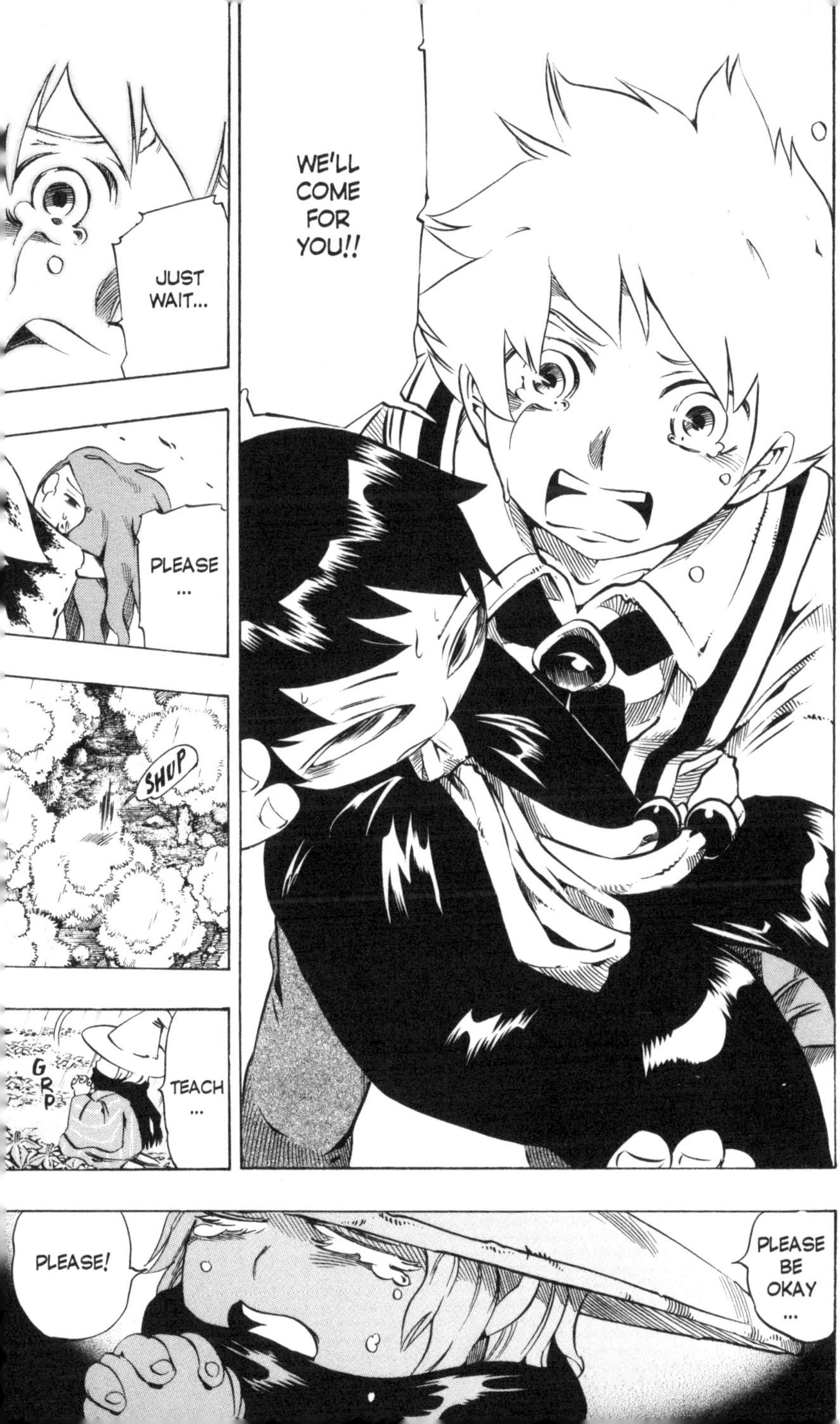
WE'LL COME FOR YOU!!
JUST WAIT...
PLEASE ...
SHUP
GRP
TEACH ...
PLEASE BE OKAY ...
PLEASE!

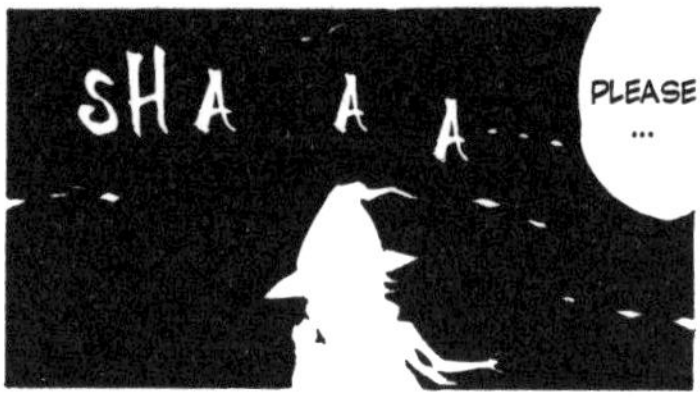
PLEASE ...
SHAAA...
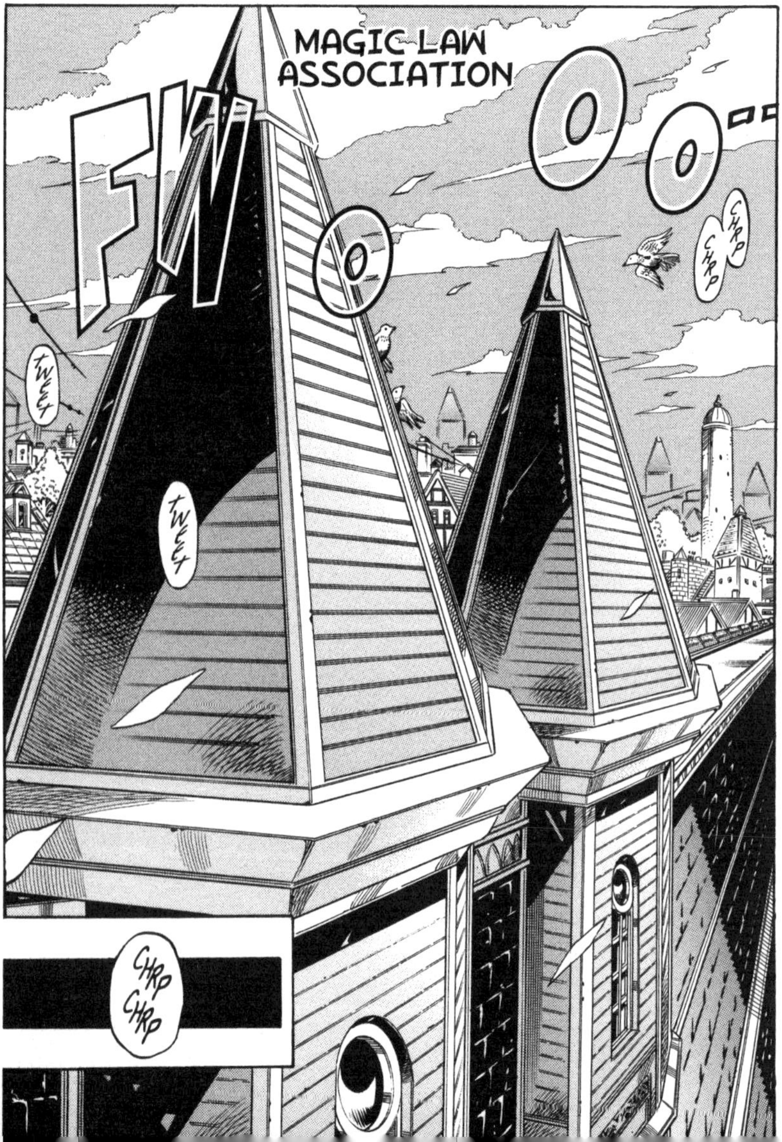
MAGIC LAW ASSOCIATION
FWOOOO...
CHRP CHRP
TWEET
TWEET
CHRP CHRP

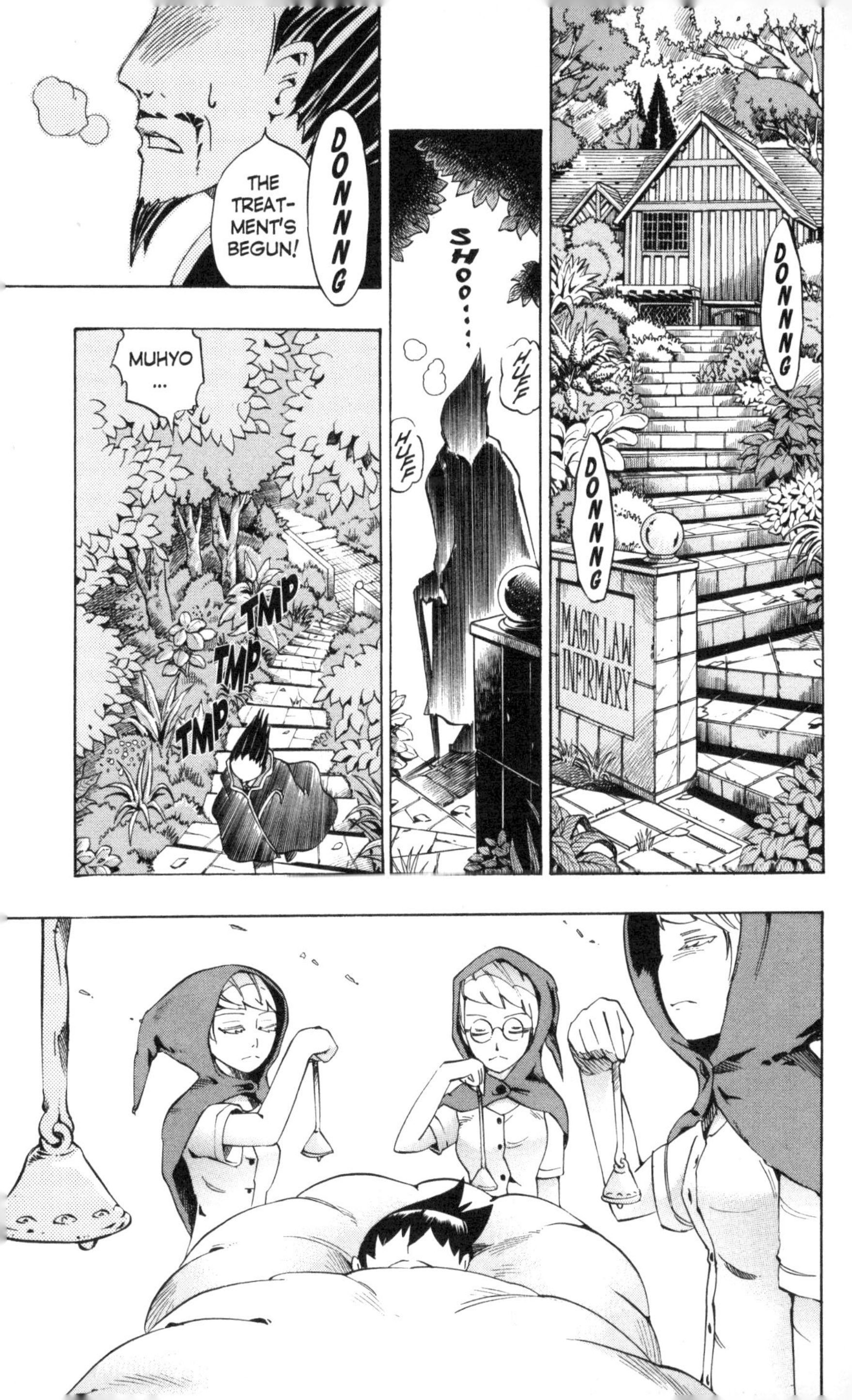
DONNNG
DONNNG
MAGIC LAW INFIRMARY
SHOO....
HUFF
HUFF
DONNNG
THE TREATMENT'S BEGUN!
MUHYO ...
TMP
TMP
TMP

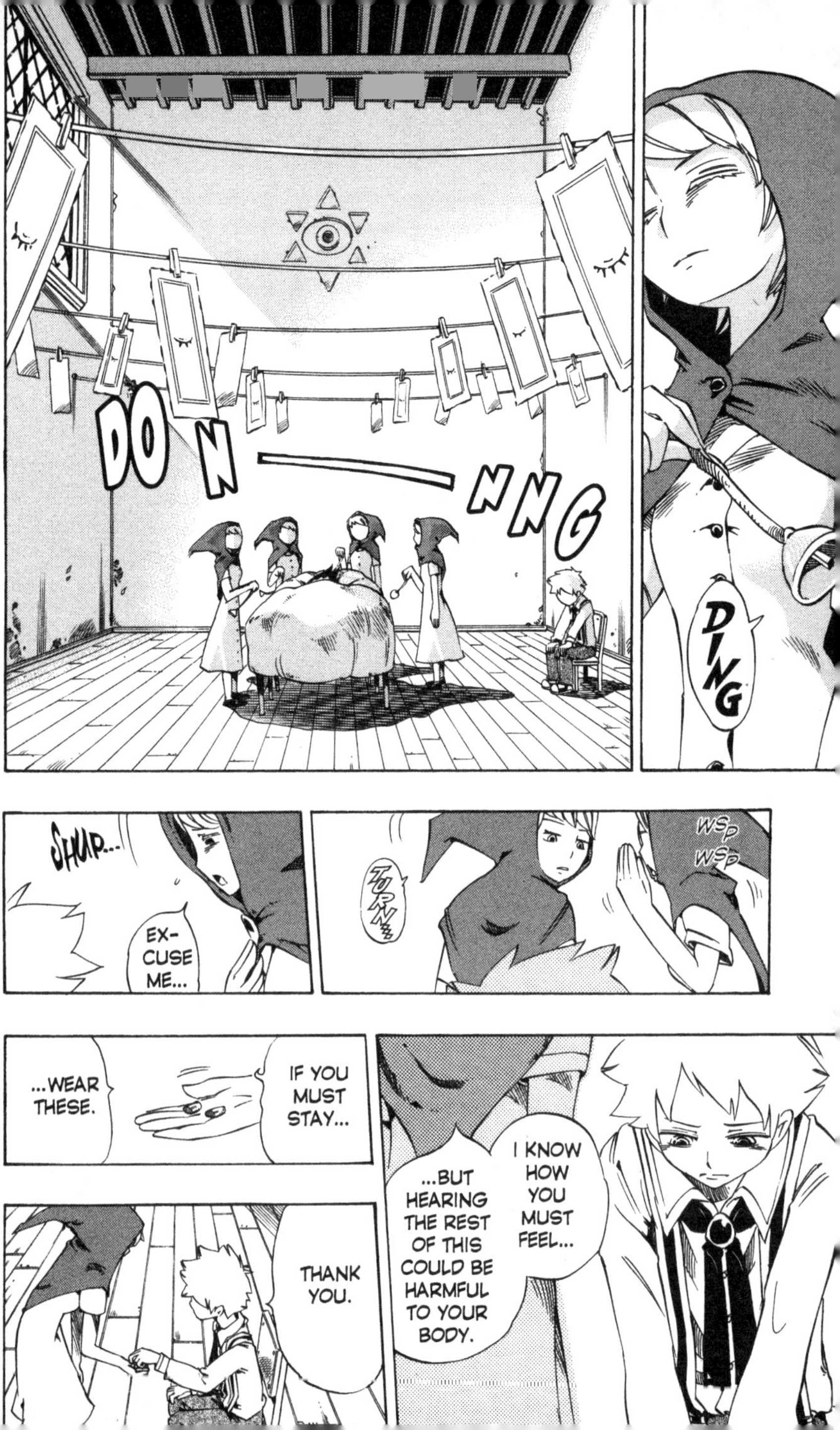
DING
DON—NNG
WSP WSP
TURN
SHUP...
EX-CUSE ME...
I KNOW HOW YOU MUST FEEL...
...BUT HEARING THE REST OF THIS COULD BE HARMFUL TO YOUR BODY.
IF YOU MUST STAY...
...WEAR THESE.
THANK YOU.

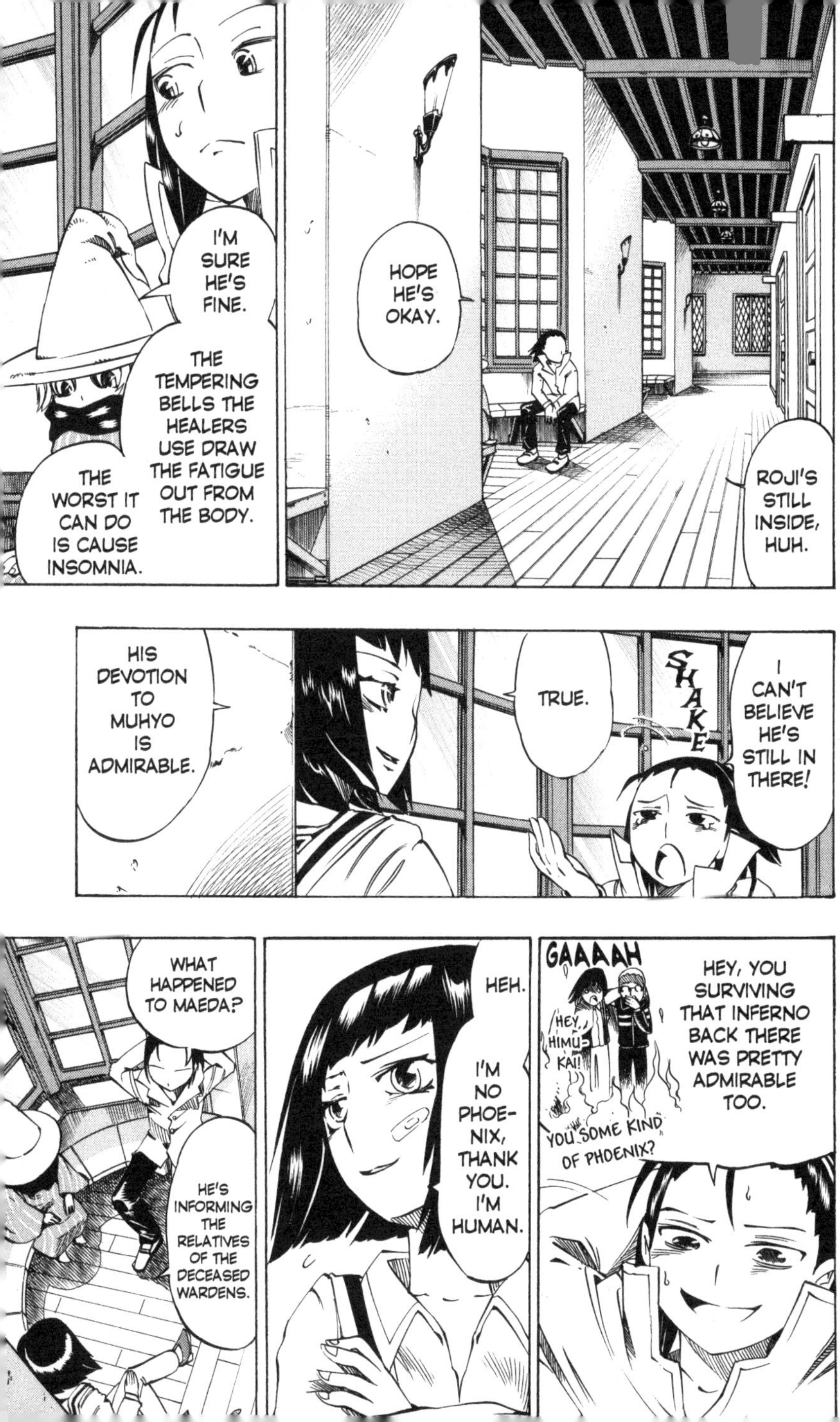
ROJI'S STILL INSIDE, HUH.
HOPE HE'S OKAY.
I'M SURE HE'S FINE.
THE TEMPERING BELLS THE HEALERS USE DRAW THE FATIGUE OUT FROM THE BODY.
THE WORST IT CAN DO IS CAUSE INSOMNIA.
SHAKE
I CAN'T BELIEVE HE'S STILL IN THERE!
TRUE.
HIS DEVOTION TO MUHYO IS ADMIRABLE.
HEY, YOU SURVIVING THAT INFERNO BACK THERE WAS PRETTY ADMIRABLE TOO.
GAAAAH
HEY, HIMUKAI!
YOU SOME KIND OF PHOENIX?
HEH.
I'M NO PHOENIX, THANK YOU. I'M HUMAN.
WHAT HAPPENED TO MAEDA?
HE'S INFORMING THE RELATIVES OF THE DECEASED WARDENS.

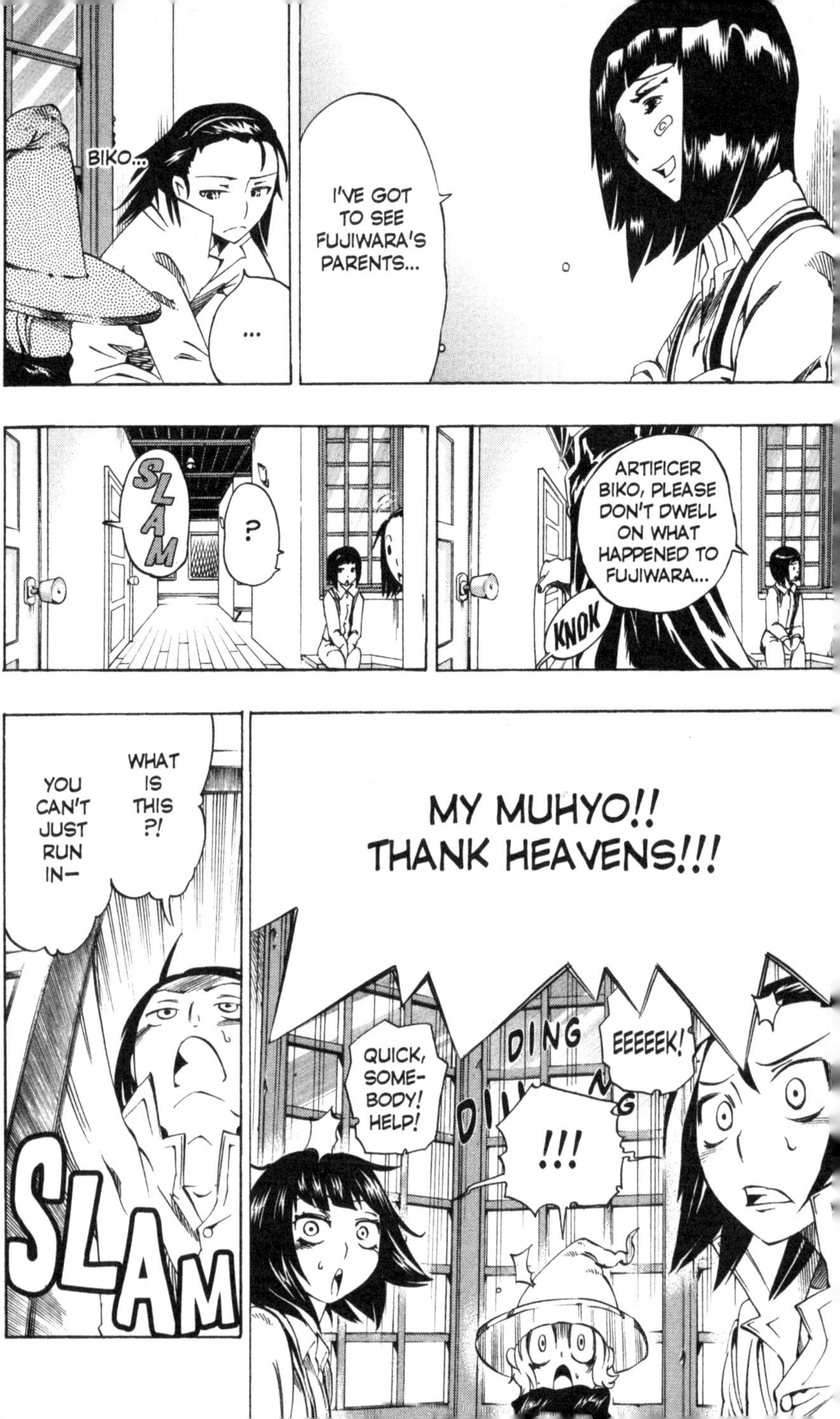
I'VE GOT TO SEE FUJIWARA'S PARENTS...
BIKO...
...
KNOK
ARTIFICER BIKO, PLEASE DON'T DWELL ON WHAT HAPPENED TO FUJIWARA...
SLAM
?
MY MUHYO!! THANK HEAVENS!!!
EEEEEK!
QUICK, SOMEBODY! HELP!
DING DING
!!!
WHAT IS THIS?!
YOU CAN'T JUST RUN IN—
SLAM

EE EEEK

EE EEEK

OH...!

CHIEF INVESTIGATOR PAGE?!

SOMEBODY!!

THANK HEAV-ENS...

THANK HEAV-ENS...

EEEK

PAGE ?!

YOUR RED HOOD MIRRORS THE BLUSH OF MY HEART...

ALLOW ME TO COMPOSE A POEM BY WAY OF APOLOGY!

VWIP

HE'S MORE THAN THAT...

HE'S AN EXECUTOR? YOUR SUPERIOR, YOICHI?

UMPH

EH?

SORRY! SORRY!

BOW

BOW

YOU WOKE HIM UP!

REALLY!

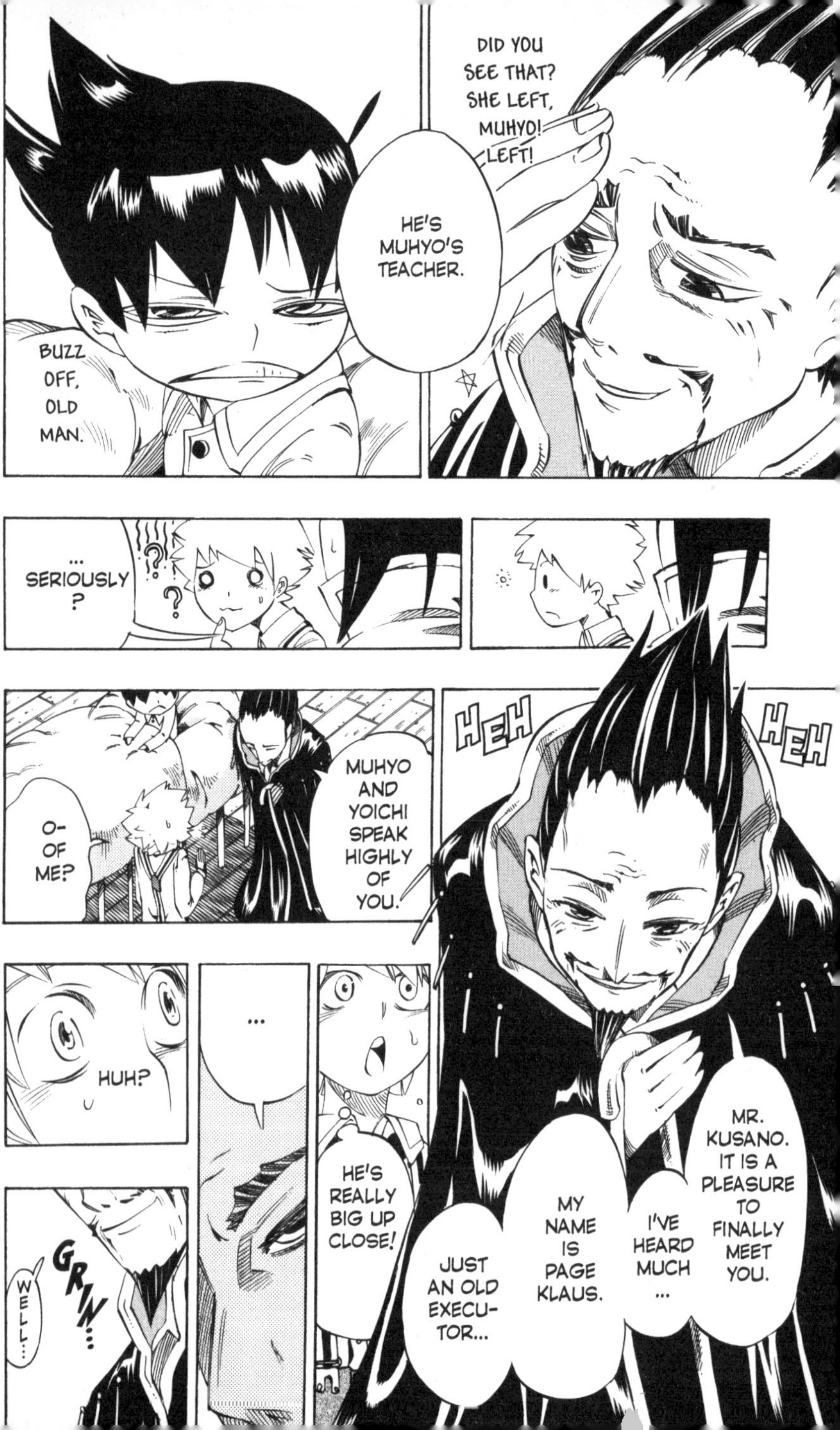
DID YOU SEE THAT? SHE LEFT, MUHYO! LEFT!
HE'S MUHYO'S TEACHER.
BUZZ OFF, OLD MAN.
...SERIOUSLY?
HEH
HEH
MR. KUSANO. IT IS A PLEASURE TO FINALLY MEET YOU.
I'VE HEARD MUCH...
MY NAME IS PAGE KLAUS.
JUST AN OLD EXECUTOR...
MUHYO AND YOICHI SPEAK HIGHLY OF YOU.
O-OF ME?
HE'S REALLY BIG UP CLOSE!
...
HUH?
GRIN...
WELL...

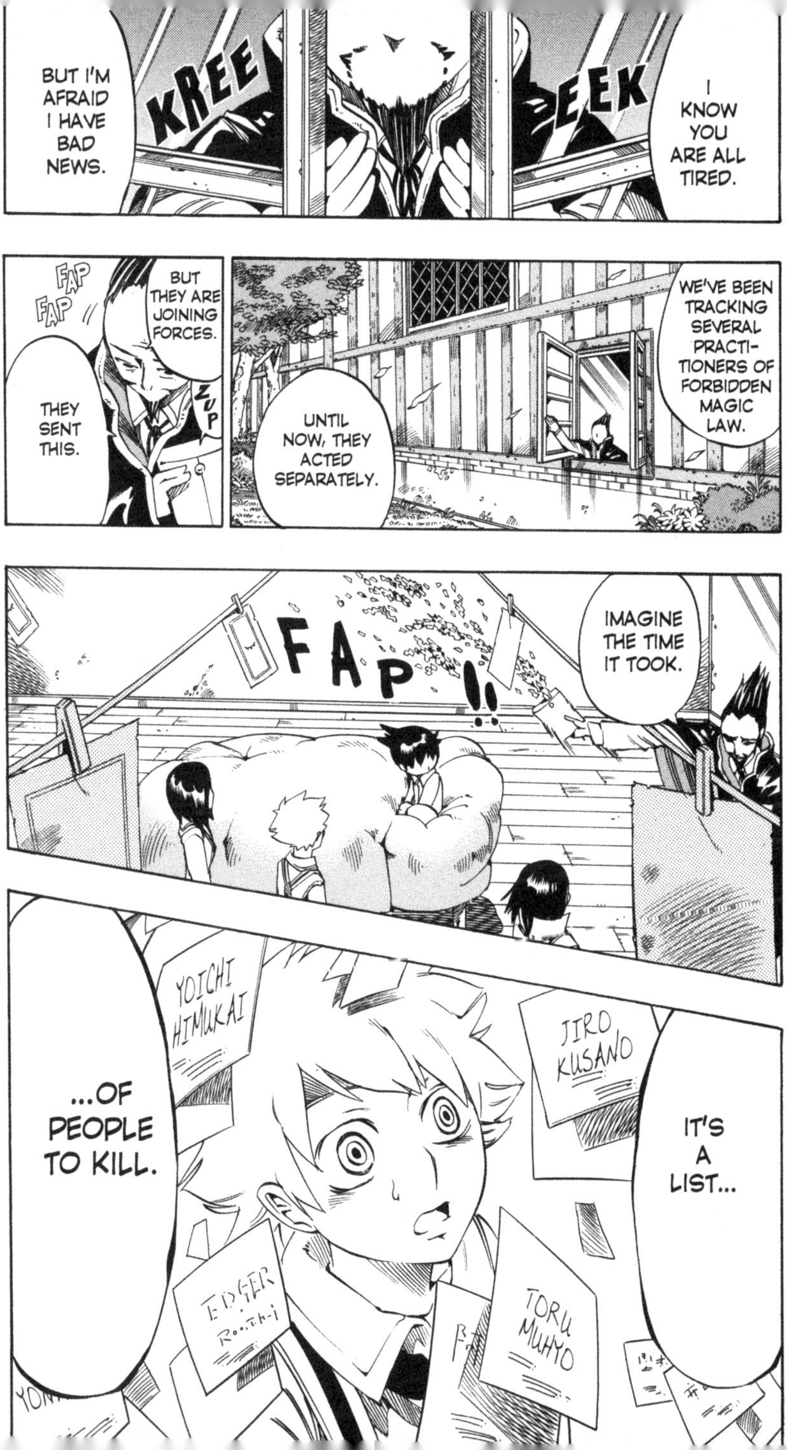
I KNOW YOU ARE ALL TIRED.
KREE EEK
BUT I'M AFRAID I HAVE BAD NEWS.
WE'VE BEEN TRACKING SEVERAL PRACTI- TIONERS OF FORBIDDEN MAGIC LAW.
UNTIL NOW, THEY ACTED SEPARATELY.
BUT THEY ARE JOINING FORCES.
ZUP
FAP FAP
THEY SENT THIS.
IMAGINE THE TIME IT TOOK.
FAP!!
IT'S A LIST...
JIRO KUSANO
YOICHI HIMUKAI
TORU MUHYO
...OF PEOPLE TO KILL.

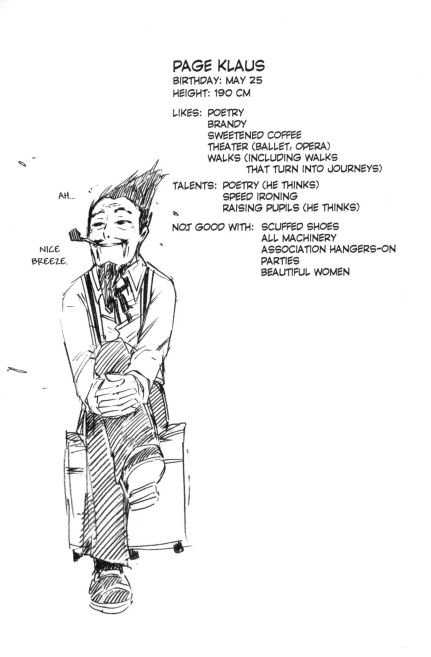

PAGE KLAUS
BIRTHDAY: MAY 25
HEIGHT: 190 CM

LIKES: POETRY
BRANDY
SWEETENED COFFEE
THEATER (BALLET, OPERA)
WALKS (INCLUDING WALKS
THAT TURN INTO JOURNEYS)

TALENTS: POETRY (HE THINKS)
SPEED IRONING
RAISING PUPILS (HE THINKS)

NOT GOOD WITH: SCUFFED SHOES
ALL MACHINERY
ASSOCIATION HANGERS-ON
PARTIES
BEAUTIFUL WOMEN

AH...

NICE
BREEZE.

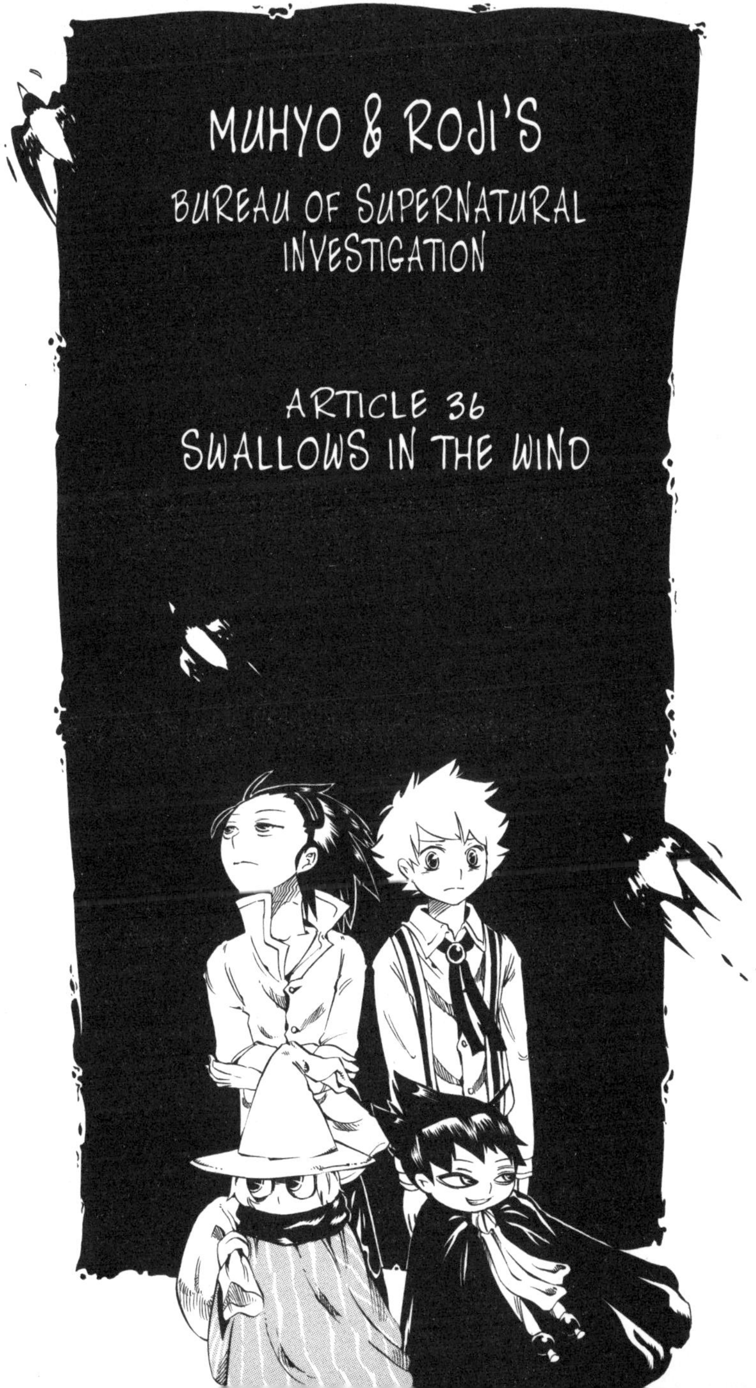
MUHYO & ROJI'S
BUREAU OF SUPERNATURAL INVESTIGATION
ARTICLE 36
SWALLOWS IN THE WIND

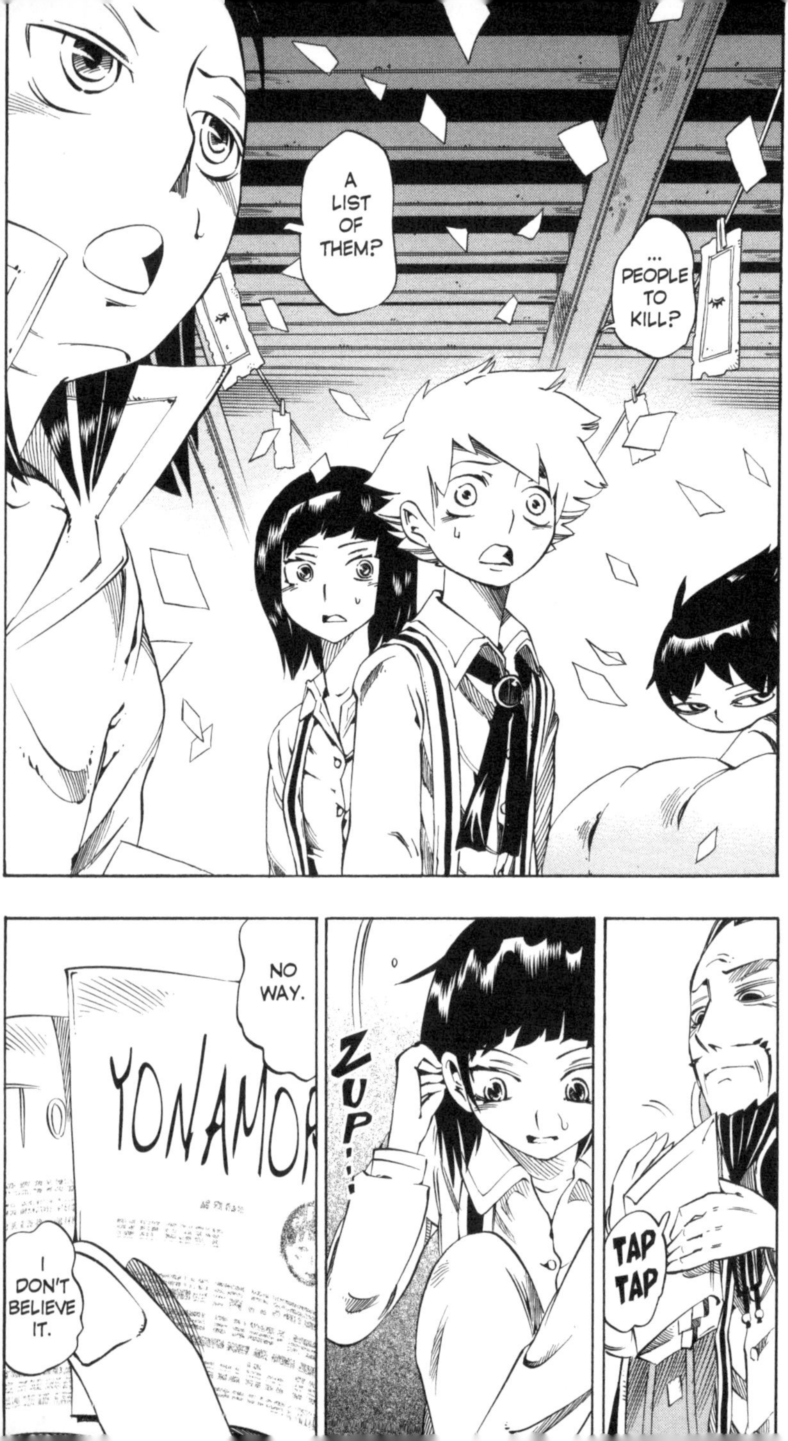
A LIST OF THEM?
... PEOPLE TO KILL?
TAP TAP
ZUP!!
NO WAY.
I DON'T BELIEVE IT.

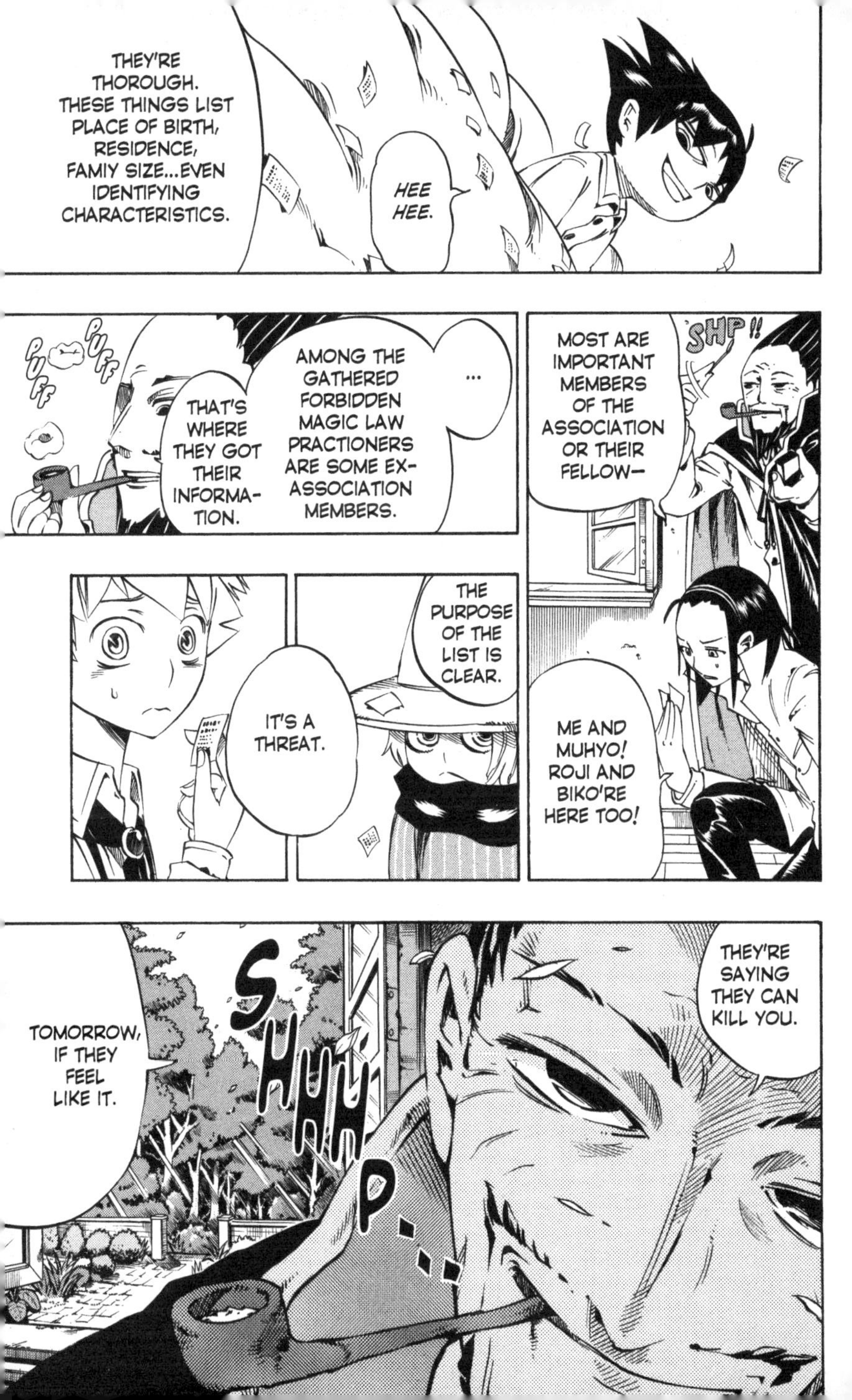
THEY'RE THOROUGH. THESE THINGS LIST PLACE OF BIRTH, RESIDENCE, FAMIY SIZE...EVEN IDENTIFYING CHARACTERISTICS.
HEE HEE.
SHP!!
MOST ARE IMPORTANT MEMBERS OF THE ASSOCIATION OR THEIR FELLOW—
ME AND MUHYO! ROJI AND BIKO'RE HERE TOO!
...
AMONG THE GATHERED FORBIDDEN MAGIC LAW PRACTIONERS ARE SOME EX-ASSOCIATION MEMBERS.
PUFF PUFF
THAT'S WHERE THEY GOT THEIR INFORMATION.
THE PURPOSE OF THE LIST IS CLEAR.
IT'S A THREAT.
THEY'RE SAYING THEY CAN KILL YOU.
SHHHP...
TOMORROW, IF THEY FEEL LIKE IT.

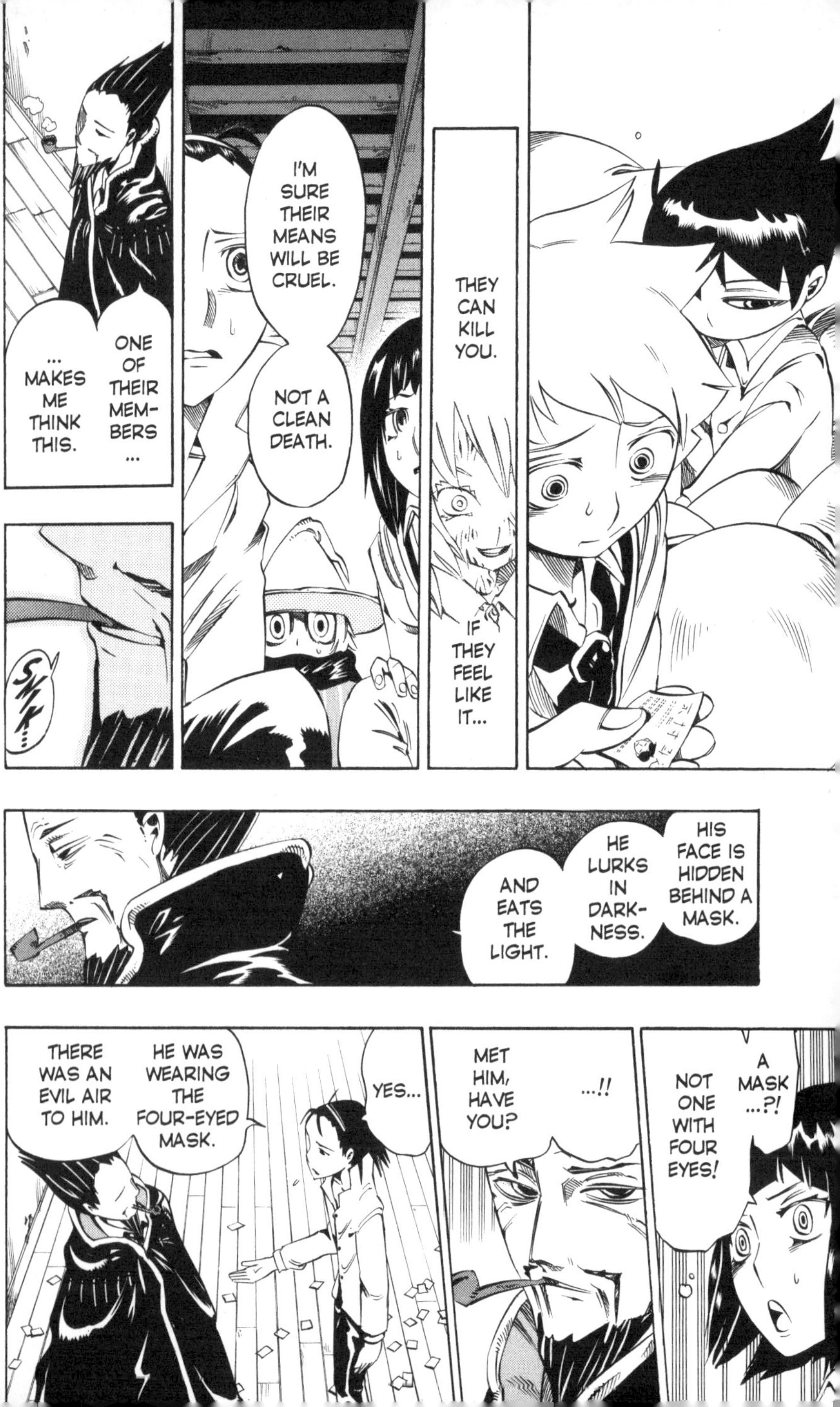
THEY CAN KILL YOU.
IF THEY FEEL LIKE IT...
I'M SURE THEIR MEANS WILL BE CRUEL.
NOT A CLEAN DEATH.
ONE OF THEIR MEMBERS...
...MAKES ME THINK THIS.
SNIK...
HIS FACE IS HIDDEN BEHIND A MASK.
HE LURKS IN DARKNESS.
AND EATS THE LIGHT.
A MASK...?!
NOT ONE WITH FOUR EYES!
...!!
MET HIM, HAVE YOU?
YES...
HE WAS WEARING THE FOUR-EYED MASK.
THERE WAS AN EVIL AIR TO HIM.

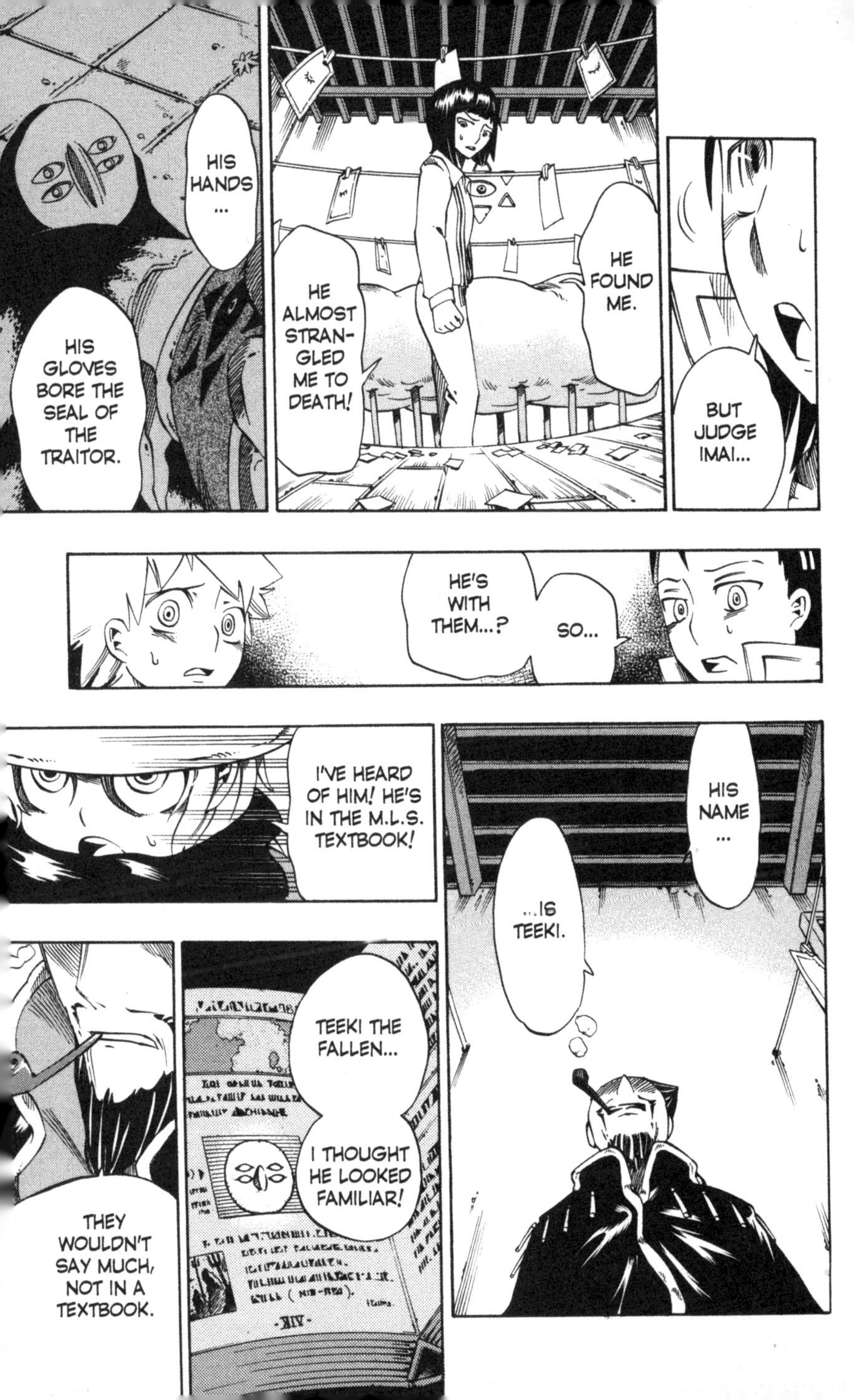
BUT JUDGE IMAI...
HE FOUND ME.
HE ALMOST STRANGLED ME TO DEATH!
HIS HANDS...
HIS GLOVES BORE THE SEAL OF THE TRAITOR.
SO...
HE'S WITH THEM...?
HIS NAME...
...IS TEEKI.
I'VE HEARD OF HIM! HE'S IN THE M.L.S. TEXTBOOK!
TEEKI THE FALLEN...
I THOUGHT HE LOOKED FAMILIAR!
THEY WOULDN'T SAY MUCH, NOT IN A TEXTBOOK.

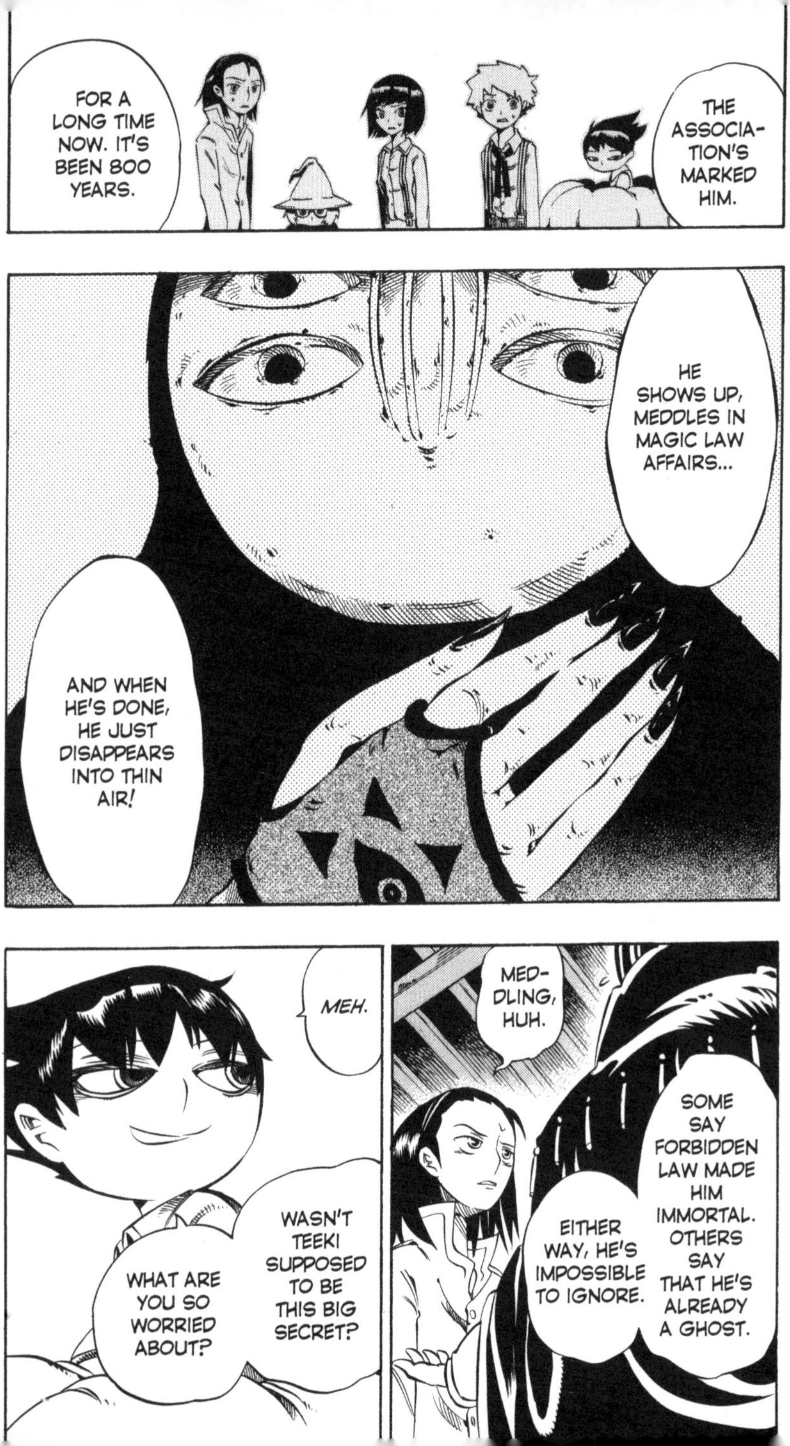
THE ASSOCIATION'S MARKED HIM.
FOR A LONG TIME NOW. IT'S BEEN 800 YEARS.
HE SHOWS UP, MEDDLES IN MAGIC LAW AFFAIRS...
AND WHEN HE'S DONE, HE JUST DISAPPEARS INTO THIN AIR!
MEDDLING, HUH.
SOME SAY FORBIDDEN LAW MADE HIM IMMORTAL. OTHERS SAY THAT HE'S ALREADY A GHOST.
EITHER WAY, HE'S IMPOSSIBLE TO IGNORE.
MEH.
WASN'T TEEKI SUPPOSED TO BE THIS BIG SECRET?
WHAT ARE YOU SO WORRIED ABOUT?

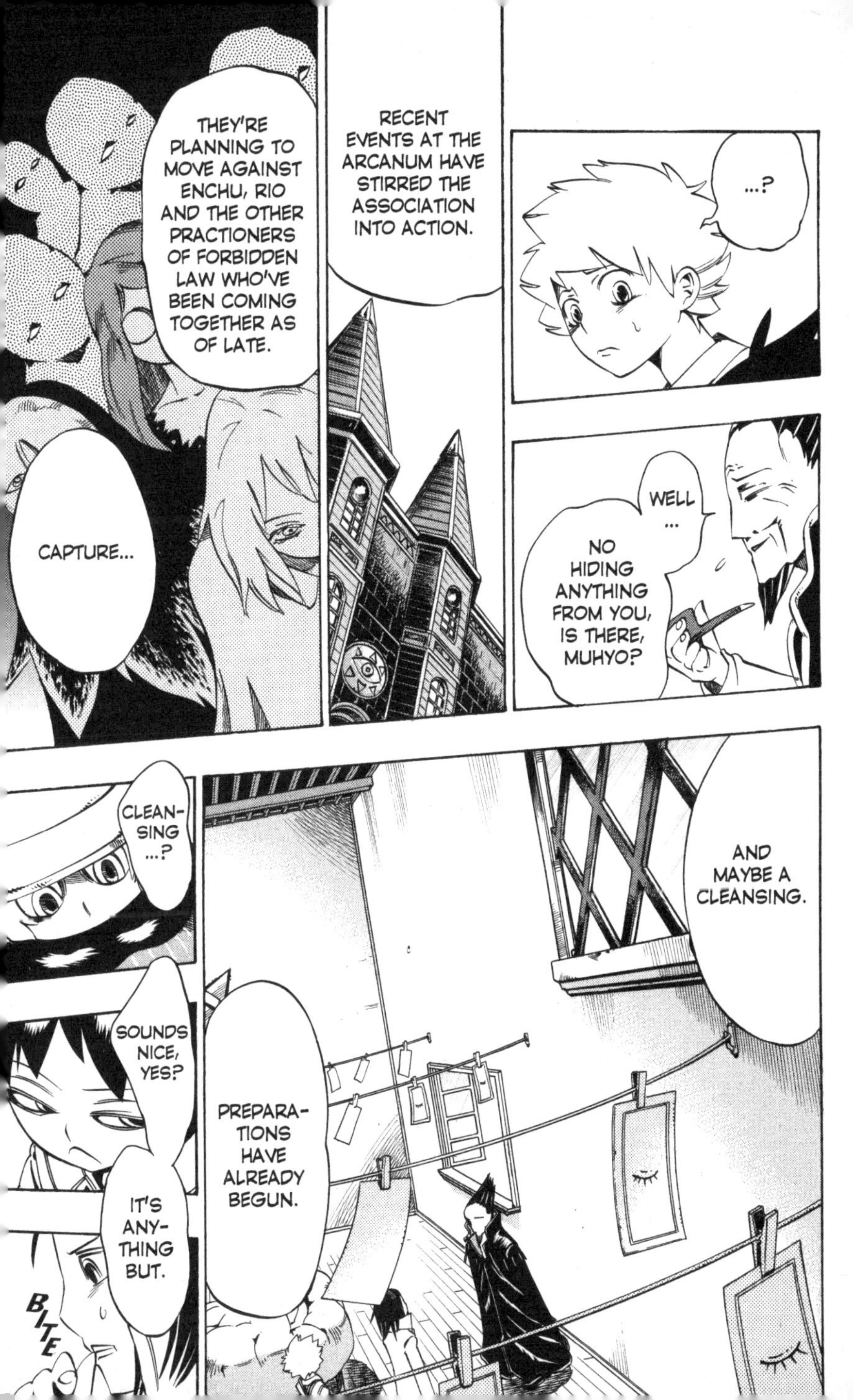
...?
WELL ...
NO HIDING ANYTHING FROM YOU, IS THERE, MUHYO?
RECENT EVENTS AT THE ARCANUM HAVE STIRRED THE ASSOCIATION INTO ACTION.
THEY'RE PLANNING TO MOVE AGAINST ENCHU, RIO AND THE OTHER PRACTIONERS OF FORBIDDEN LAW WHO'VE BEEN COMING TOGETHER AS OF LATE.
CAPTURE...
AND MAYBE A CLEANSING.
PREPARATIONS HAVE ALREADY BEGUN.
CLEANSING ...?
SOUNDS NICE, YES?
IT'S ANYTHING BUT.
BITE

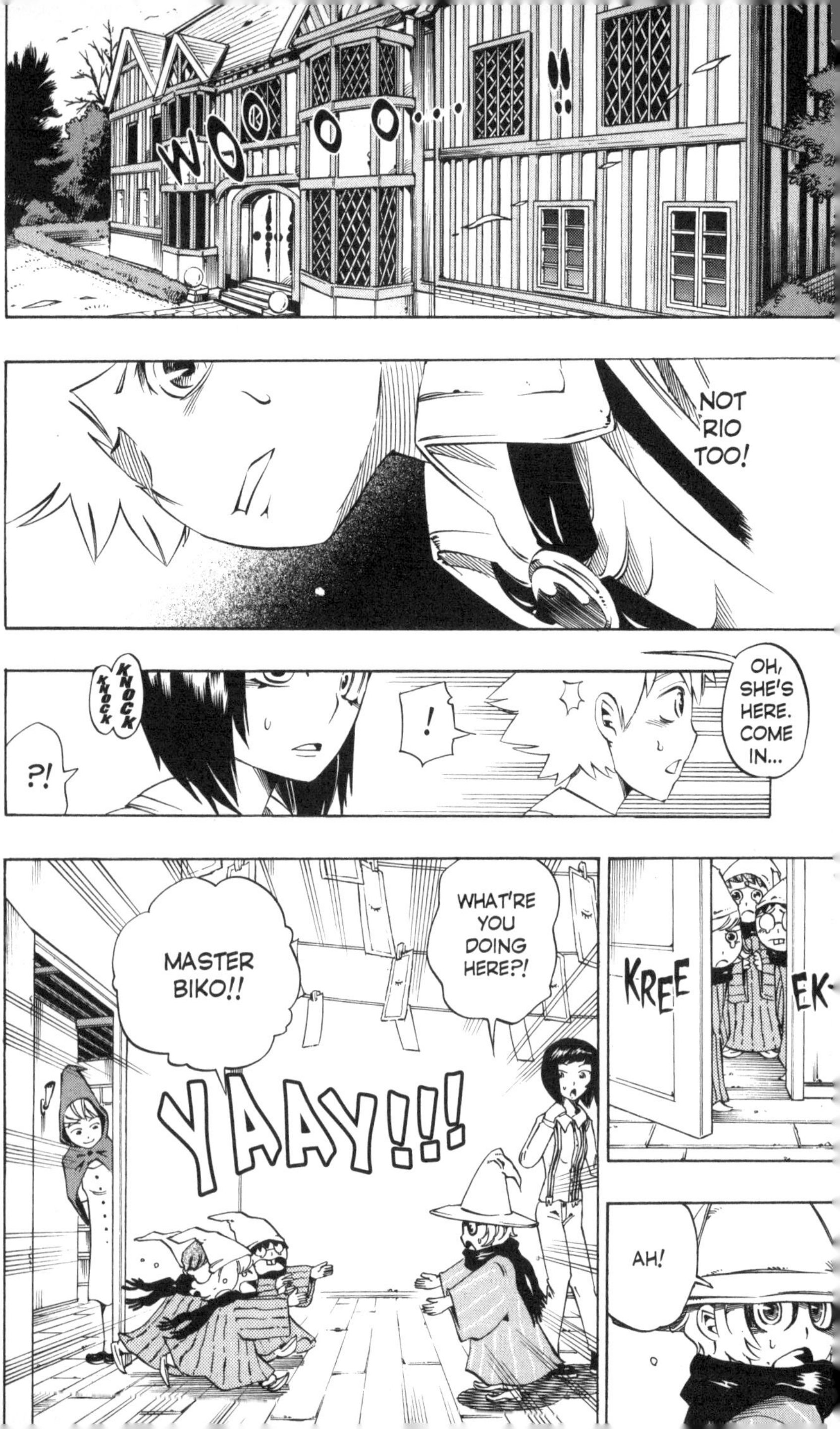
WOOO....!!
NOT RIO TOO!
OH, SHE'S HERE. COME IN...
!
KNOCK KNOCK
?!
KREEEK
AH!
WHAT'RE YOU DOING HERE?!
MASTER BIKO!!
YAAY!!!

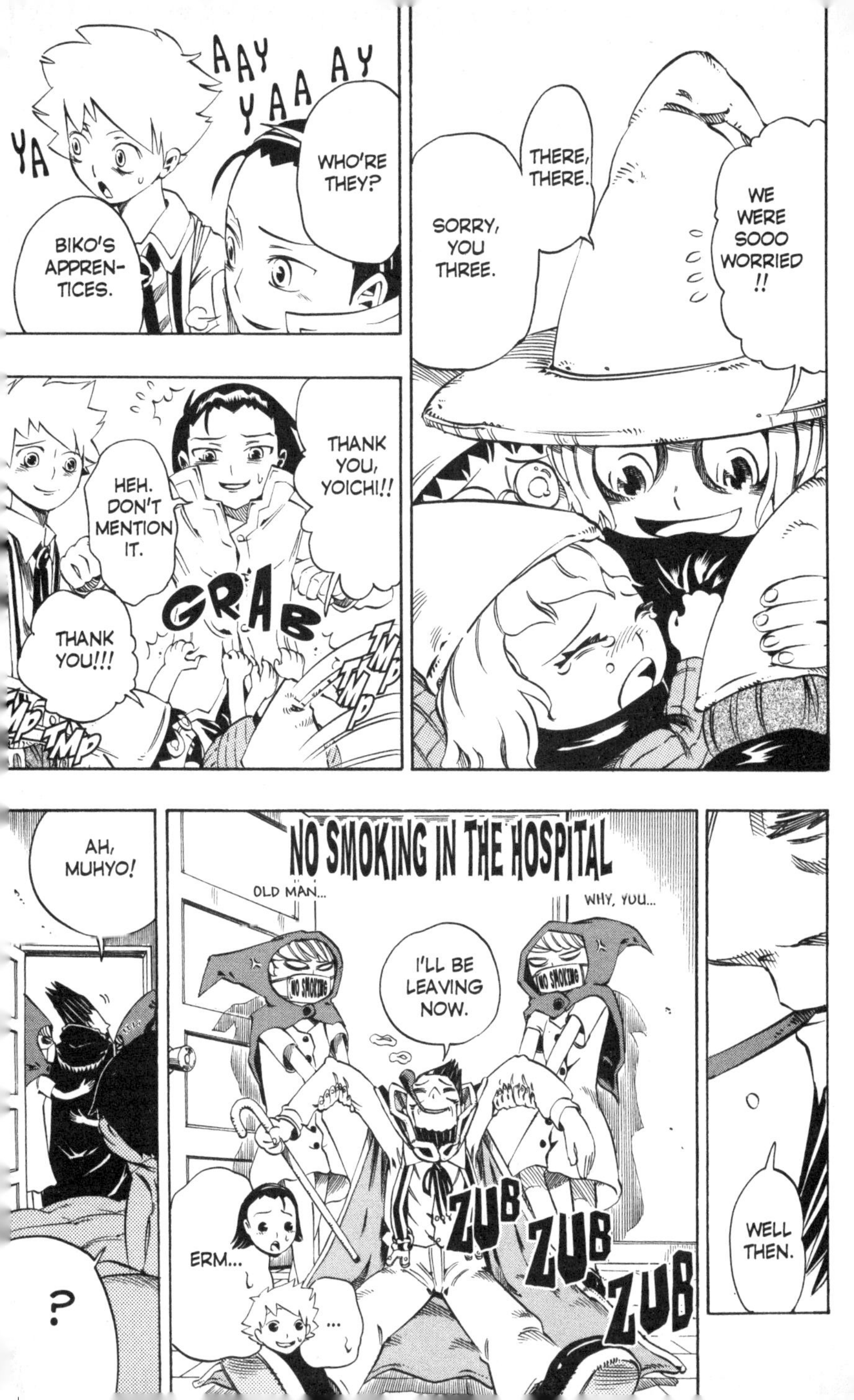
WE WERE SOOO WORRIED!!
THERE, THERE.
SORRY, YOU THREE.
AAY YAAA AY YA
WHO'RE THEY?
BIKO'S APPREN-TICES.
THANK YOU, YOICHI!!
HEH. DON'T MENTION IT.
GRAB
THANK YOU!!!
TMP TMP TMP
TMP TMP
WELL THEN.
NO SMOKING IN THE HOSPITAL
WHY, YOU...
NO SMOKING
I'LL BE LEAVING NOW.
NO SMOKING
OLD MAN...
ZUB ZUB ZUB
ERM...
...
AH, MUHYO!
?

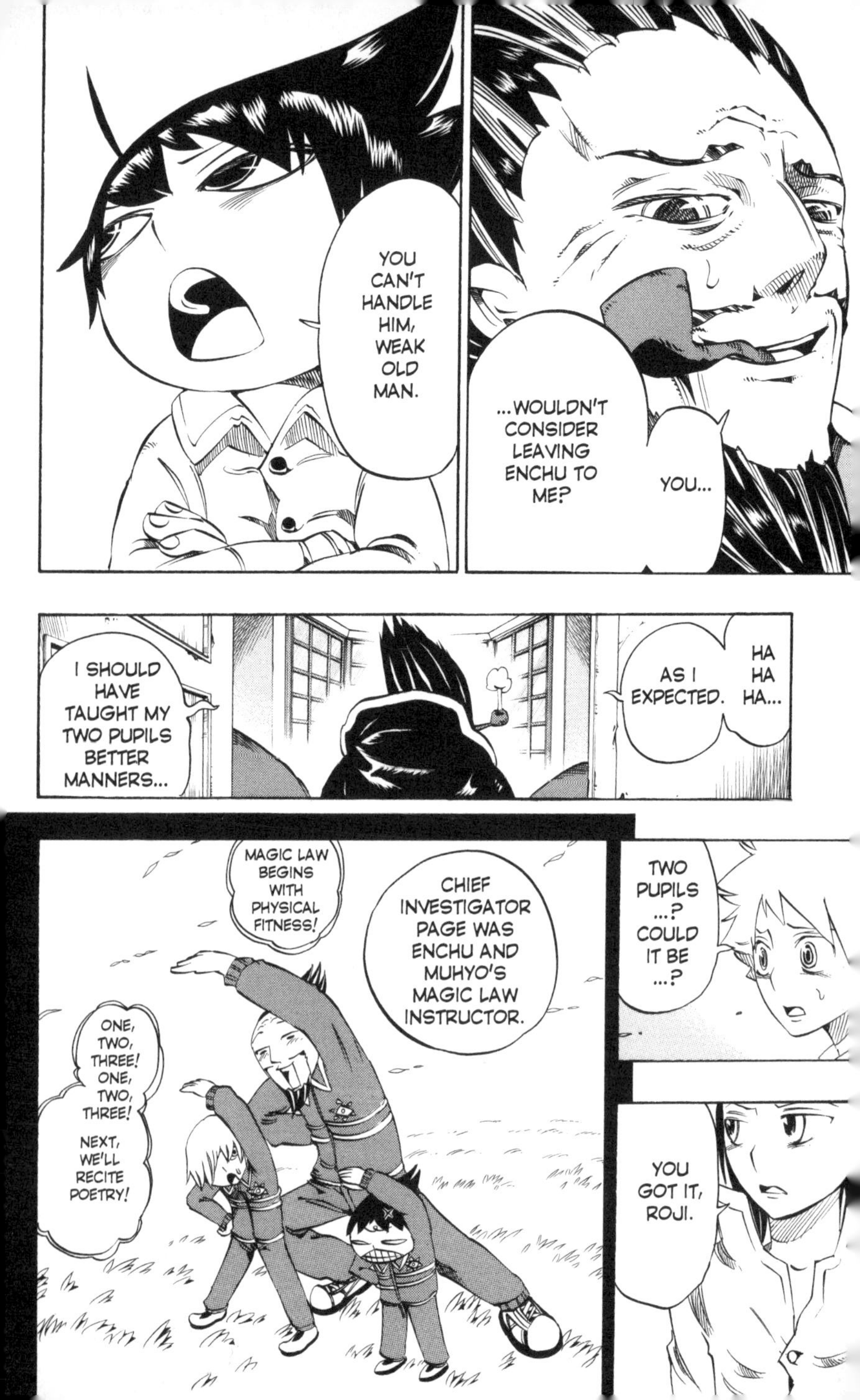

YOU...
...WOULDN'T CONSIDER LEAVING ENCHU TO ME?
YOU CAN'T HANDLE HIM, WEAK OLD MAN.
HA HA HA...
AS I EXPECTED.
I SHOULD HAVE TAUGHT MY TWO PUPILS BETTER MANNERS...
TWO PUPILS ...? COULD IT BE ...?
YOU GOT IT, ROJI.
CHIEF INVESTIGATOR PAGE WAS ENCHU AND MUHYO'S MAGIC LAW INSTRUCTOR.
MAGIC LAW BEGINS WITH PHYSICAL FITNESS!
ONE, TWO, THREE! ONE, TWO, THREE!
NEXT, WE'LL RECITE POETRY!

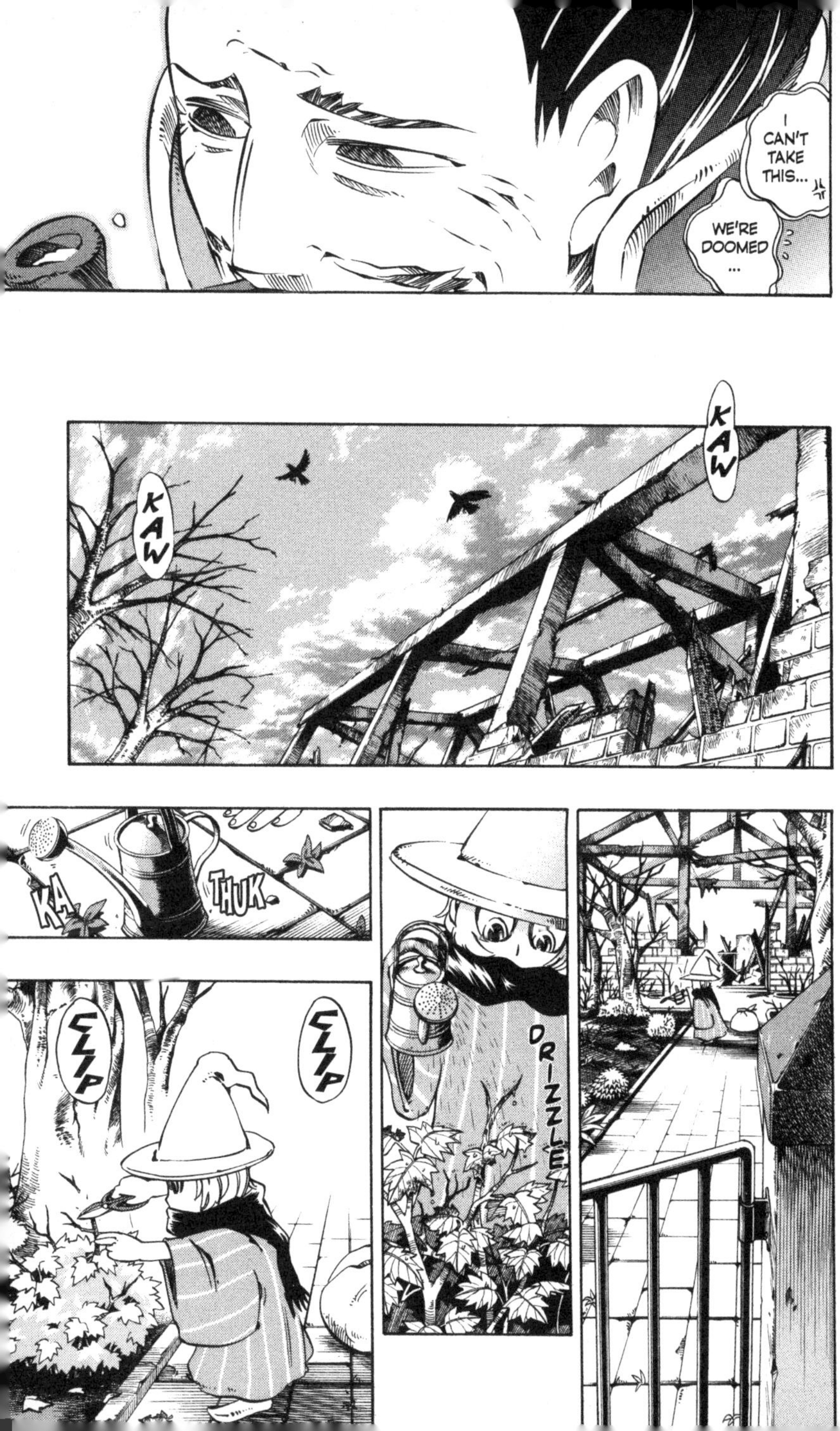
I CAN'T TAKE THIS...
WE'RE DOOMED ...
KAW
KAW
DRIZZLE
KA THUK
CLIP
CLIP

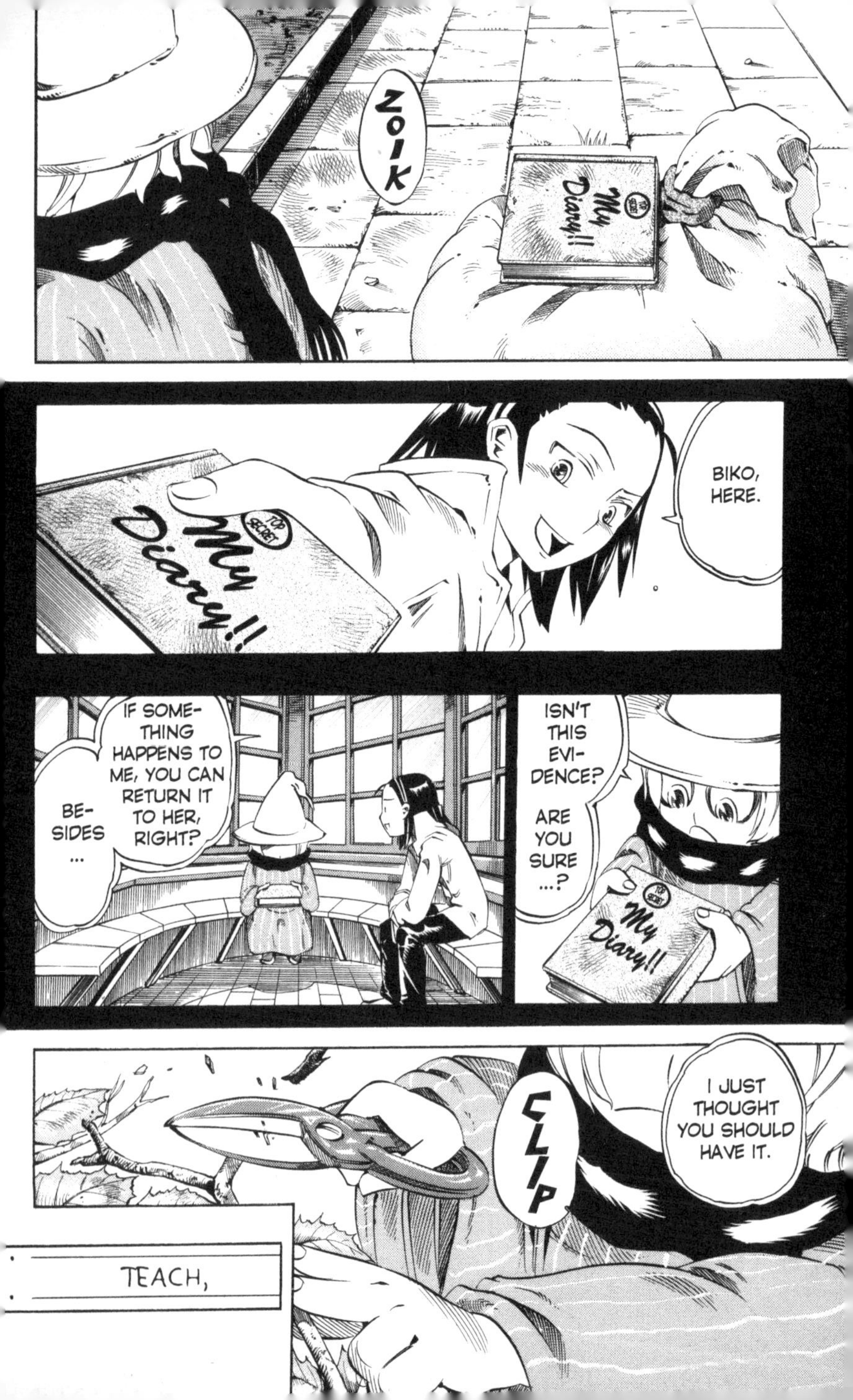
ZOIK
TOP SECRET
My Diary!!
BIKO, HERE.
TOP SECRET
My Diary!!
ISN'T THIS EVIDENCE?
ARE YOU SURE ...?
My Diary!!
IF SOMETHING HAPPENS TO ME, YOU CAN RETURN IT TO HER, RIGHT?
BESIDES ...
I JUST THOUGHT YOU SHOULD HAVE IT.
CLIP
TEACH,

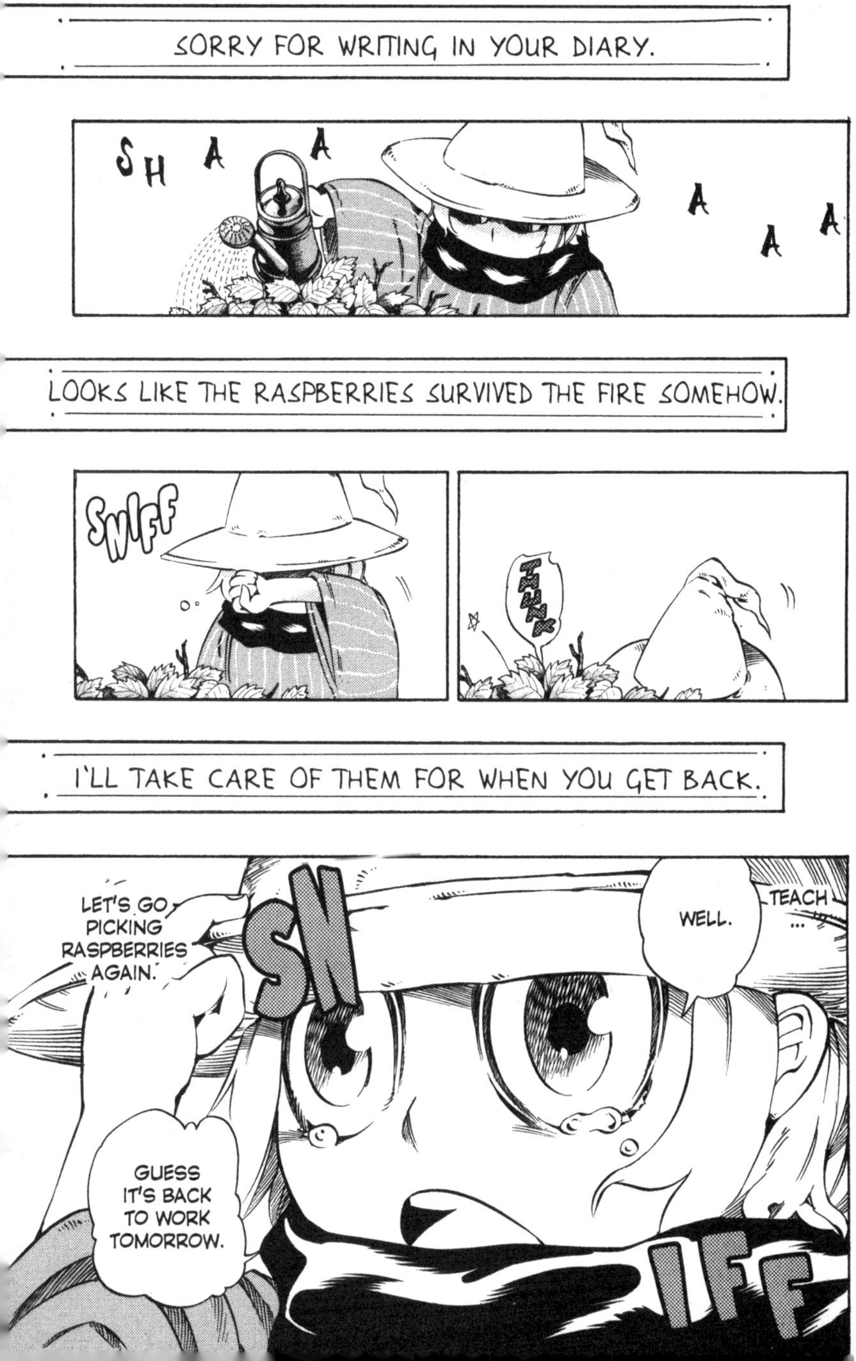
SORRY FOR WRITING IN YOUR DIARY.
SHAAAAAA
LOOKS LIKE THE RASPBERRIES SURVIVED THE FIRE SOMEHOW.
THUNK
SNIFF
I'LL TAKE CARE OF THEM FOR WHEN YOU GET BACK.
TEACH ...
WELL.
SN
LET'S GO PICKING RASPBERRIES AGAIN.
IFF
GUESS IT'S BACK TO WORK TOMORROW.

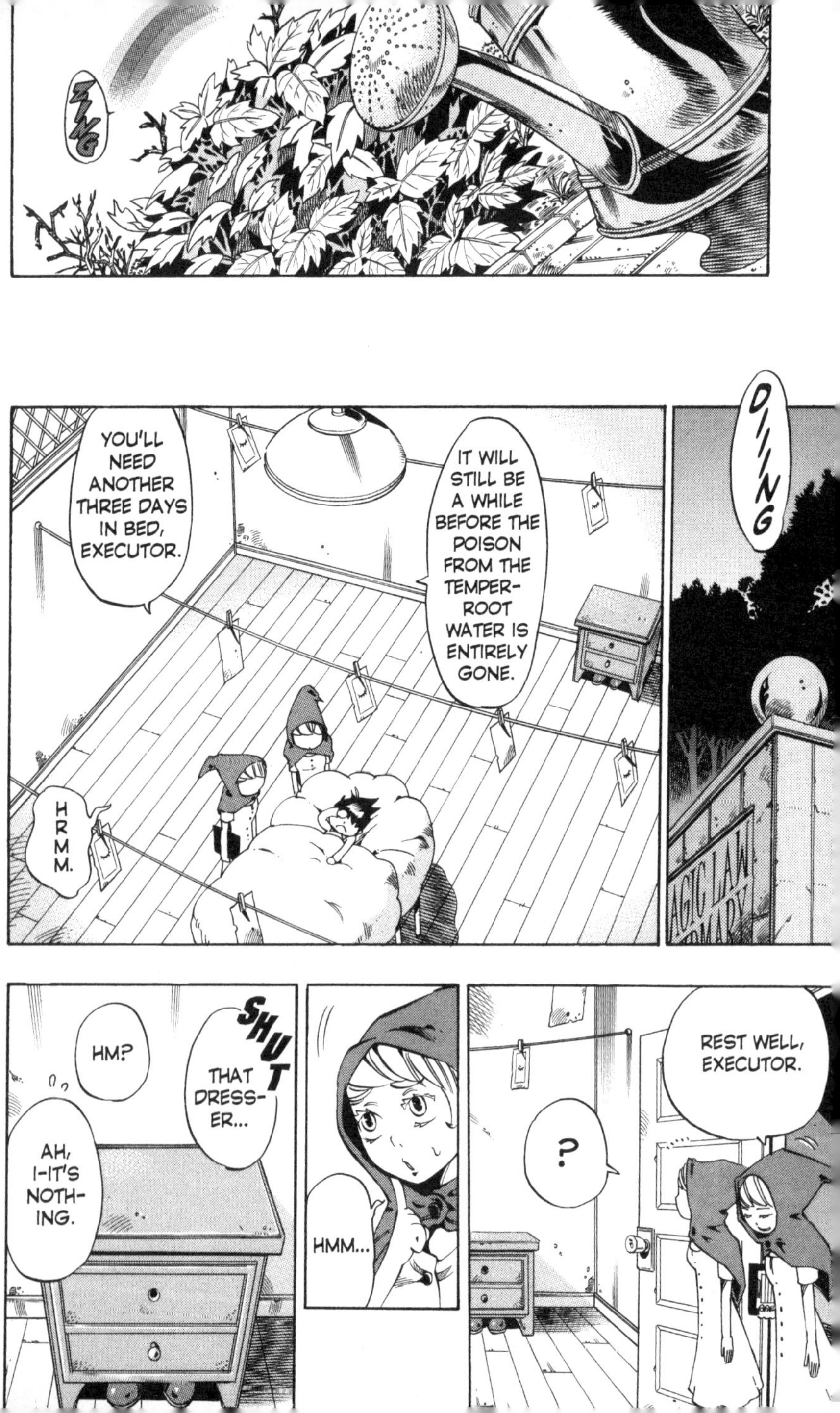
ZING
DIIING
YOU'LL NEED ANOTHER THREE DAYS IN BED, EXECUTOR.
IT WILL STILL BE A WHILE BEFORE THE POISON FROM THE TEMPER-ROOT WATER IS ENTIRELY GONE.
HRMM.
REST WELL, EXECUTOR.
?
HMM...
SHUT
THAT DRESS-ER...
HM?
AH, I-IT'S NOTH-ING.

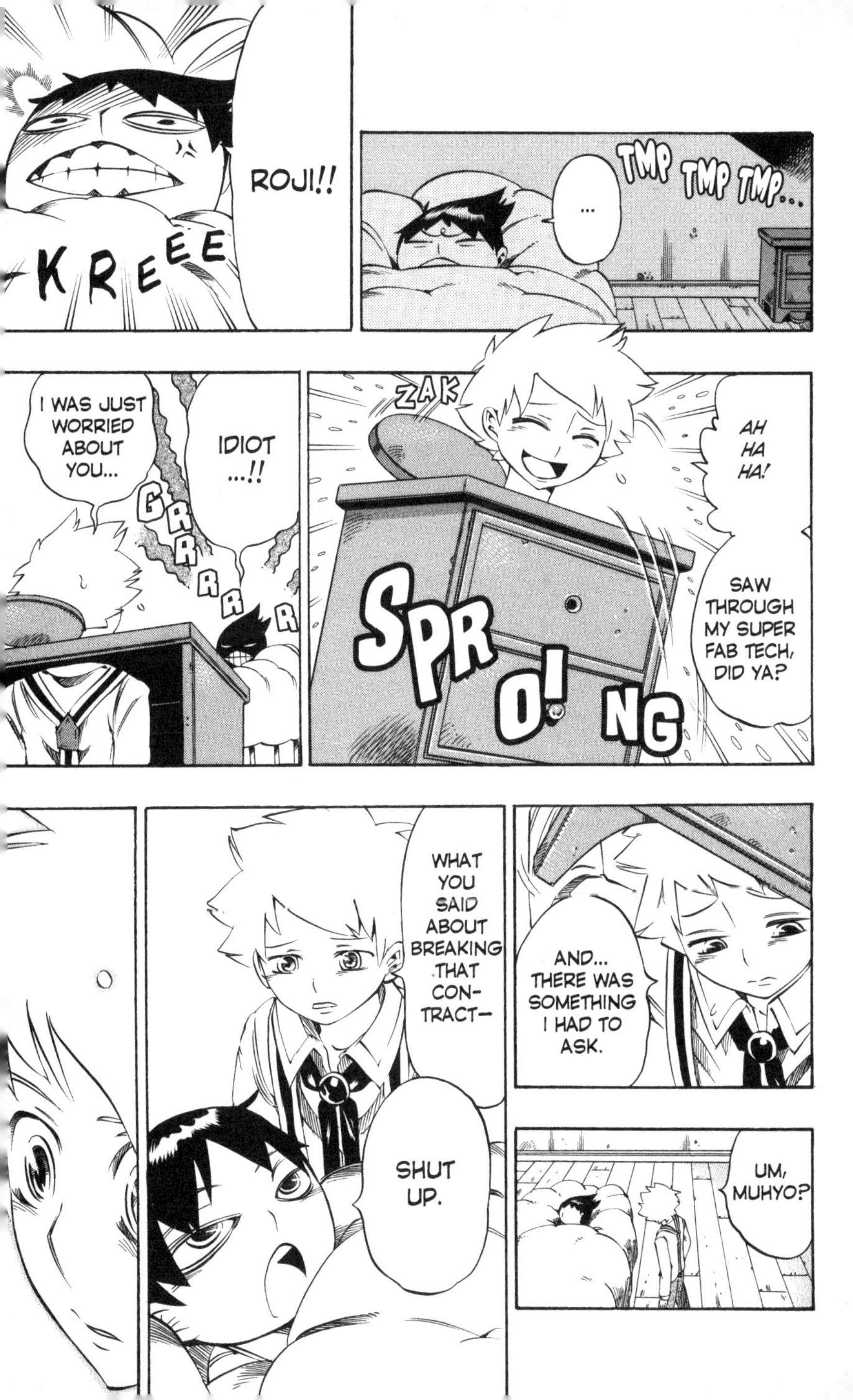
TMP TMP TMP...
...
ROJI!!
KREEE
ZAK
AH HA HA!
SAW THROUGH MY SUPER FAB TECH, DID YA?
SPROING
I WAS JUST WORRIED ABOUT YOU...
IDIOT ...!!
GRRRRR
AND... THERE WAS SOMETHING I HAD TO ASK.
UM, MUHYO?
WHAT YOU SAID ABOUT BREAKING THAT CON-TRACT—
SHUT UP.

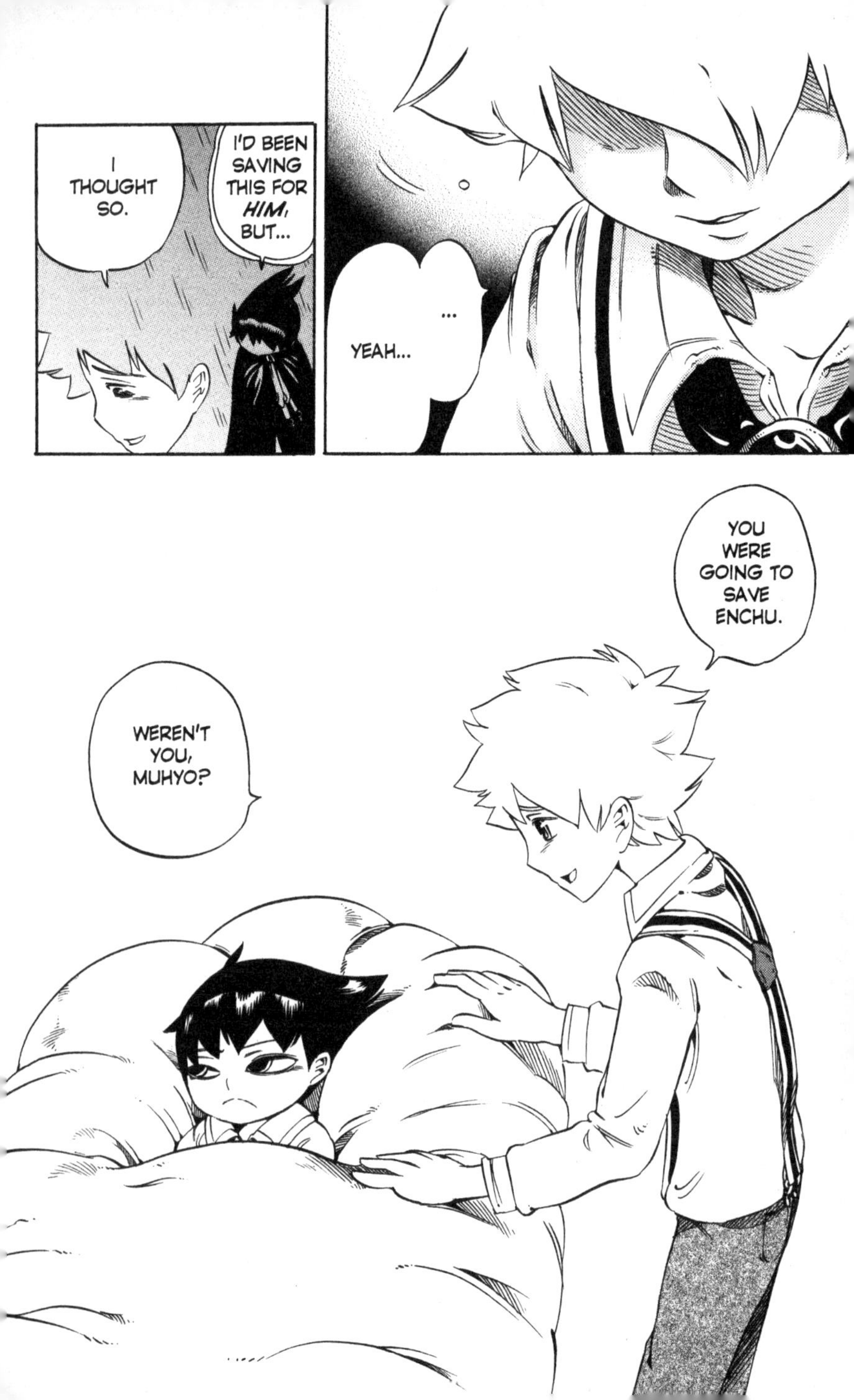
...
YEAH...
I'D BEEN SAVING THIS FOR *HIM*, BUT...
I THOUGHT SO.
YOU WERE GOING TO SAVE ENCHU.
WEREN'T YOU, MUHYO?

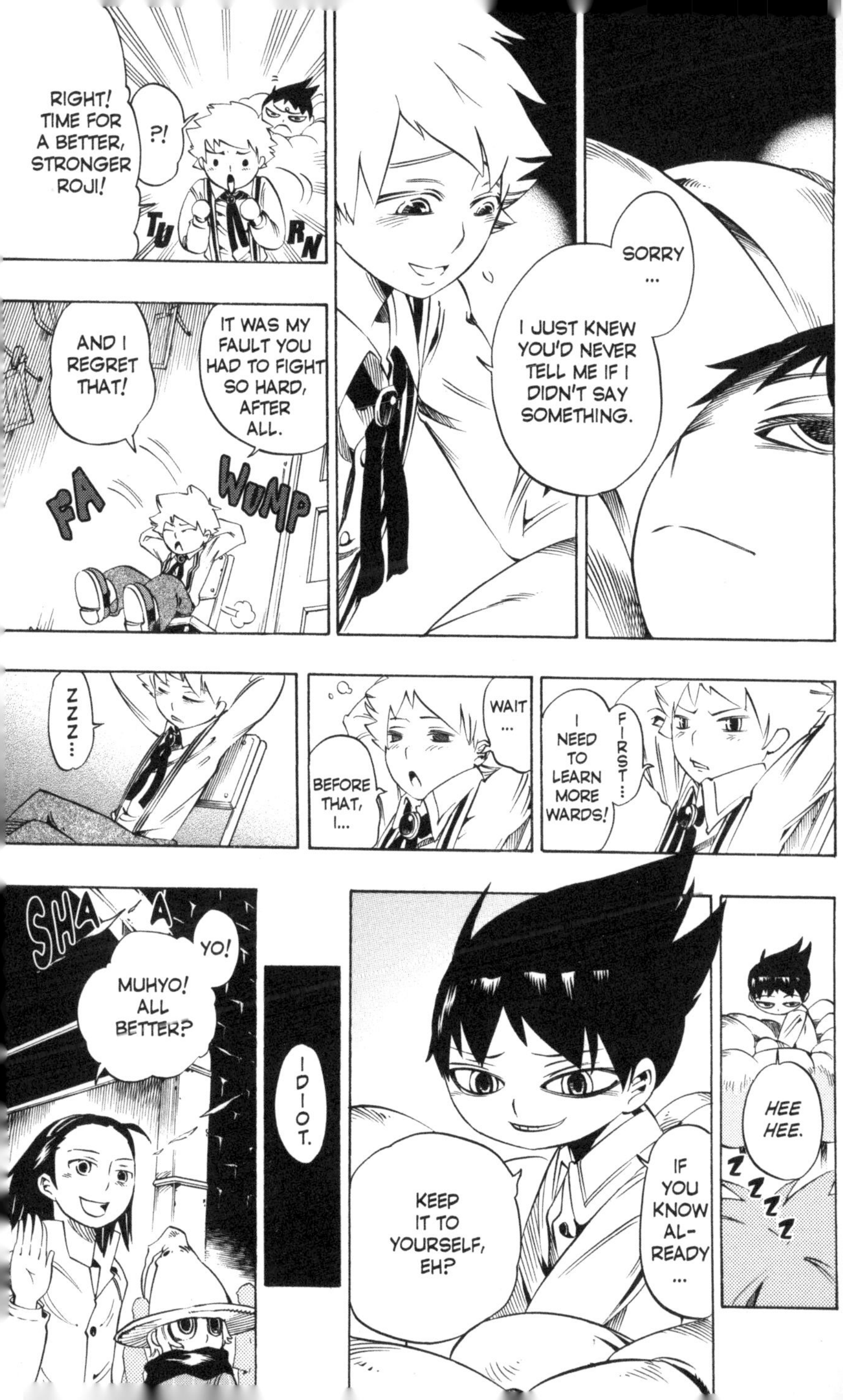
SORRY...
I JUST KNEW YOU'D NEVER TELL ME IF I DIDN'T SAY SOMETHING.
?!
RIGHT! TIME FOR A BETTER, STRONGER ROJI!
TURN
IT WAS MY FAULT YOU HAD TO FIGHT SO HARD, AFTER ALL.
AND I REGRET THAT!
FA WUMP
FIRST...
I NEED TO LEARN MORE WARDS!
WAIT...
BEFORE THAT, I...
ZZZ...
HEE HEE.
Z Z Z Z
IF YOU KNOW AL-READY...
KEEP IT TO YOURSELF, EH?
IDIOT.
SHA A A
YO!
MUHYO! ALL BETTER?

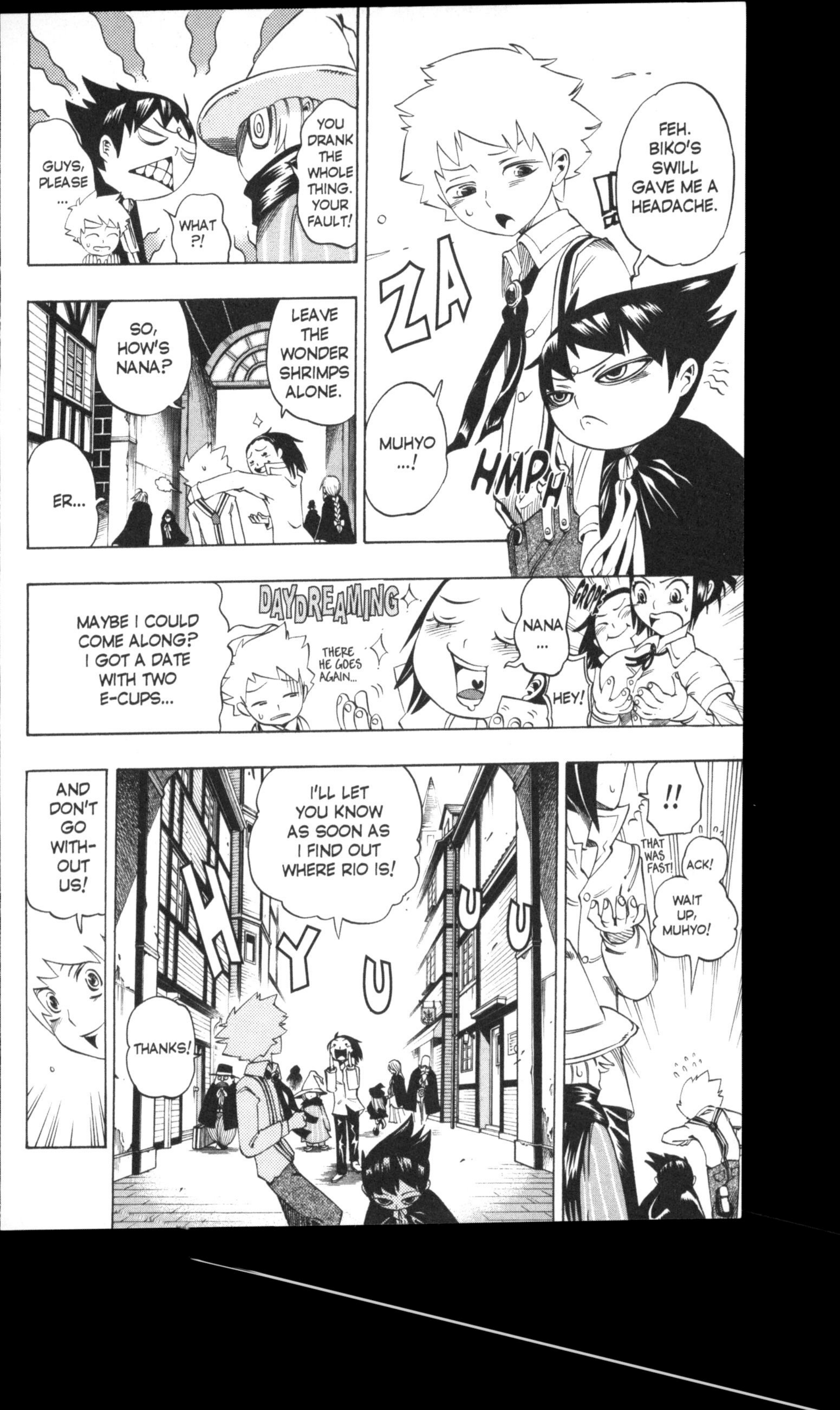

FEH. BIKO'S SWILL GAVE ME A HEADACHE.
!!
ZA
MUHYO ...!
HMPH
YOU DRANK THE WHOLE THING. YOUR FAULT!
WHAT ?!
GUYS, PLEASE ...
LEAVE THE WONDER SHRIMPS ALONE.
SO, HOW'S NANA?
ER...
GROPE
NANA ...
HEY!
DAYDREAMING
THERE HE GOES AGAIN...
MAYBE I COULD COME ALONG? I GOT A DATE WITH TWO E-CUPS...
!!
THAT WAS FAST!
ACK!
WAIT UP, MUHYO!
I'LL LET YOU KNOW AS SOON AS I FIND OUT WHERE RIO IS!
HYUUU
THANKS!
AND DON'T GO WITH-OUT US!

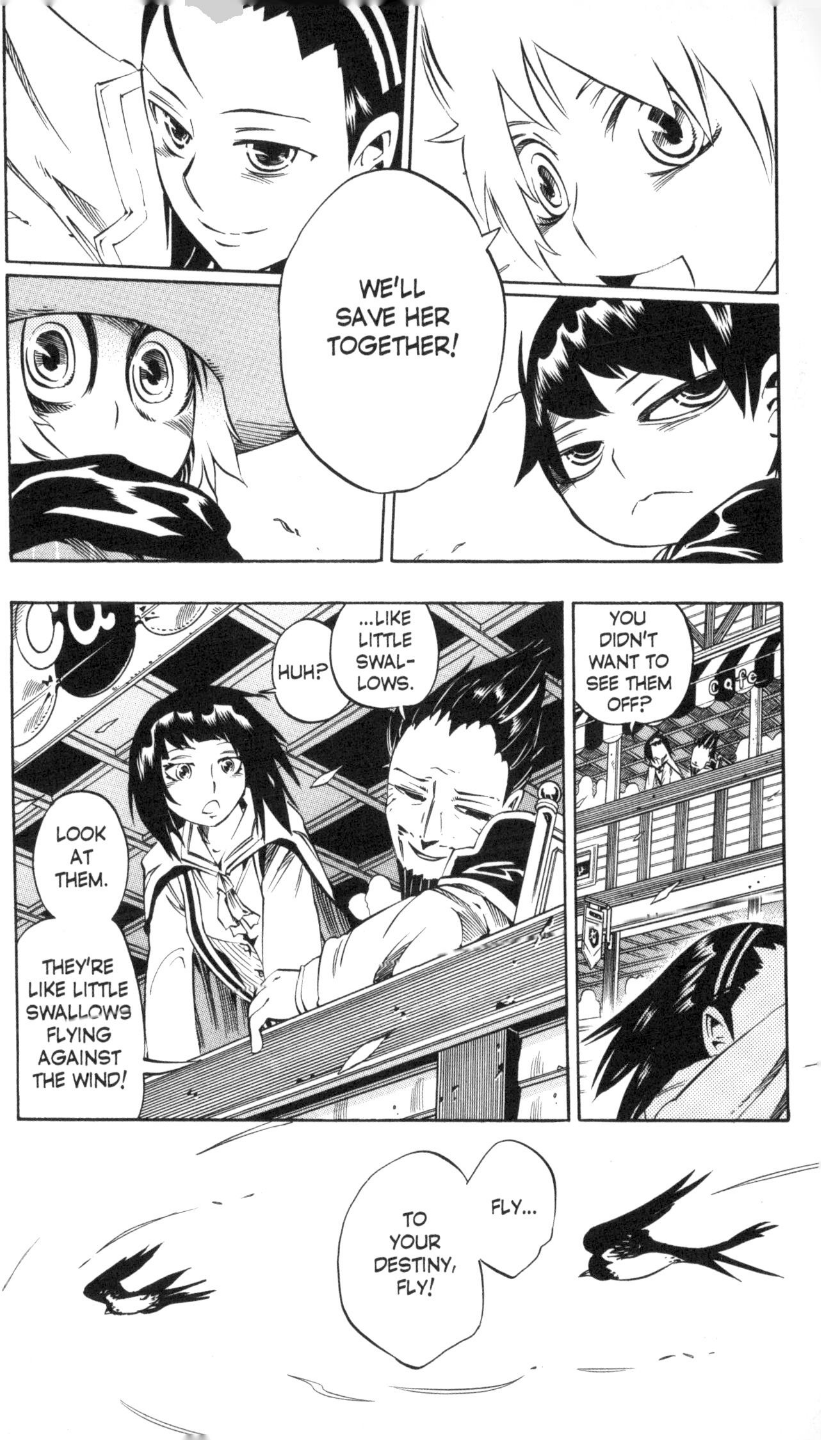
WE'LL SAVE HER TOGETHER!
YOU DIDN'T WANT TO SEE THEM OFF?
...LIKE LITTLE SWALLOWS.
HUH?
LOOK AT THEM.
THEY'RE LIKE LITTLE SWALLOWS FLYING AGAINST THE WIND!
FLY...
TO YOUR DESTINY, FLY!

ARTICLE 37
KOKKURI

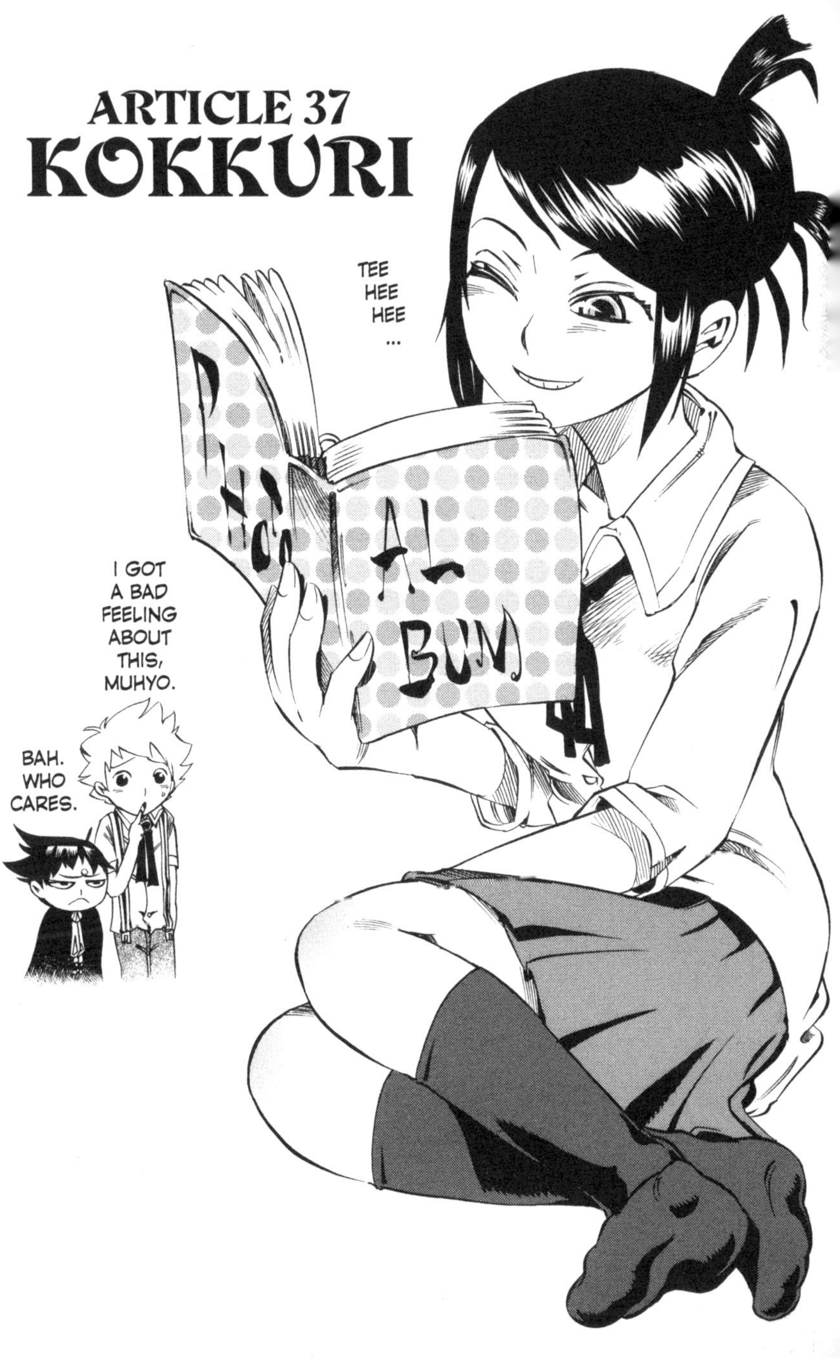
TEE HEE HEE ...
I GOT A BAD FEELING ABOUT THIS, MUHYO.
BAH. WHO CARES.

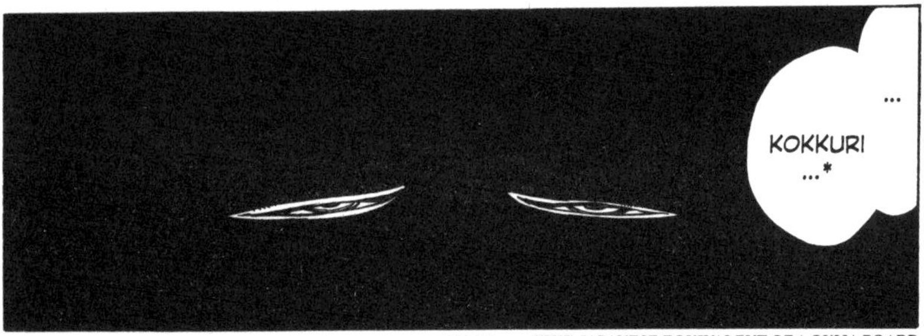
... KOKKURI ...*

*THE JAPANESE EQUIVALENT OF A OUIJA BOARD

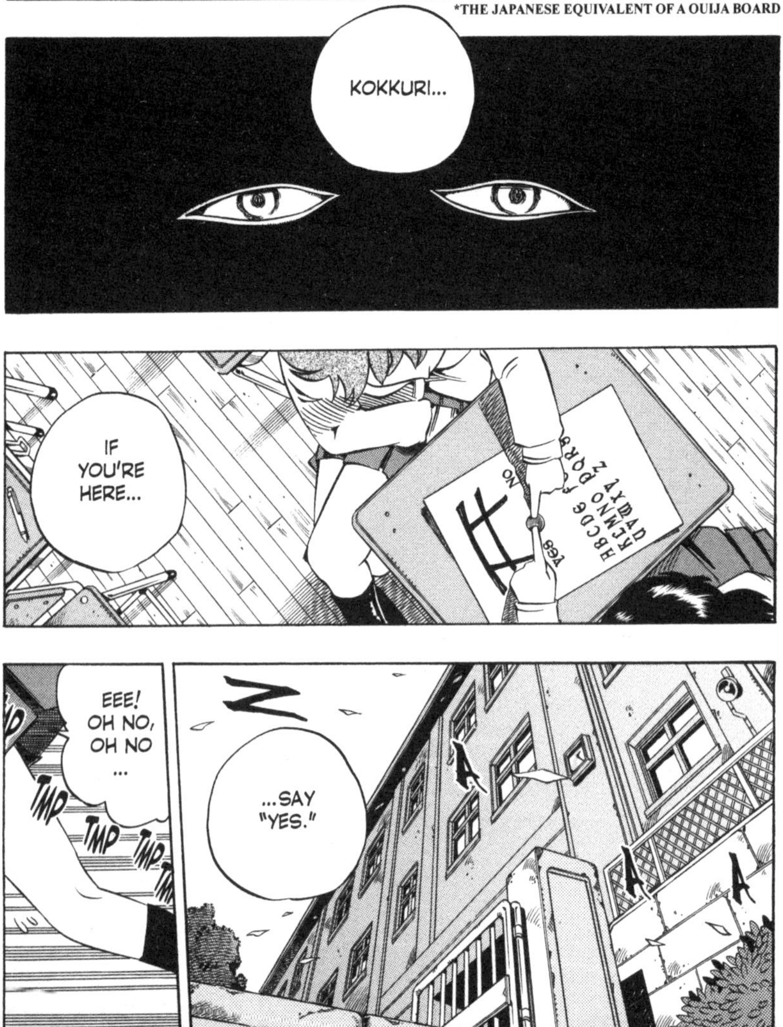
KOKKURI...
IF YOU'RE HERE...
...SAY "YES."
EEE! OH NO, OH NO ...
TMP
TMP
TMP
TMP

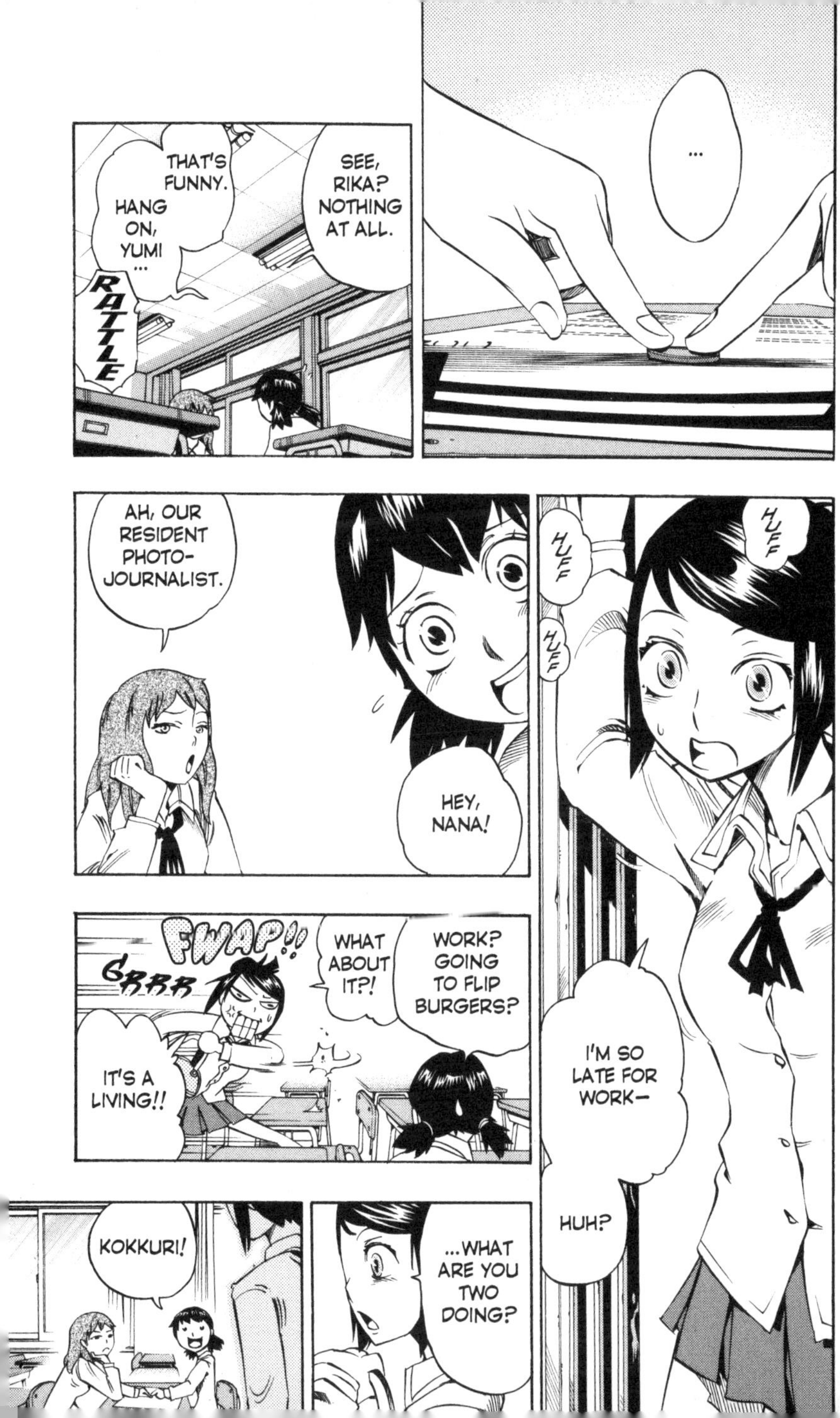
...
SEE, RIKA? NOTHING AT ALL.
THAT'S FUNNY. HANG ON, YUMI ...
RATTLE
HUFF HUFF
HUFF
I'M SO LATE FOR WORK—
HUH?
HEY, NANA!
AH, OUR RESIDENT PHOTO-JOURNALIST.
WORK? GOING TO FLIP BURGERS?
WHAT ABOUT IT?!
FWAP!!
GRRR
IT'S A LIVING!!
...WHAT ARE YOU TWO DOING?
KOKKURI!

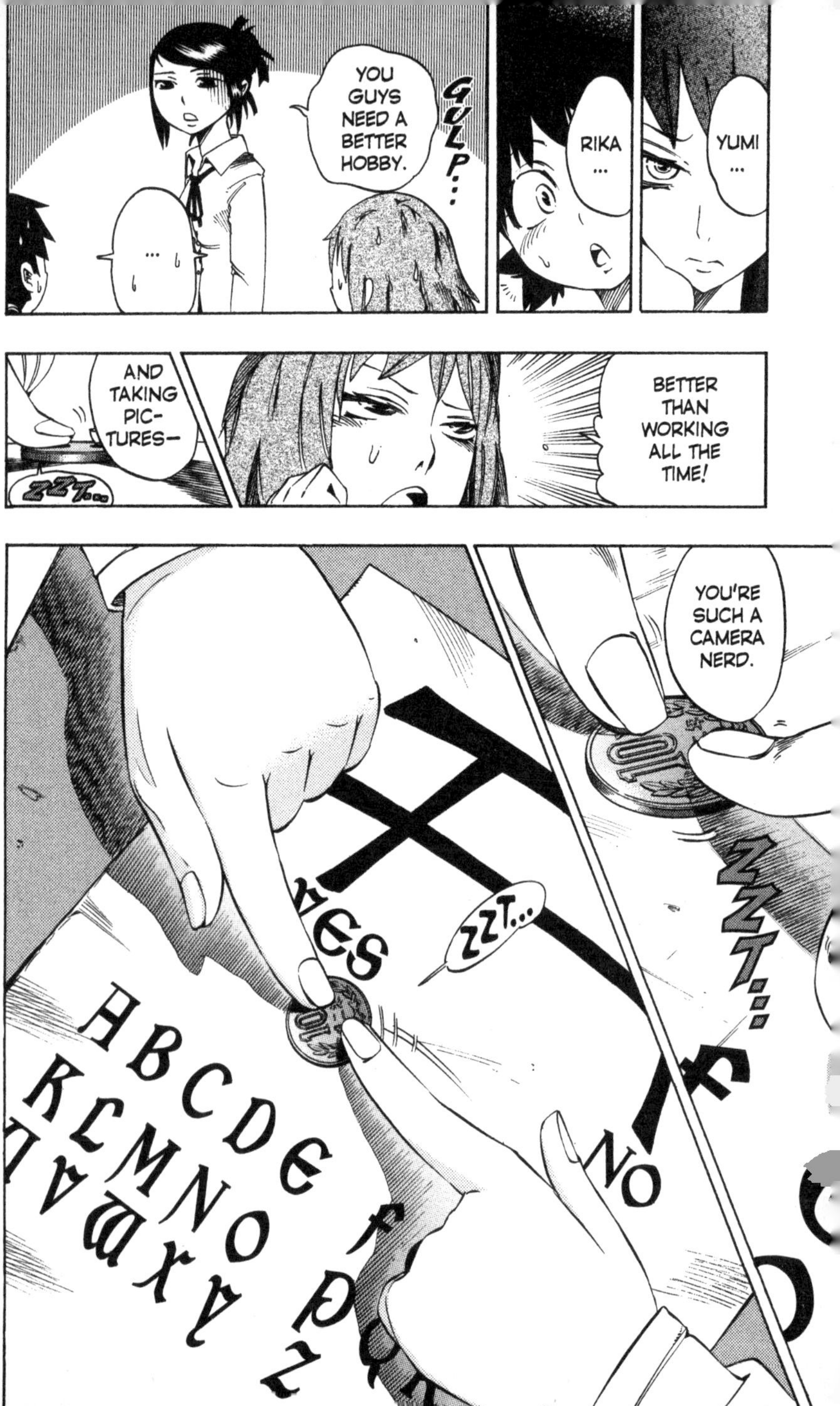
YUMI ...
RIKA ...
YOU GUYS NEED A BETTER HOBBY.
GULP...
...
BETTER THAN WORKING ALL THE TIME!
AND TAKING PICTURES—
ZZT...
YOU'RE SUCH A CAMERA NERD.
ZZZT...
ZZT...
YES
NO

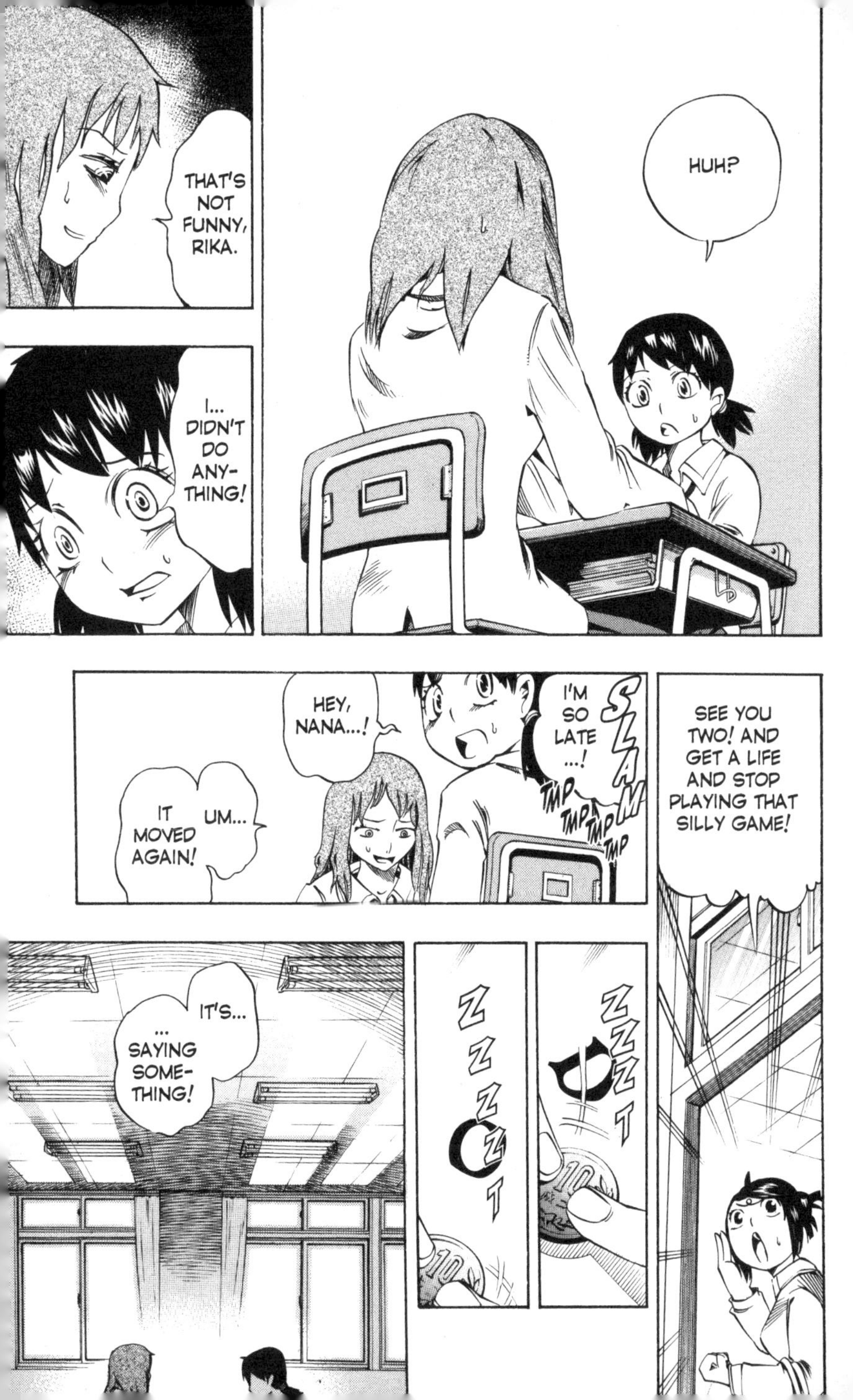
HUH?
THAT'S NOT FUNNY, RIKA.
I... DIDN'T DO ANY-THING!
SEE YOU TWO! AND GET A LIFE AND STOP PLAYING THAT SILLY GAME!
SLAM
TMP TMP TMP TMP TMP
I'M SO LATE ...!
HEY, NANA...!
UM...
IT MOVED AGAIN!
ZZZZT
ZZZZT
IT'S...
... SAYING SOME-THING!

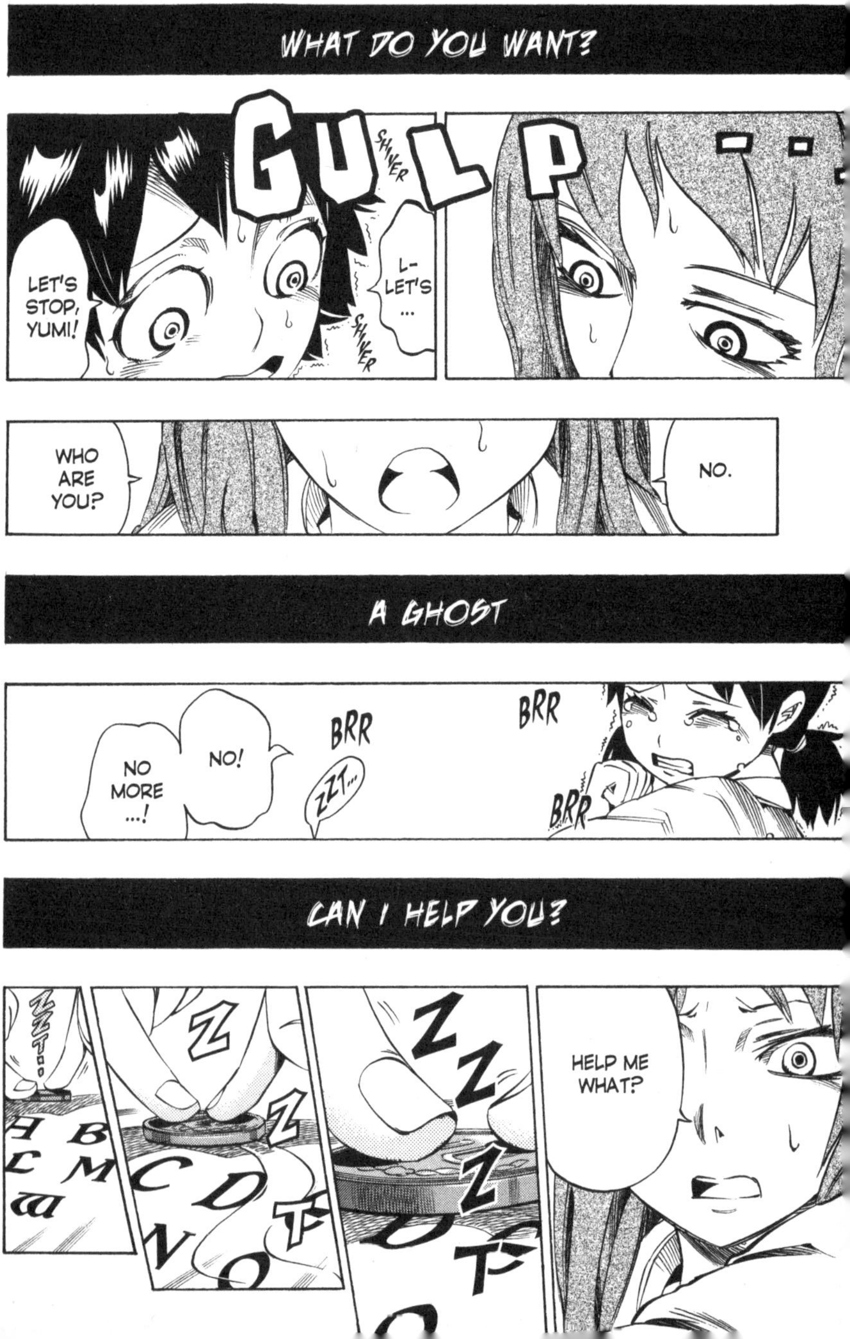
WHAT DO YOU WANT?
GULP
SHIVER
L- LET'S ...
SHIVER
LET'S STOP, YUMI!
NO.
WHO ARE YOU?
A GHOST
BRR
BRR
BRR
ZZT...
NO!
NO MORE ...!
CAN I HELP YOU?
HELP ME WHAT?
Z
Z
Z
Z
Z
ZZT...

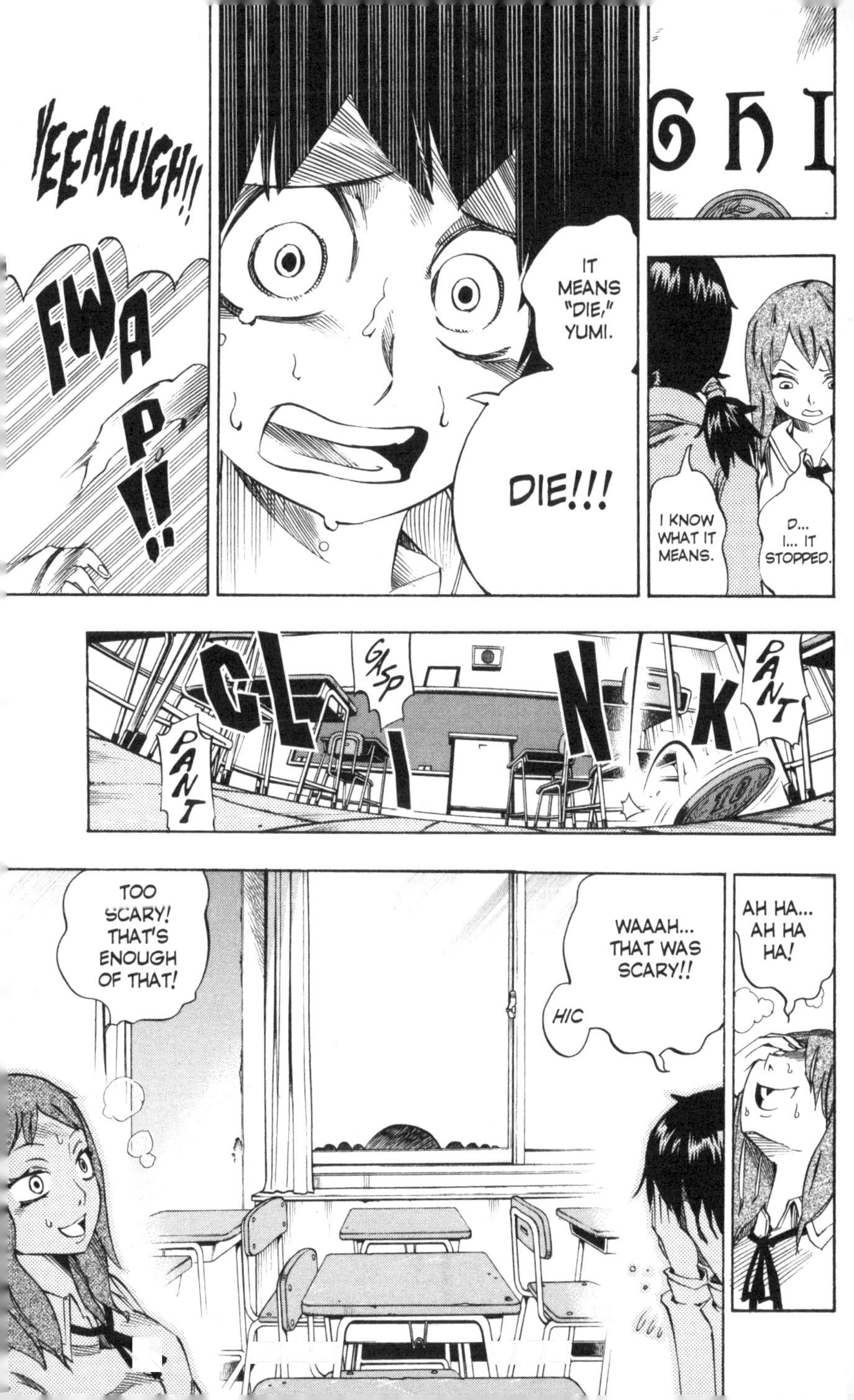
GHI
D... I... IT STOPPED.
I KNOW WHAT IT MEANS.
IT MEANS "DIE," YUMI.
DIE!!!
YEEAAUGH!!
FWAP!!
PANT
PANT
CLINK
GASP
PANT
AH HA... AH HA HA!
WAAAH... THAT WAS SCARY!!
HIC
TOO SCARY! THAT'S ENOUGH OF THAT!

I FEEL SICK. LET'S GO, RIKA.
OKAY...
TA DA!
PANDORA BLDG
DINNER IS SERVED!
LOTS OF NOODLES!
LOTS OF VEGGIES!
GOTTA LOVE INSTANT RAMEN...
SLURP
SLURP
MM
MUNCH
YOUR COOKING SPREE ONLY LASTED ONE DAY, I SEE.
MICROWAVE FOOD CITY...
HMF

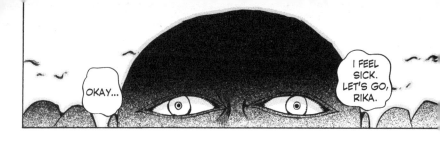

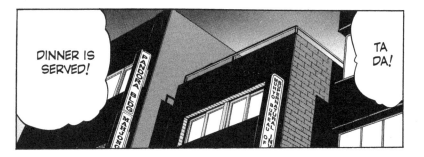

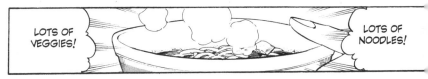

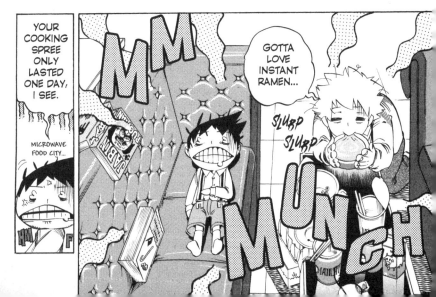

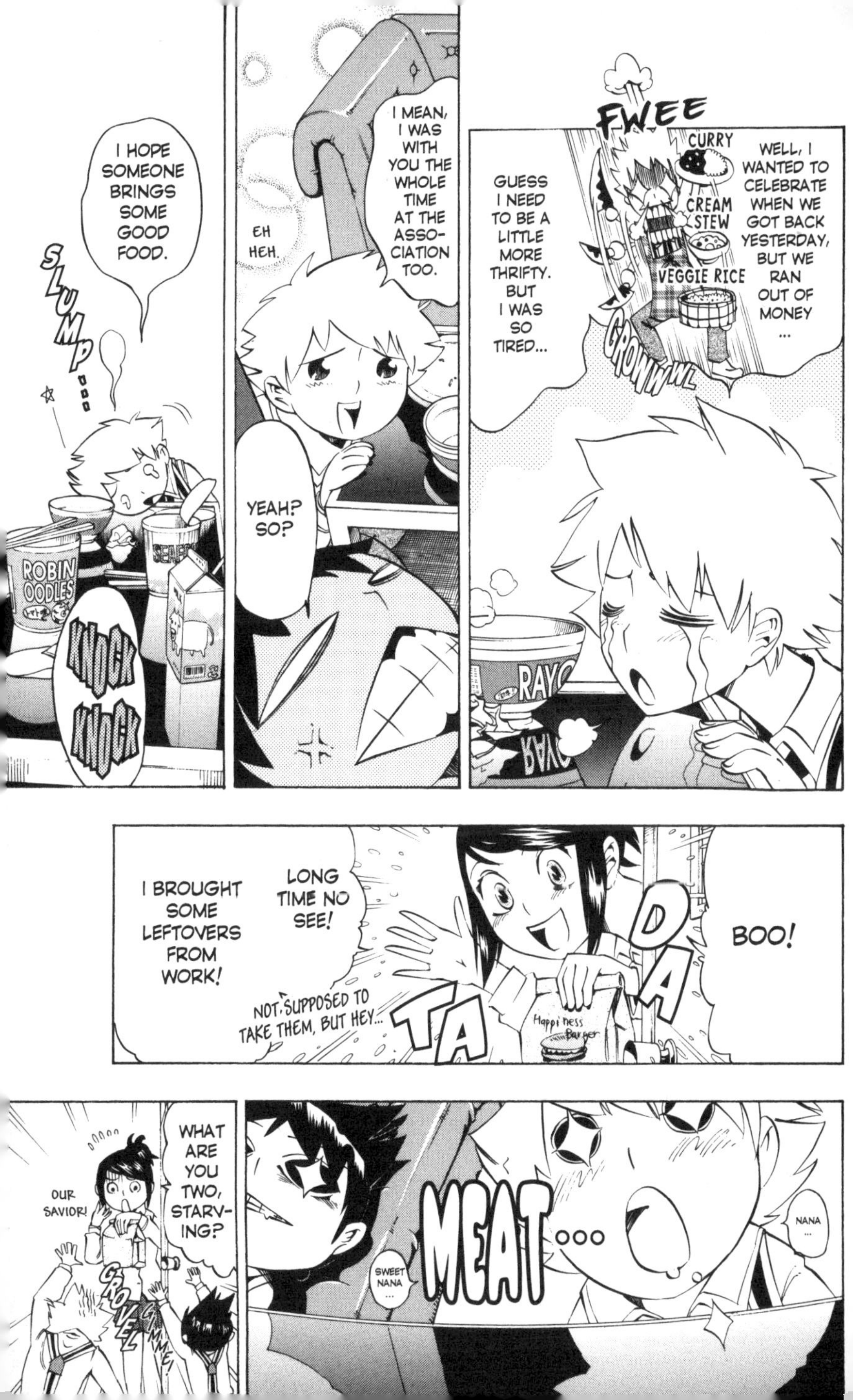
FWEE
CURRY
CREAM STEW
VEGGIE RICE
WELL, I WANTED TO CELEBRATE WHEN WE GOT BACK YESTERDAY, BUT WE RAN OUT OF MONEY ...
GUESS I NEED TO BE A LITTLE MORE THRIFTY. BUT I WAS SO TIRED...
GROWWWL
RAYO
I MEAN, I WAS WITH YOU THE WHOLE TIME AT THE ASSO-CIATION TOO.
EH HEH.
YEAH? SO?
I HOPE SOMEONE BRINGS SOME GOOD FOOD.
SLUMP...
ROBIN OODLES
KNOCK KNOCK
BOO!
DA
TA
LONG TIME NO SEE!
I BROUGHT SOME LEFTOVERS FROM WORK!
NOT SUPPOSED TO TAKE THEM, BUT HEY...
Happiness Burger
NANA ...
MEAT...
SWEET NANA ...
WHAT ARE YOU TWO, STARV-ING?
OUR SAVIOR!
GROVEL
GIMME!

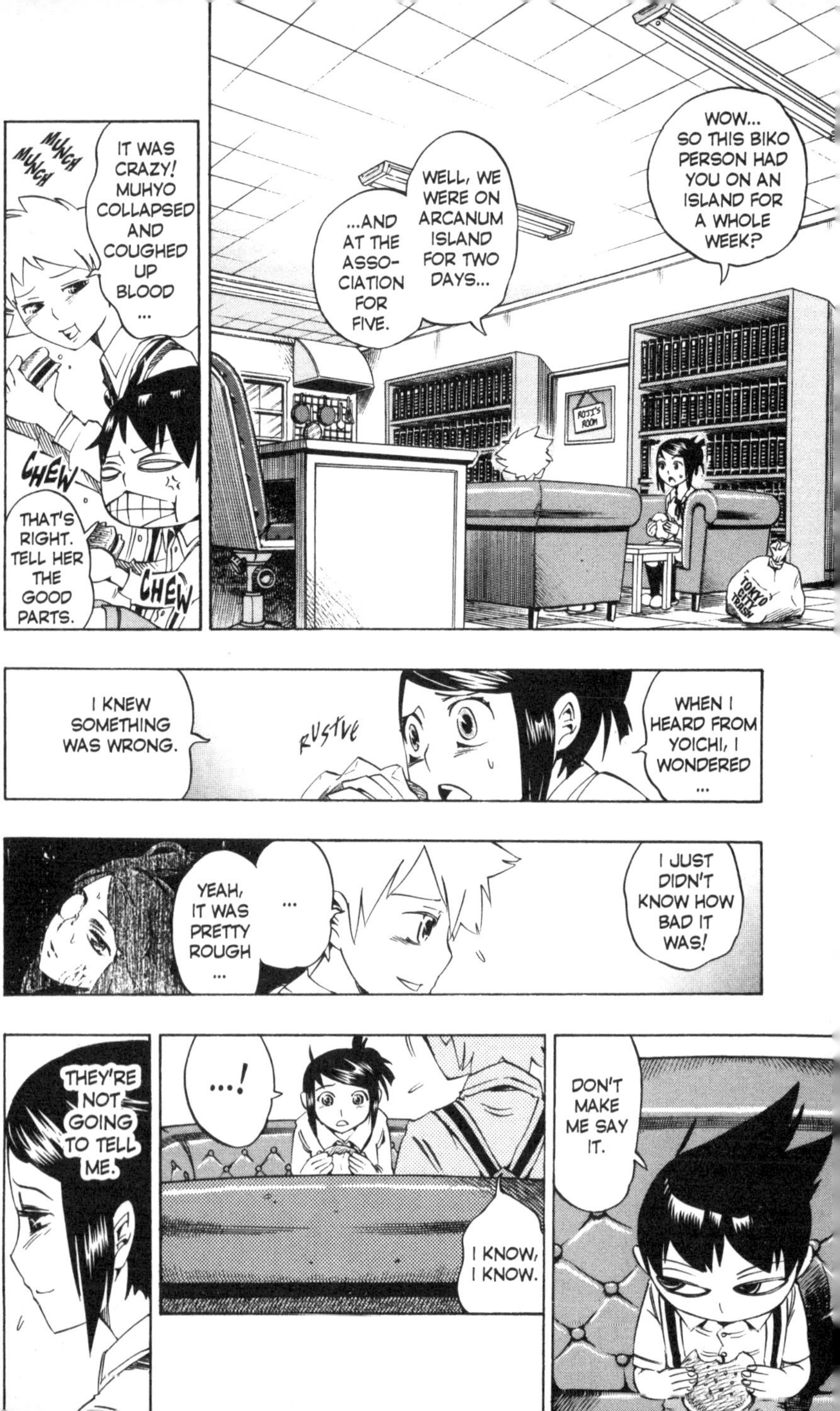
WOW... SO THIS BIKO PERSON HAD YOU ON AN ISLAND FOR A WHOLE WEEK?
ROJI'S ROOM
TOKYO CITY TRASH
WELL, WE WERE ON ARCANUM ISLAND FOR TWO DAYS...
...AND AT THE ASSOCIATION FOR FIVE.
MUNCH MUNCH
IT WAS CRAZY! MUHYO COLLAPSED AND COUGHED UP BLOOD...
CHEW
THAT'S RIGHT. TELL HER THE GOOD PARTS.
CHEW
WHEN I HEARD FROM YOICHI, I WONDERED...
RUSTLE
I KNEW SOMETHING WAS WRONG.
I JUST DIDN'T KNOW HOW BAD IT WAS!
...
YEAH, IT WAS PRETTY ROUGH...
DON'T MAKE ME SAY IT.
...!
I KNOW, I KNOW.
THEY'RE NOT GOING TO TELL ME.

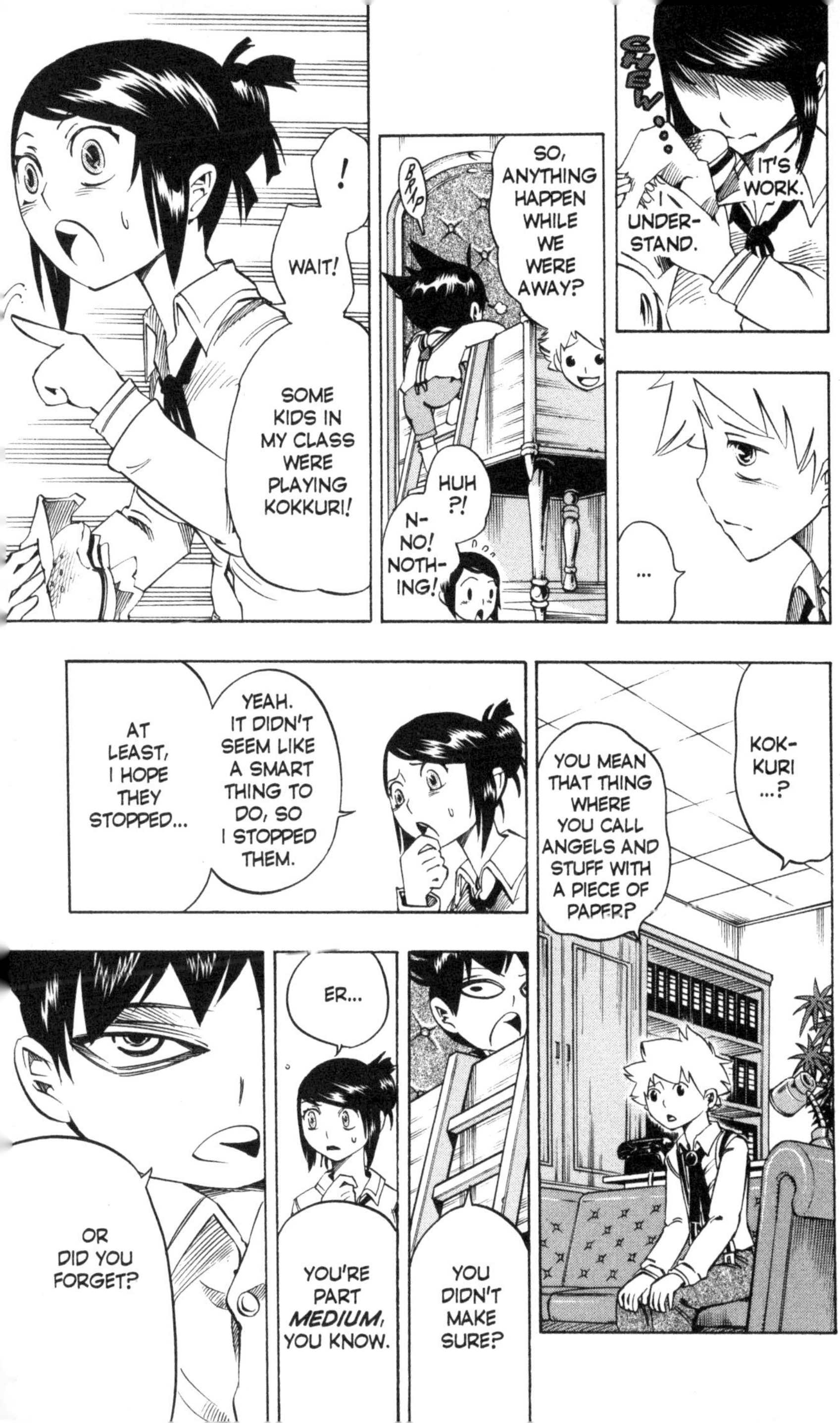
CHEW...
IT'S WORK.
I UNDERSTAND.
...
BRAP
SO, ANYTHING HAPPEN WHILE WE WERE AWAY?
HUH?!
N-NO! NOTHING!
!
WAIT!
SOME KIDS IN MY CLASS WERE PLAYING KOKKURI!
KOK-KURI...?
YOU MEAN THAT THING WHERE YOU CALL ANGELS AND STUFF WITH A PIECE OF PAPER?
YEAH. IT DIDN'T SEEM LIKE A SMART THING TO DO, SO I STOPPED THEM.
AT LEAST, I HOPE THEY STOPPED...
YOU DIDN'T MAKE SURE?
ER...
YOU'RE PART *MEDIUM*, YOU KNOW.
OR DID YOU FORGET?

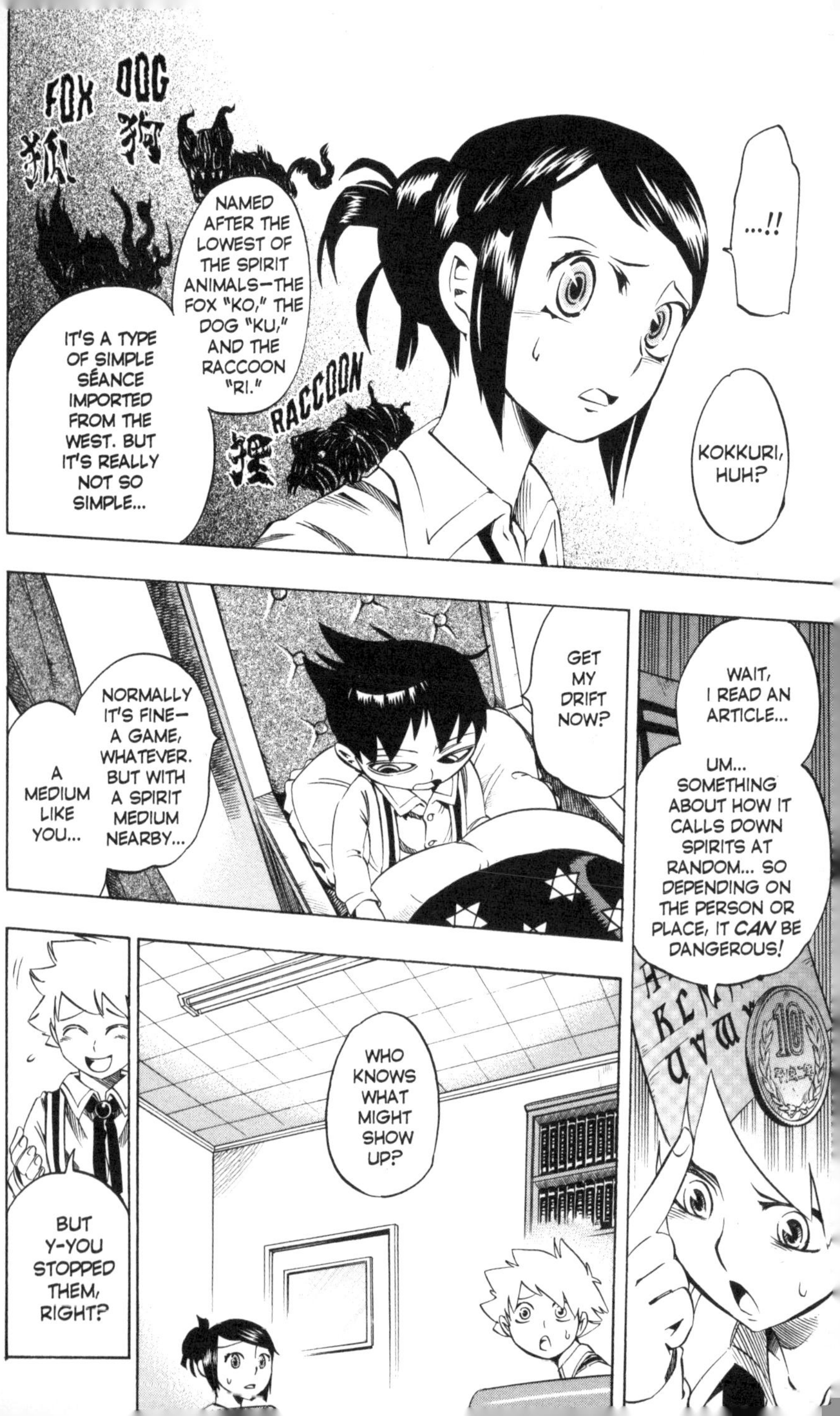

...!!
KOKKURI, HUH?
FOX 狐
DOG 狗
NAMED AFTER THE LOWEST OF THE SPIRIT ANIMALS—THE FOX "KO," THE DOG "KU," AND THE RACCOON "RI."
RACCOON 狸
IT'S A TYPE OF SIMPLE SÉANCE IMPORTED FROM THE WEST. BUT IT'S REALLY NOT SO SIMPLE...
WAIT, I READ AN ARTICLE...
UM... SOMETHING ABOUT HOW IT CALLS DOWN SPIRITS AT RANDOM... SO DEPENDING ON THE PERSON OR PLACE, IT *CAN* BE DANGEROUS!
GET MY DRIFT NOW?
NORMALLY IT'S FINE— A GAME, WHATEVER. BUT WITH A SPIRIT MEDIUM NEARBY...
A MEDIUM LIKE YOU...
10
WHO KNOWS WHAT MIGHT SHOW UP?
BUT Y-YOU STOPPED THEM, RIGHT?

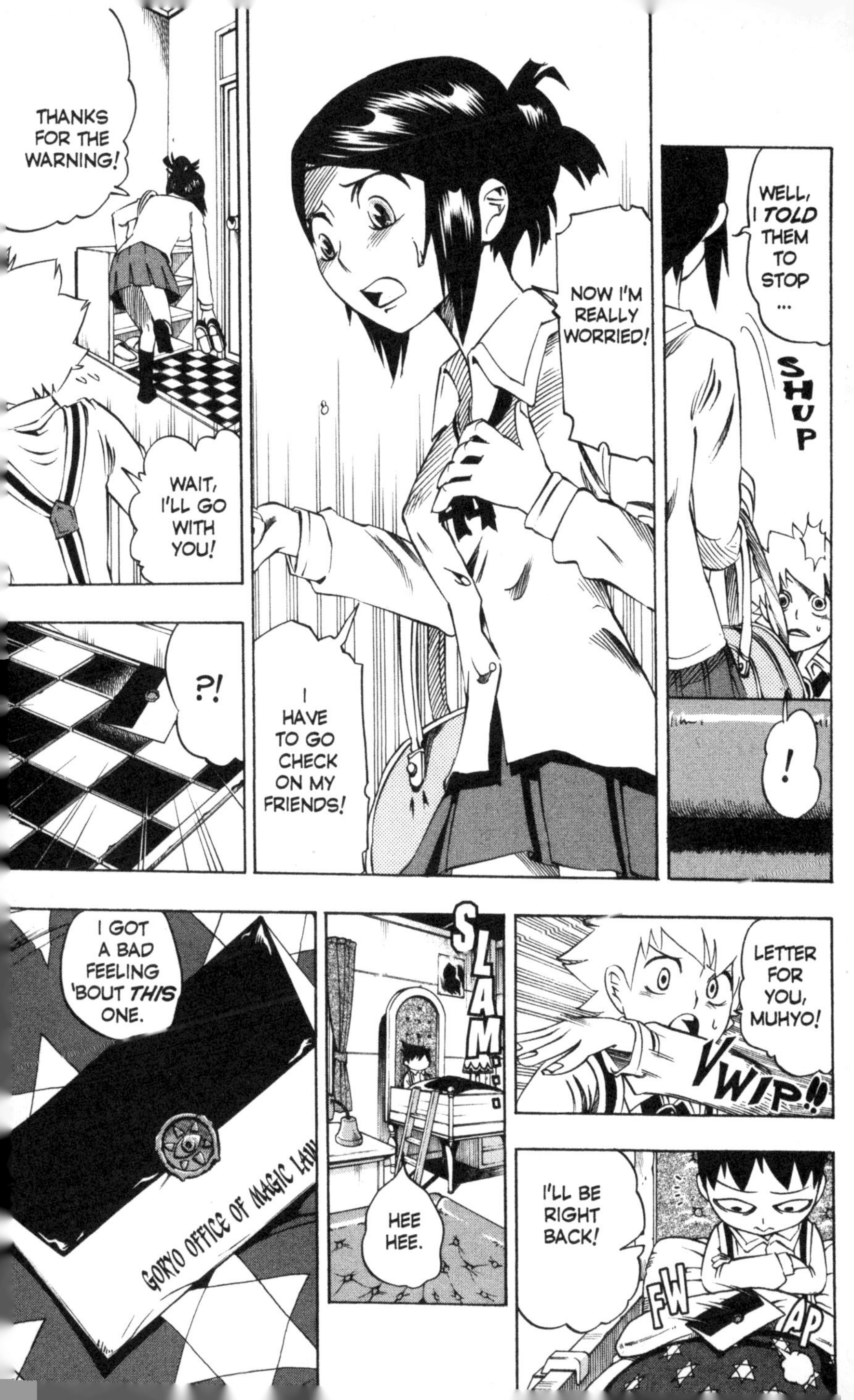
WELL, I *TOLD* THEM TO STOP ...
SHUP
!
NOW I'M REALLY WORRIED!
I HAVE TO GO CHECK ON MY FRIENDS!
THANKS FOR THE WARNING!
WAIT, I'LL GO WITH YOU!
?!
LETTER FOR YOU, MUHYO!
VWIP!!
I'LL BE RIGHT BACK!
FWAP
SLAM
HEE HEE.
I GOT A BAD FEELING 'BOUT *THIS* ONE.
GORYO OFFICE OF MAGIC LAW

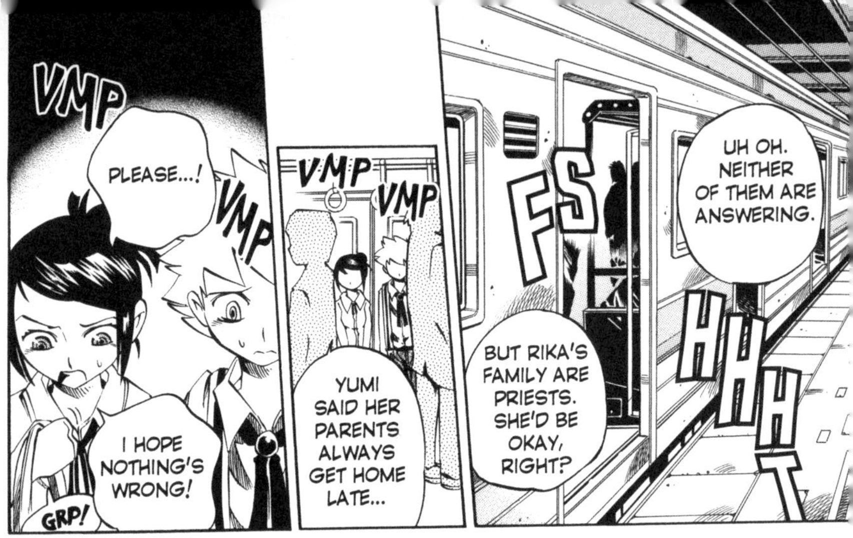
UH OH. NEITHER OF THEM ARE ANSWERING.
FS
HHHT
BUT RIKA'S FAMILY ARE PRIESTS. SHE'D BE OKAY, RIGHT?
VMP
VMP
YUMI SAID HER PARENTS ALWAYS GET HOME LATE...
VMP
PLEASE...!
VMP
I HOPE NOTHING'S WRONG!
GRP!

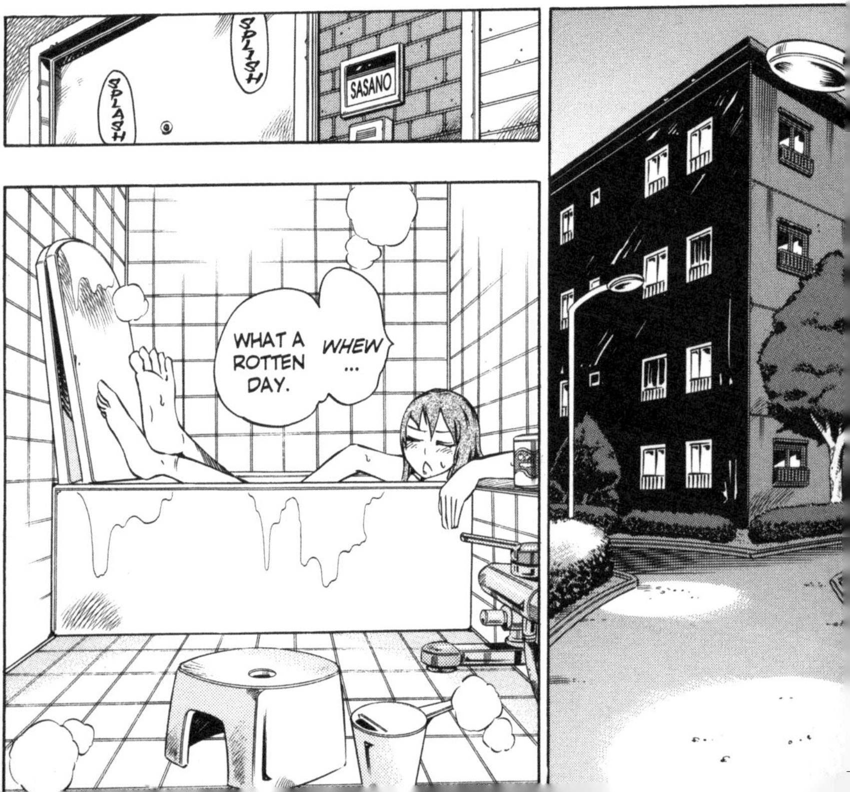
SPLISH
SASANO
SPLASH
WHEW...
WHAT A ROTTEN DAY.

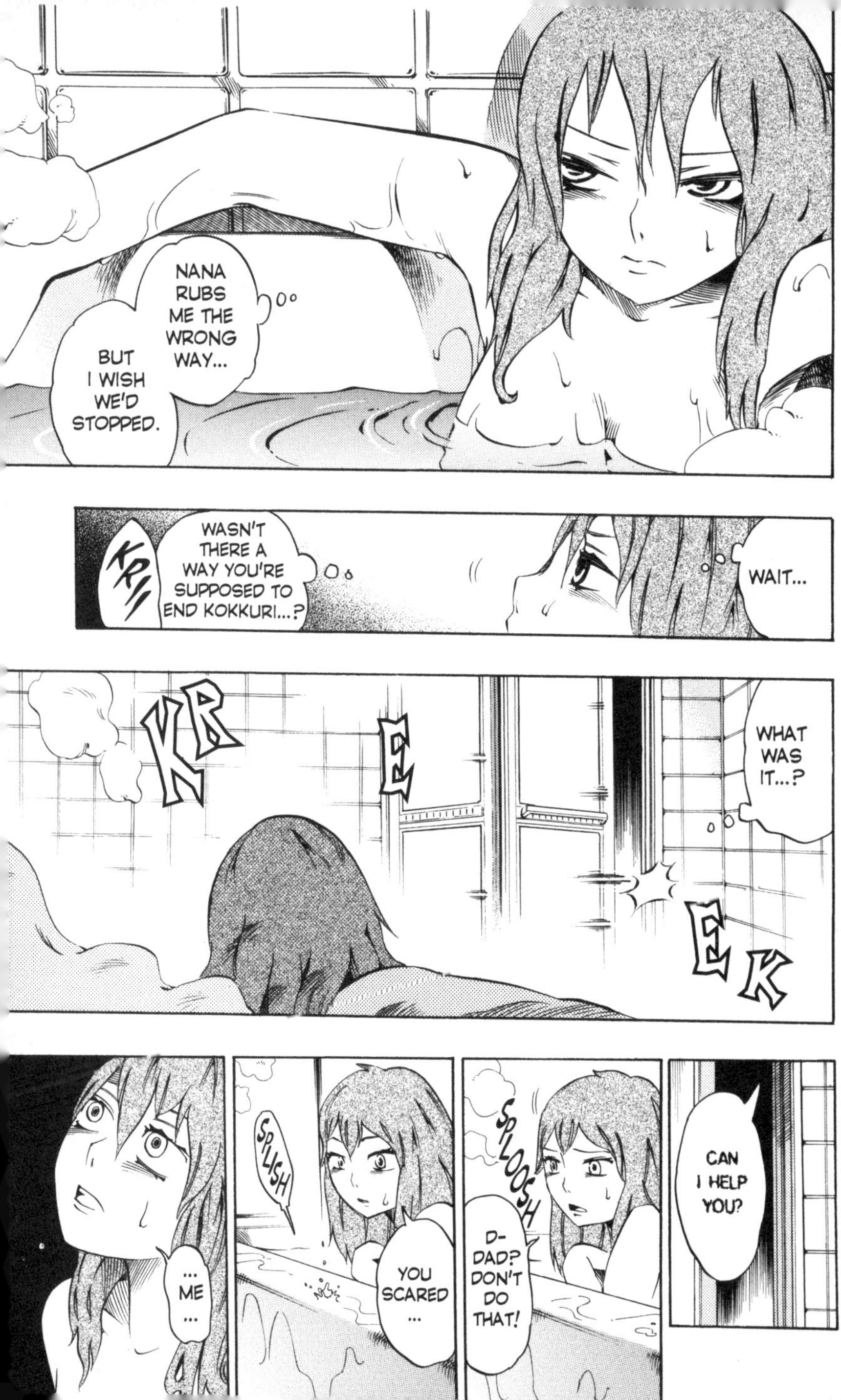
NANA RUBS ME THE WRONG WAY...
BUT I WISH WE'D STOPPED.
WAIT...
WASN'T THERE A WAY YOU'RE SUPPOSED TO END KOKKURI...?
KRI
WHAT WAS IT...?
KR E E K
CAN I HELP YOU?
SPLOOSH
D-DAD? DON'T DO THAT!
SPLISH
YOU SCARED ...
... ME ...

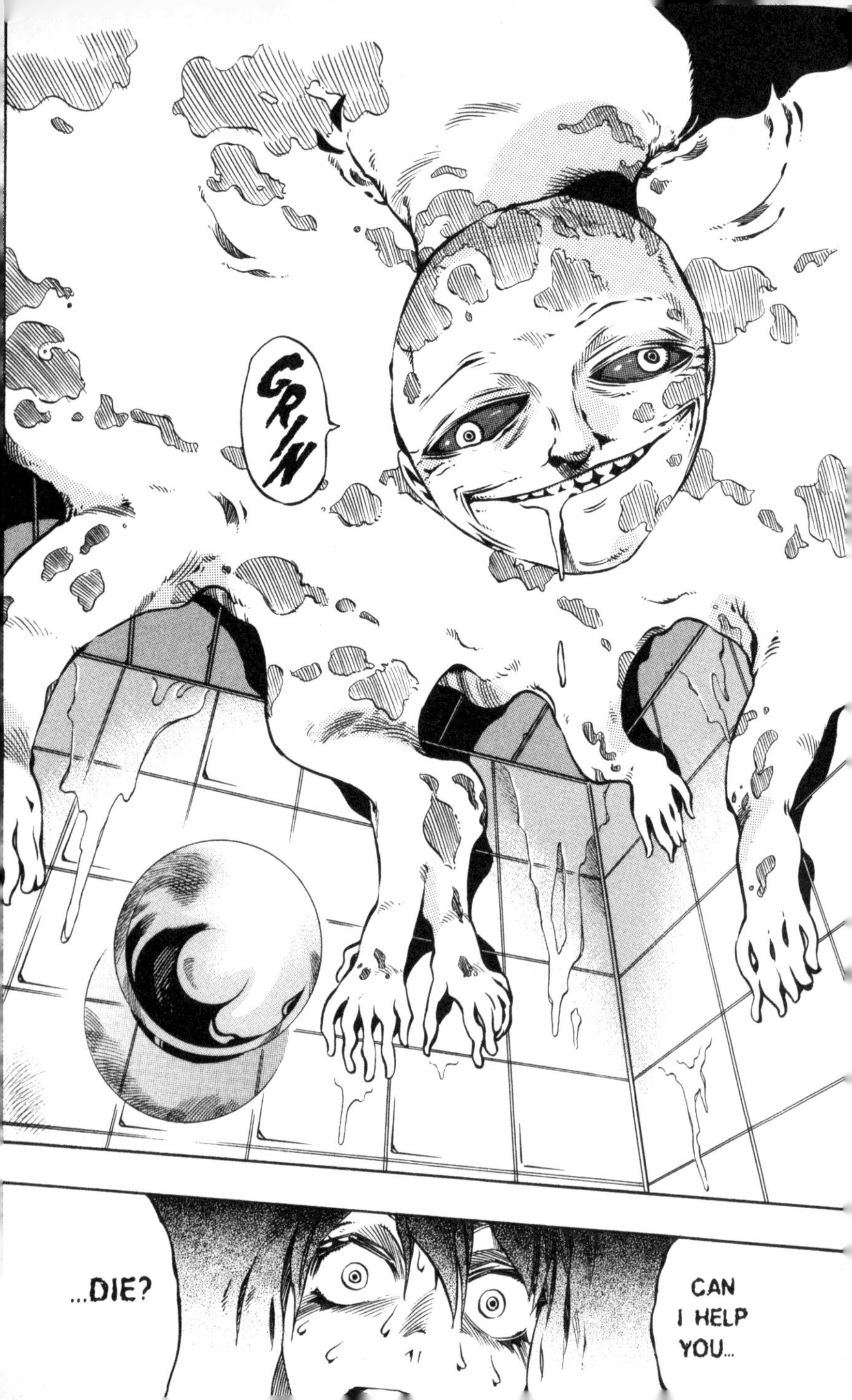
GRIN
CAN I HELP YOU...
...DIE?

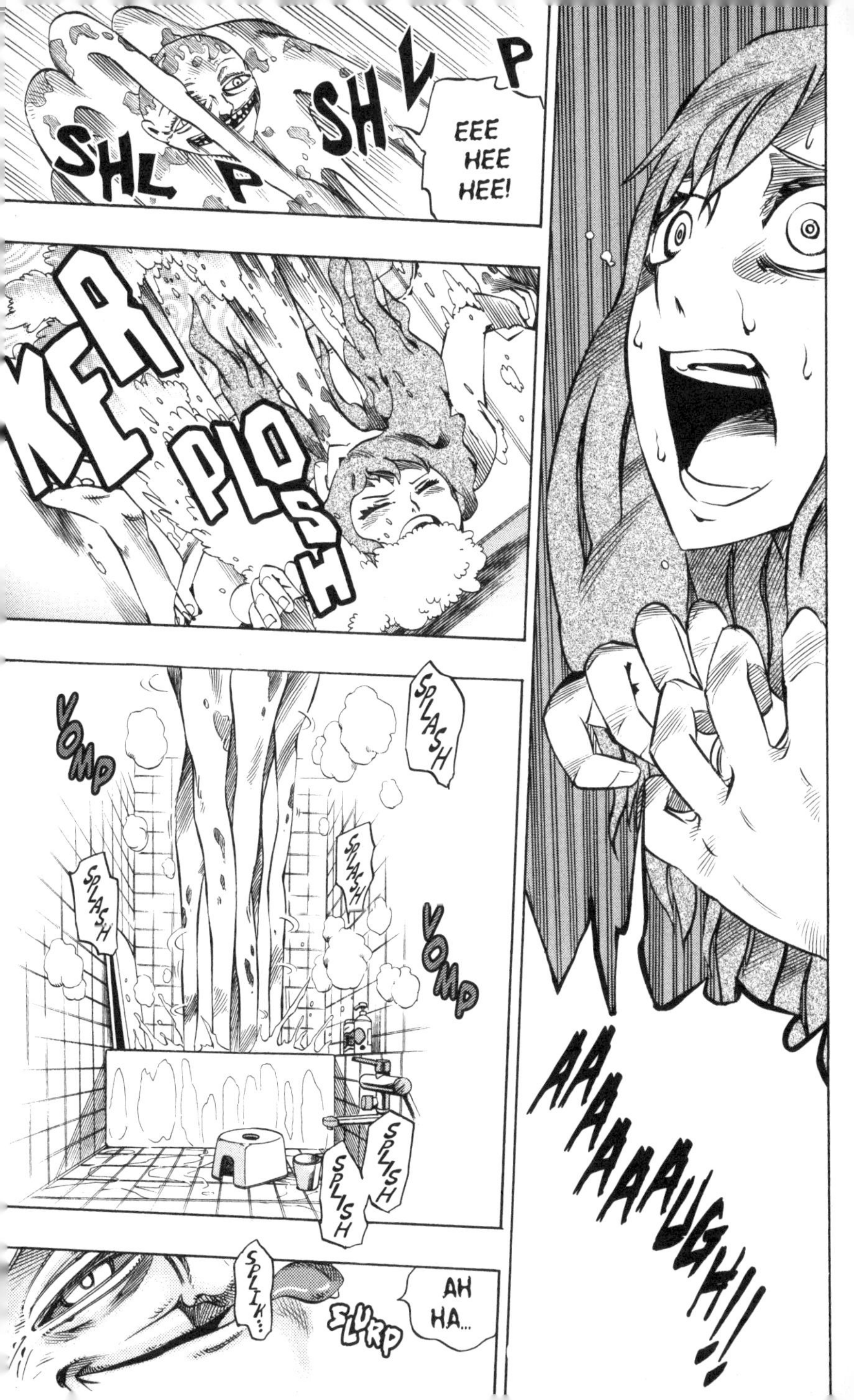
AAAAAAAUGH!!
EEE HEE HEE!
SHUP
SHLP
KER
PLOSH
SPLASH
VOMP
SPLASH
SPLASH
VOMP
SPLISH
SPLISH
AH HA...
SLURP
SPLIK...

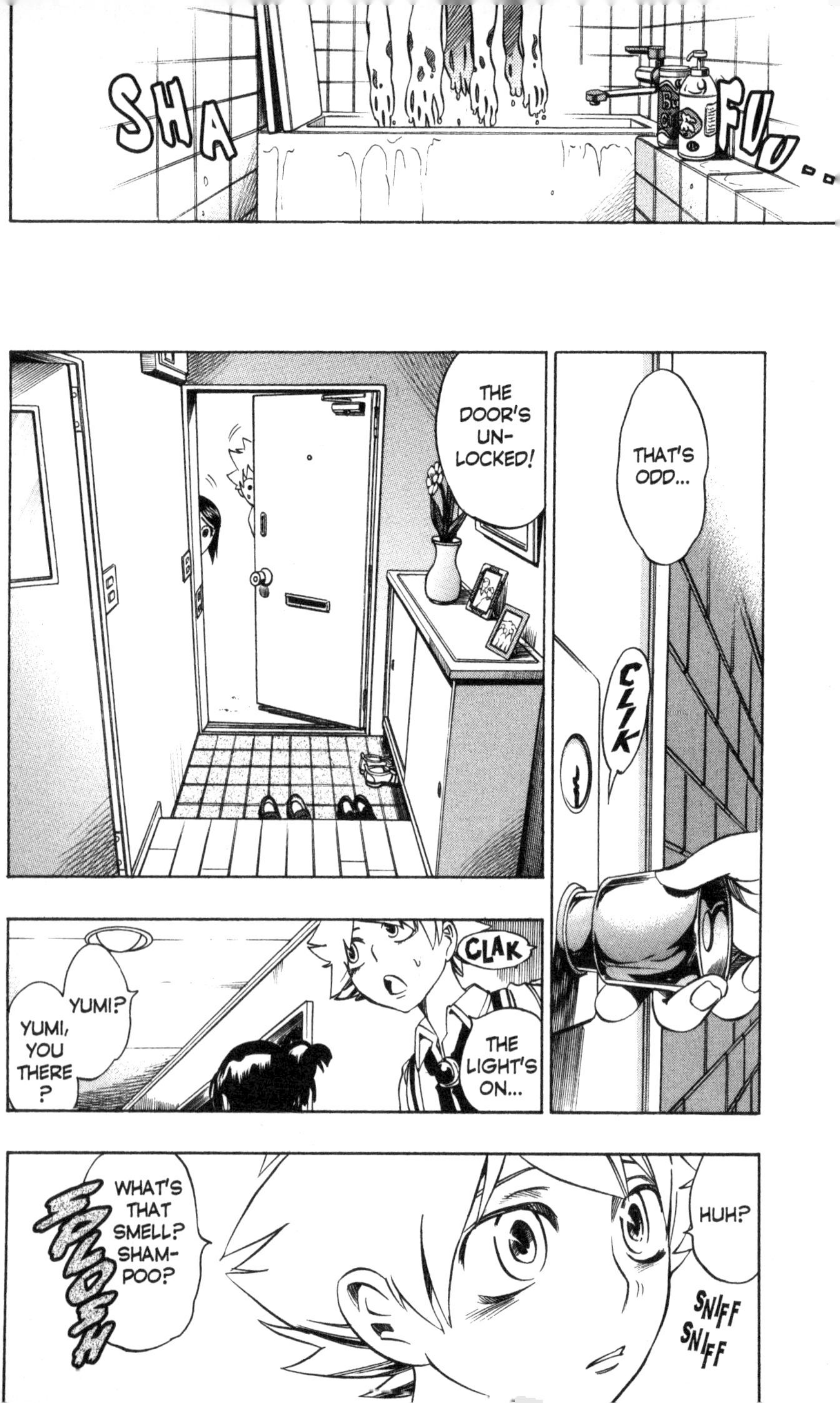
FUU...
SHA
THAT'S ODD...
CLIK
THE DOOR'S UN-LOCKED!
CLAK
THE LIGHT'S ON...
YUMI?
YUMI, YOU THERE?
HUH?
SNIFF SNIFF
WHAT'S THAT SMELL? SHAMPOO?

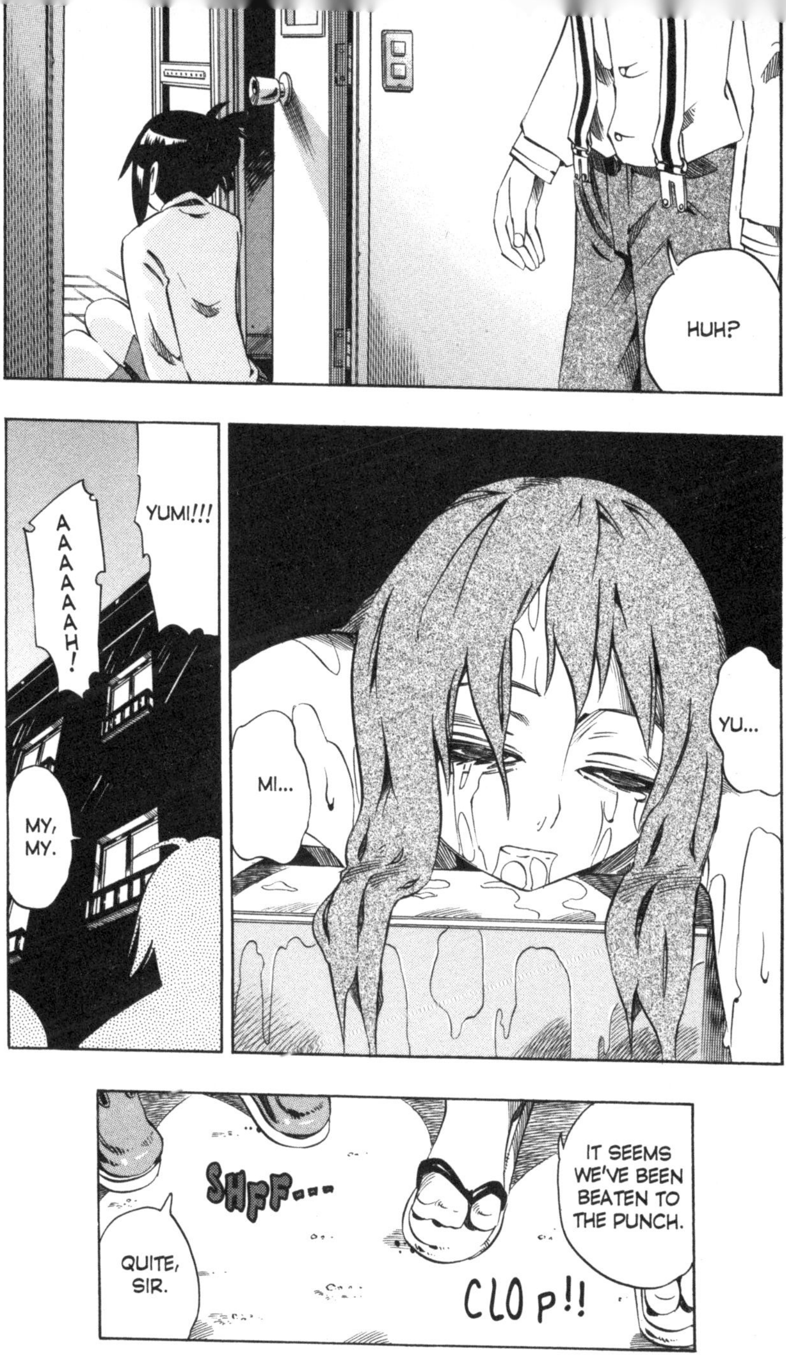
HUH?
YU...
MI...
YUMI!!!
AAAAAAAH!
MY, MY.
IT SEEMS WE'VE BEEN BEATEN TO THE PUNCH.
SHFF...
CLOP!!
QUITE, SIR.

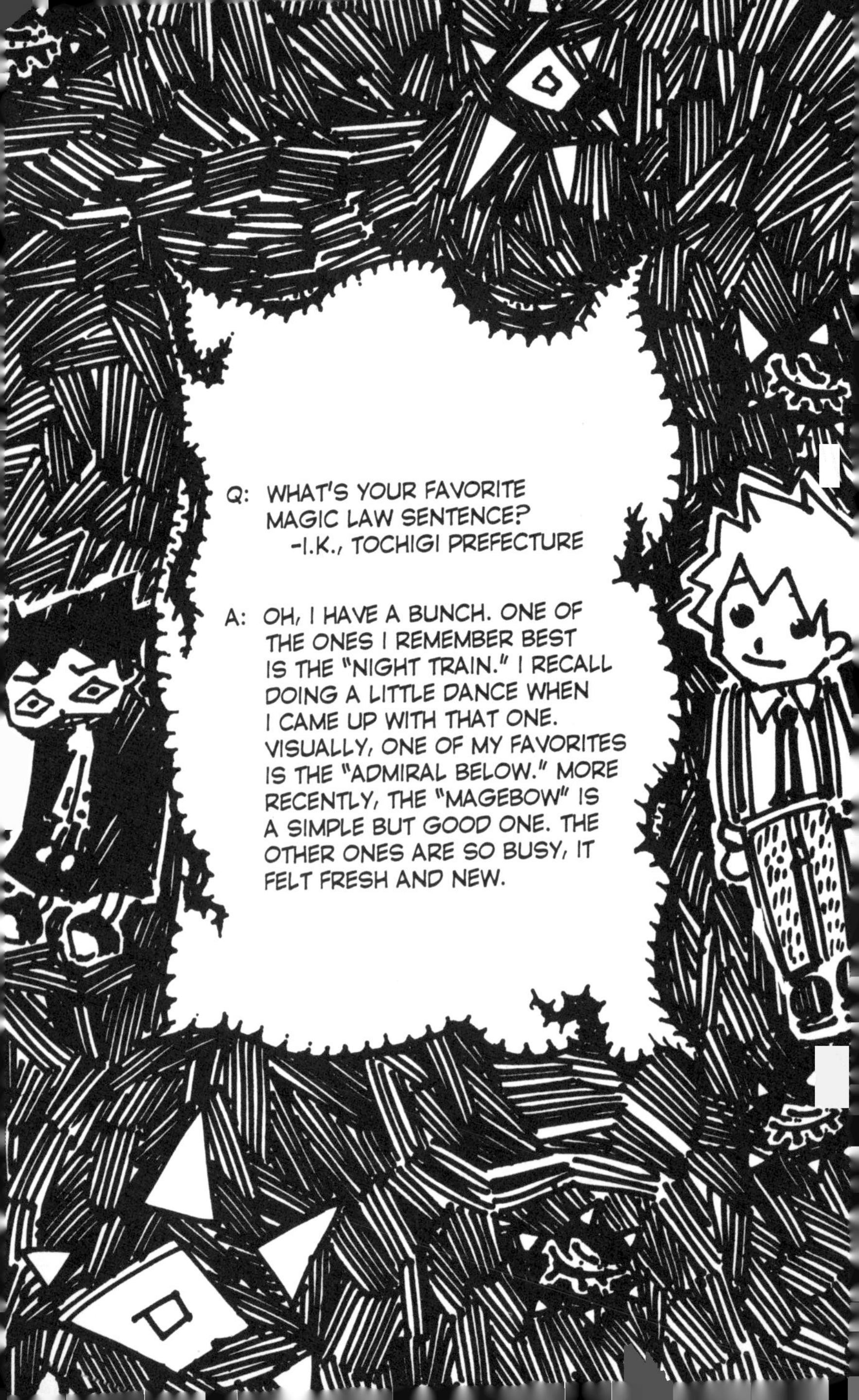

Q: WHAT'S YOUR FAVORITE MAGIC LAW SENTENCE?
-I.K., TOCHIGI PREFECTURE

A: OH, I HAVE A BUNCH. ONE OF THE ONES I REMEMBER BEST IS THE "NIGHT TRAIN." I RECALL DOING A LITTLE DANCE WHEN I CAME UP WITH THAT ONE. VISUALLY, ONE OF MY FAVORITES IS THE "ADMIRAL BELOW." MORE RECENTLY, THE "MAGEBOW" IS A SIMPLE BUT GOOD ONE. THE OTHER ONES ARE SO BUSY, IT FELT FRESH AND NEW.

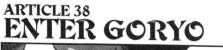

ARTICLE 38
ENTER GORYO

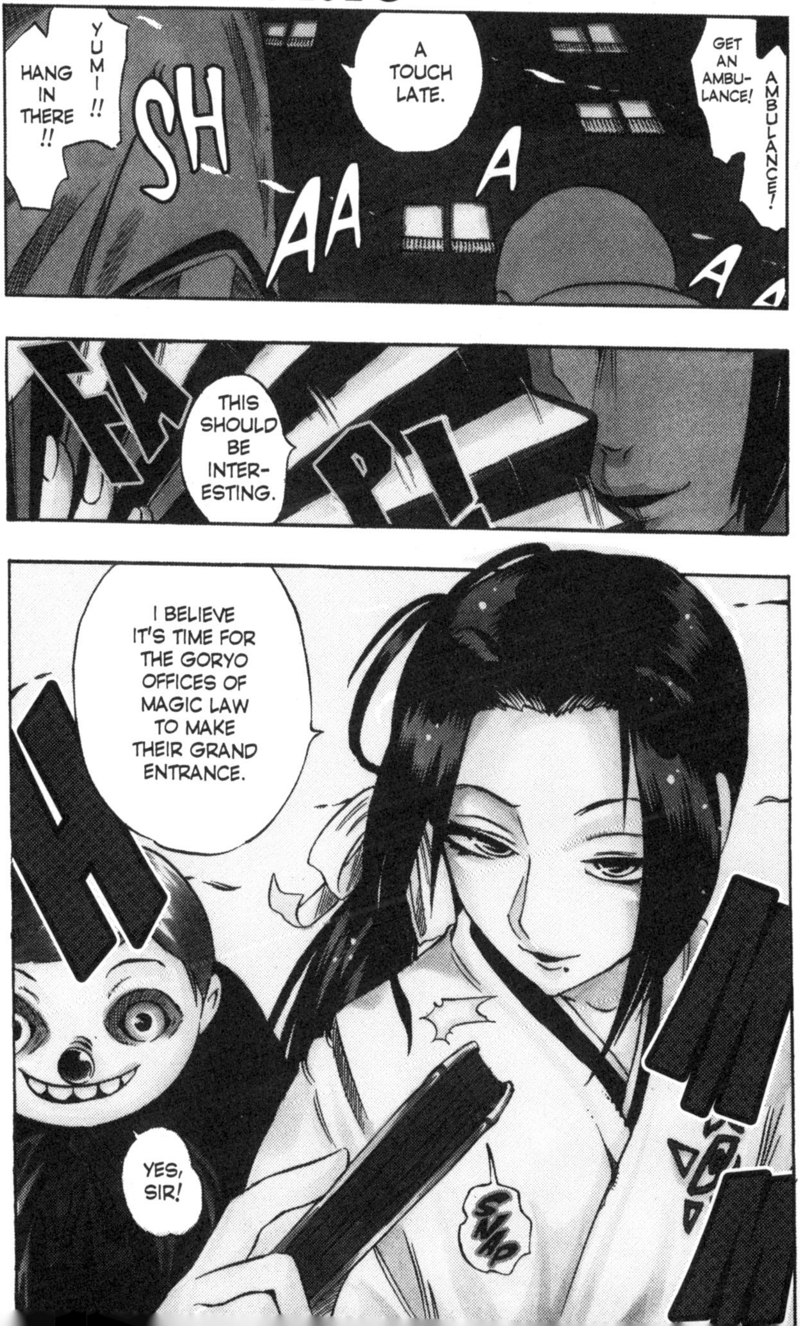
GET AN AMBULANCE!
AMBULANCE!
A TOUCH LATE.
YUMI!!
HANG IN THERE!!
SH AA A A
THIS SHOULD BE INTERESTING.
I BELIEVE IT'S TIME FOR THE GORYO OFFICES OF MAGIC LAW TO MAKE THEIR GRAND ENTRANCE.
YES, SIR!
SNAP

ARTICLE 38
ENTER GORYO

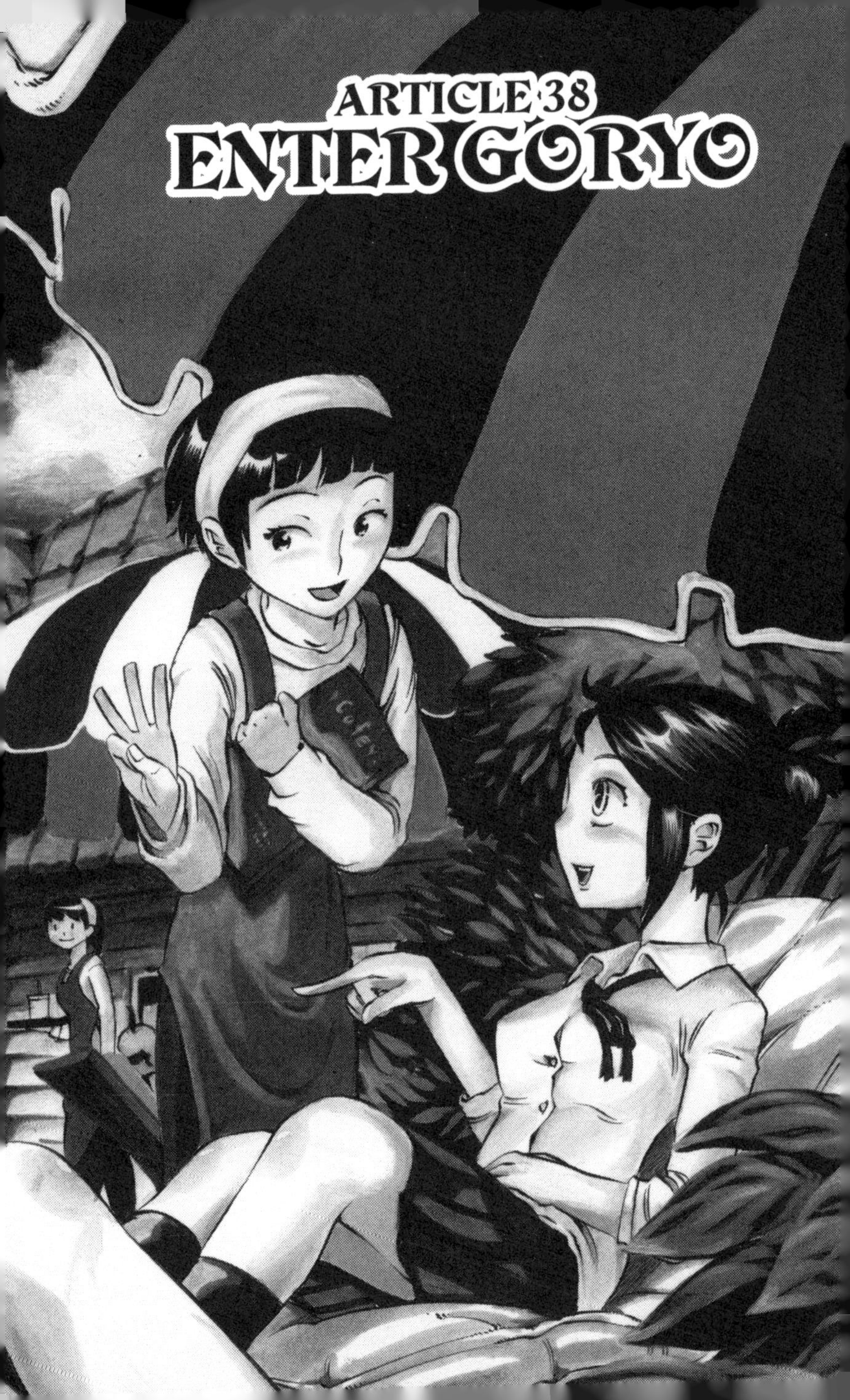

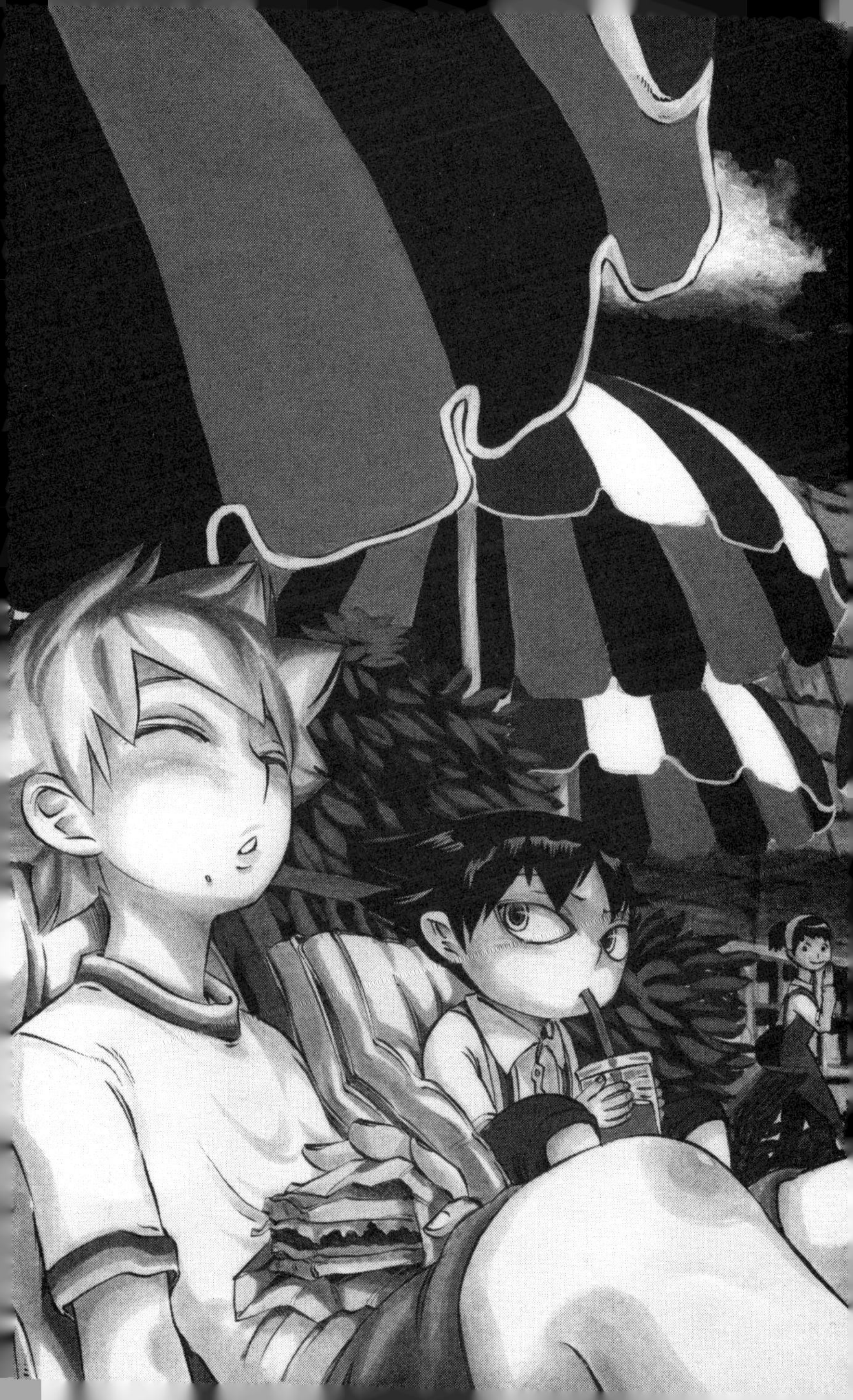

A HAPPY WORK-PLACE...

THE STAFF

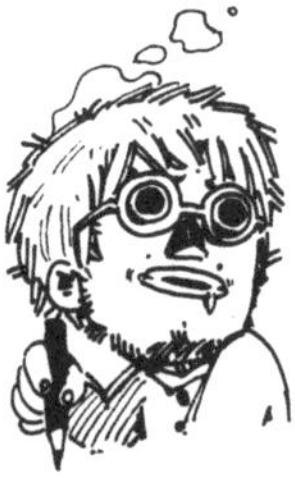

THE AUTHOR

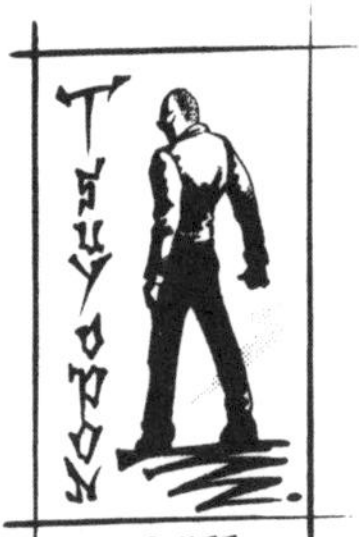

CHIEF ILLUSTRATOR #1

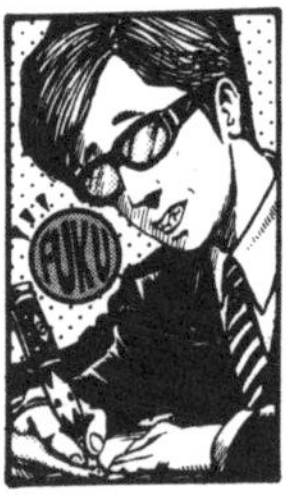
FUKU

CHIEF ILLUSTRATOR #2

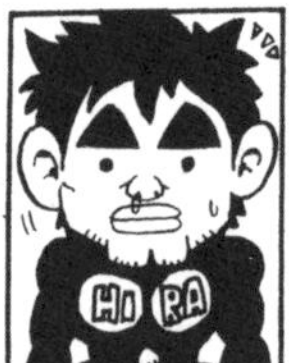
HI RA

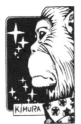

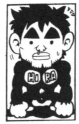

ASSISTANT HIRAISHI

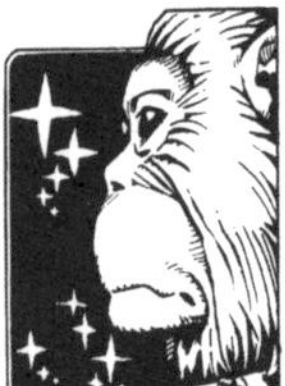
KIMURA

ASSISTANT KIMURA

ADDITIONAL ASSISTANTS:

TATSUYA ENDO
SATOKO NAKAMURA

...BEGINS WITH SMILING FACES!

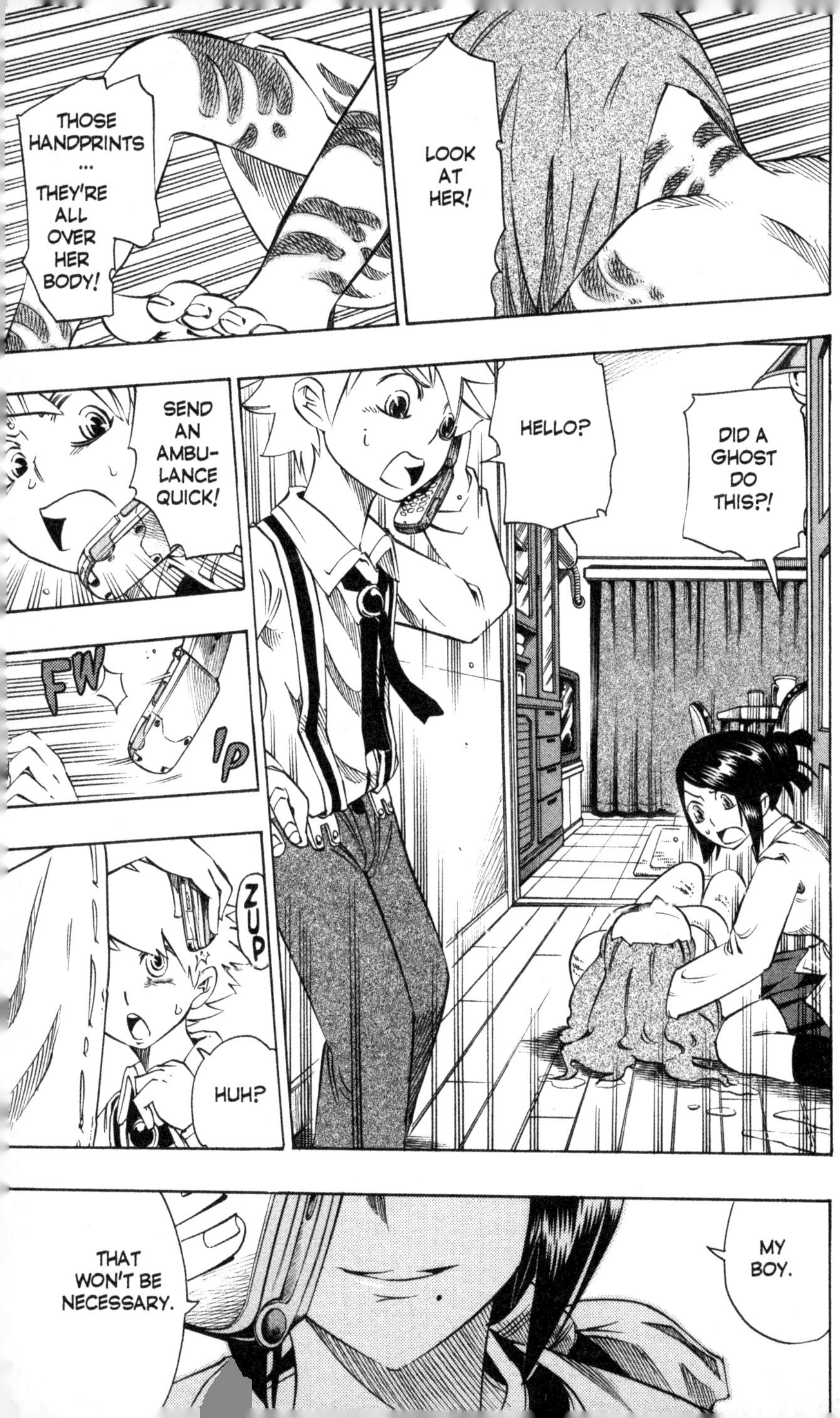
LOOK AT HER!
THOSE HANDPRINTS ... THEY'RE ALL OVER HER BODY!
DID A GHOST DO THIS?!
HELLO?
SEND AN AMBULANCE QUICK!
FWIP
ZUP
HUH?
MY BOY.
THAT WON'T BE NECESSARY.

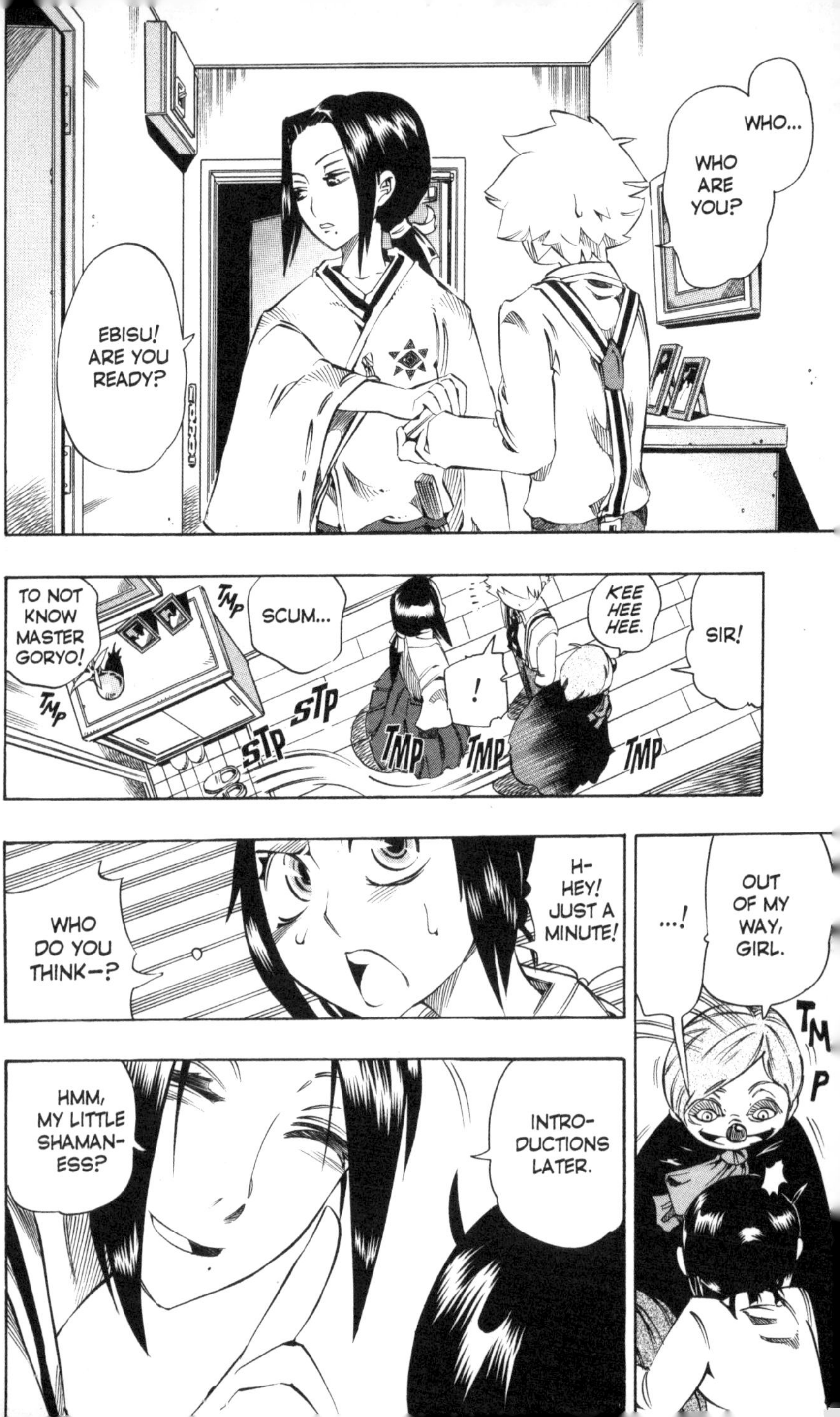
WHO... WHO ARE YOU?
EBISU! ARE YOU READY?
SIR!
KEE HEE HEE.
TMP
!
TMP
TMP
SCUM...
STP
STP
TMP
TO NOT KNOW MASTER GORYO!
TMP
OUT OF MY WAY, GIRL.
TMP
...!
H-HEY! JUST A MINUTE!
WHO DO YOU THINK—?
INTRO-DUCTIONS LATER.
HMM, MY LITTLE SHAMAN-ESS?

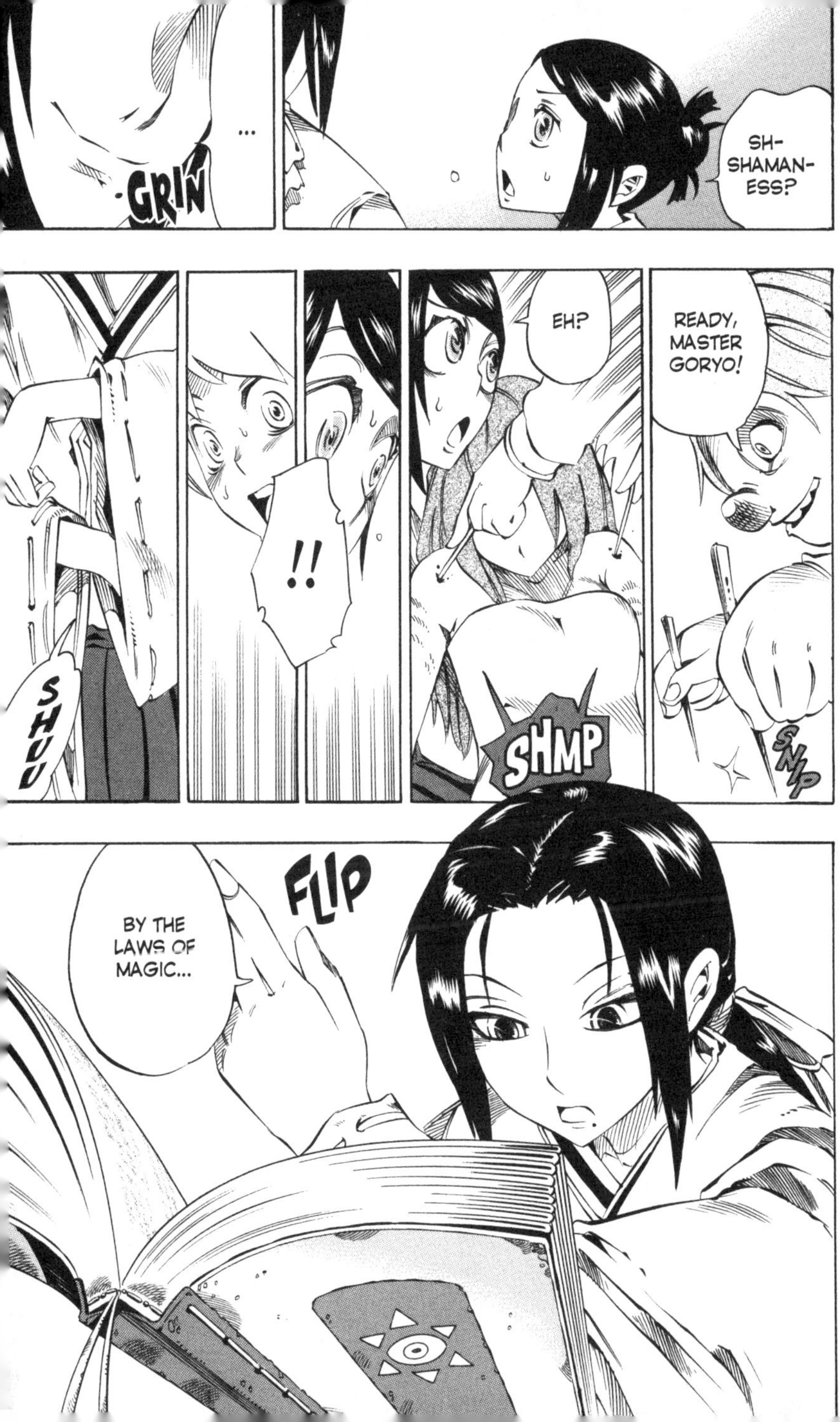
SH-
SHAMAN-
ESS?
...
GRIN
READY, MASTER GORYO!
SNIP
EH?
SHMP
!!
SHUU
FLIP
BY THE LAWS OF MAGIC...

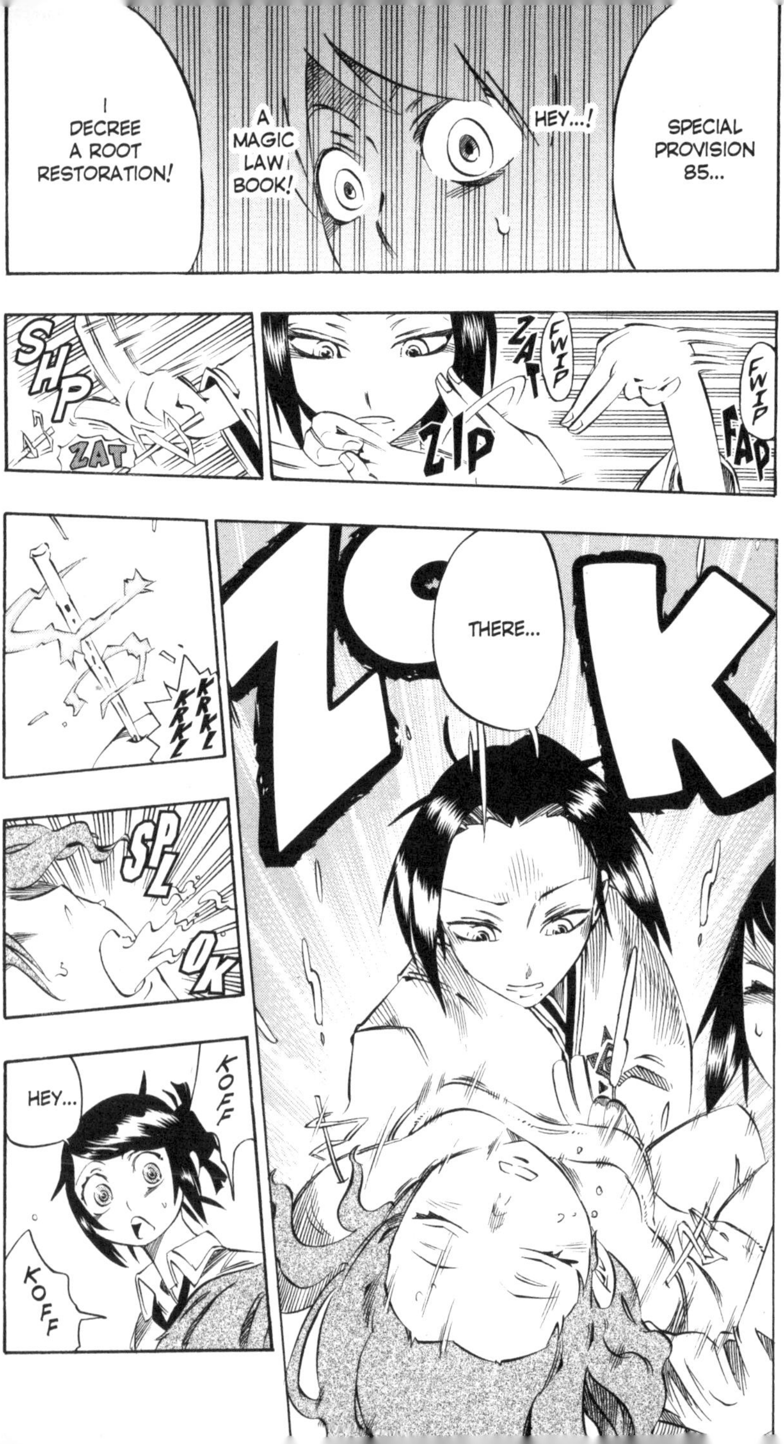
SPECIAL PROVISION 85...
HEY...!
A MAGIC LAW BOOK!
I DECREE A ROOT RESTORATION!
FWIP
FAP
FWIP
ZAT
ZIP
SHP
ZAT
ZOK
THERE...
KRKL KRKL
SPLOK
KOFF
HEY...
KOFF

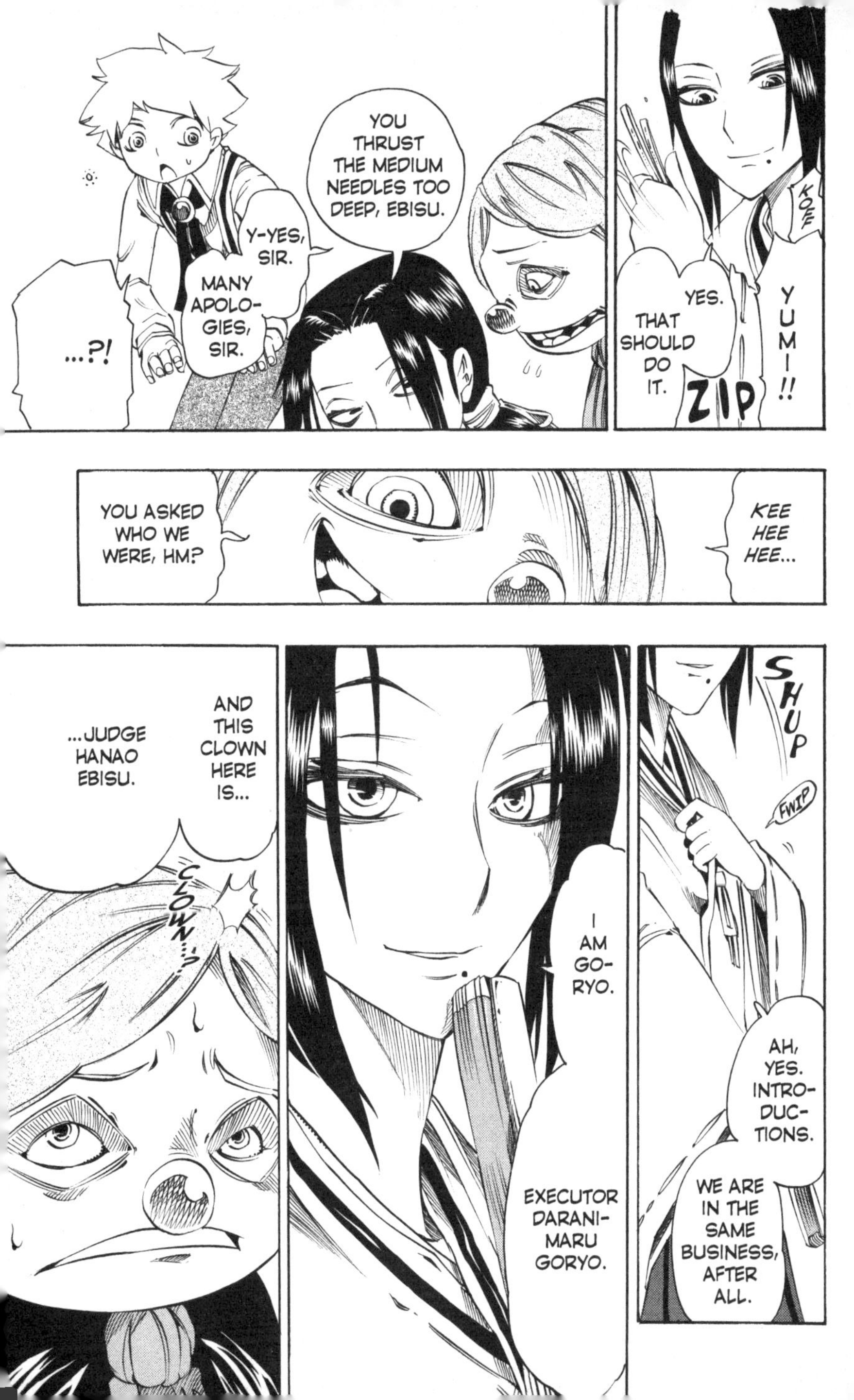
KOFF
YUMI!!
YES. THAT SHOULD DO IT.
ZIP
YOU THRUST THE MEDIUM NEEDLES TOO DEEP, EBISU.
Y-YES, SIR.
MANY APOLO-GIES, SIR.
...?!
KEE HEE HEE...
YOU ASKED WHO WE WERE, HM?
SHUP
FWIP
AH, YES. INTRO-DUC-TIONS.
WE ARE IN THE SAME BUSINESS, AFTER ALL.
I AM GO-RYO.
EXECUTOR DARANI-MARU GORYO.
AND THIS CLOWN HERE IS...
...JUDGE HANAO EBISU.
CLOWN...?

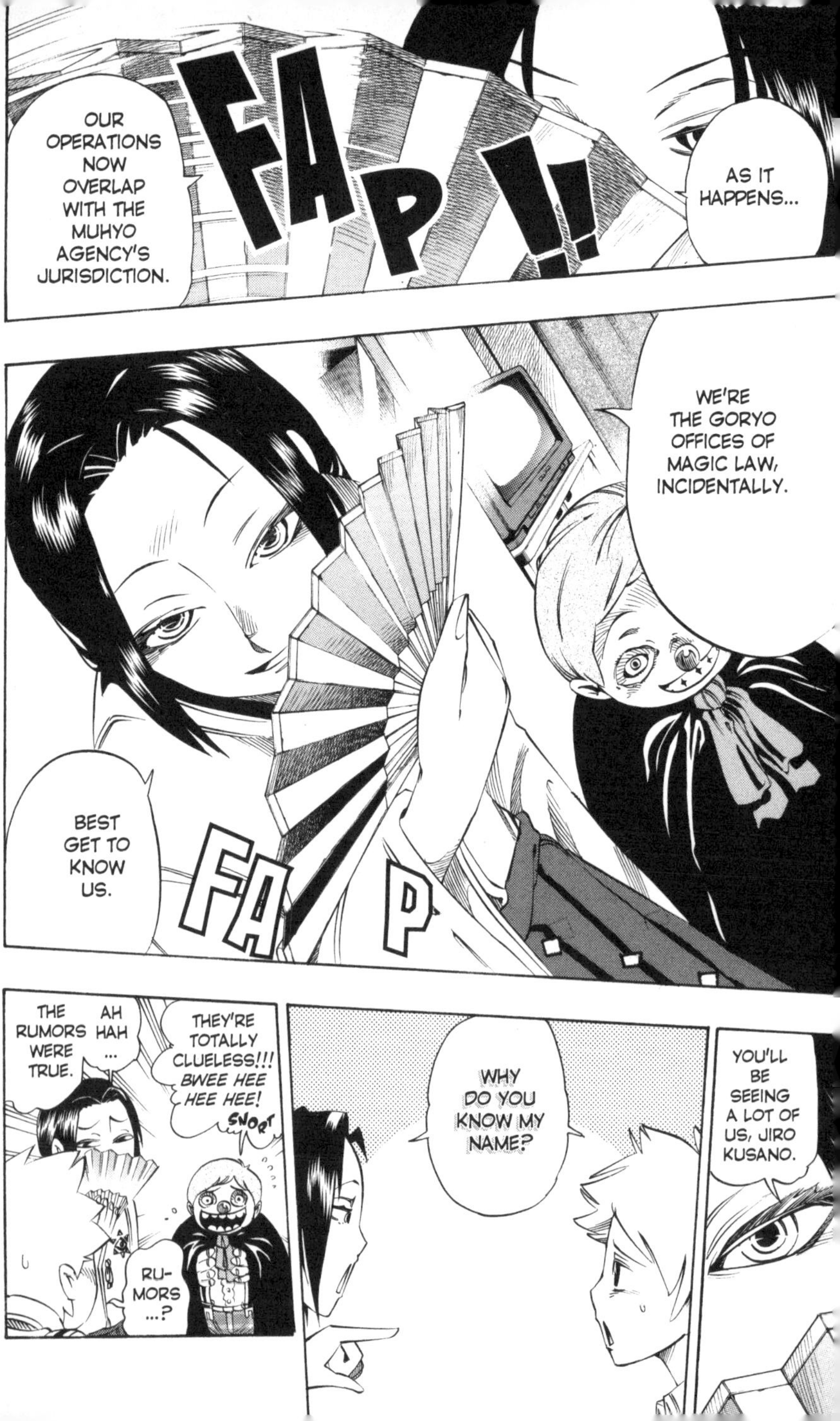
AS IT HAPPENS...
FAP!!
OUR OPERATIONS NOW OVERLAP WITH THE MUHYO AGENCY'S JURISDICTION.
WE'RE THE GORYO OFFICES OF MAGIC LAW, INCIDENTALLY.
BEST GET TO KNOW US.
FAP
YOU'LL BE SEEING A LOT OF US, JIRO KUSANO.
WHY DO YOU KNOW MY NAME?
THEY'RE TOTALLY CLUELESS!!! BWEE HEE HEE HEE!
SNORT
AH HAH ...
THE RUMORS WERE TRUE.
RU-MORS ...?

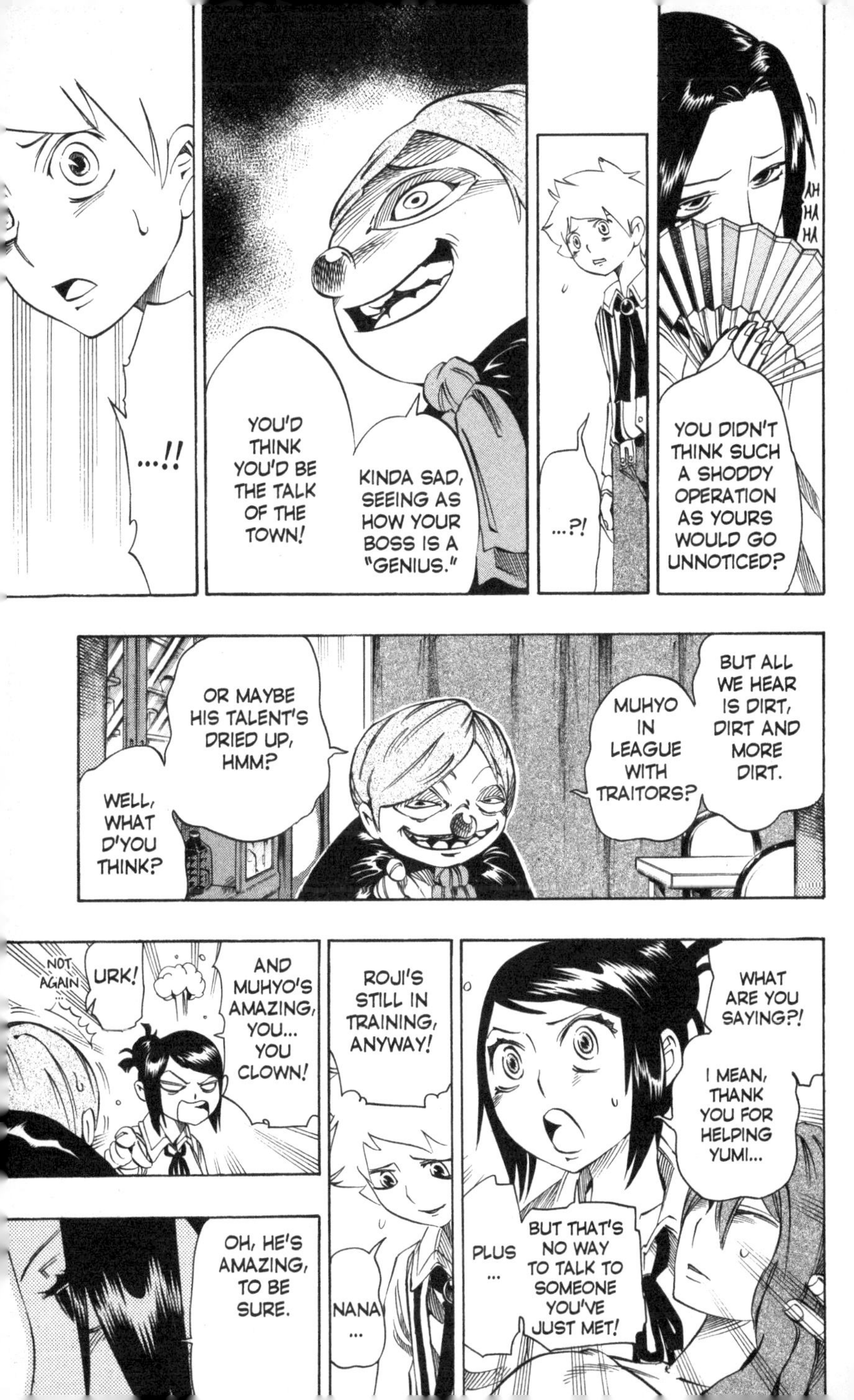
AH HA HA
YOU DIDN'T THINK SUCH A SHODDY OPERATION AS YOURS WOULD GO UNNOTICED?
...?!
KINDA SAD, SEEING AS HOW YOUR BOSS IS A "GENIUS."
YOU'D THINK YOU'D BE THE TALK OF THE TOWN!
...!!
BUT ALL WE HEAR IS DIRT, DIRT AND MORE DIRT.
MUHYO IN LEAGUE WITH TRAITORS?
OR MAYBE HIS TALENT'S DRIED UP, HMM?
WELL, WHAT D'YOU THINK?
WHAT ARE YOU SAYING?!
I MEAN, THANK YOU FOR HELPING YUMI...
BUT THAT'S NO WAY TO TALK TO SOMEONE YOU'VE JUST MET!
PLUS...
ROJI'S STILL IN TRAINING, ANYWAY!
NANA...
AND MUHYO'S AMAZING, YOU... YOU CLOWN!
URK!
NOT AGAIN...
OH, HE'S AMAZING, TO BE SURE.

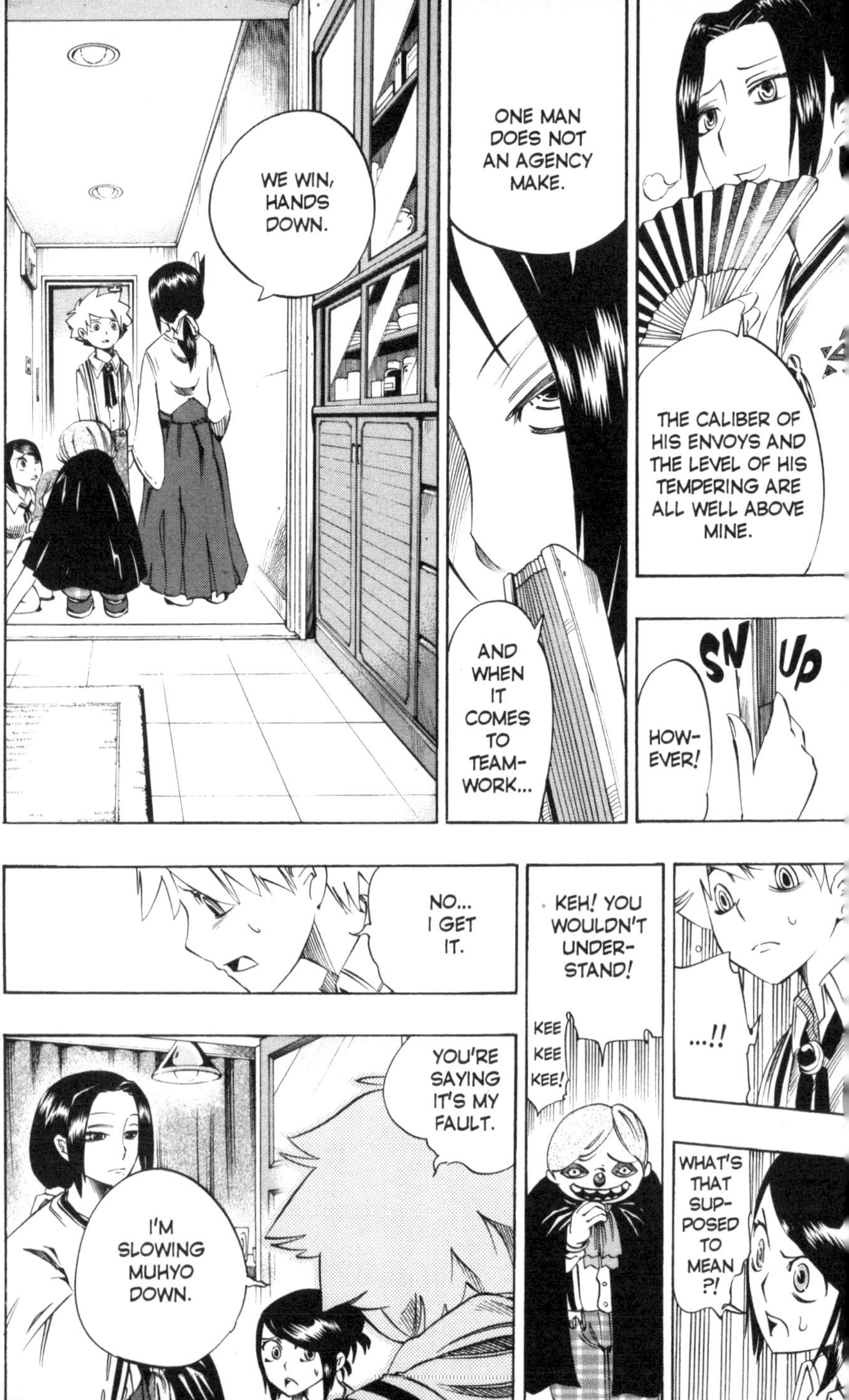
THE CALIBER OF HIS ENVOYS AND THE LEVEL OF HIS TEMPERING ARE ALL WELL ABOVE MINE.
SNUP
HOW-EVER!
ONE MAN DOES NOT AN AGENCY MAKE.
AND WHEN IT COMES TO TEAM-WORK...
WE WIN, HANDS DOWN.
...!!
WHAT'S THAT SUP-POSED TO MEAN?!
KEH! YOU WOULDN'T UNDER-STAND!
KEE KEE KEE!
NO... I GET IT.
YOU'RE SAYING IT'S MY FAULT.
I'M SLOWING MUHYO DOWN.

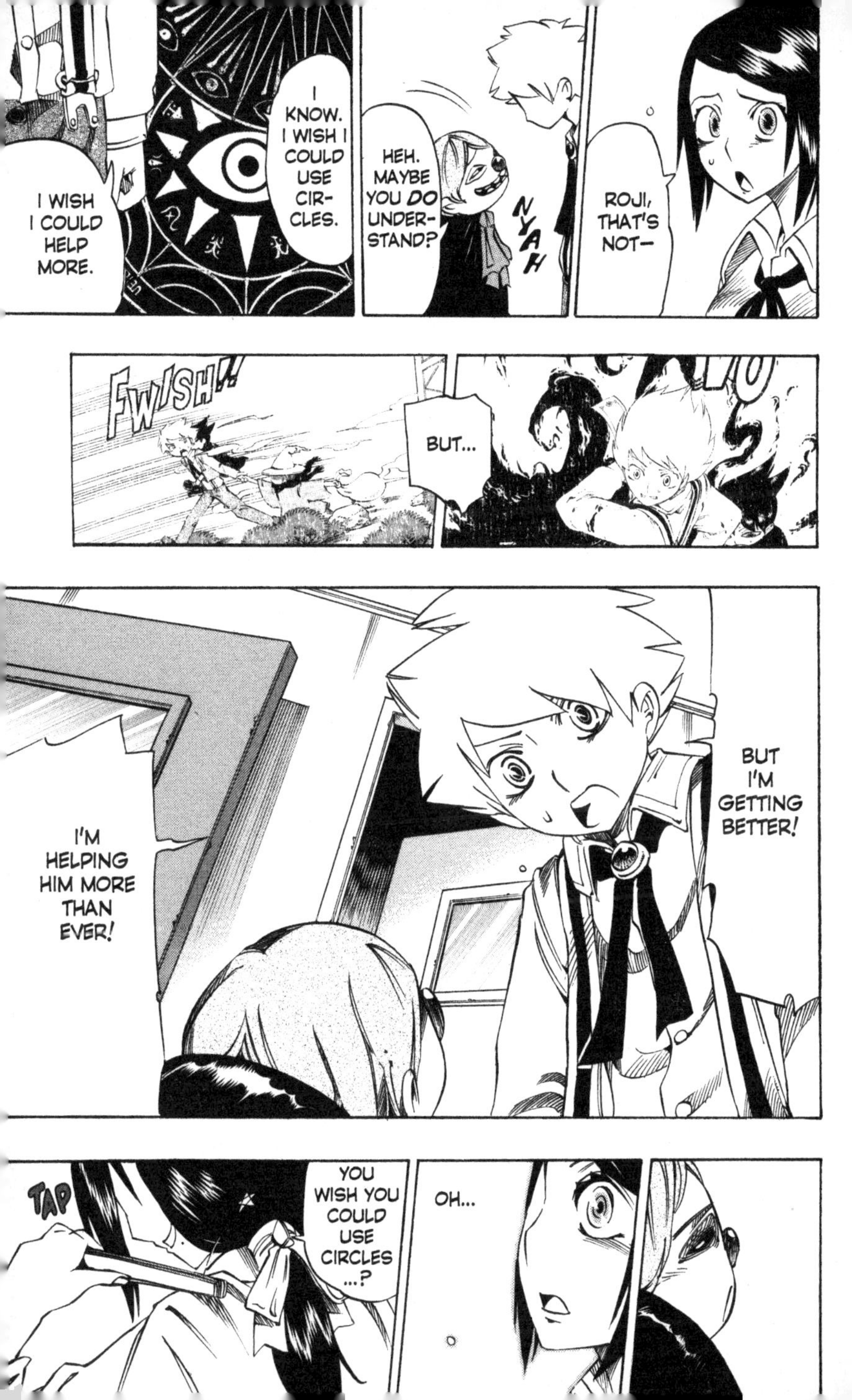
ROJI, THAT'S NOT—
HEH. MAYBE YOU DO UNDERSTAND?
NYAH
I KNOW. I WISH I COULD USE CIR-CLES.
I WISH I COULD HELP MORE.
BUT...
FWISH!!
BUT I'M GETTING BETTER!
I'M HELPING HIM MORE THAN EVER!
OH...
YOU WISH YOU COULD USE CIRCLES ...?
TAP

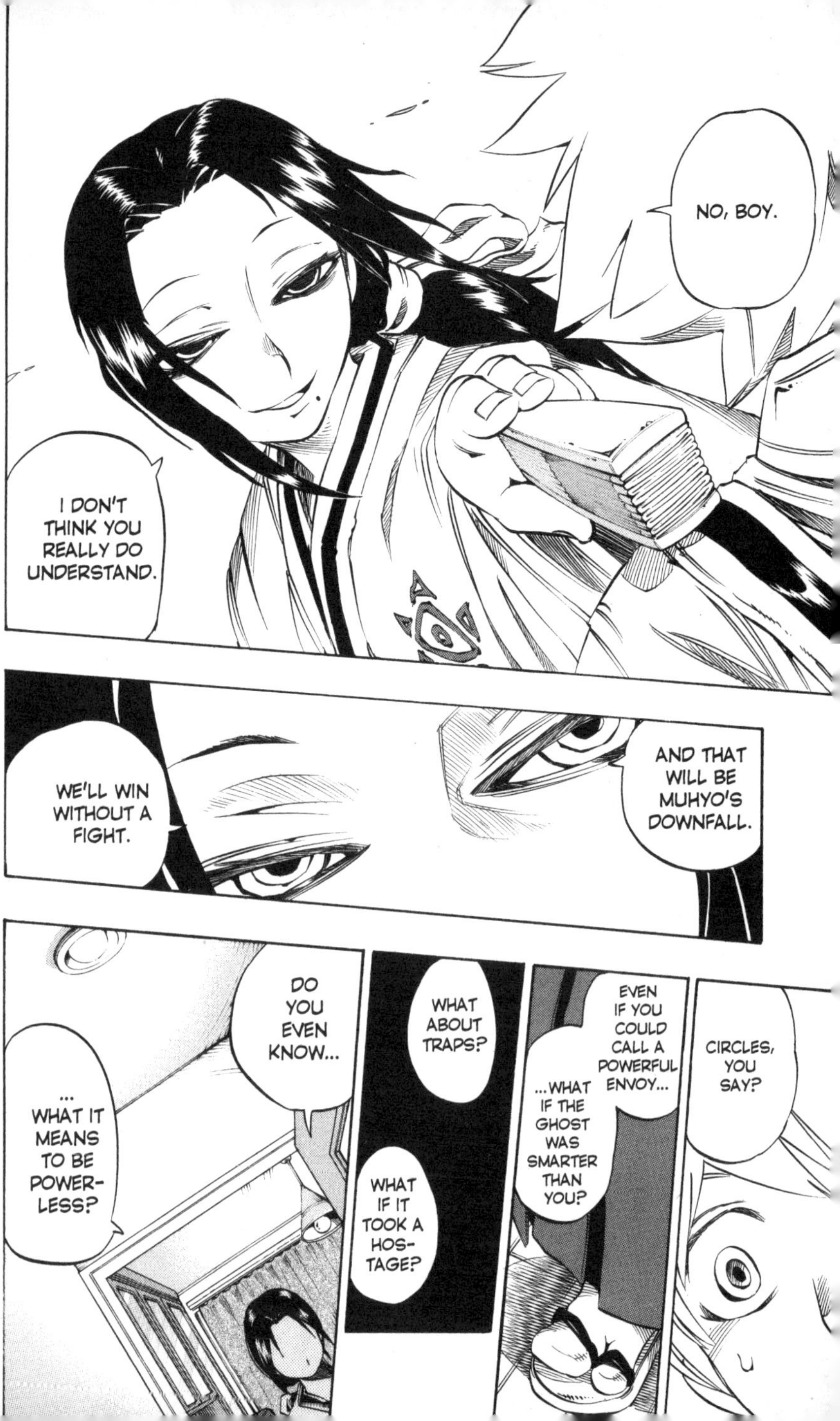
NO, BOY.
I DON'T THINK YOU REALLY DO UNDERSTAND.
AND THAT WILL BE MUHYO'S DOWNFALL.
WE'LL WIN WITHOUT A FIGHT.
CIRCLES, YOU SAY?
EVEN IF YOU COULD CALL A POWERFUL ENVOY...
...WHAT IF THE GHOST WAS SMARTER THAN YOU?
WHAT ABOUT TRAPS?
WHAT IF IT TOOK A HOSTAGE?
DO YOU EVEN KNOW...
...WHAT IT MEANS TO BE POWERLESS?

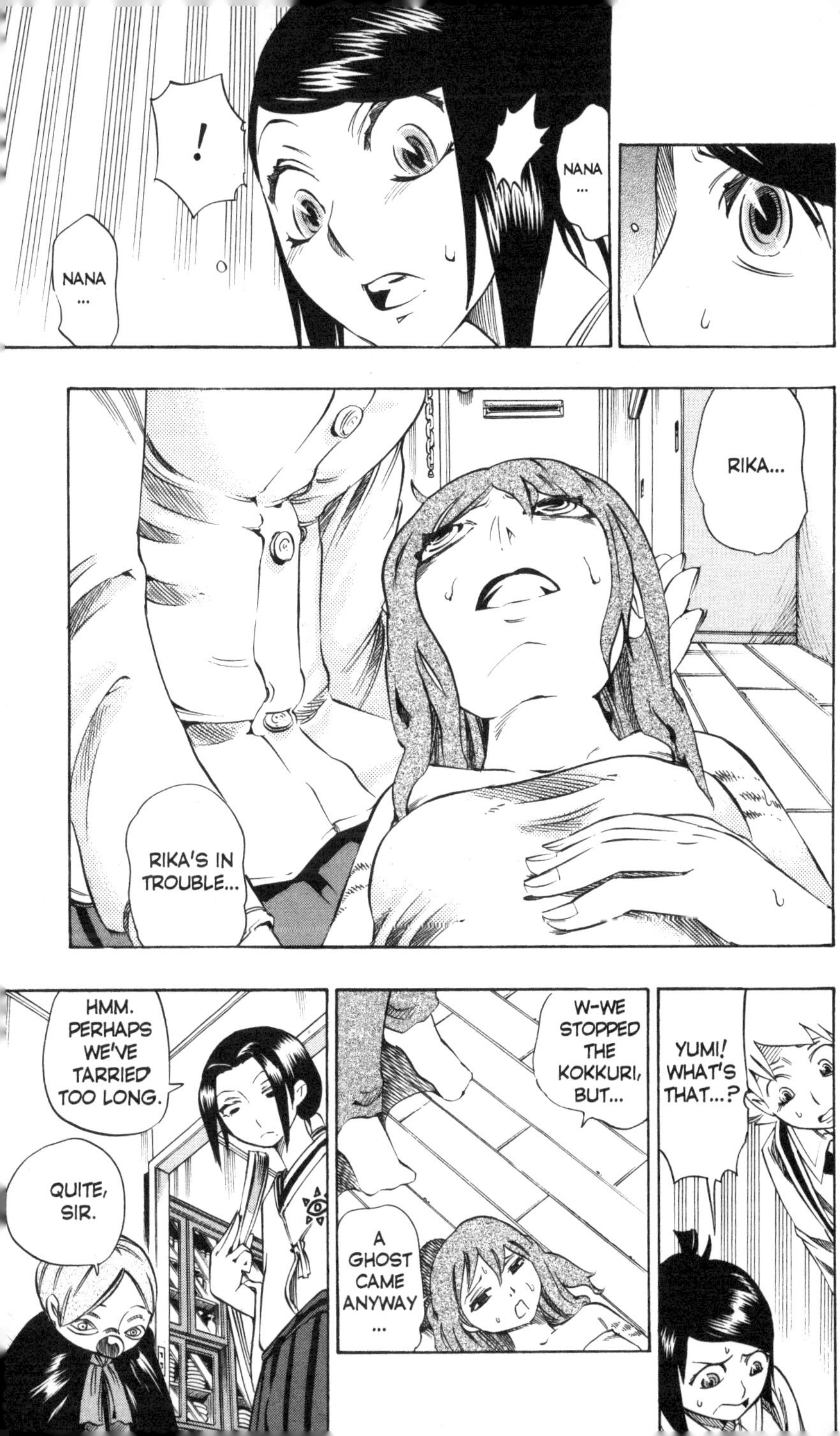
NANA ...
!
NANA ...
RIKA...
RIKA'S IN TROUBLE...
YUMI! WHAT'S THAT...?
W-WE STOPPED THE KOKKURI, BUT...
A GHOST CAME ANYWAY ...
HMM. PERHAPS WE'VE TARRIED TOO LONG.
QUITE, SIR.

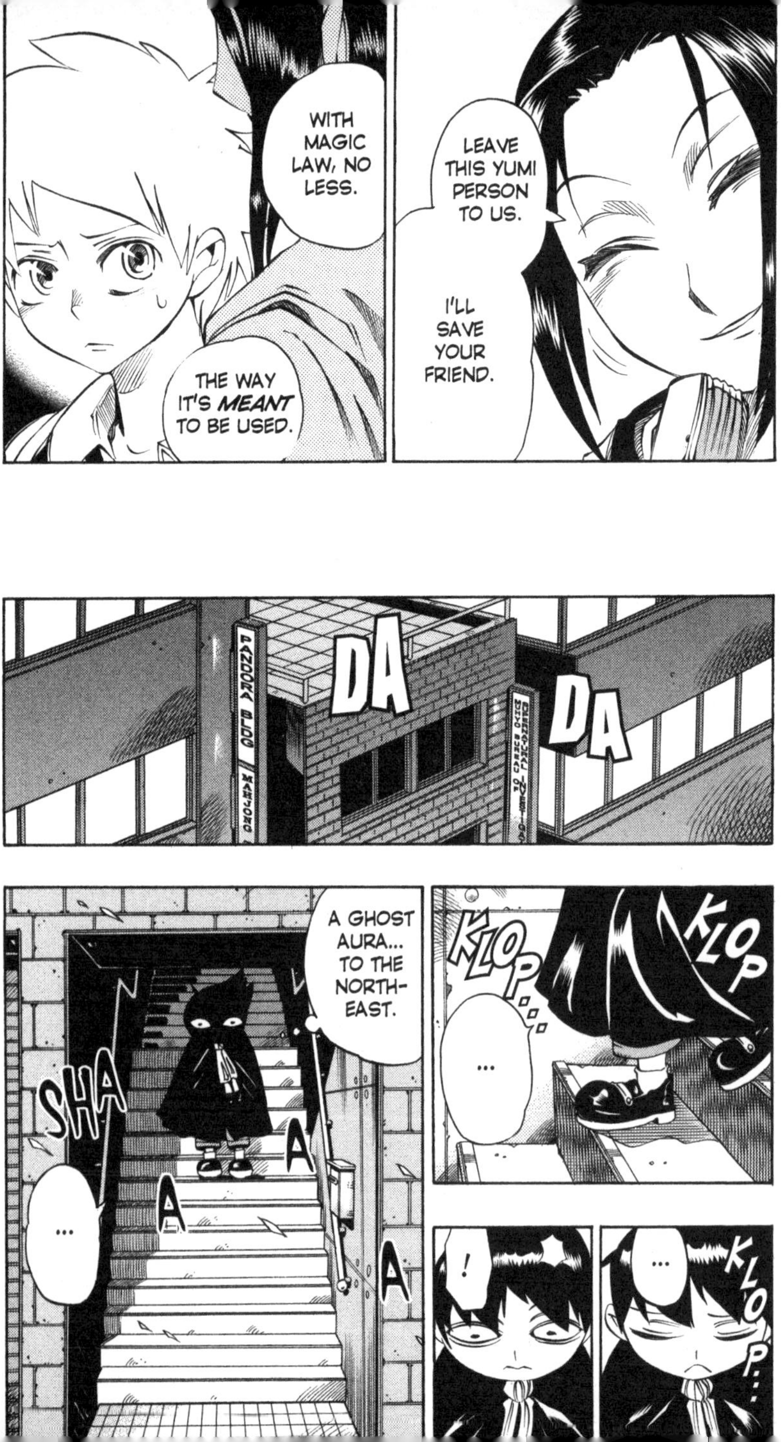
LEAVE THIS YUMI PERSON TO US.
I'LL SAVE YOUR FRIEND.
WITH MAGIC LAW, NO LESS.
THE WAY IT'S *MEANT* TO BE USED.
DA
DA
PANDORA BLDG
MAHJONG
KLOP
KLOP...
...
KLOP...
...
!
A GHOST AURA... TO THE NORTH-EAST.
SHA
A
A
A
...

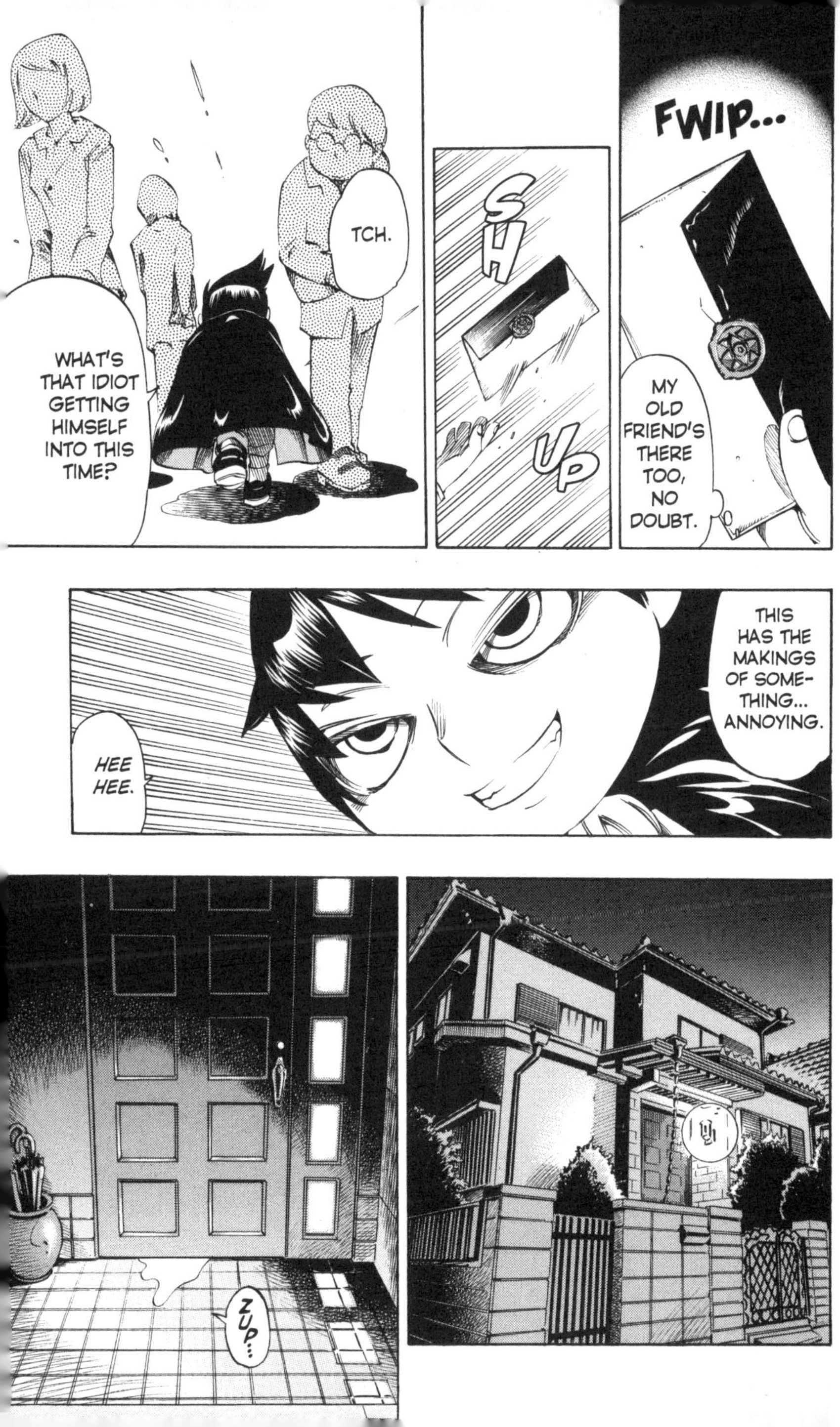
FWIP...
MY OLD FRIEND'S THERE TOO, NO DOUBT.
SHUP
TCH.
WHAT'S THAT IDIOT GETTING HIMSELF INTO THIS TIME?
THIS HAS THE MAKINGS OF SOME-THING... ANNOYING.
HEE HEE.
ZUP...

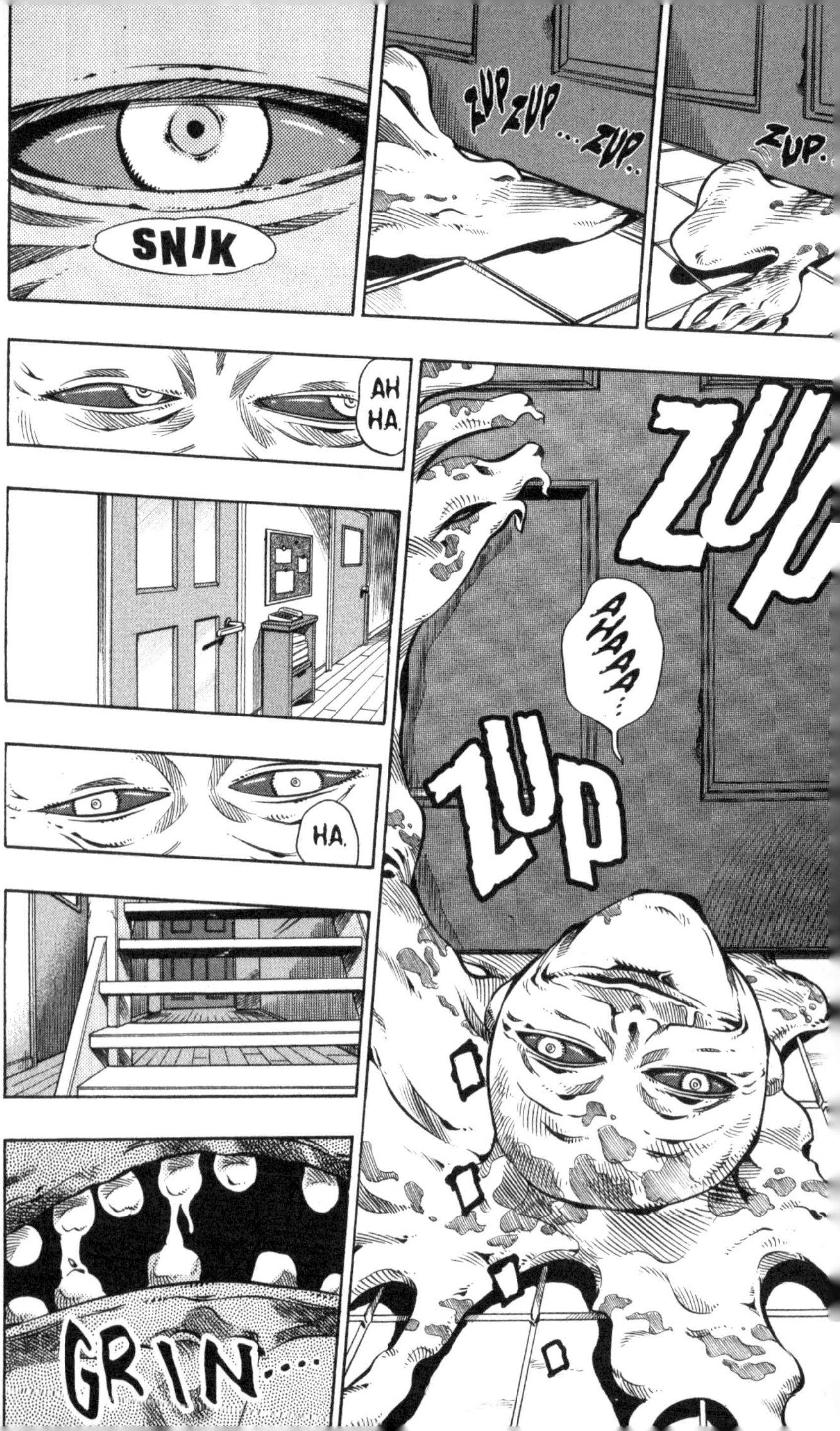
ZUP...
ZUP ZUP... ZUP..
SNIK
ZUP
AHAAA...
ZUP
AH HA.
HA.
GRIN....

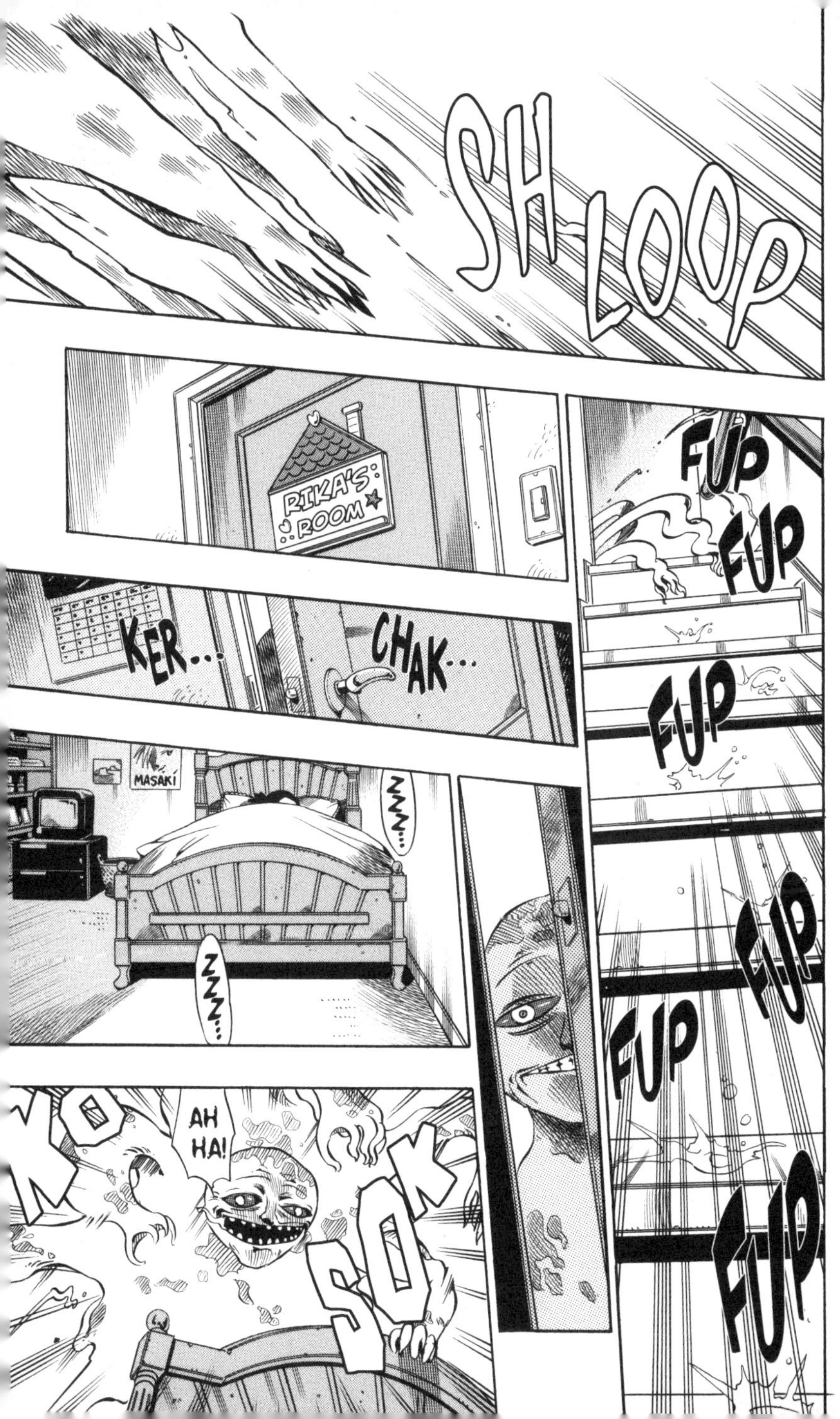
SHLOOP
FUP
FUP
FUP
FUP
FUP
FUP
RIKA'S ROOM
KER... CHAK...
MASAKI
ZZZ...
ZZZ...
SOK
AH HA!

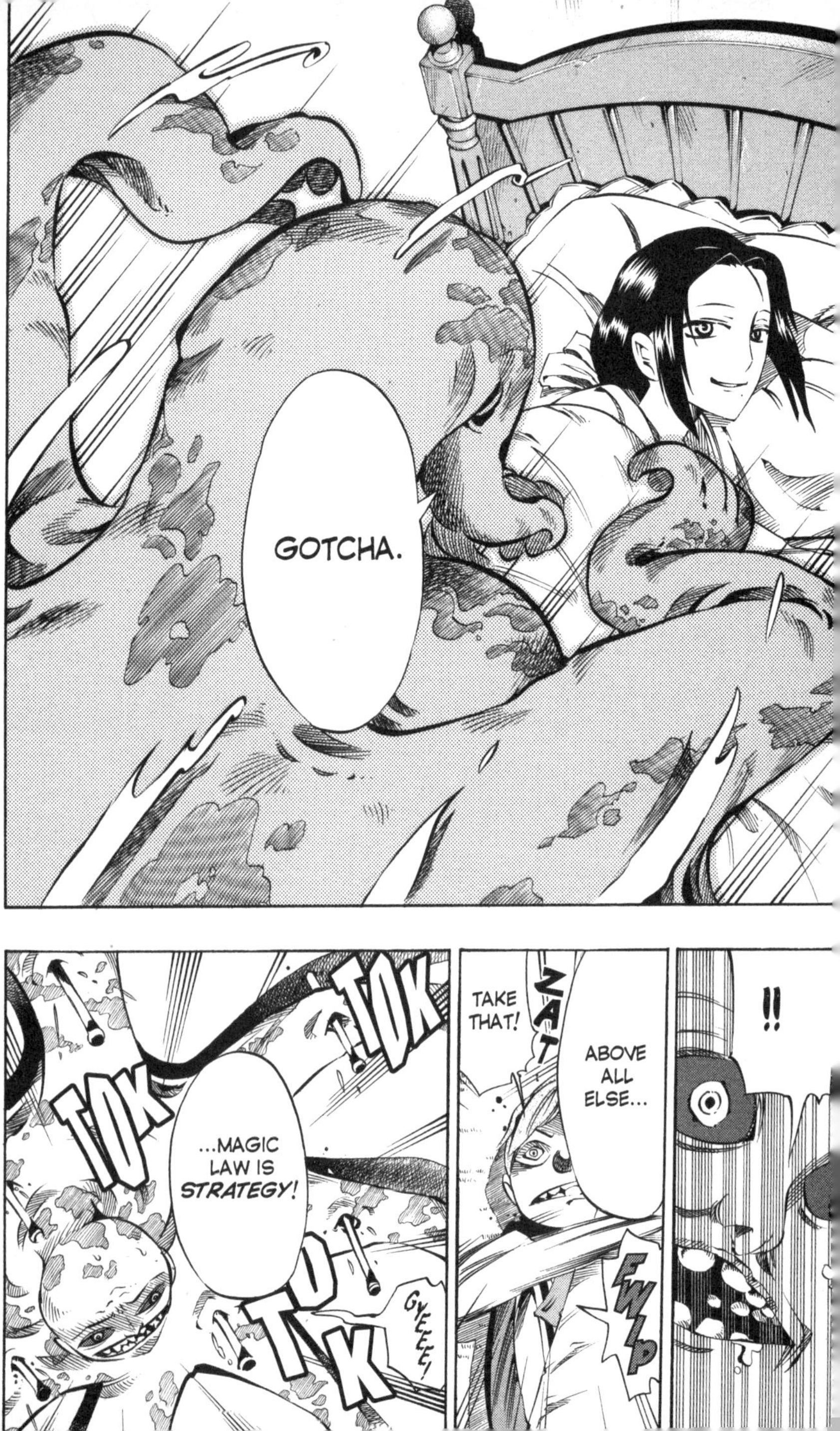
GOTCHA.
!!
TAKE THAT!
ZAT
ABOVE ALL ELSE...
FWIP
TOK
TOK
...MAGIC LAW IS STRATEGY!
TOK
GYEEE!

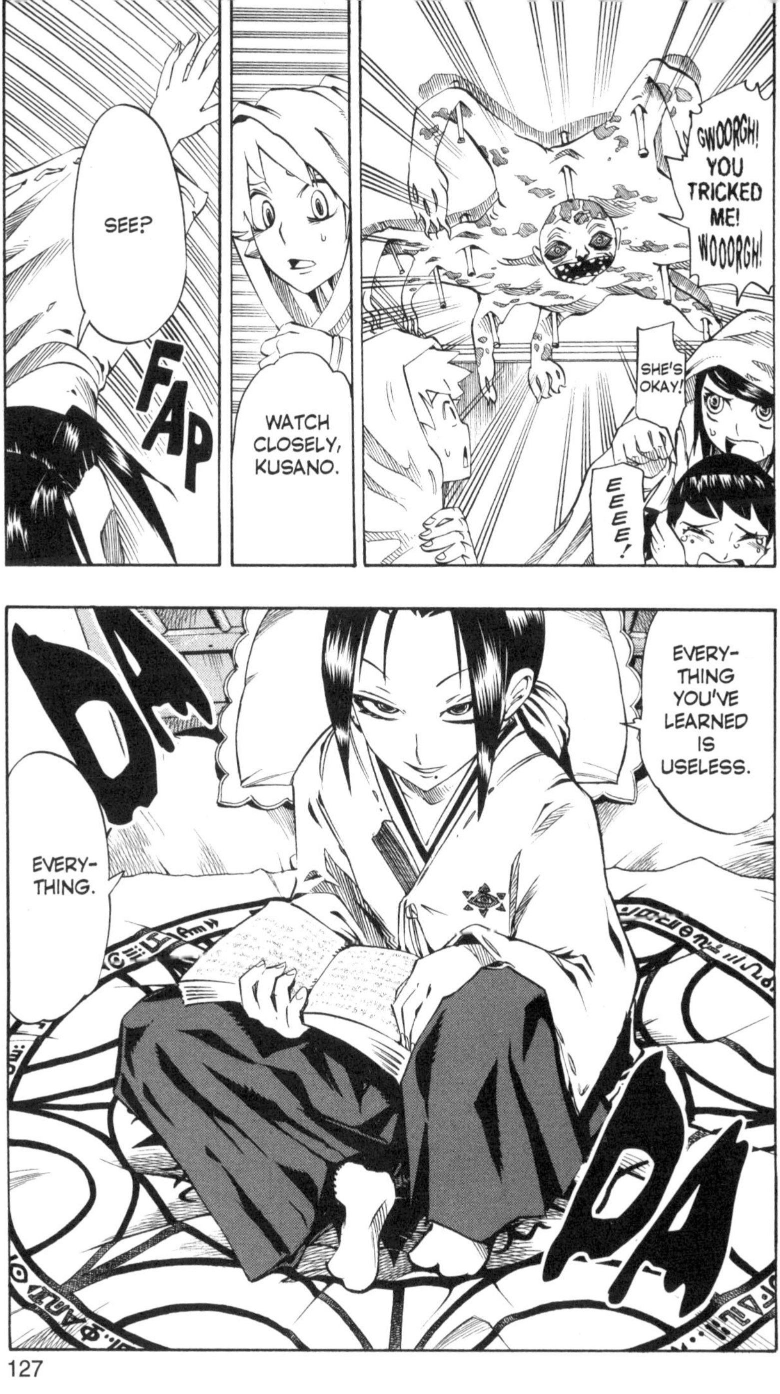
GWOORGH! YOU TRICKED ME! WOOORGH!
SHE'S OKAY!
EEEE!
WATCH CLOSELY, KUSANO.
SEE?
FAP
EVERY-THING YOU'VE LEARNED IS USELESS.
EVERY-THING.
DA
DA

DARANIMARU GORYO

BIRTHDAY: DECEMBER 12
HEIGHT: 178 CM

LIKES: YOKAN SWEETS
OSHIRUKO MOCHI WITH AZUKI BEANS
SOBA NOODLES
TEA
WALKING THE GARDENS
(AT THE GORYO RESIDENCE)

TALENTS: WRITING (ALL BY BRUSH,
MASTER CALLIGRAPHER)
HEARING EVERYTHING SAID ABOUT HIM
STRATEGIZING

NOT GOOD WITH: BUDGETING MONEY
LOUD NOISE
TRAINS
OILY FOODS
RAW-SMELLING FOODS, ETC.
(A PICKY EATER)

ARTICLE 39
THE PLAN

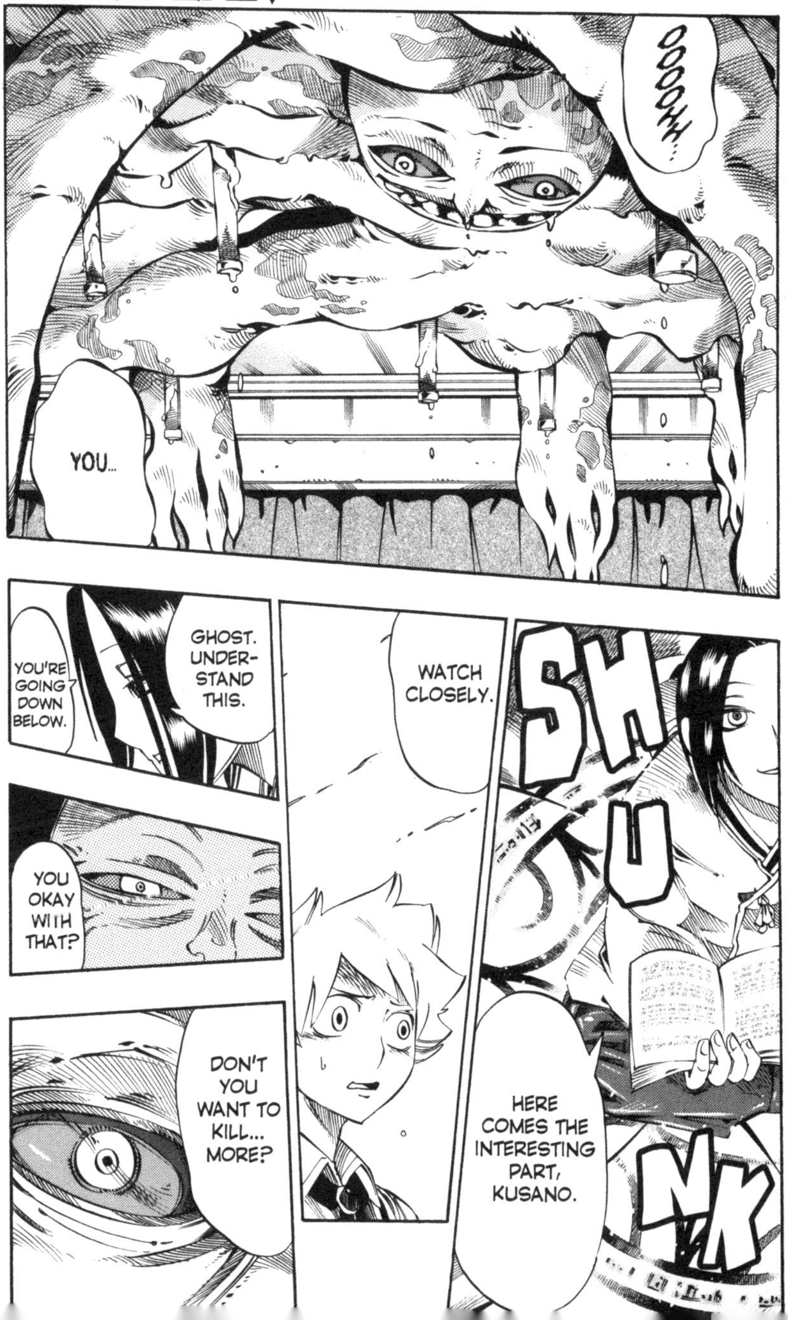
OOOOHH...
YOU...
SHUNK
HERE COMES THE INTERESTING PART, KUSANO.
WATCH CLOSELY.
GHOST. UNDER-STAND THIS.
YOU'RE GOING DOWN BELOW.
YOU OKAY WITH THAT?
DON'T YOU WANT TO KILL... MORE?

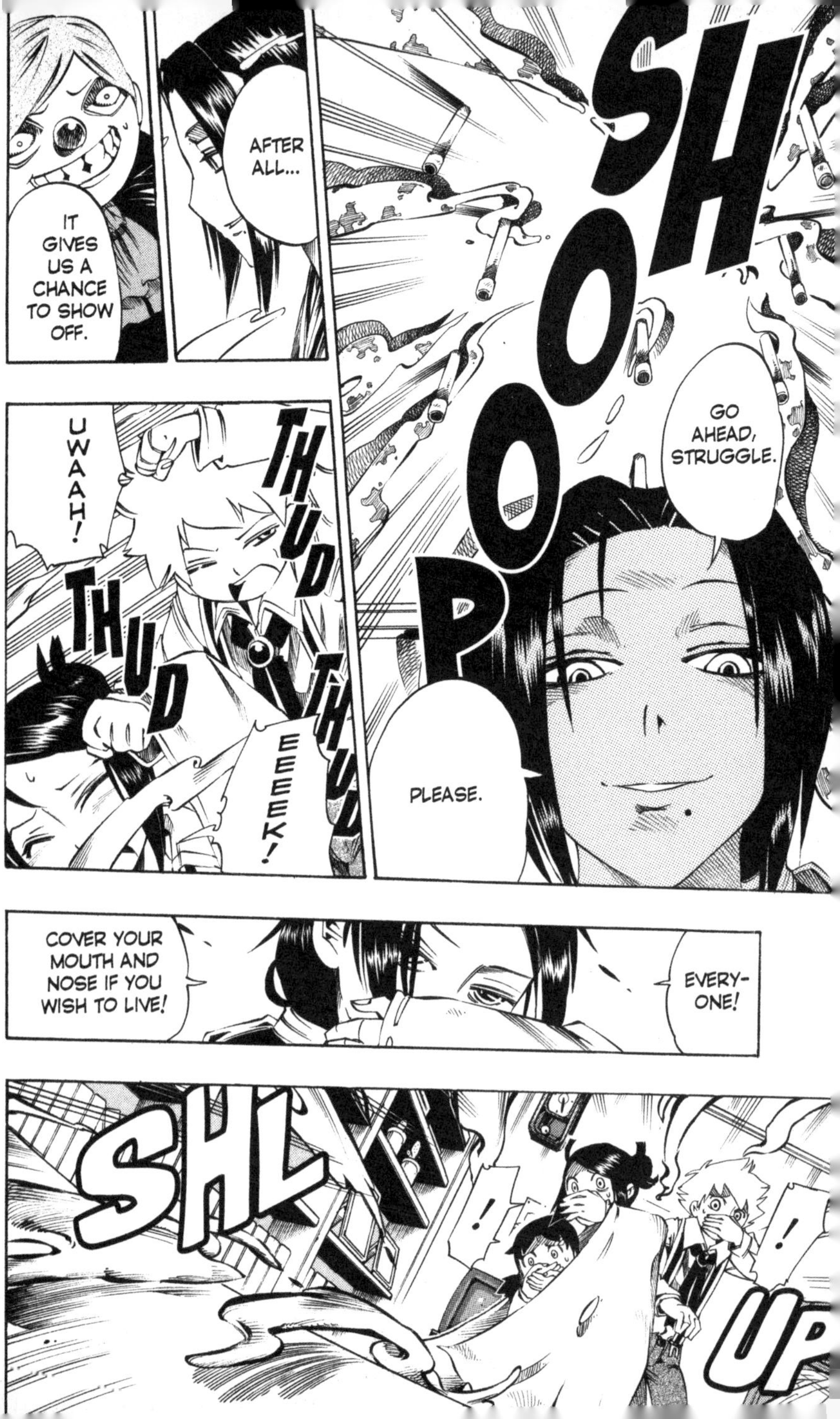
SHOOOP
GO AHEAD, STRUGGLE.
PLEASE.
AFTER ALL...
IT GIVES US A CHANCE TO SHOW OFF.
THUD THUD
UWAAH!
EEEEK!
THUD THUD
EVERY-ONE!
COVER YOUR MOUTH AND NOSE IF YOU WISH TO LIVE!
SHLUP
!
!

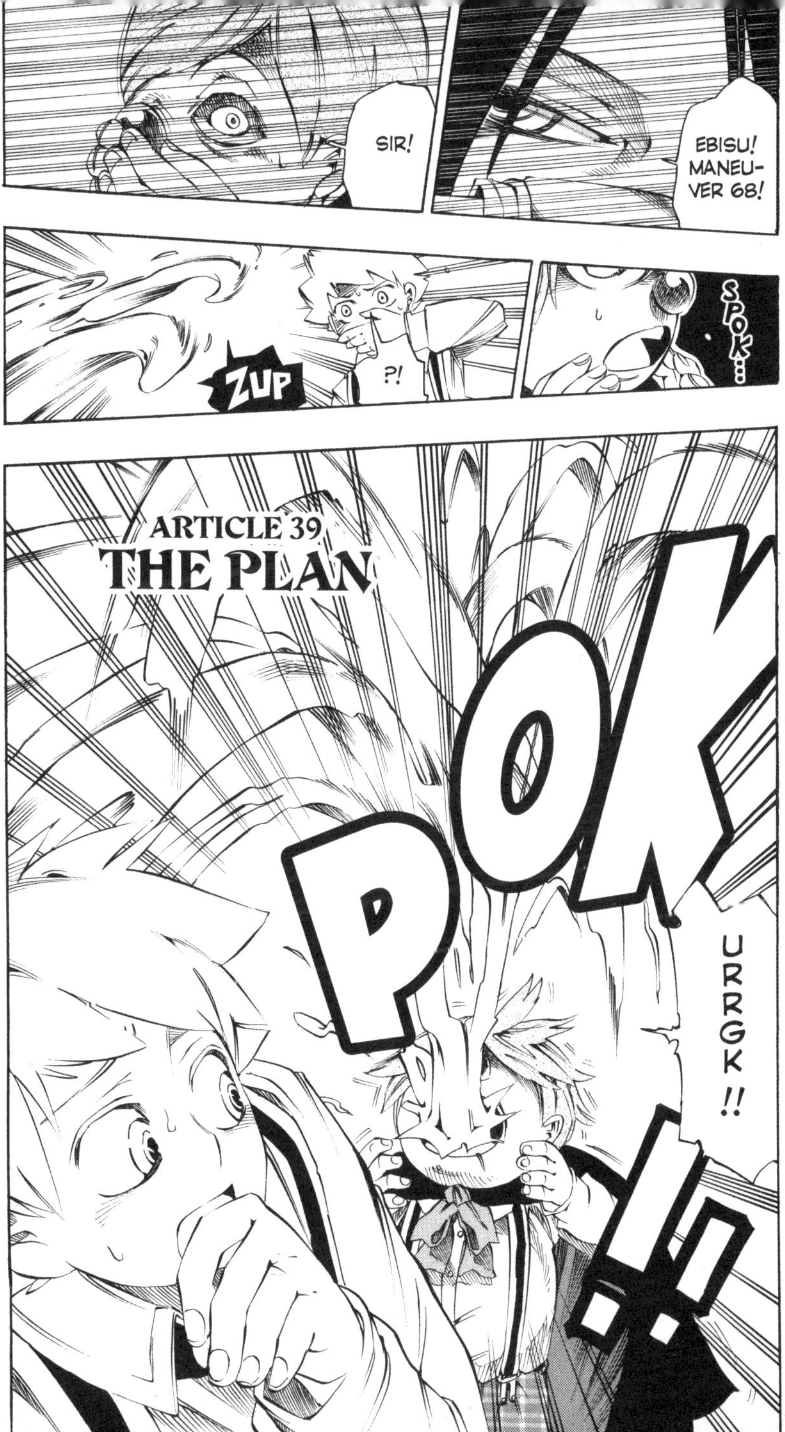
EBISU! MANEUVER 68!
SIR!
SPOK...
?!
ZUP
ARTICLE 39
THE PLAN
POK!!
URRGK!!

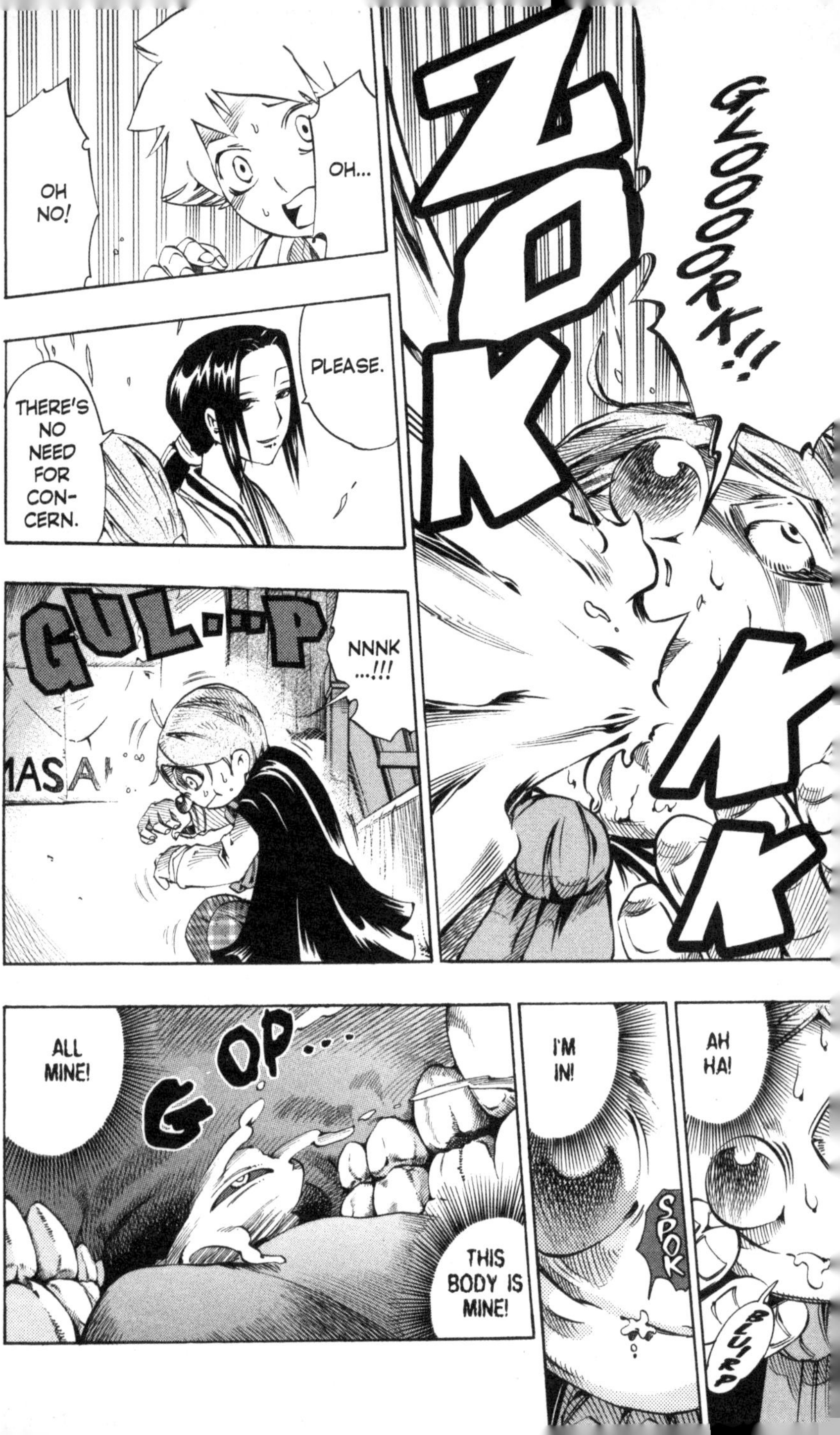

ZOK
GLOOOORK!!
KKK
OH...
OH NO!
PLEASE.
THERE'S NO NEED FOR CON-CERN.
GUL...P
NNNK ...!!!
AH HA!
SPOK
I'M IN!
THIS BODY IS MINE!
ALL MINE!
GOP...

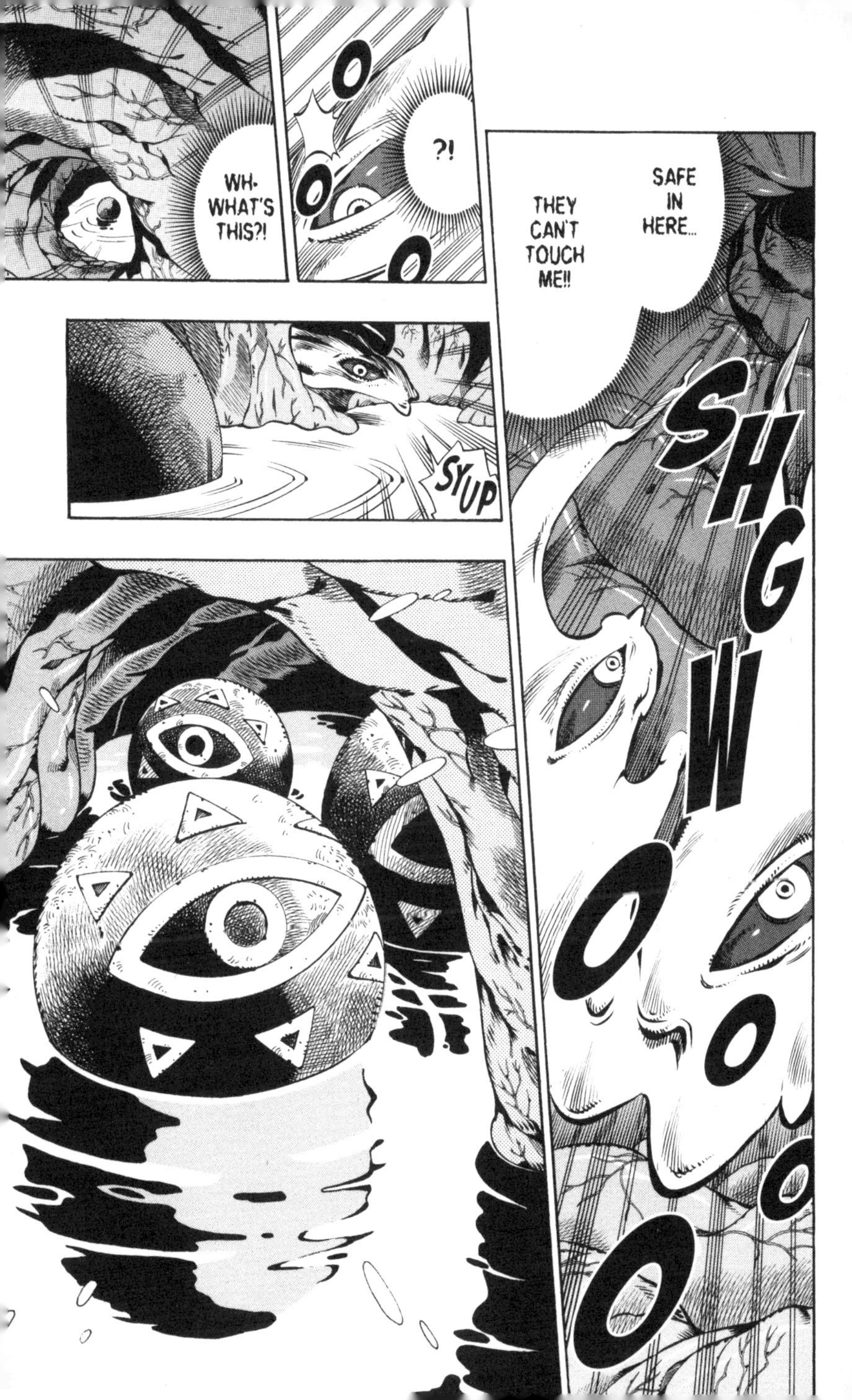
SAFE IN HERE...
THEY CAN'T TOUCH ME!!
SHGWOOOOO
OOO
?!
WH-WHAT'S THIS?!
SYUP

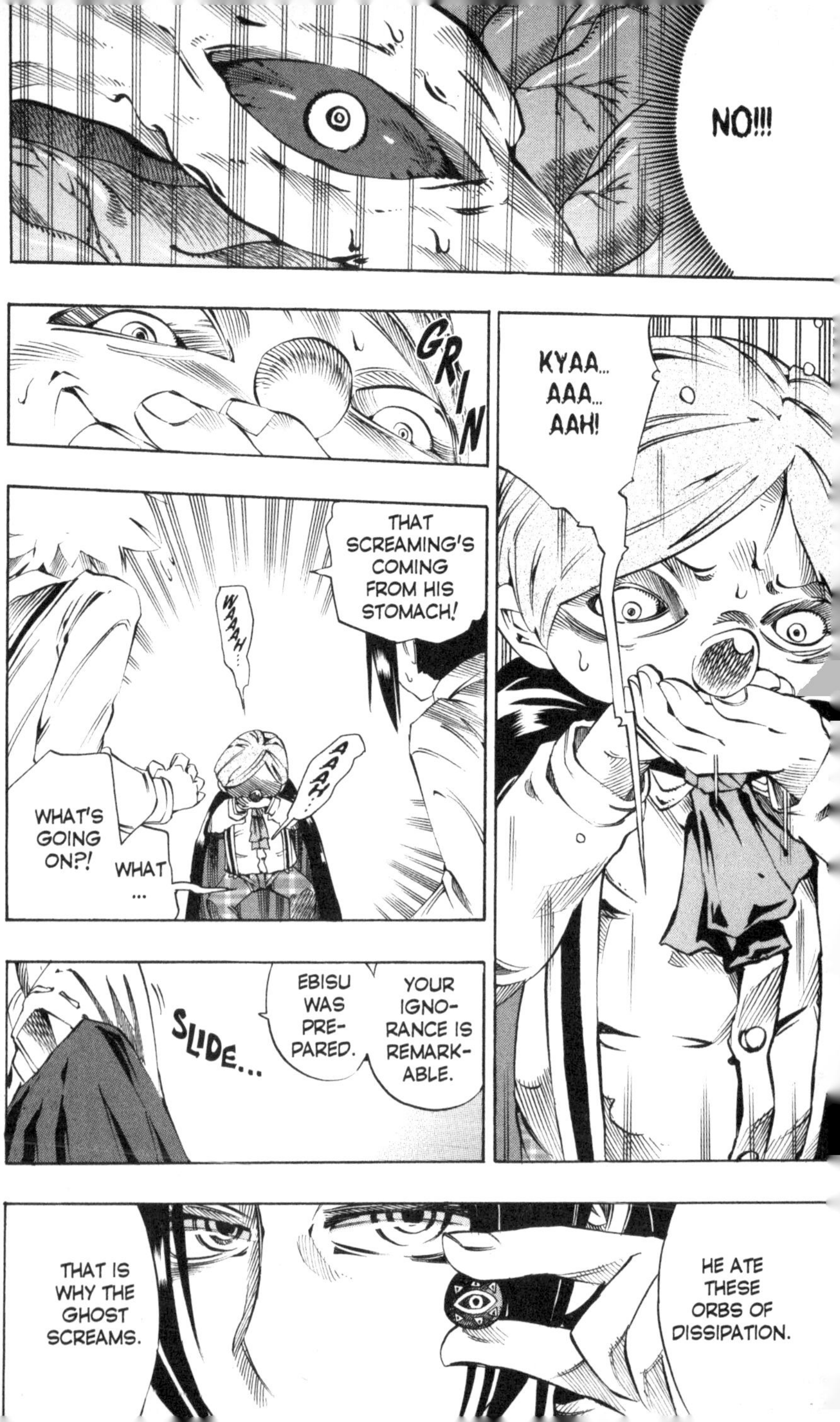
NO!!!
KYAA... AAA... AAH!
GRIN
THAT SCREAMING'S COMING FROM HIS STOMACH!
WAAAH...
AAAH...
WHAT'S GOING ON?!
WHAT...
YOUR IGNO-RANCE IS REMARK-ABLE.
EBISU WAS PRE-PARED.
SLIDE...
HE ATE THESE ORBS OF DISSIPATION.
THAT IS WHY THE GHOST SCREAMS.

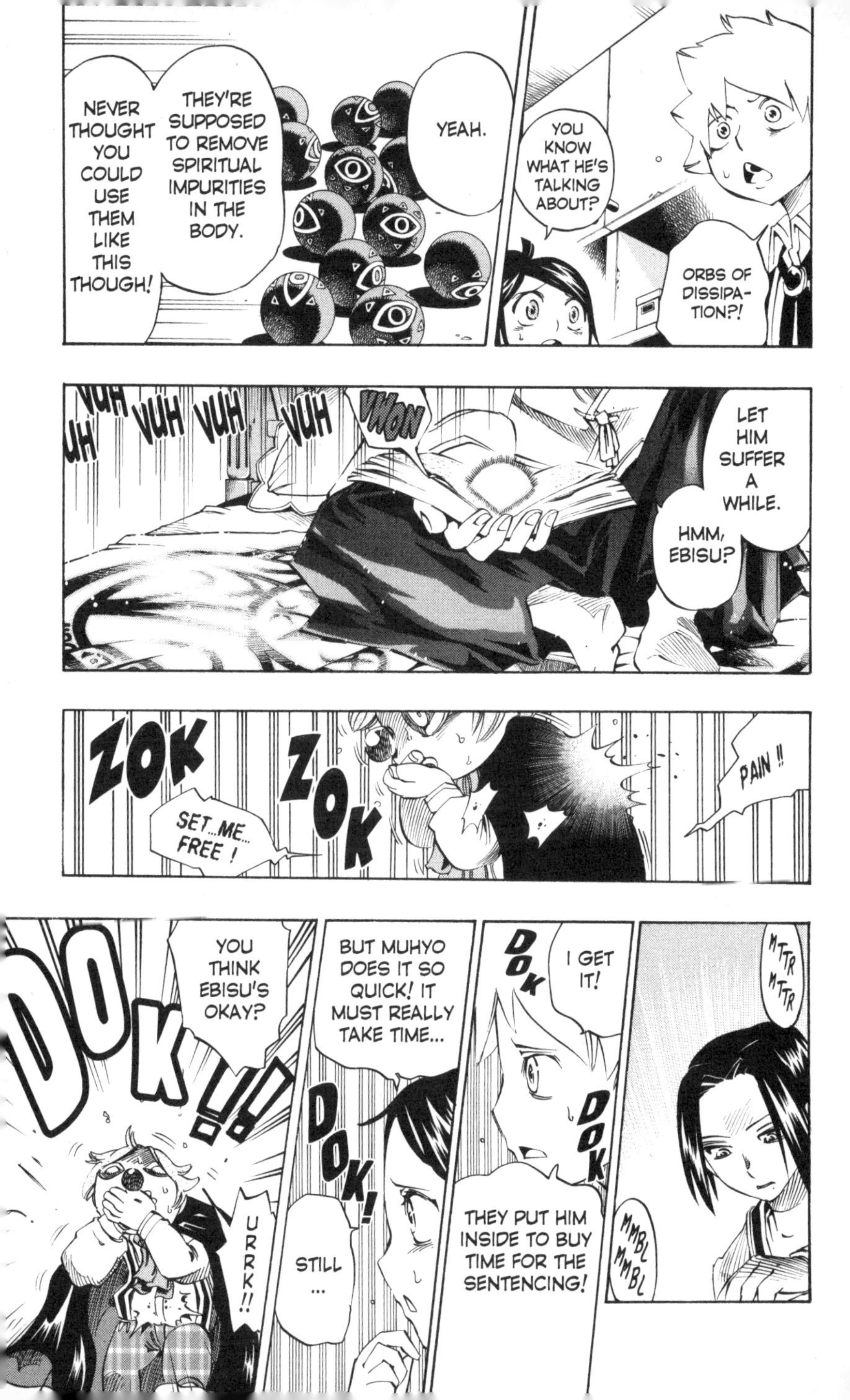
YOU KNOW WHAT HE'S TALKING ABOUT?
ORBS OF DISSIPATION?!
YEAH.
THEY'RE SUPPOSED TO REMOVE SPIRITUAL IMPURITIES IN THE BODY.
NEVER THOUGHT YOU COULD USE THEM LIKE THIS THOUGH!
LET HIM SUFFER A WHILE.
HMM, EBISU?
VWON
VUH VUH VUH VUH VUH
PAIN!!
ZOK
ZOK
SET...ME... FREE!
MTTR MTTR
MMBL MMBL
I GET IT!
DOK DOK
THEY PUT HIM INSIDE TO BUY TIME FOR THE SENTENCING!
BUT MUHYO DOES IT SO QUICK! IT MUST REALLY TAKE TIME...
DOK!
STILL...
YOU THINK EBISU'S OKAY?
DOKU!!
URRK!!

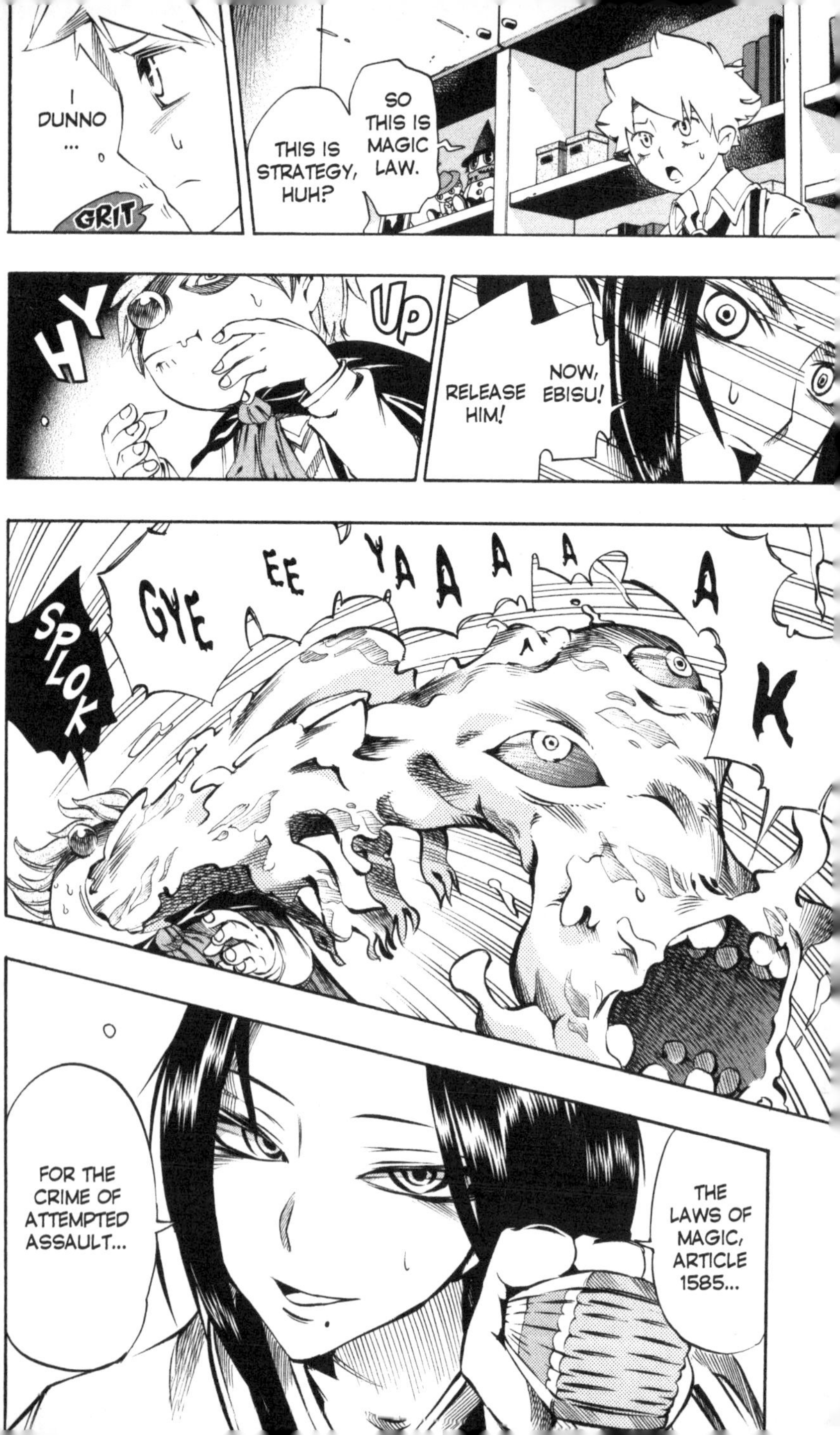
SO THIS IS MAGIC LAW.
THIS IS STRATEGY, HUH?
I DUNNO...
GRIT
NOW, EBISU!
RELEASE HIM!
UP
HY
GYE EE YAAAAA A K
SPLOK
THE LAWS OF MAGIC, ARTICLE 1585...
FOR THE CRIME OF ATTEMPTED ASSAULT...

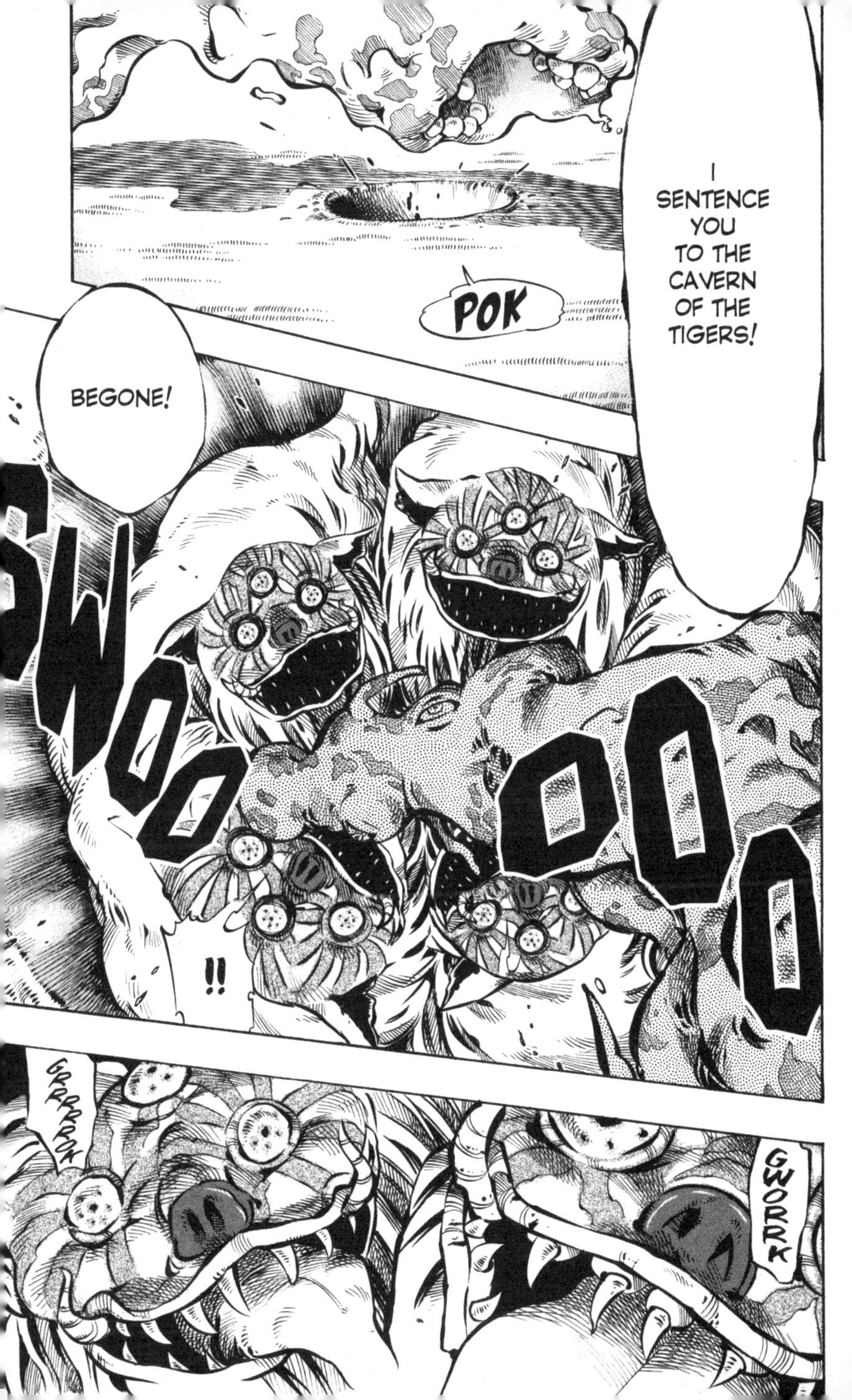
I SENTENCE YOU TO THE CAVERN OF THE TIGERS!
POK
BEGONE!
SWOOOOO
!!
GWORRK
GRRRROK

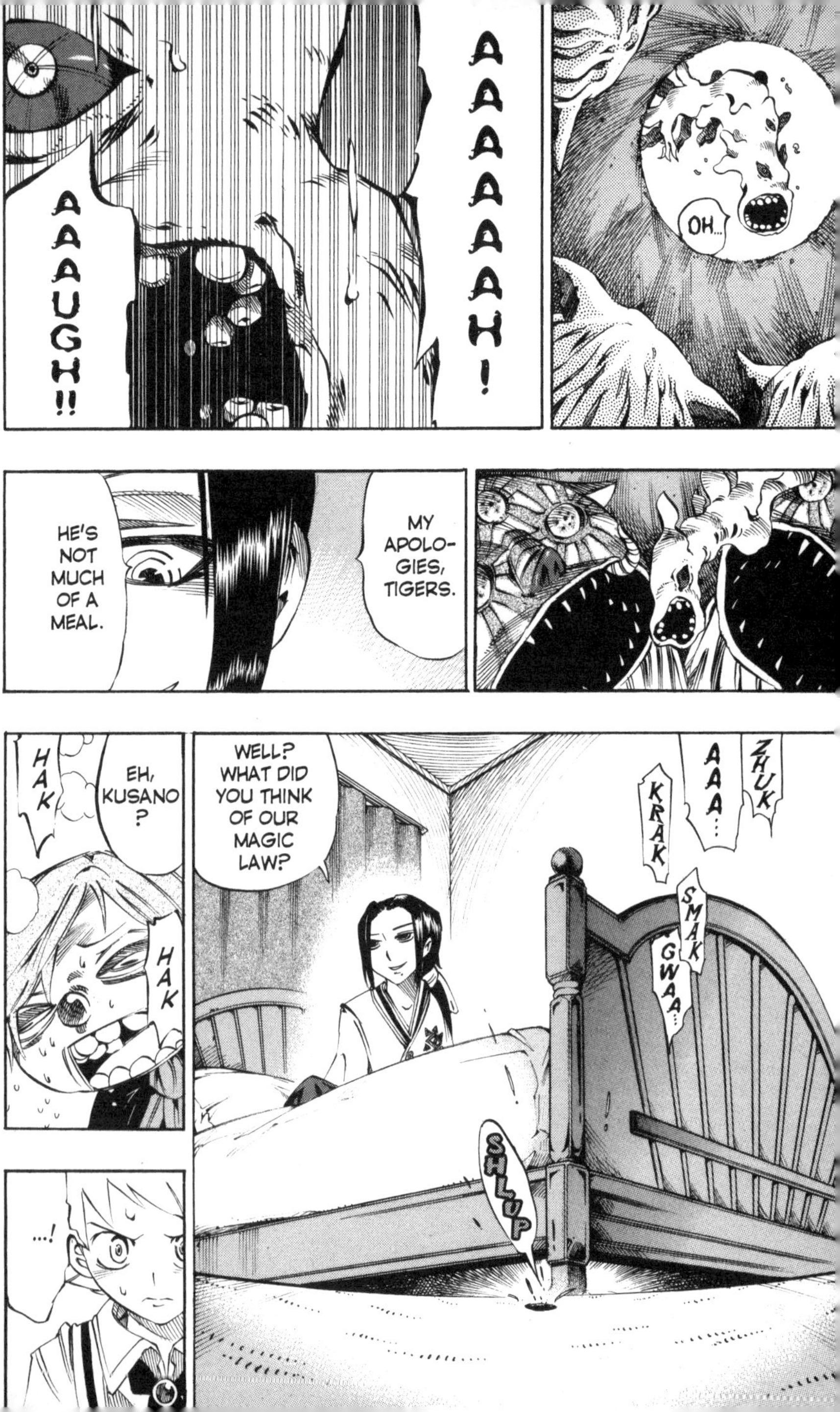
OH...
AAAAAAAH!
AAAUGH!!
MY APOLOGIES, TIGERS.
HE'S NOT MUCH OF A MEAL.
ZHUK
AAA...
KRAK
SMAK
GWAA...
WELL? WHAT DID YOU THINK OF OUR MAGIC LAW?
SHLUP
EH, KUSANO?
HAK
HAK
...!

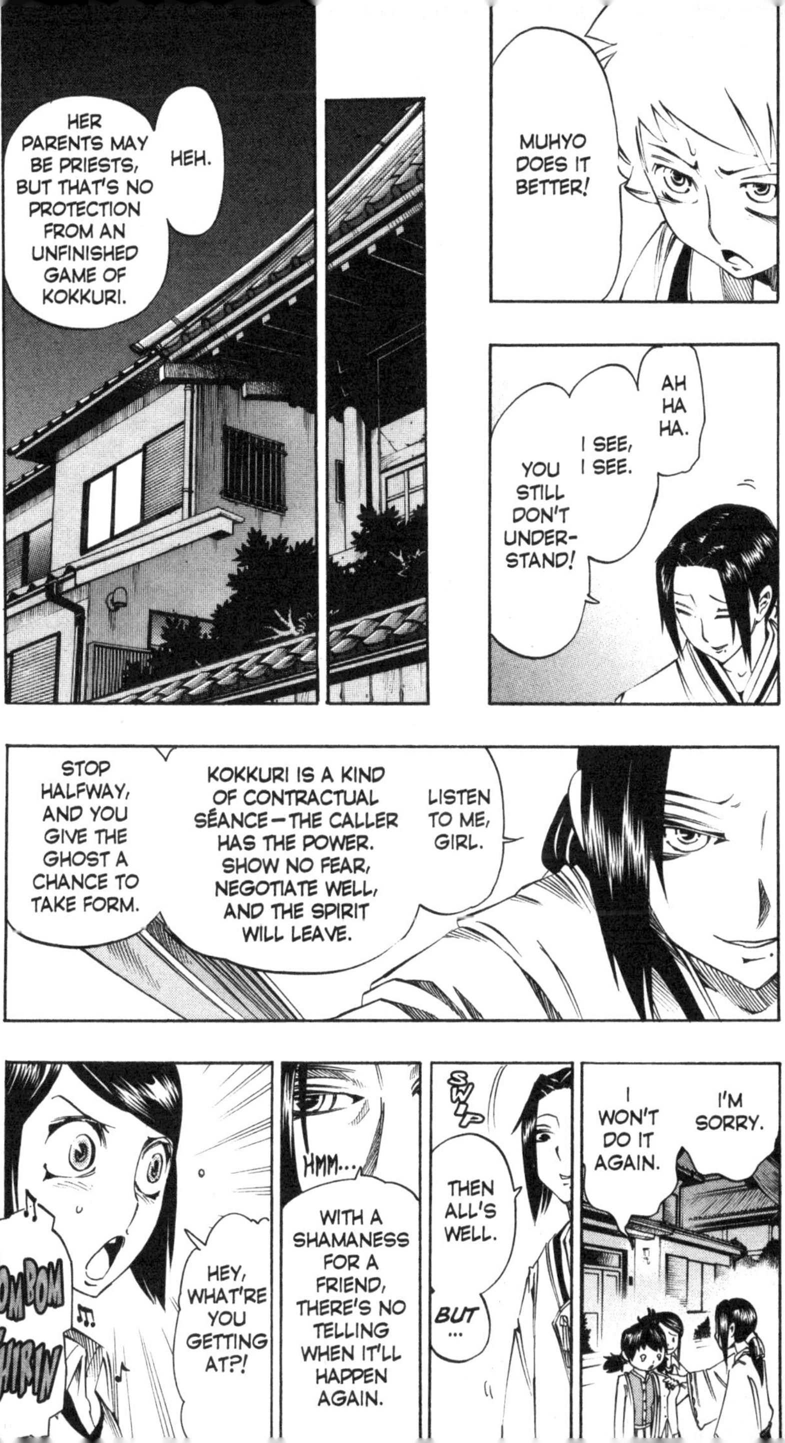
MUHYO DOES IT BETTER!
AH HA HA.
I SEE, I SEE.
YOU STILL DON'T UNDER-STAND!
HEH.
HER PARENTS MAY BE PRIESTS, BUT THAT'S NO PROTECTION FROM AN UNFINISHED GAME OF KOKKURI.
LISTEN TO ME, GIRL.
KOKKURI IS A KIND OF CONTRACTUAL SÉANCE—THE CALLER HAS THE POWER. SHOW NO FEAR, NEGOTIATE WELL, AND THE SPIRIT WILL LEAVE.
STOP HALFWAY, AND YOU GIVE THE GHOST A CHANCE TO TAKE FORM.
I'M SORRY.
I WON'T DO IT AGAIN.
SWIP
THEN ALL'S WELL.
BUT ...
HMM...
WITH A SHAMANESS FOR A FRIEND, THERE'S NO TELLING WHEN IT'LL HAPPEN AGAIN.
HEY, WHAT'RE YOU GETTING AT?!
BOM BOM CHIRIN

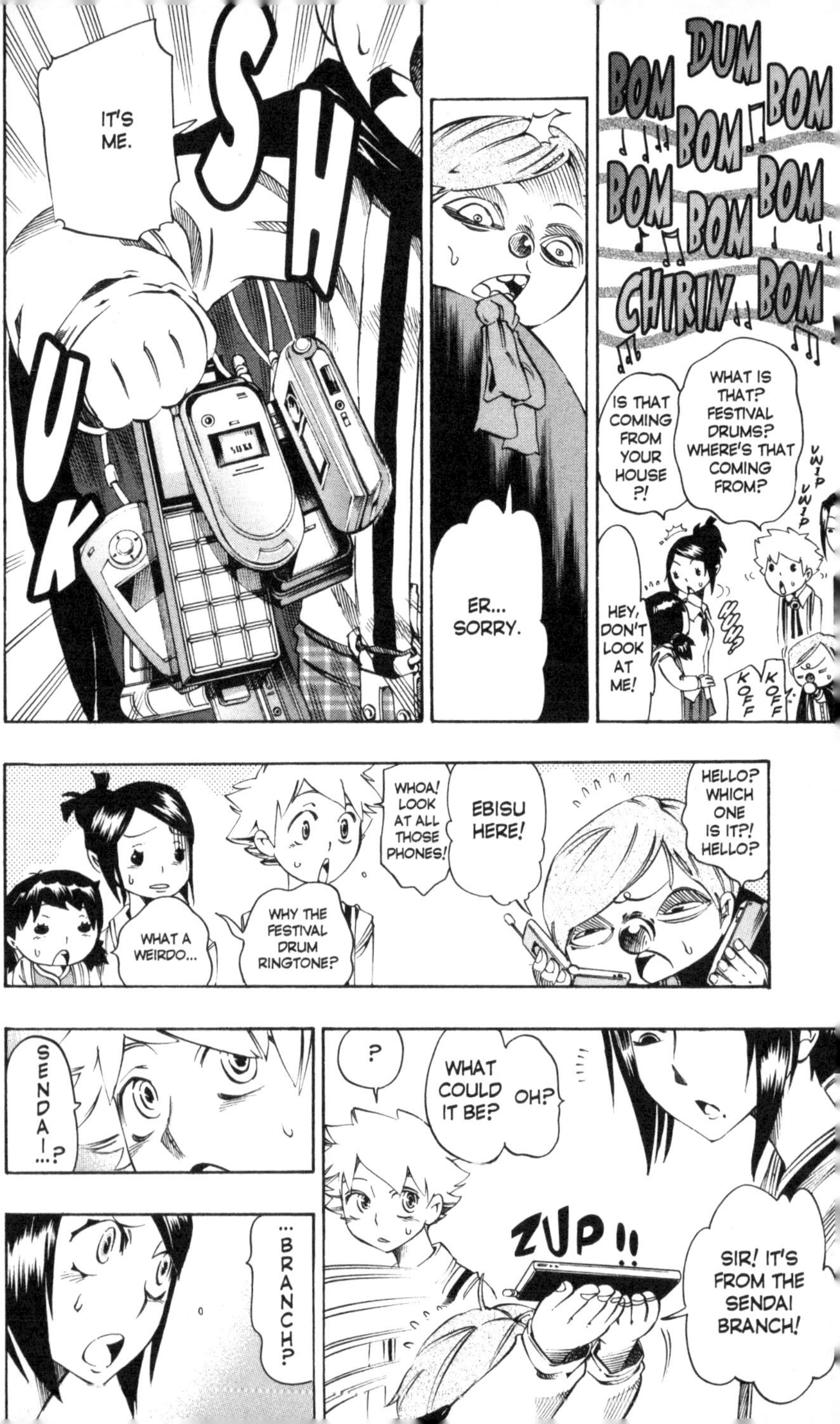
BOM DUM BOM BOM BOM BOM BOM BOM CHIRIN BOM
WHAT IS THAT? FESTIVAL DRUMS? WHERE'S THAT COMING FROM?
IS THAT COMING FROM YOUR HOUSE?!
VWIP VWIP
HEY, DON'T LOOK AT ME!
KOFF KOFF
ER... SORRY.
IT'S ME.
SHUK
HELLO? WHICH ONE IS IT?! HELLO?
EBISU HERE!
WHOA! LOOK AT ALL THOSE PHONES!
WHY THE FESTIVAL DRUM RINGTONE?
WHAT A WEIRDO...
OH?
WHAT COULD IT BE?
?
ZUP!!
SIR! IT'S FROM THE SENDAI BRANCH!
SENDAI...?
...BRANCH?

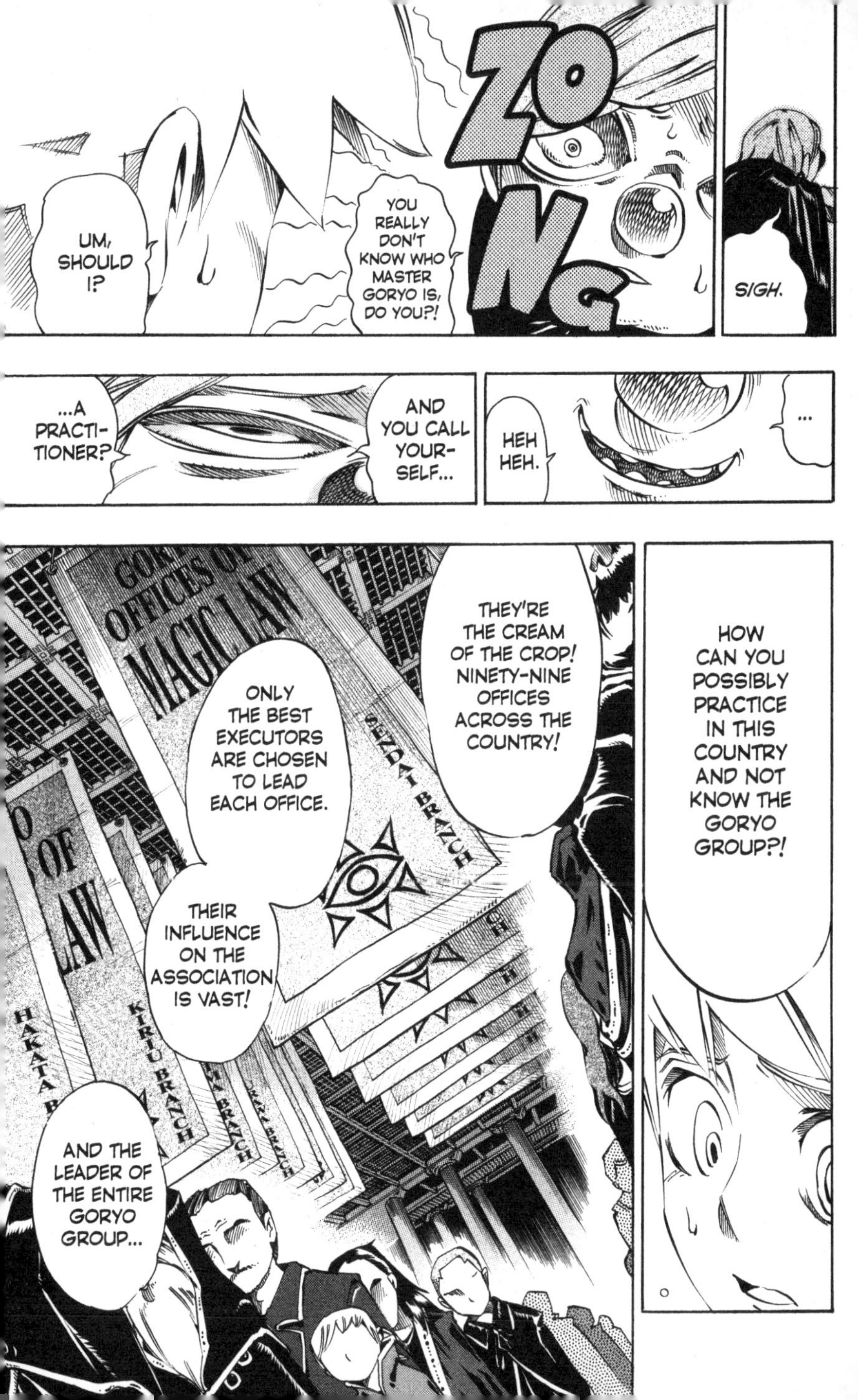
SIGH.
ZONG
YOU REALLY DON'T KNOW WHO MASTER GORYO IS, DO YOU?!
UM, SHOULD I?
...
HEH HEH.
AND YOU CALL YOURSELF...
...A PRACTITIONER?
HOW CAN YOU POSSIBLY PRACTICE IN THIS COUNTRY AND NOT KNOW THE GORYO GROUP?!
THEY'RE THE CREAM OF THE CROP! NINETY-NINE OFFICES ACROSS THE COUNTRY!
OFFICES OF MAGIC LAW
SENDAI BRANCH
ONLY THE BEST EXECUTORS ARE CHOSEN TO LEAD EACH OFFICE.
THEIR INFLUENCE ON THE ASSOCIATION IS VAST!
KIRIU BRANCH
AND THE LEADER OF THE ENTIRE GORYO GROUP...

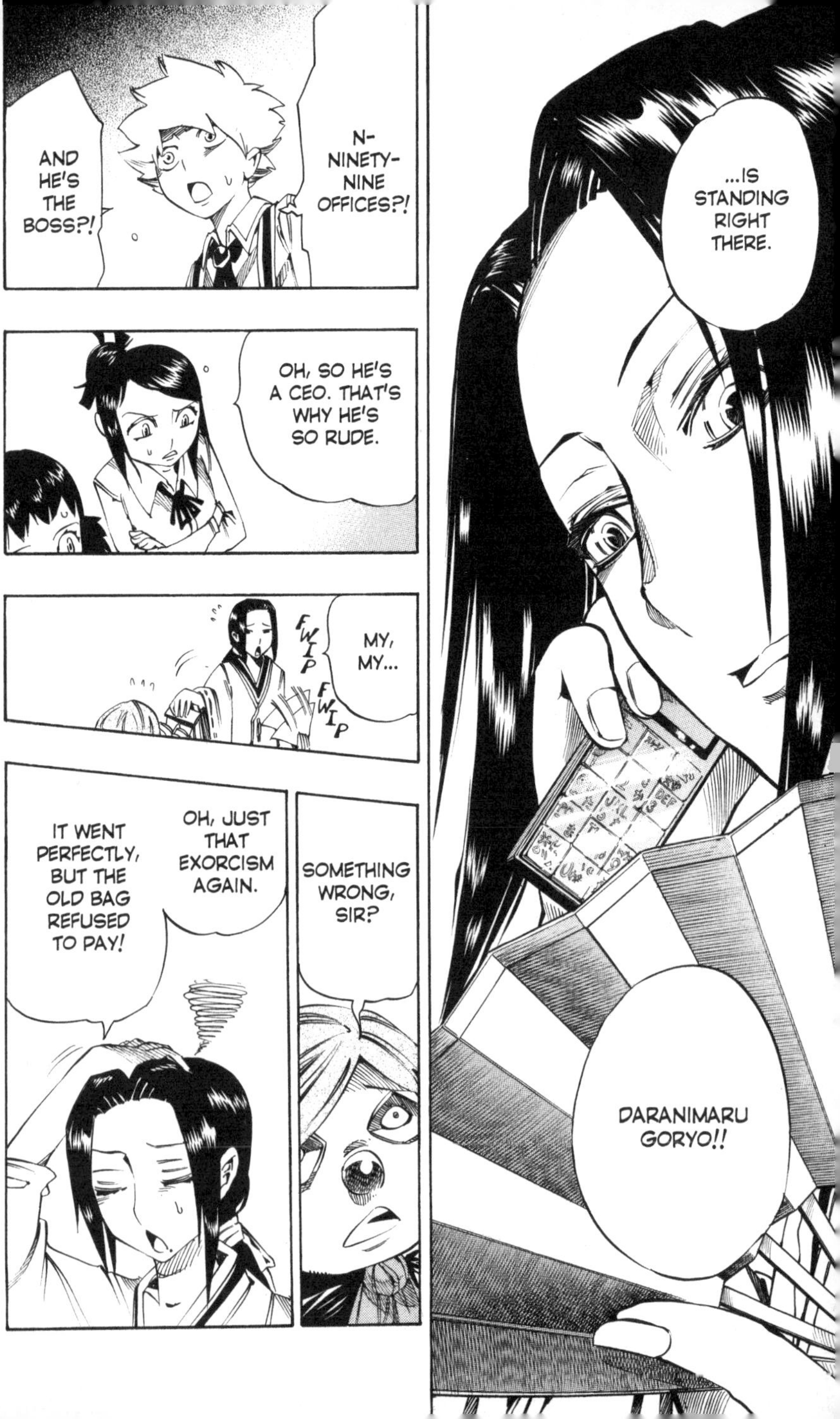
...IS STANDING RIGHT THERE.
DARANIMARU GORYO!!
N-NINETY-NINE OFFICES?!
AND HE'S THE BOSS?!
OH, SO HE'S A CEO. THAT'S WHY HE'S SO RUDE.
MY, MY...
FWIP
FWIP
SOMETHING WRONG, SIR?
OH, JUST THAT EXORCISM AGAIN.
IT WENT PERFECTLY, BUT THE OLD BAG REFUSED TO PAY!

READ THIS WAY

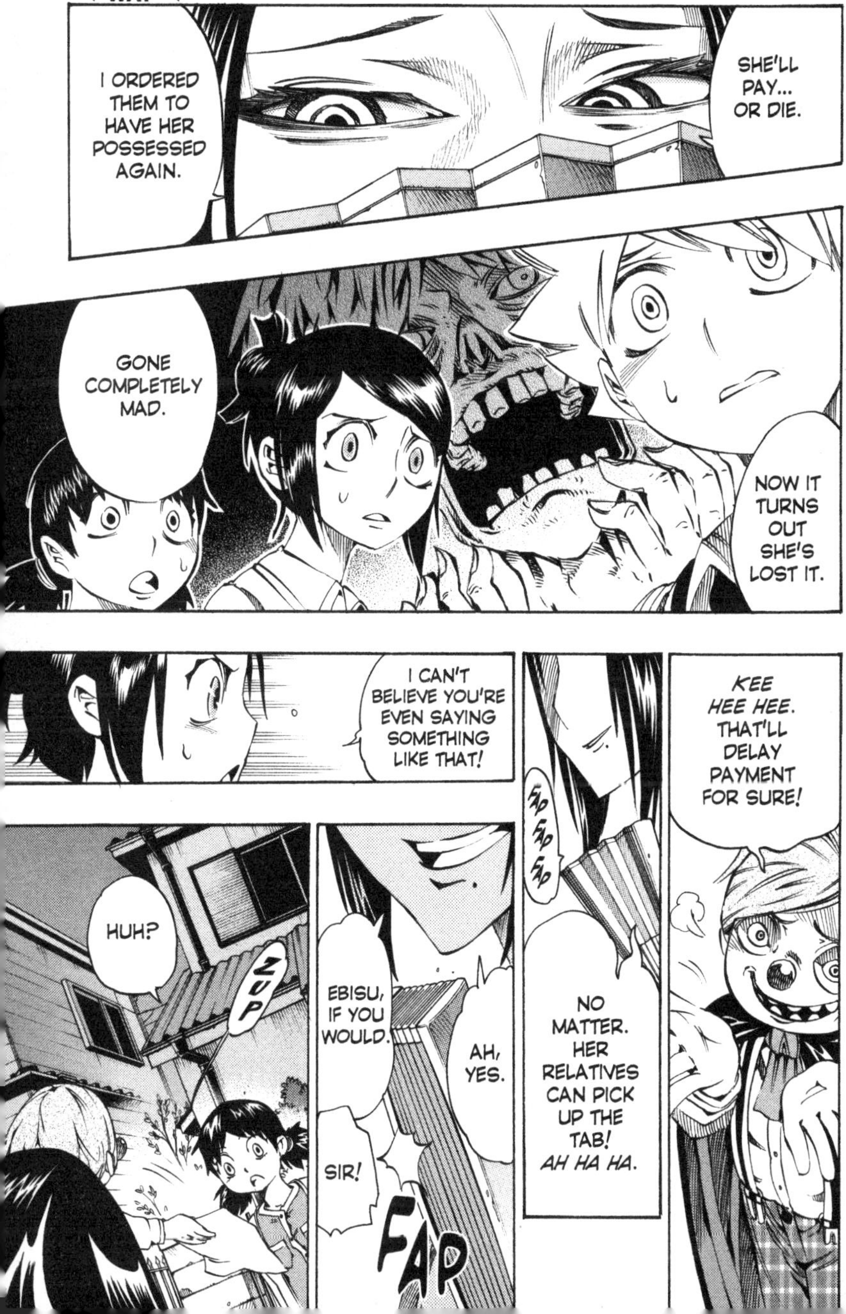
SHE'LL PAY... OR DIE.
I ORDERED THEM TO HAVE HER POSSESSED AGAIN.
NOW IT TURNS OUT SHE'S LOST IT.
GONE COMPLETELY MAD.
KEE HEE HEE. THAT'LL DELAY PAYMENT FOR SURE!
FAP FAP FAP
NO MATTER. HER RELATIVES CAN PICK UP THE TAB! *AH HA HA.*
I CAN'T BELIEVE YOU'RE EVEN SAYING SOMETHING LIKE THAT!
EBISU, IF YOU WOULD.
AH, YES.
SIR!
FAP
HUH?
ZUP

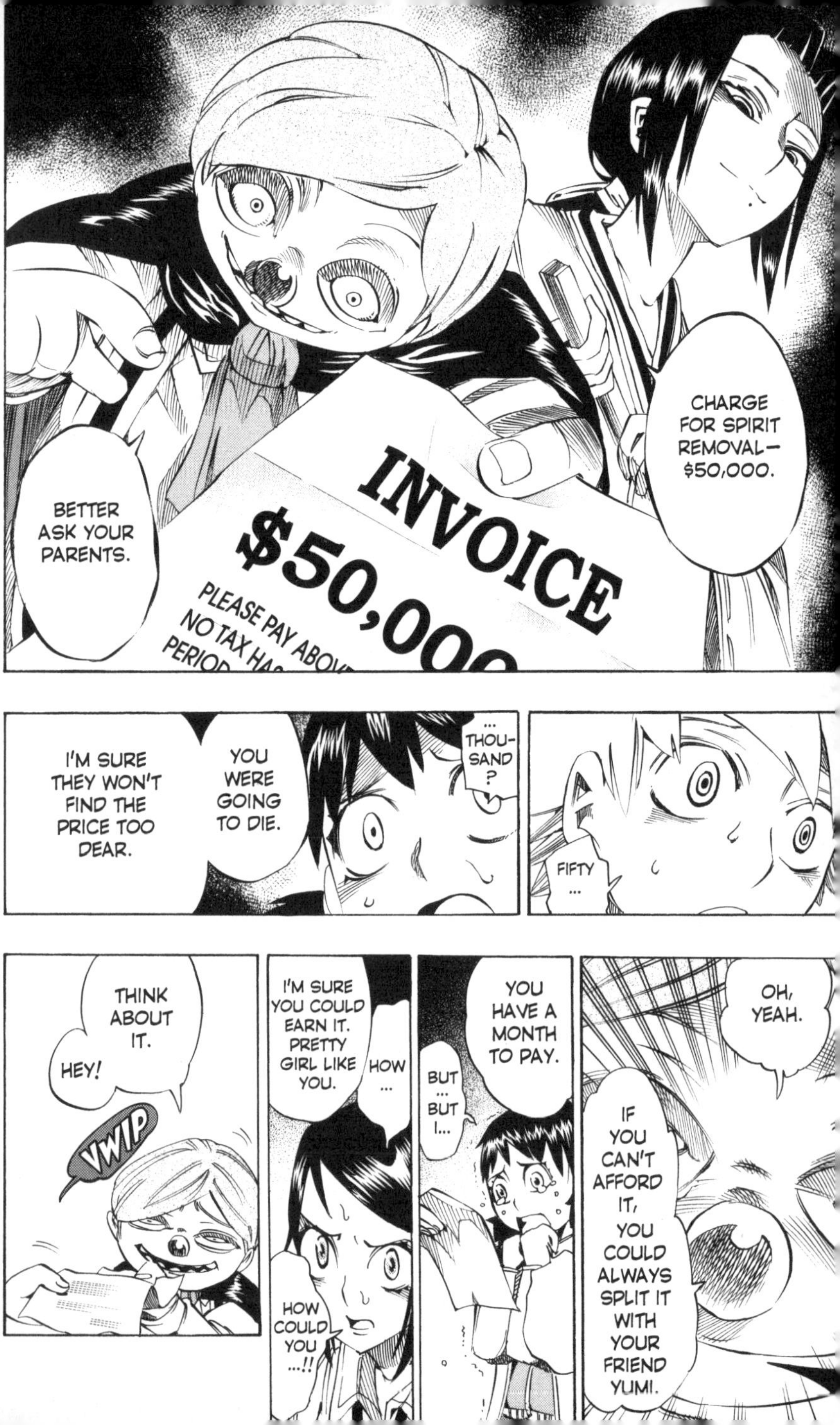
CHARGE FOR SPIRIT REMOVAL—$50,000.
INVOICE
$50,00
PLEASE PAY ABOV
NO TAX HA
PERIOD
BETTER ASK YOUR PARENTS.
FIFTY ...
... THOUSAND?
YOU WERE GOING TO DIE.
I'M SURE THEY WON'T FIND THE PRICE TOO DEAR.
OH, YEAH.
IF YOU CAN'T AFFORD IT, YOU COULD ALWAYS SPLIT IT WITH YOUR FRIEND YUMI.
YOU HAVE A MONTH TO PAY.
BUT ... BUT I...
I'M SURE YOU COULD EARN IT. PRETTY GIRL LIKE YOU.
HOW ...
HOW COULD YOU ...!!
THINK ABOUT IT.
HEY!
VWIP

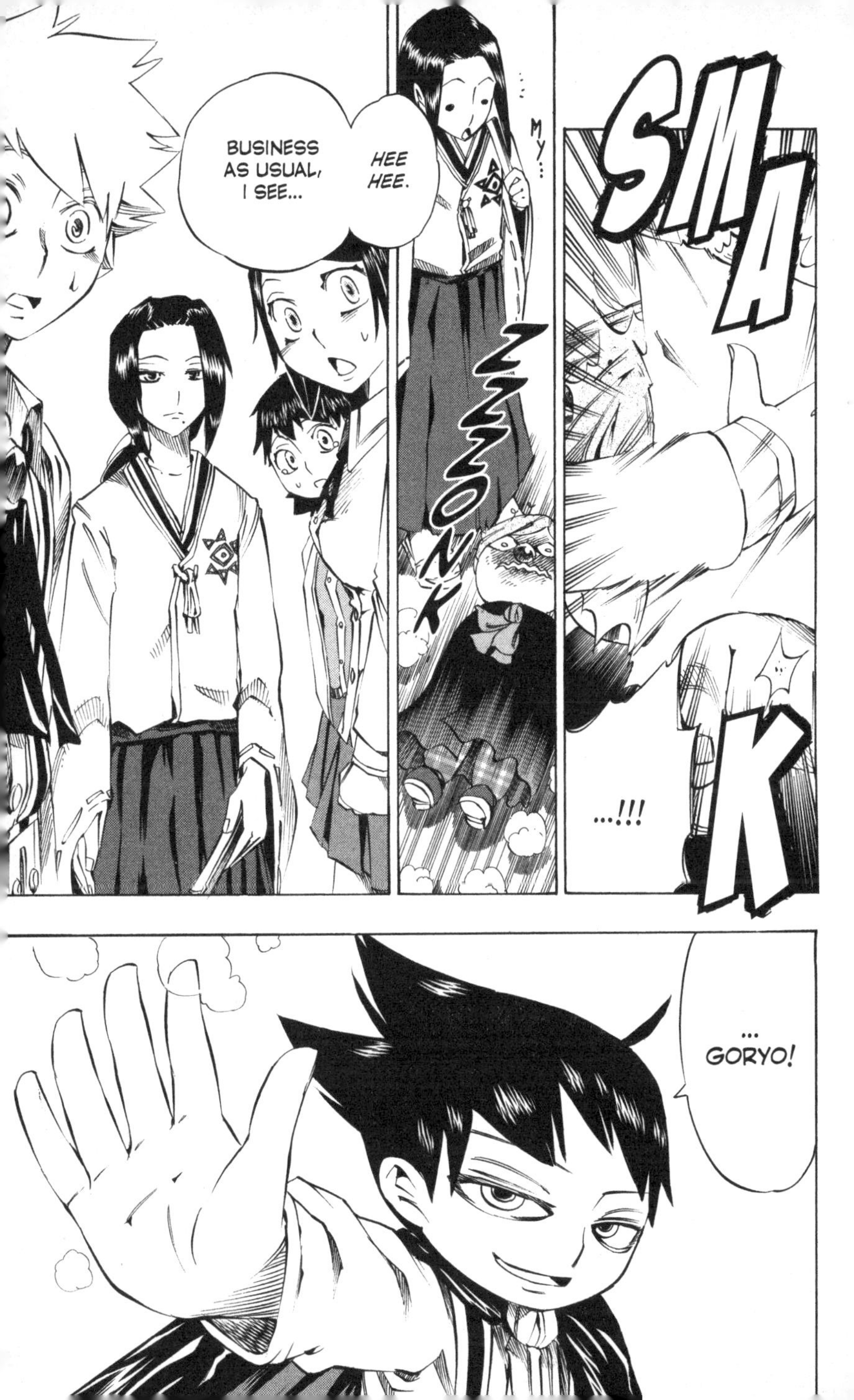
SMACK
...!!!
MY...
ZZZONK
HEE HEE.
BUSINESS AS USUAL, I SEE...
... GORYO!

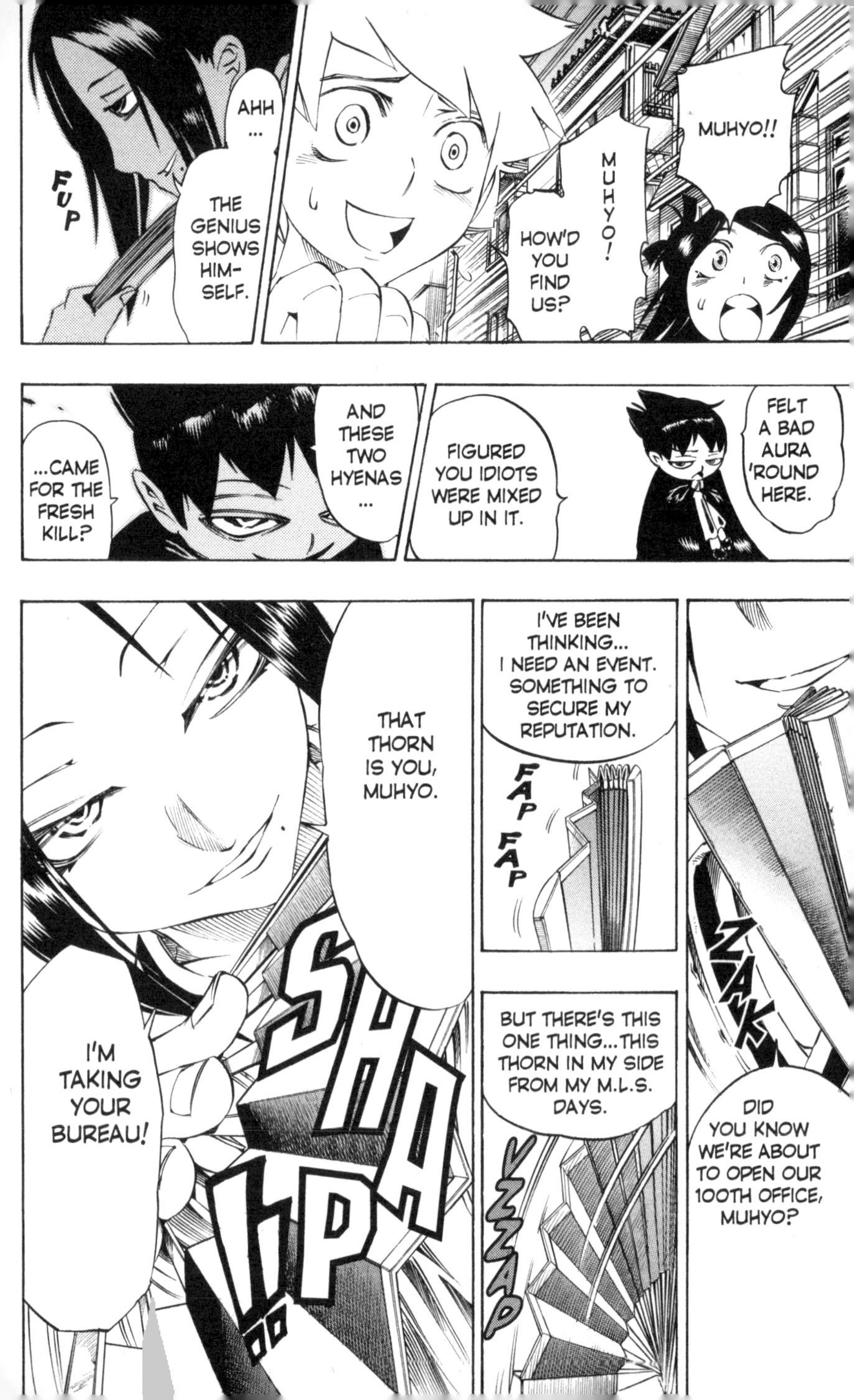
MUHYO!!
MUHYO! HOW'D YOU FIND US?
AHH...
FUP
THE GENIUS SHOWS HIMSELF.
FELT A BAD AURA 'ROUND HERE.
FIGURED YOU IDIOTS WERE MIXED UP IN IT.
AND THESE TWO HYENAS...
...CAME FOR THE FRESH KILL?
ZAK
DID YOU KNOW WE'RE ABOUT TO OPEN OUR 100TH OFFICE, MUHYO?
I'VE BEEN THINKING... I NEED AN EVENT. SOMETHING TO SECURE MY REPUTATION.
FAP FAP FAP
BUT THERE'S THIS ONE THING...THIS THORN IN MY SIDE FROM MY M.L.S. DAYS.
VZZZAP
THAT THORN IS YOU, MUHYO.
I'M TAKING YOUR BUREAU!
SHA PA!!

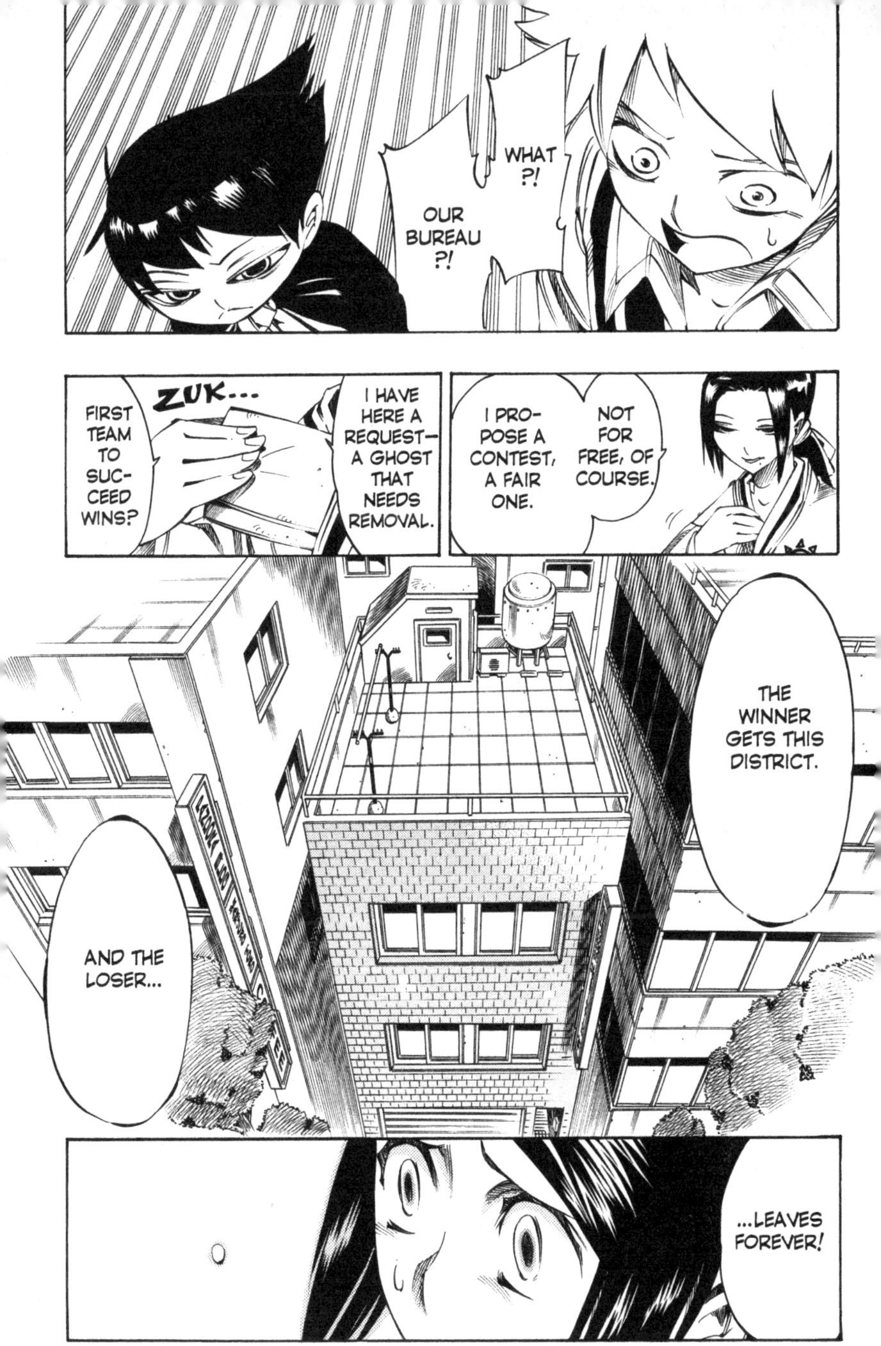
WHAT ?!
OUR BUREAU ?!
NOT FOR FREE, OF COURSE.
I PROPOSE A CONTEST, A FAIR ONE.
I HAVE HERE A REQUEST— A GHOST THAT NEEDS REMOVAL.
ZUK...
FIRST TEAM TO SUCCEED WINS?
THE WINNER GETS THIS DISTRICT.
AND THE LOSER...
...LEAVES FOREVER!

HANAO EBISU

BIRTHDAY: DECEMBER 21
HEIGHT: 130 CM

LIKES: RAMEN
CHINESE BUNS (PARTICULARLY WITH MEAT FILLING)
TAIYAKI SWEET WAFFLE
TAKOYAKI OCTOPUS BALLS
OKONOMIYAKI JAPANESE PANCAKE

TALENTS: ASSISTING IN GORYO'S PERSONAL AFFAIRS (SO HE THINKS, THOUGH SO DOES EVERYONE ELSE IN THE GORYO GROUP)
THIS INCLUDES:

- PREPARING CLOTHES AND DRESSING
- SCHEDULING
- DRIVING
- ARRANGING MEALS

EARLY RISER (DOESN'T NEED ALARM CLOCK)

NOT GOOD WITH: ANGRY GORYO
CRAMPED SPACES
HIGH PLACES

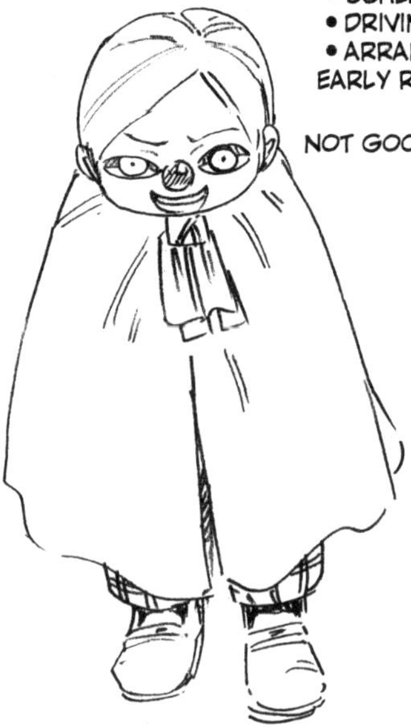

ARTICLE 40

AKAGAWA APARTMENTS

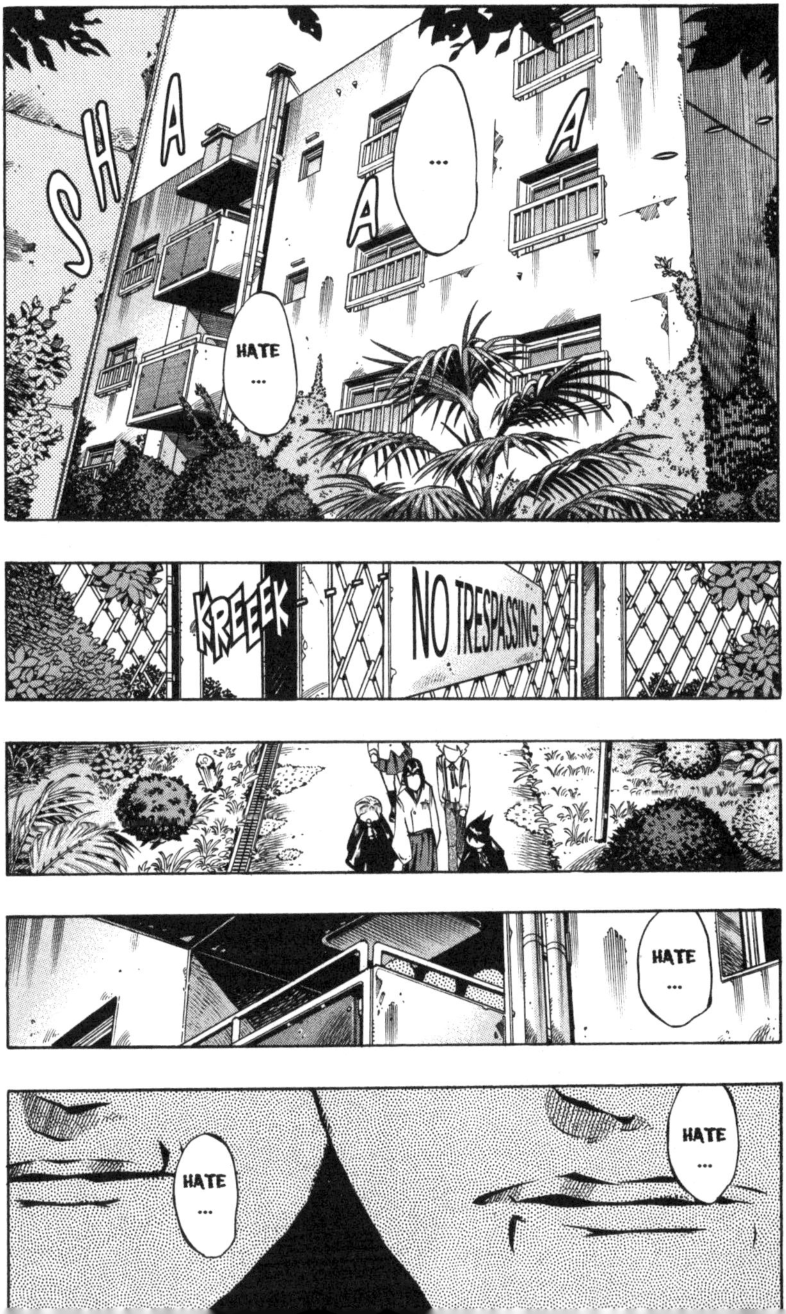
SHAAAA
...
HATE ...
NO TRESPASSING
KREEEK
HATE ...
HATE ...
HATE ...

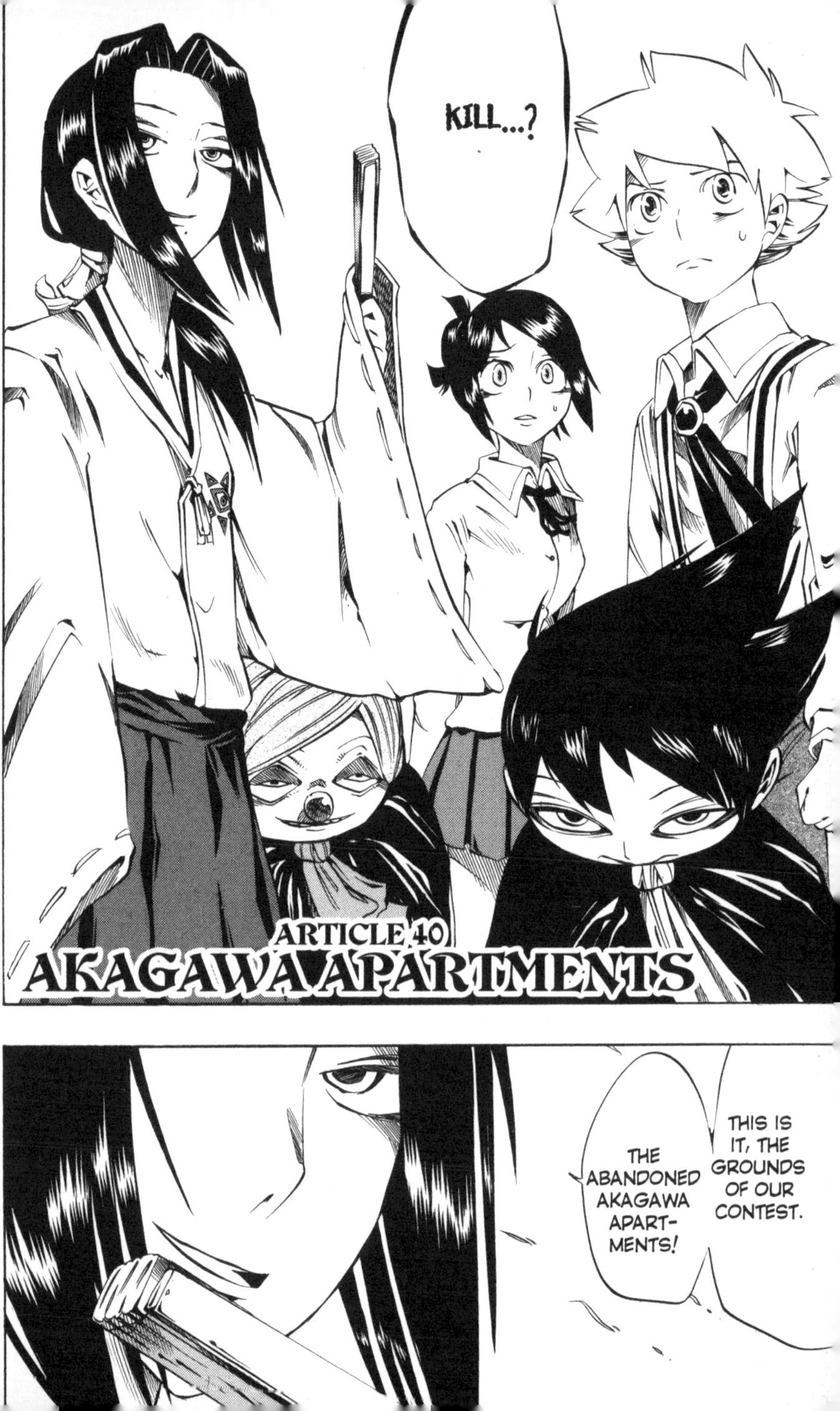
KILL...?
ARTICLE 40
AKAGAWA APARTMENTS
THIS IS IT, THE GROUNDS OF OUR CONTEST.
THE ABANDONED AKAGAWA APART-MENTS!

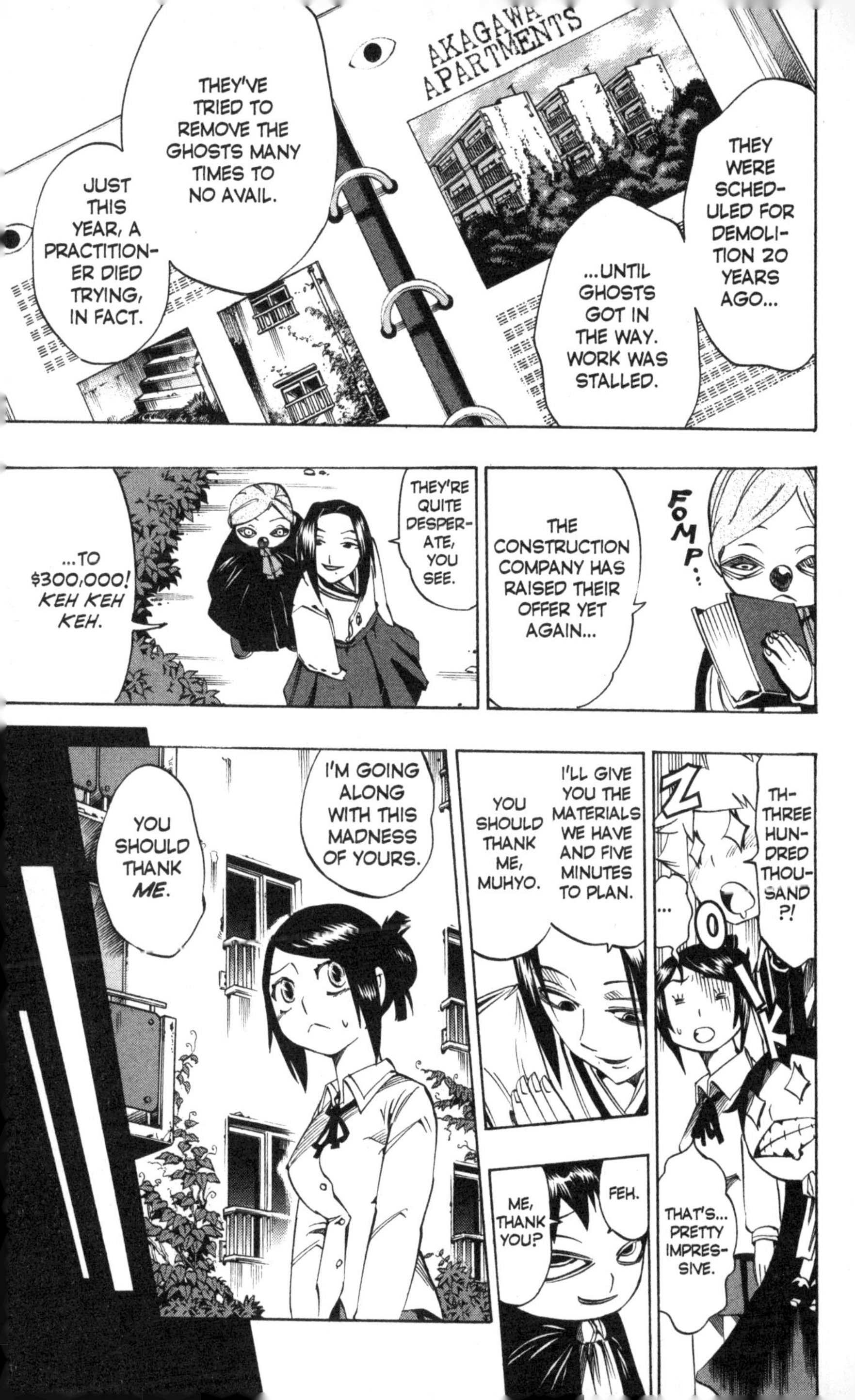
AKAGAWA APARTMENTS
THEY WERE SCHEDULED FOR DEMOLITION 20 YEARS AGO...
...UNTIL GHOSTS GOT IN THE WAY. WORK WAS STALLED.
THEY'VE TRIED TO REMOVE THE GHOSTS MANY TIMES TO NO AVAIL.
JUST THIS YEAR, A PRACTITIONER DIED TRYING, IN FACT.
FOMP...
THE CONSTRUCTION COMPANY HAS RAISED THEIR OFFER YET AGAIN...
THEY'RE QUITE DESPERATE, YOU SEE.
...TO $300,000! *KEH KEH KEH.*
TH-THREE HUNDRED THOUSAND?!
...
THAT'S... PRETTY IMPRESSIVE.
I'LL GIVE YOU THE MATERIALS WE HAVE AND FIVE MINUTES TO PLAN.
YOU SHOULD THANK ME, MUHYO.
FEH.
ME, THANK YOU?
I'M GOING ALONG WITH THIS MADNESS OF YOURS.
YOU SHOULD THANK *ME*.

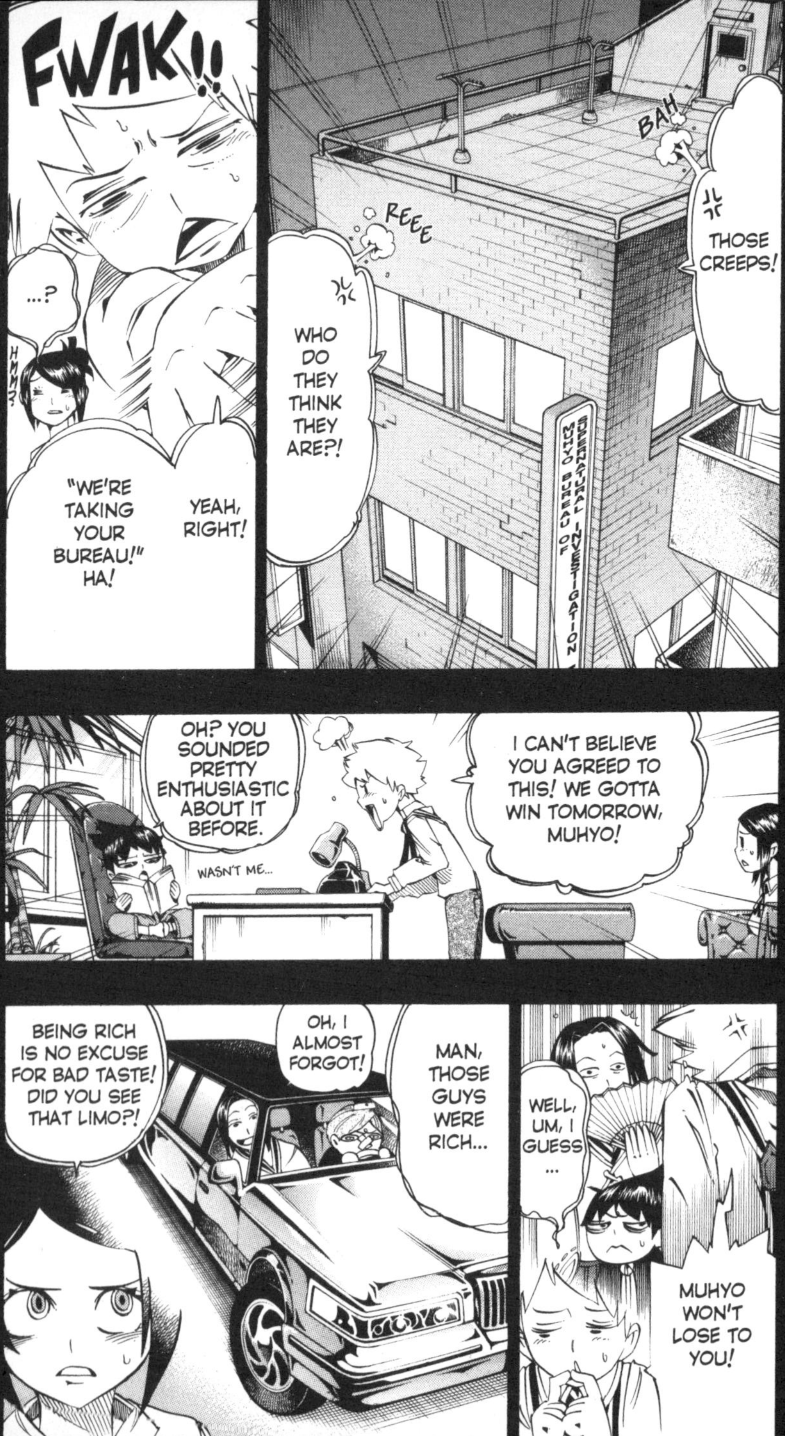
BAH
THOSE CREEPS!
REEE
WHO DO THEY THINK THEY ARE?!
MUHYO BUREAU OF SUPERNATURAL INVESTIGATION
FWAK!!
...?
HMM?
"WE'RE TAKING YOUR BUREAU!" HA!
YEAH, RIGHT!
I CAN'T BELIEVE YOU AGREED TO THIS! WE GOTTA WIN TOMORROW, MUHYO!
OH? YOU SOUNDED PRETTY ENTHUSIASTIC ABOUT IT BEFORE.
WASN'T ME...
WELL, UM, I GUESS...
MUHYO WON'T LOSE TO YOU!
MAN, THOSE GUYS WERE RICH...
OH, I ALMOST FORGOT!
BEING RICH IS NO EXCUSE FOR BAD TASTE! DID YOU SEE THAT LIMO?!

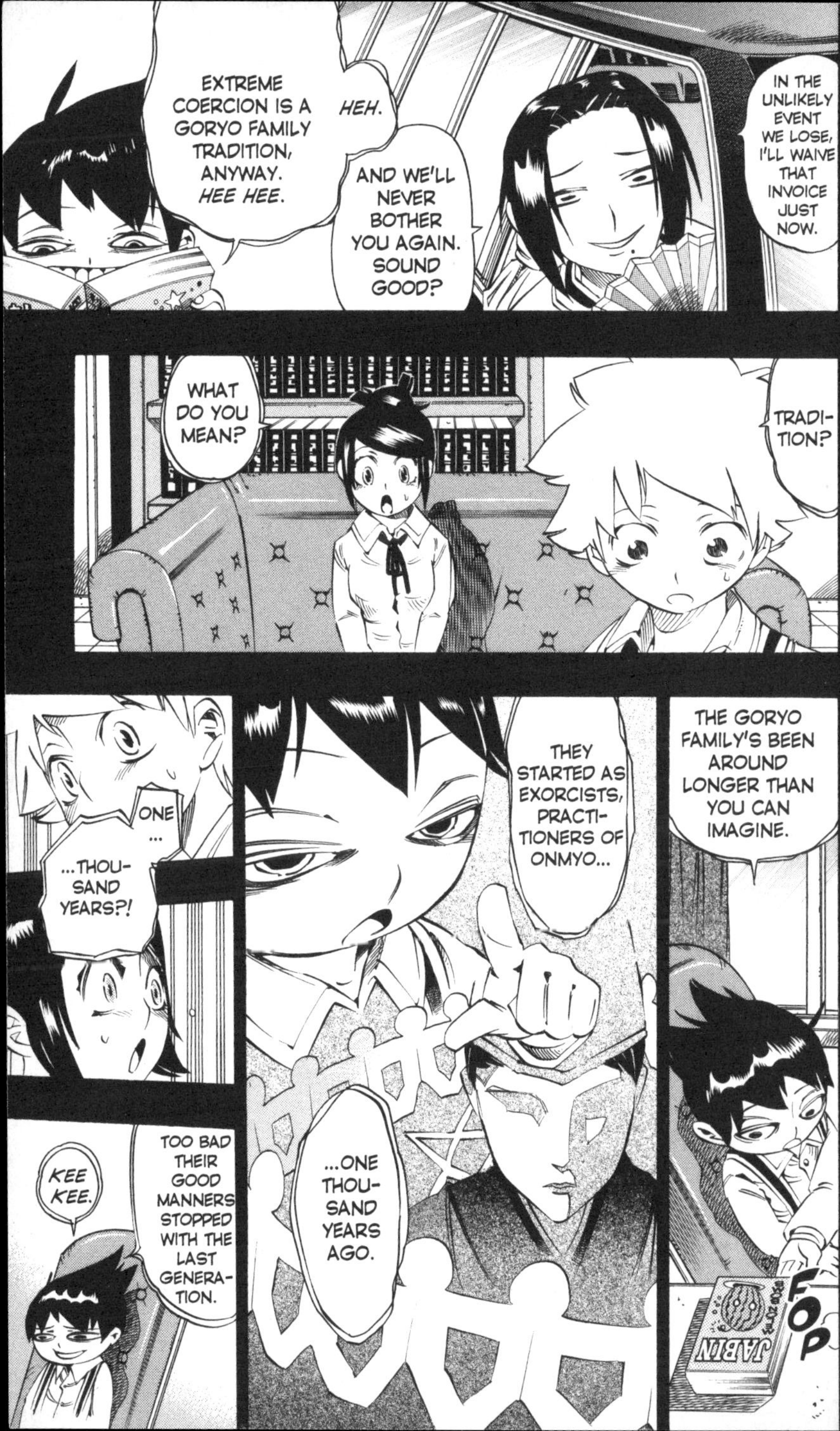
IN THE UNLIKELY EVENT WE LOSE, I'LL WAIVE THAT INVOICE JUST NOW.
HEH.
AND WE'LL NEVER BOTHER YOU AGAIN. SOUND GOOD?
EXTREME COERCION IS A GORYO FAMILY TRADITION, ANYWAY. HEE HEE.
TRADI-TION?
WHAT DO YOU MEAN?
THE GORYO FAMILY'S BEEN AROUND LONGER THAN YOU CAN IMAGINE.
FOP
JABIN
THEY STARTED AS EXORCISTS, PRACTI-TIONERS OF ONMYO...
...ONE THOU-SAND YEARS AGO.
ONE ...
...THOU-SAND YEARS?!
TOO BAD THEIR GOOD MANNERS STOPPED WITH THE LAST GENERA-TION.
KEE KEE.

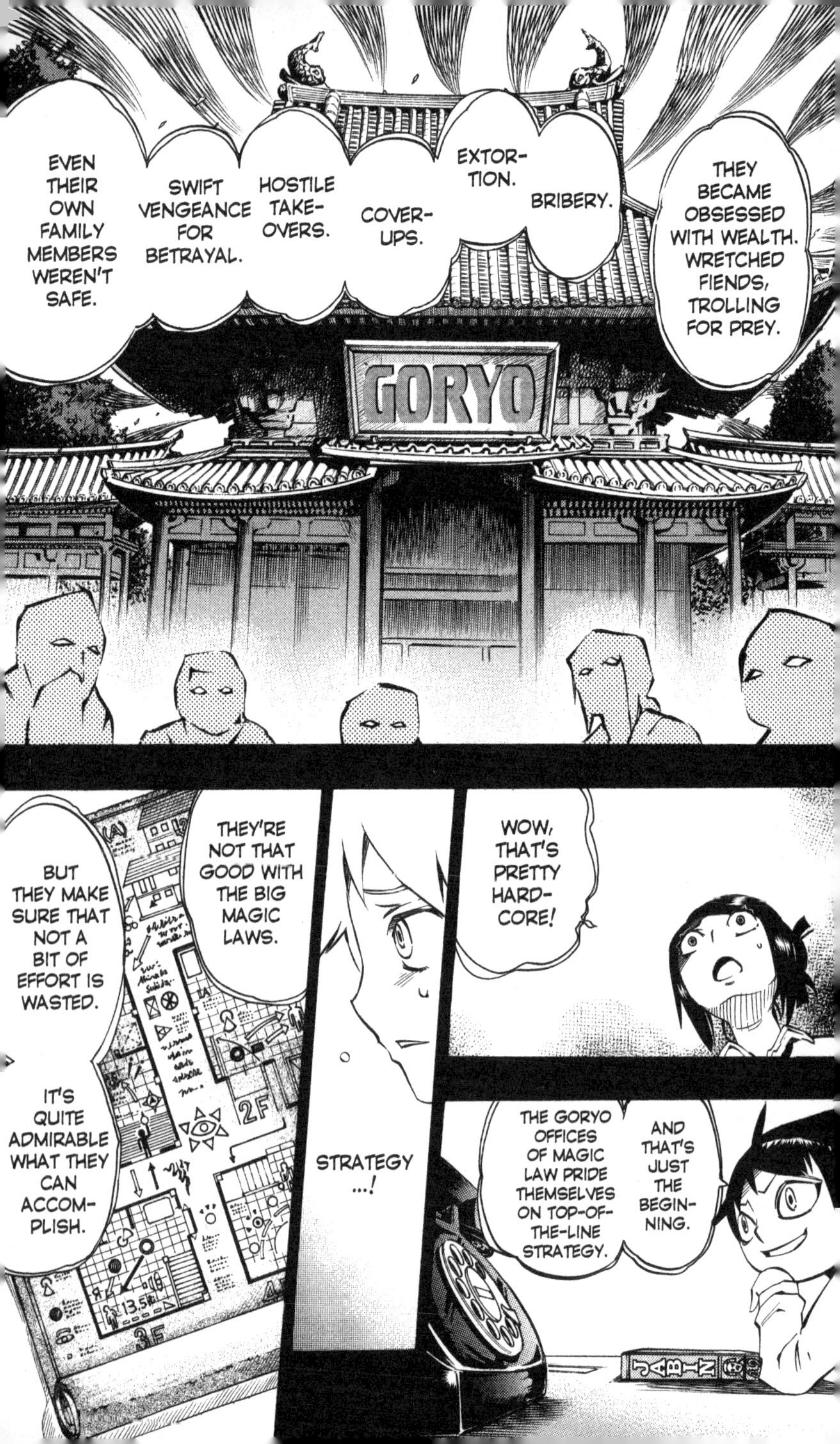
THEY BECAME OBSESSED WITH WEALTH. WRETCHED FIENDS, TROLLING FOR PREY.
BRIBERY.
EXTOR-TION.
COVER-UPS.
HOSTILE TAKE-OVERS.
SWIFT VENGEANCE FOR BETRAYAL.
EVEN THEIR OWN FAMILY MEMBERS WEREN'T SAFE.
GORYO
WOW, THAT'S PRETTY HARD-CORE!
AND THAT'S JUST THE BEGIN-NING.
THE GORYO OFFICES OF MAGIC LAW PRIDE THEMSELVES ON TOP-OF-THE-LINE STRATEGY.
JABIN
STRATEGY ...!
THEY'RE NOT THAT GOOD WITH THE BIG MAGIC LAWS.
BUT THEY MAKE SURE THAT NOT A BIT OF EFFORT IS WASTED.
IT'S QUITE ADMIRABLE WHAT THEY CAN ACCOMPLISH.
2F
3F

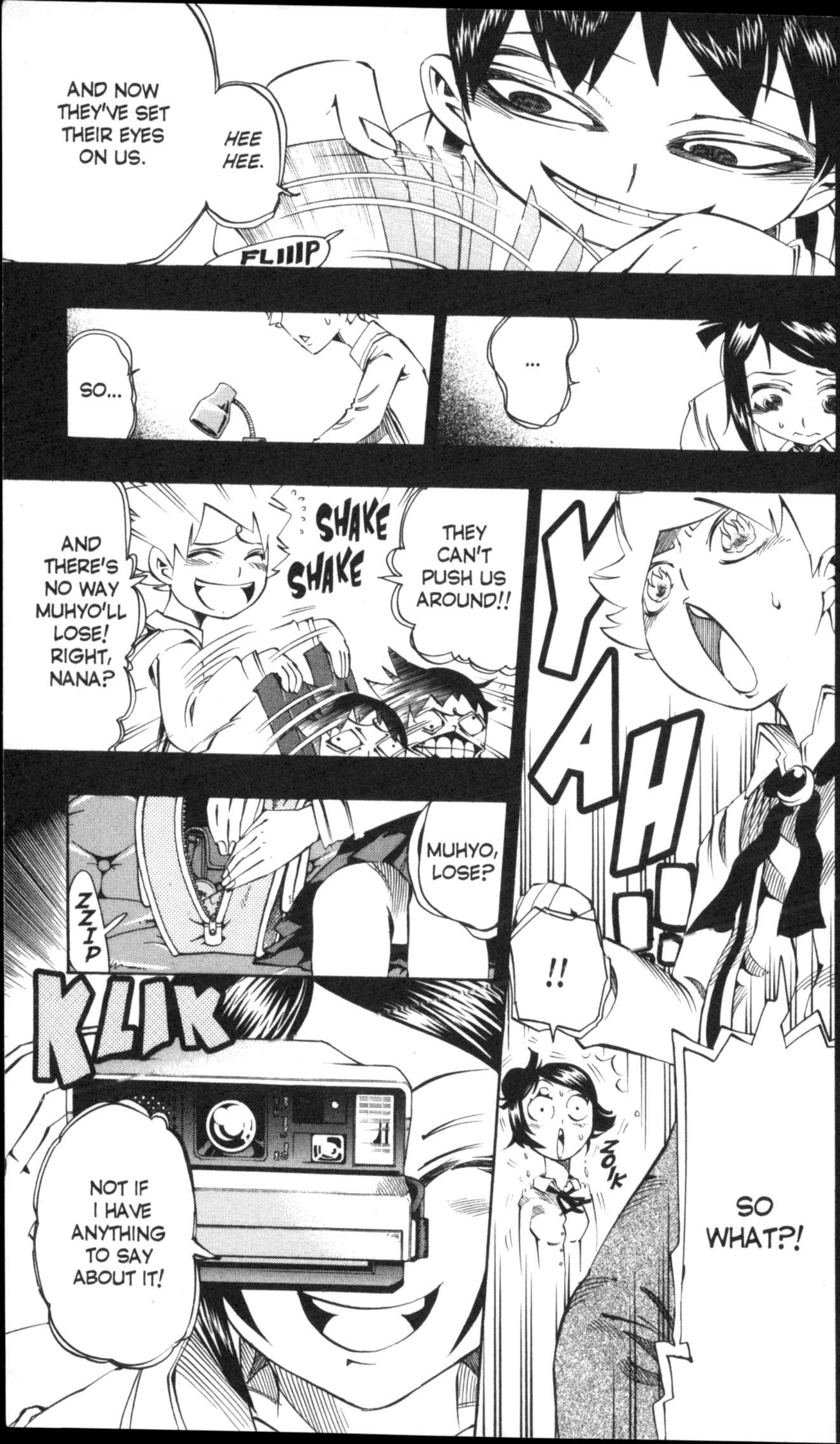

AND NOW THEY'VE SET THEIR EYES ON US.
HEE HEE.
FLIIIP
...
SO...
YAH!!
!!
THEY CAN'T PUSH US AROUND!!
SHAKE SHAKE
AND THERE'S NO WAY MUHYO'LL LOSE! RIGHT, NANA?
MUHYO, LOSE?
ZZZIP
SO WHAT?!
ZOIK
KLIK
NOT IF I HAVE ANYTHING TO SAY ABOUT IT!

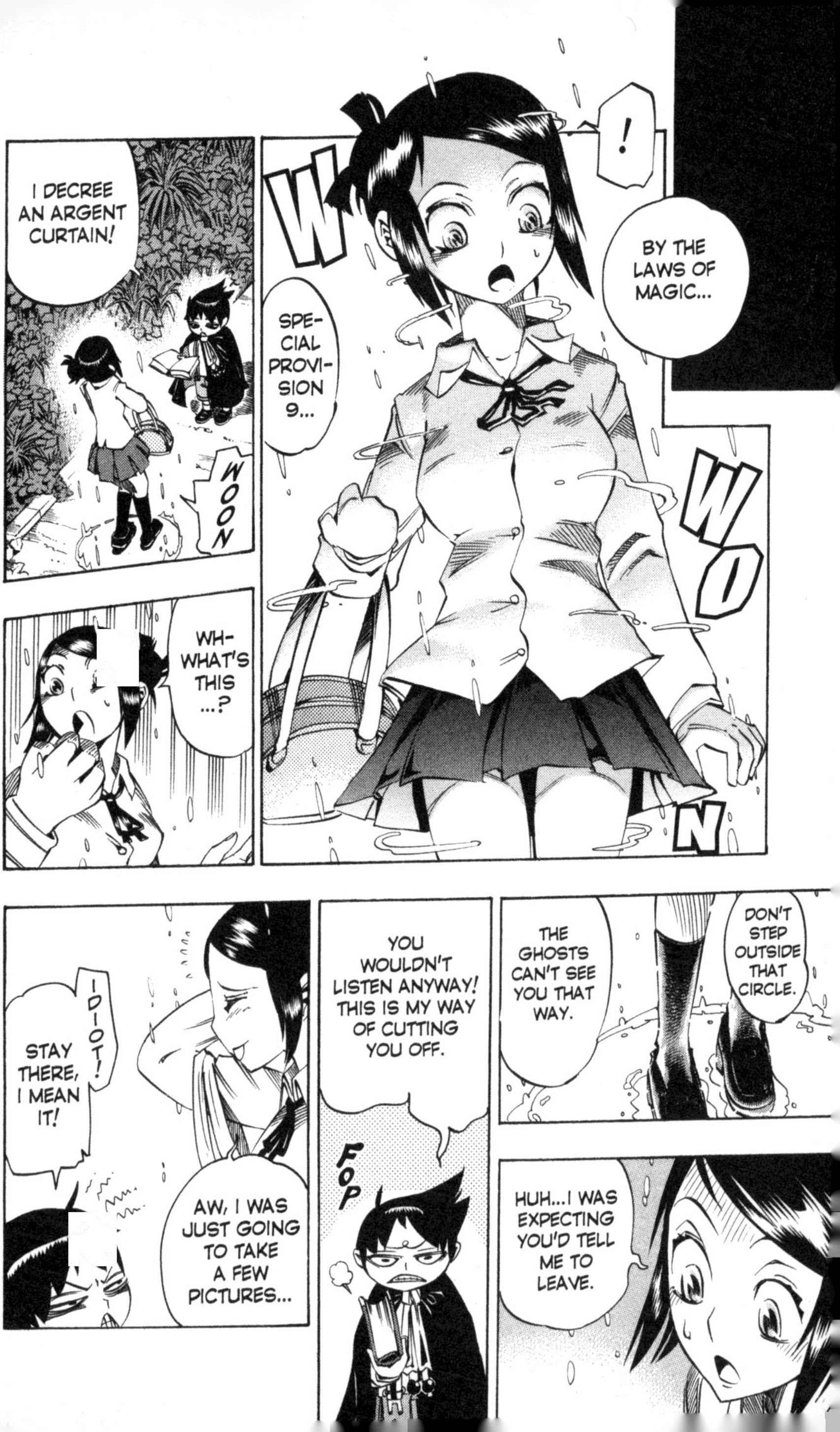
!
BY THE LAWS OF MAGIC...
SPE-CIAL PROVI-SION 9...
W
WO
N
I DECREE AN ARGENT CURTAIN!
WOON
WH-WHAT'S THIS ...?
DON'T STEP OUTSIDE THAT CIRCLE.
THE GHOSTS CAN'T SEE YOU THAT WAY.
HUH...I WAS EXPECTING YOU'D TELL ME TO LEAVE.
YOU WOULDN'T LISTEN ANYWAY! THIS IS MY WAY OF CUTTING YOU OFF.
FOP
IDIOT!
STAY THERE, I MEAN IT!
AW, I WAS JUST GOING TO TAKE A FEW PICTURES...

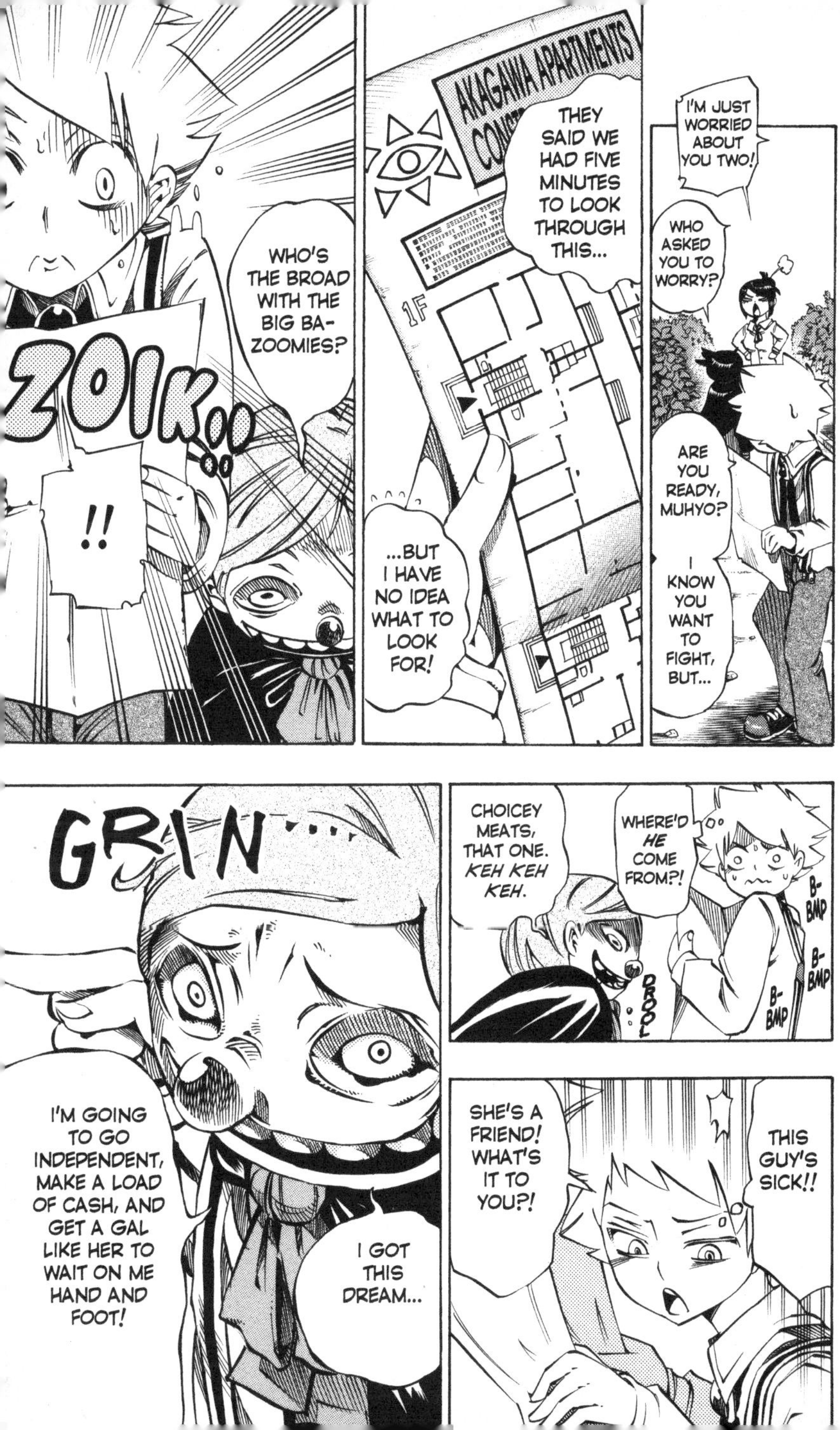

I'M JUST WORRIED ABOUT YOU TWO!
WHO ASKED YOU TO WORRY?
ARE YOU READY, MUHYO?
I KNOW YOU WANT TO FIGHT, BUT...
AKAGAWA APARTMENTS
THEY SAID WE HAD FIVE MINUTES TO LOOK THROUGH THIS...
1F
...BUT I HAVE NO IDEA WHAT TO LOOK FOR!
WHO'S THE BROAD WITH THE BIG BA-ZOOMIES?
ZOIK!!
!!
WHERE'D *HE* COME FROM?!
B-BMP B-BMP B-BMP
CHOICEY MEATS, THAT ONE. *KEH KEH KEH.*
DROOL
THIS GUY'S SICK!!
SHE'S A FRIEND! WHAT'S IT TO YOU?!
GRIN...
I GOT THIS DREAM...
I'M GOING TO GO INDEPENDENT, MAKE A LOAD OF CASH, AND GET A GAL LIKE HER TO WAIT ON ME HAND AND FOOT!

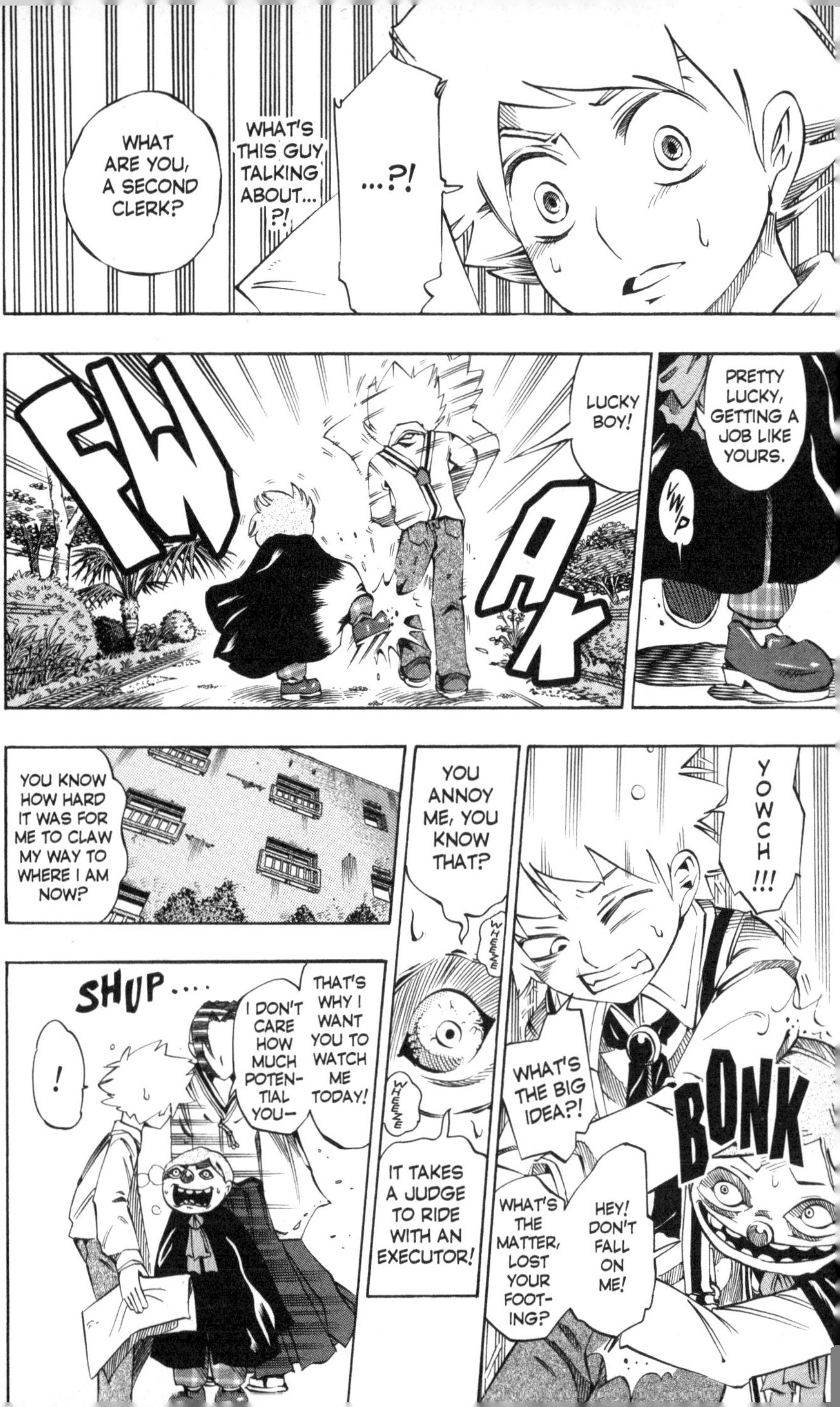
...?!
WHAT'S THIS GUY TALKING ABOUT...?!
WHAT ARE YOU, A SECOND CLERK?
PRETTY LUCKY, GETTING A JOB LIKE YOURS.
VWIP
LUCKY BOY!
FWAK
YOWCH!!!
BONK
HEY! DON'T FALL ON ME!
WHAT'S THE MATTER, LOST YOUR FOOTING?
WHAT'S THE BIG IDEA?!
YOU ANNOY ME, YOU KNOW THAT?
WHEEZE
WHEEZE
IT TAKES A JUDGE TO RIDE WITH AN EXECUTOR!
YOU KNOW HOW HARD IT WAS FOR ME TO CLAW MY WAY TO WHERE I AM NOW?
THAT'S WHY I WANT YOU TO WATCH ME TODAY!
I DON'T CARE HOW MUCH POTEN-TIAL YOU—
SHUP....
!

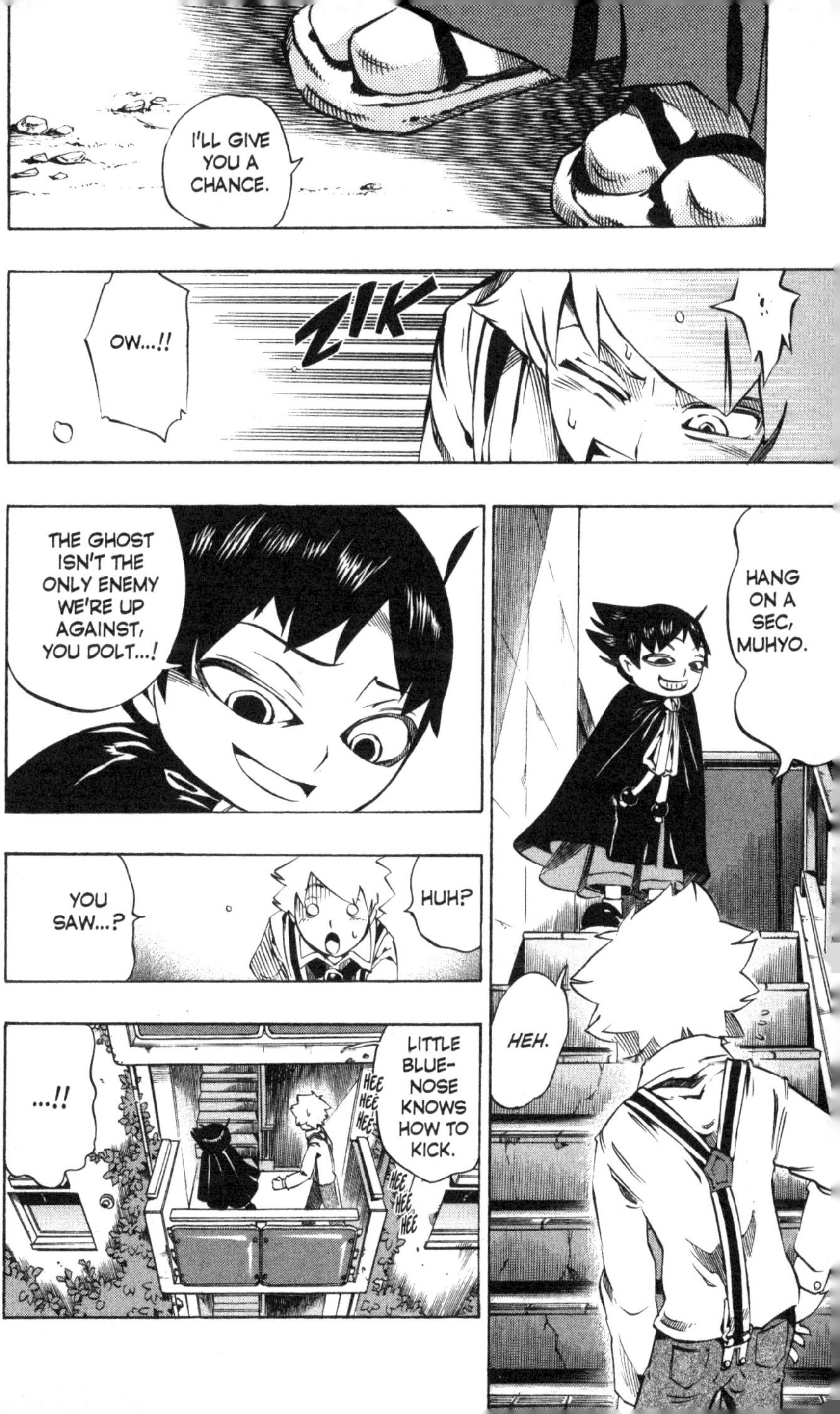
I'LL GIVE YOU A CHANCE.
ZIK
OW...!!
HANG ON A SEC, MUHYO.
HEH.
THE GHOST ISN'T THE ONLY ENEMY WE'RE UP AGAINST, YOU DOLT...!
HUH?
YOU SAW...?
LITTLE BLUE-NOSE KNOWS HOW TO KICK.
HEE HEE HEE
HEE HEE HEE
...!!

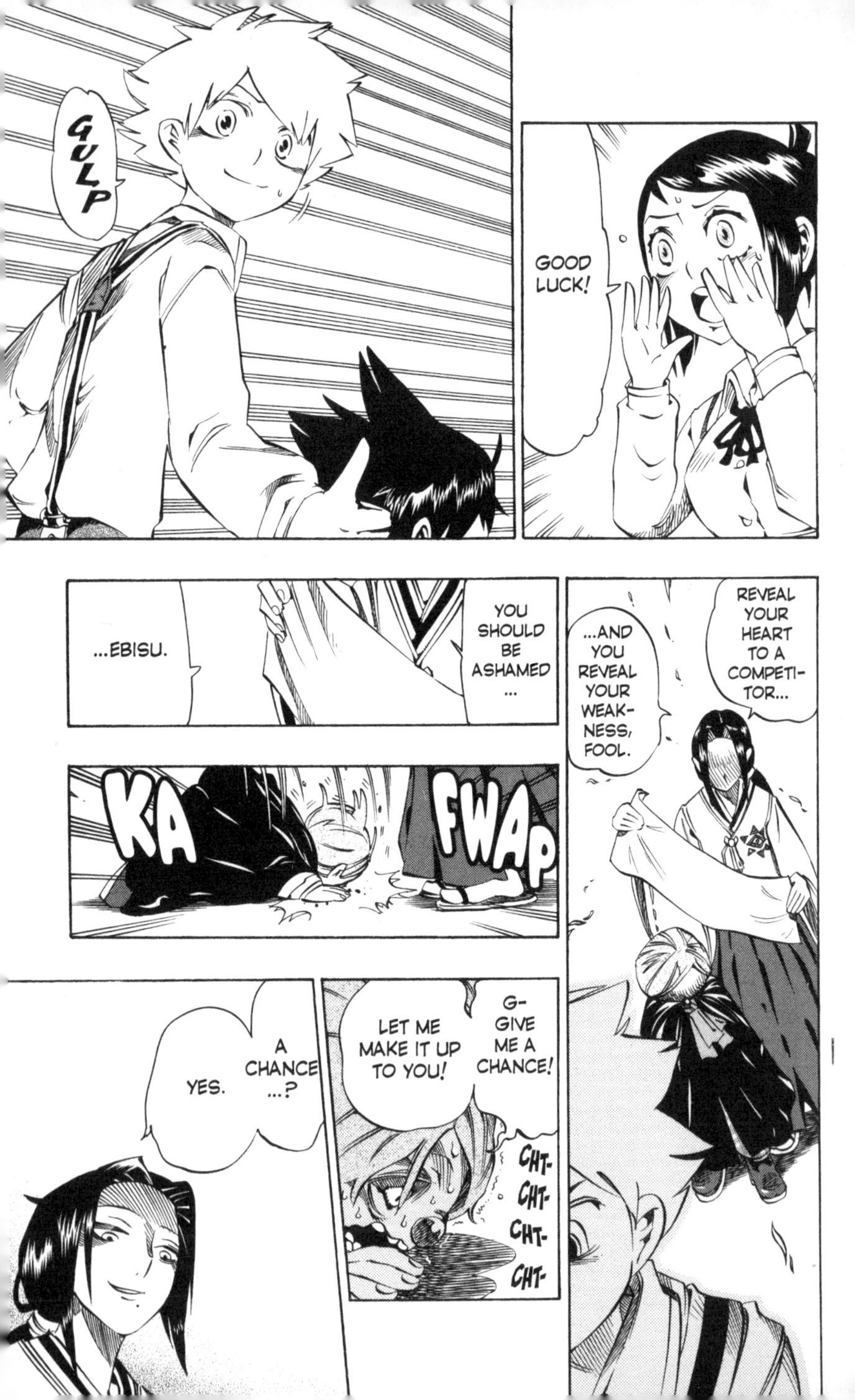

GOOD LUCK!
GULP
REVEAL YOUR HEART TO A COMPETITOR...
...AND YOU REVEAL YOUR WEAKNESS, FOOL.
YOU SHOULD BE ASHAMED...
...EBISU.
KA FWAP
G-GIVE ME A CHANCE!
LET ME MAKE IT UP TO YOU!
CHT- CHT- CHT- CHT-
A CHANCE...?
YES.

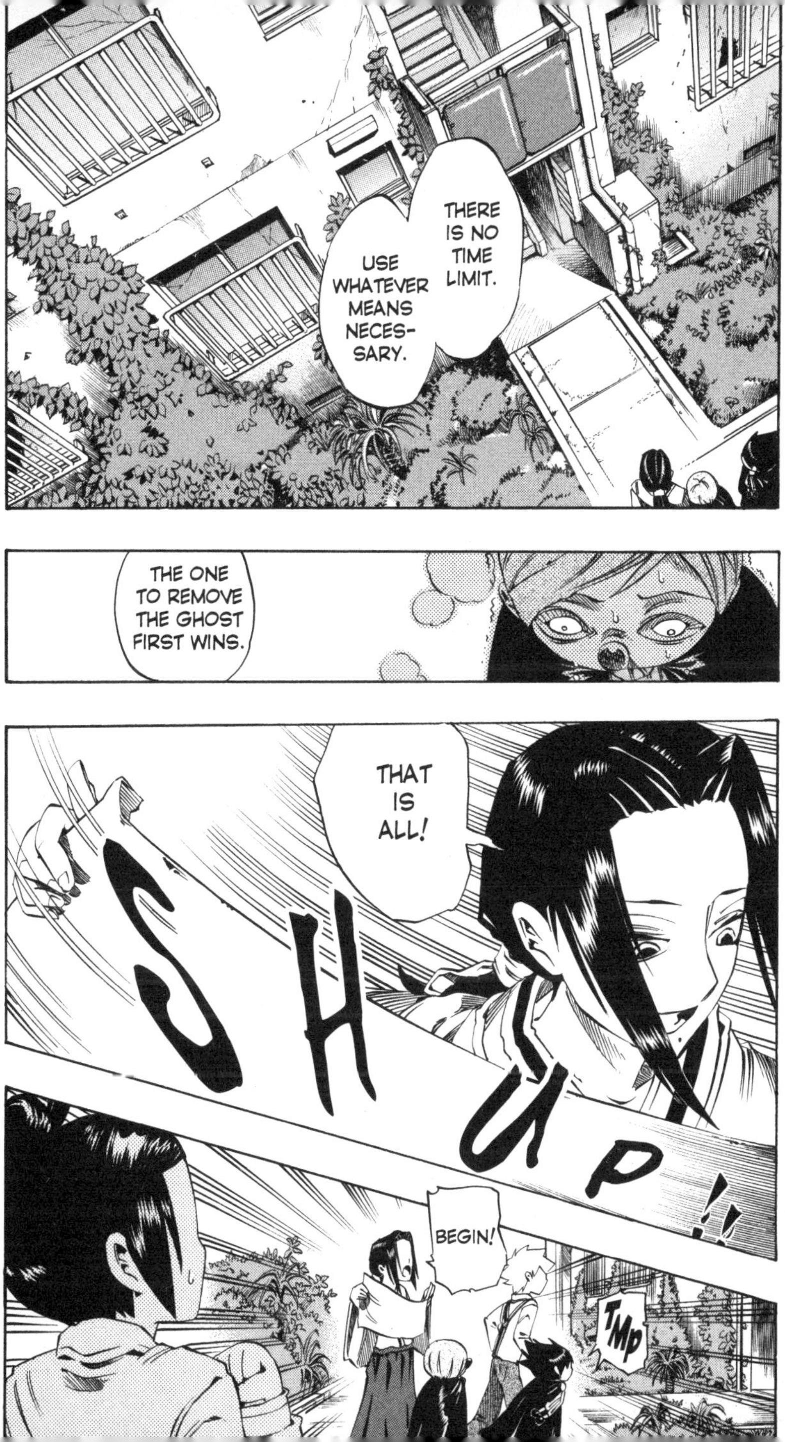
THERE IS NO TIME LIMIT.
USE WHATEVER MEANS NECES-SARY.
THE ONE TO REMOVE THE GHOST FIRST WINS.
THAT IS ALL!
SHUP!!
BEGIN!
TMP

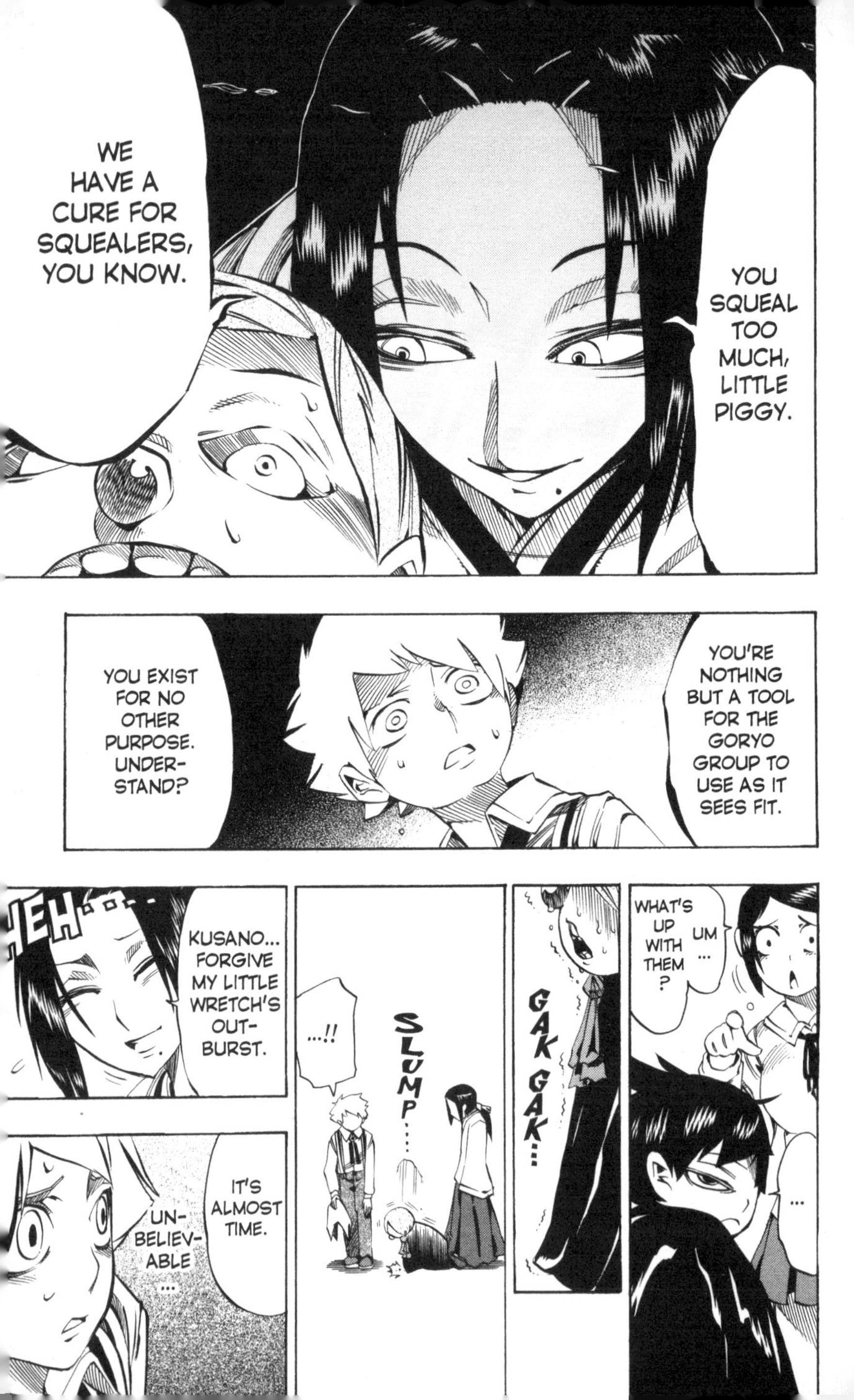
YOU SQUEAL TOO MUCH, LITTLE PIGGY.
WE HAVE A CURE FOR SQUEALERS, YOU KNOW.
YOU'RE NOTHING BUT A TOOL FOR THE GORYO GROUP TO USE AS IT SEES FIT.
YOU EXIST FOR NO OTHER PURPOSE. UNDER-STAND?
WHAT'S UP WITH THEM?
UM ...
...
GAK GAK GAK...
SLUMP....
...!!
HEH...
KUSANO... FORGIVE MY LITTLE WRETCH'S OUT-BURST.
IT'S ALMOST TIME.
UN-BELIEV-ABLE ...

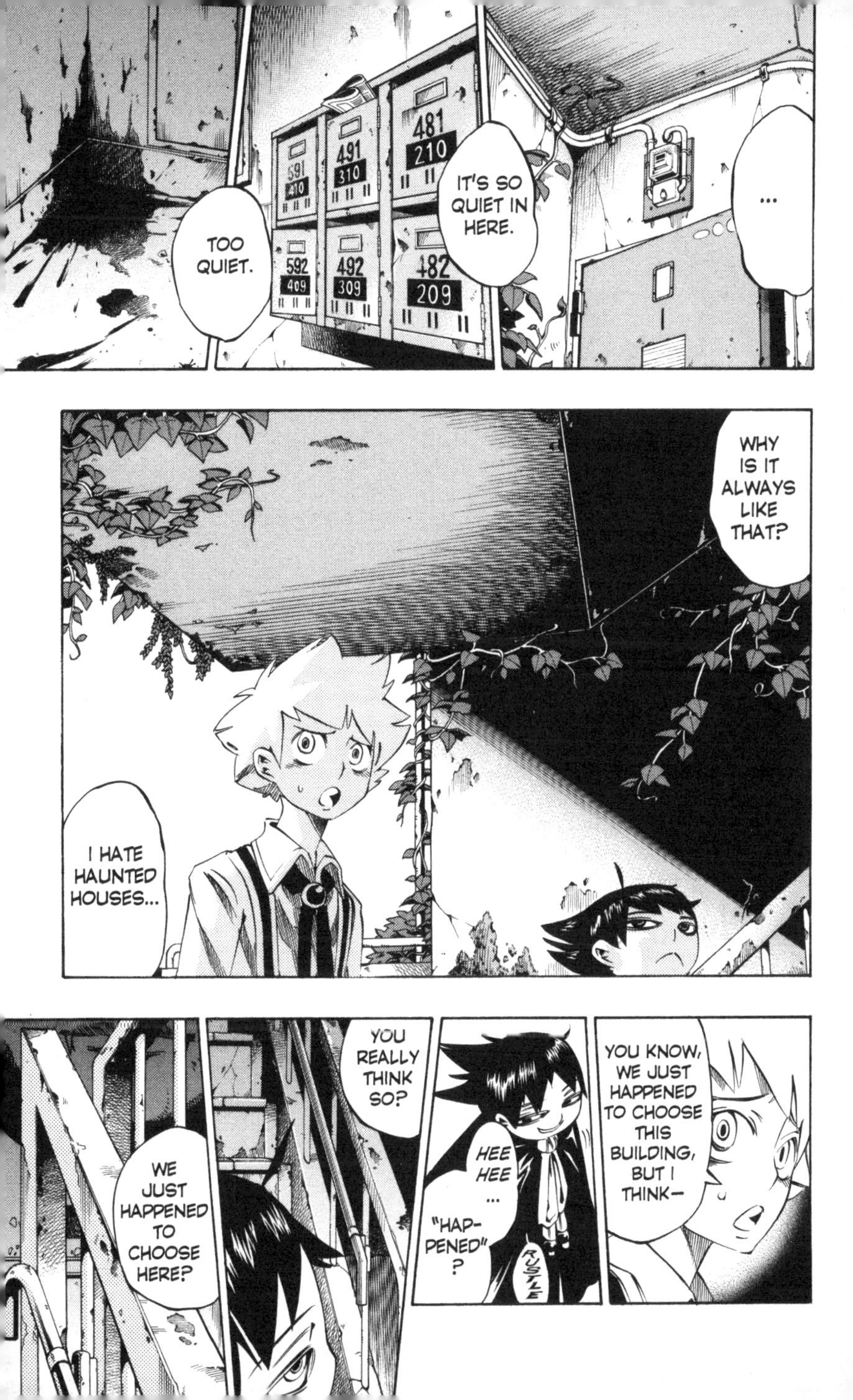
...
IT'S SO QUIET IN HERE.
TOO QUIET.
WHY IS IT ALWAYS LIKE THAT?
I HATE HAUNTED HOUSES...
YOU KNOW, WE JUST HAPPENED TO CHOOSE THIS BUILDING, BUT I THINK—
HEE HEE ...
"HAP-PENED"?
RUSTLE
YOU REALLY THINK SO?
WE JUST HAPPENED TO CHOOSE HERE?

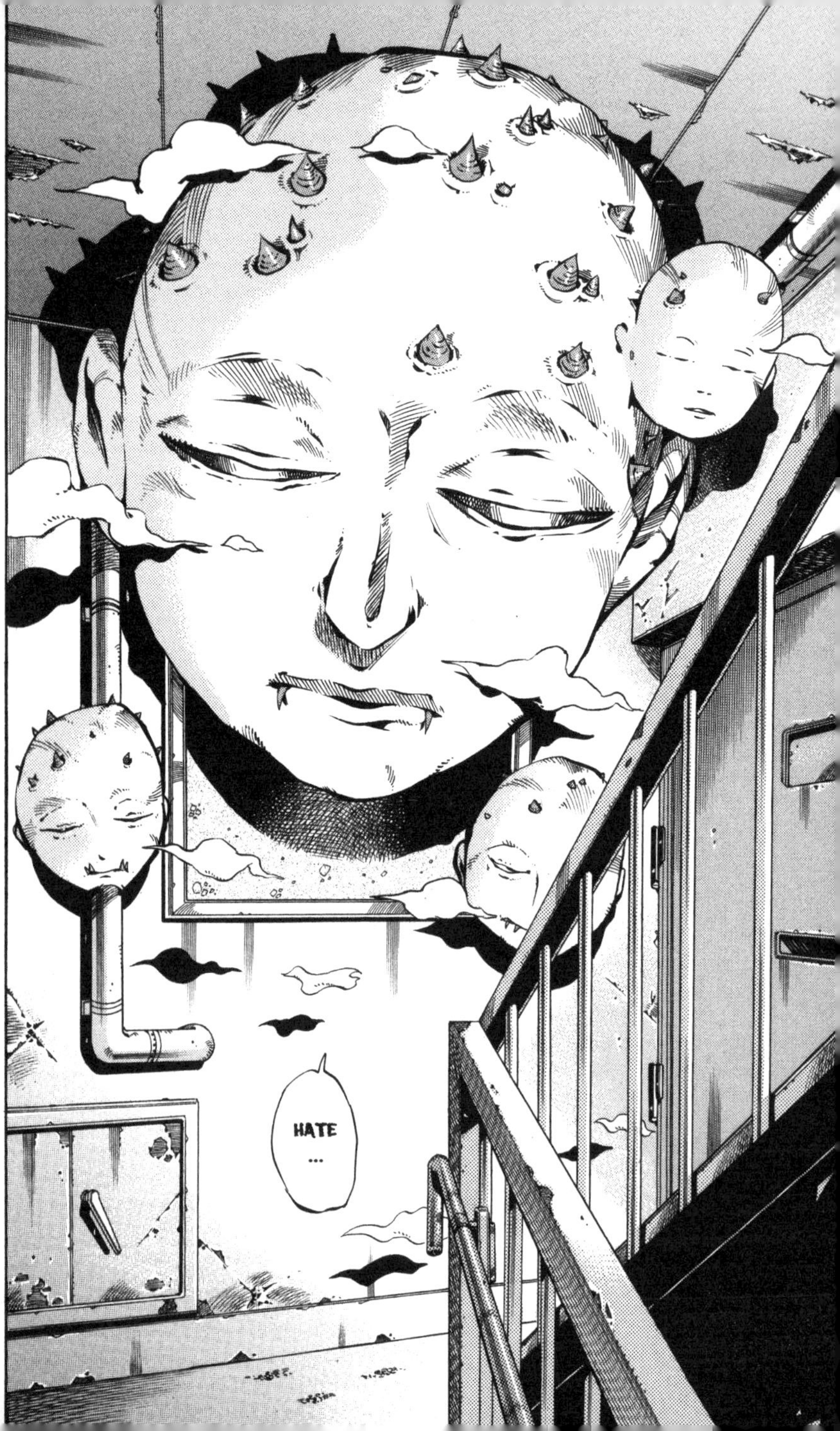
HATE ...

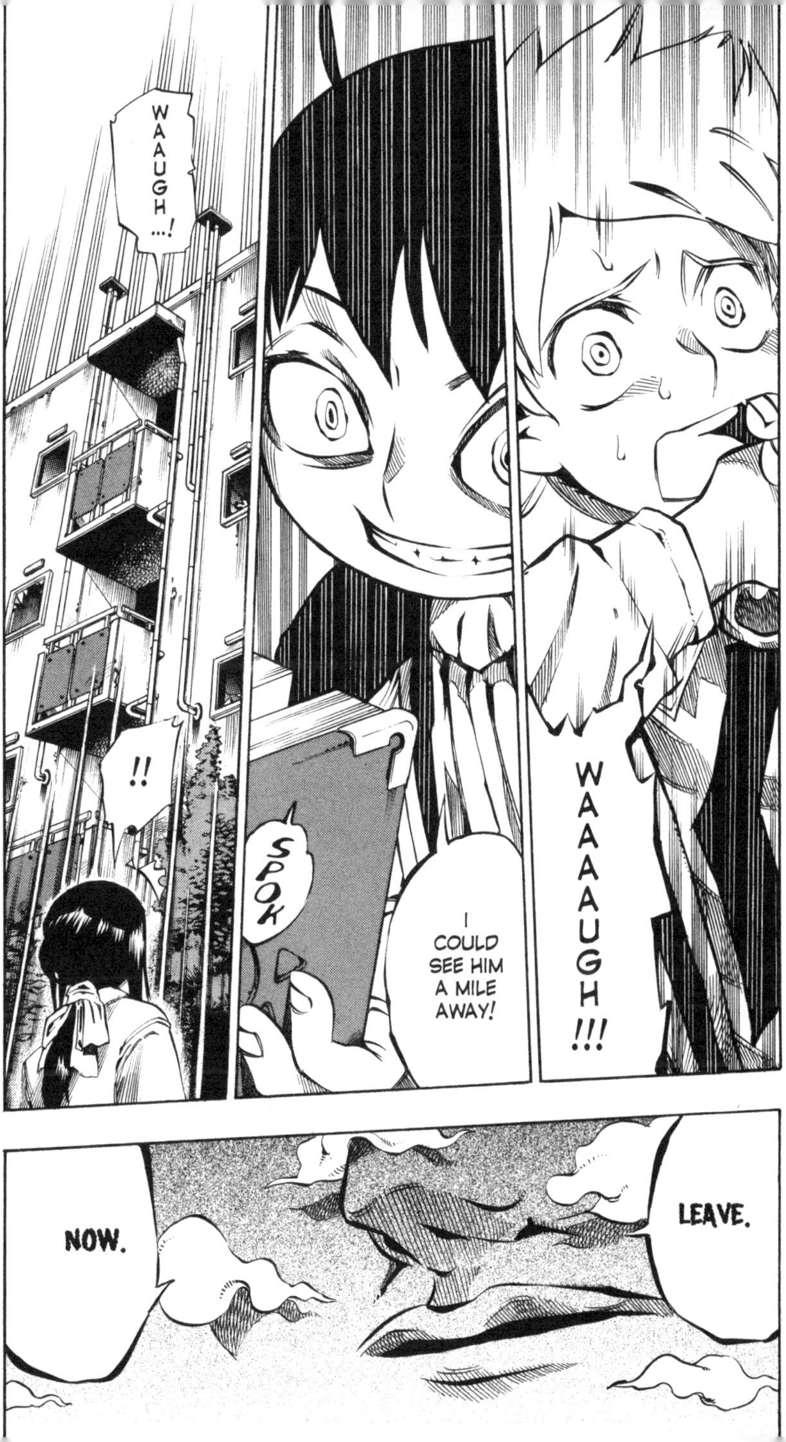
WAAAAUGH!!!
I COULD SEE HIM A MILE AWAY!
SPOK
WAAUGH...!
!!
LEAVE.
NOW.

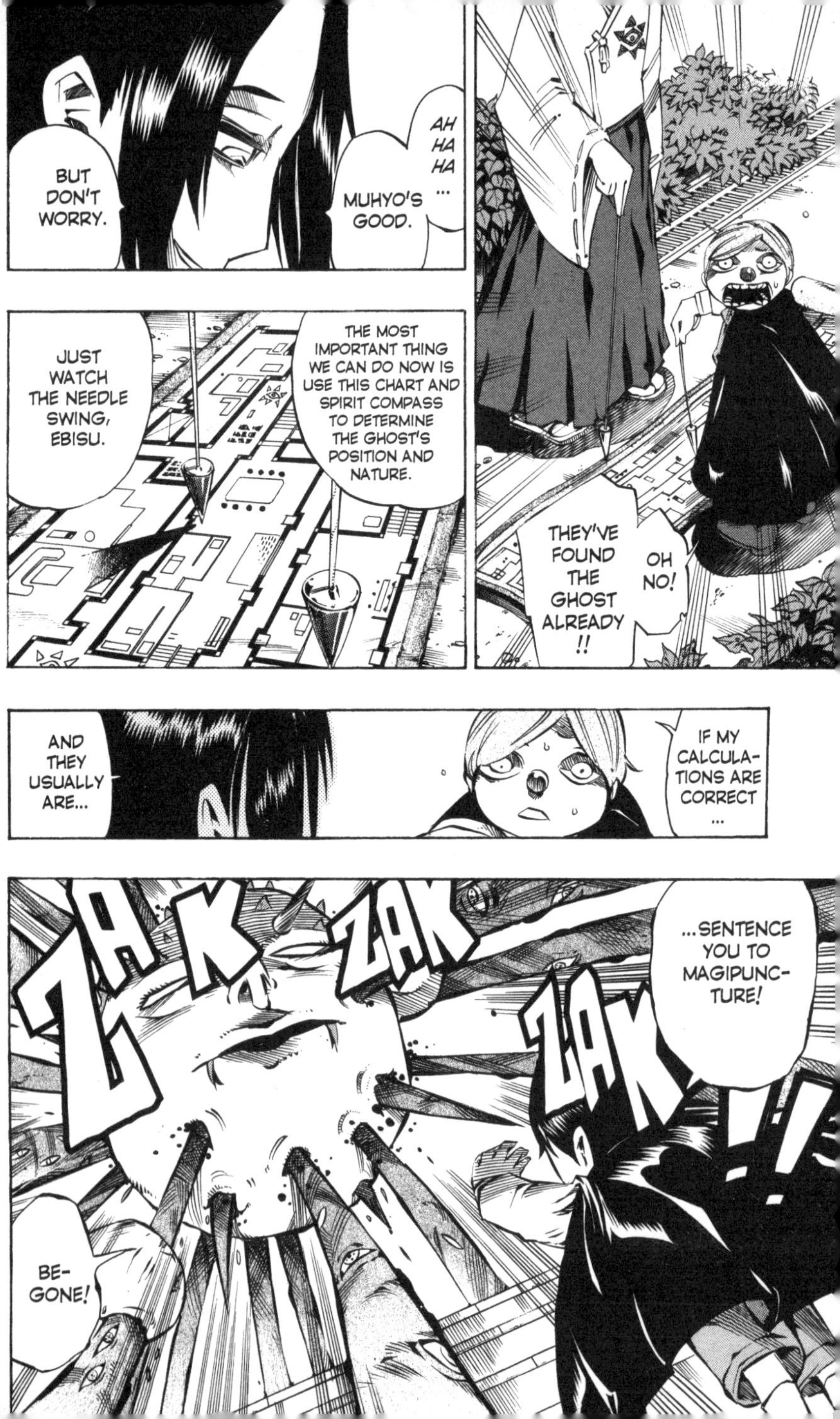
OH NO!
THEY'VE FOUND THE GHOST ALREADY!!
AH HA HA...
MUHYO'S GOOD.
BUT DON'T WORRY.
THE MOST IMPORTANT THING WE CAN DO NOW IS USE THIS CHART AND SPIRIT COMPASS TO DETERMINE THE GHOST'S POSITION AND NATURE.
JUST WATCH THE NEEDLE SWING, EBISU.
IF MY CALCULATIONS ARE CORRECT...
AND THEY USUALLY ARE...
...SENTENCE YOU TO MAGIPUNCTURE!
ZAK
ZAK
ZAK
ZAK
BE-GONE!

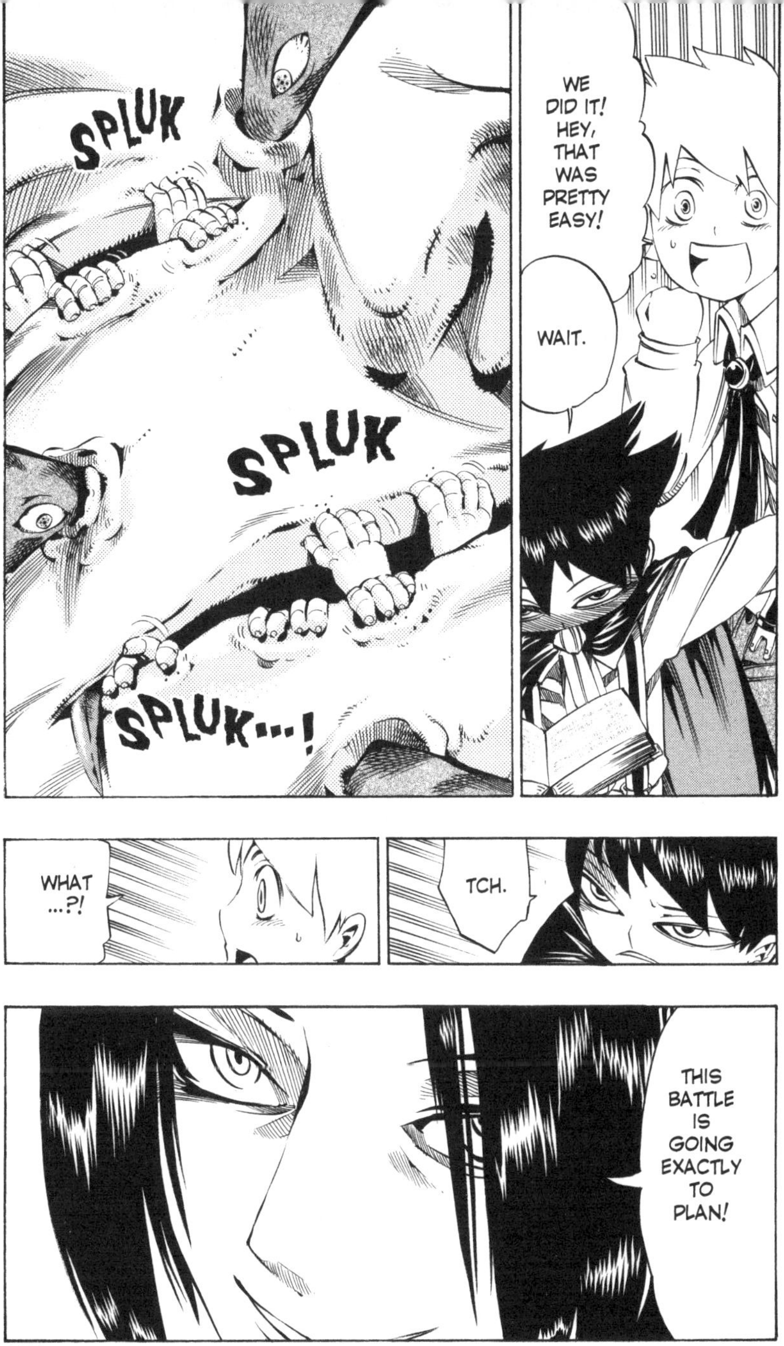
WE DID IT! HEY, THAT WAS PRETTY EASY!
WAIT.
SPLUK
SPLUK
SPLUK...!
TCH.
WHAT ...?!
THIS BATTLE IS GOING EXACTLY TO PLAN!

FAN MAIL WANTED!

HAVE A MESSAGE FOR THE AUTHOR? SEND IT HERE, AND SEND LOTS!

YOSHIYUKI NISHI
C/O MUHYO & ROJI'S
BSI EDITOR
VIZ MEDIA
P.O. BOX 77010
SAN FRANCISCO, CA 94107

HEE HEE... DON'T MESS UP THE ADDRESS NOW.

ARTICLE 41
DOLLS

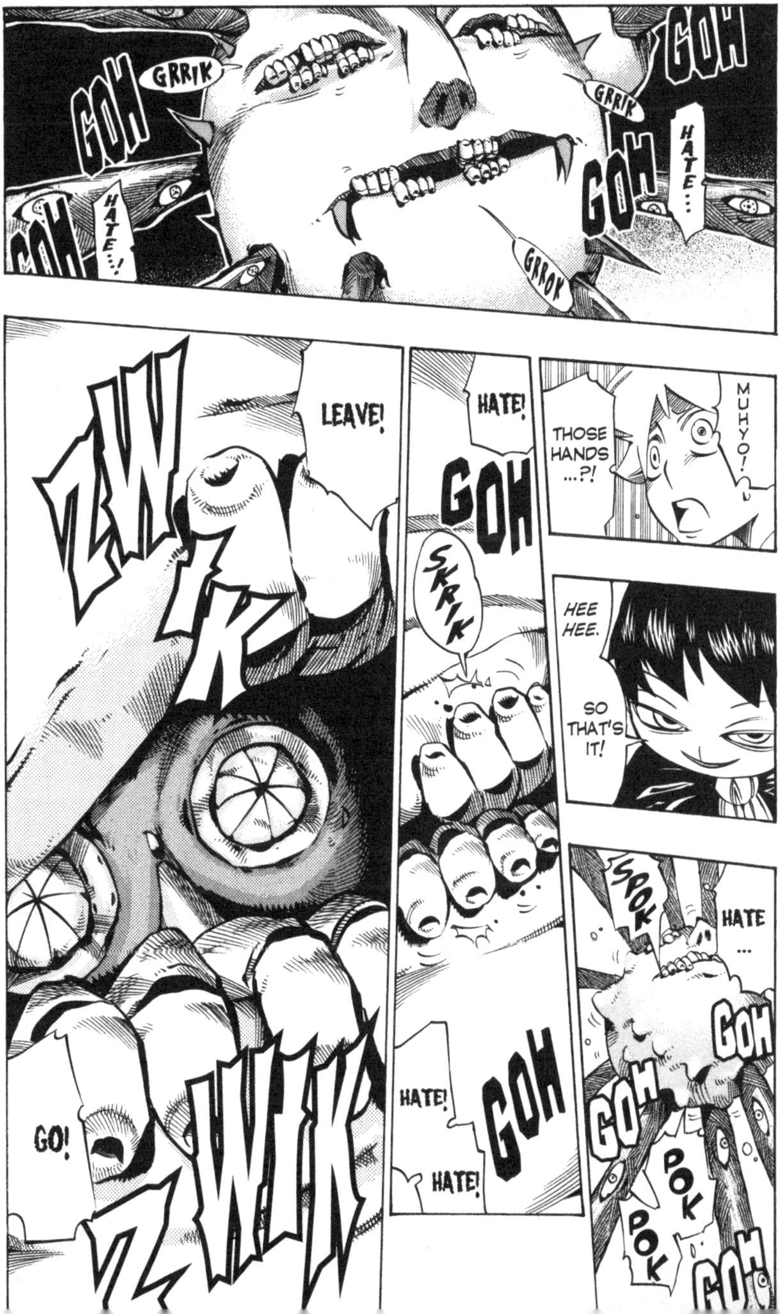
GOH
GRRIK
GOH
HATE...
GRROK
GRRIK
GOH
GOH
HATE...!
MUHYO!
THOSE HANDS ...?!
HEE HEE.
SO THAT'S IT!
SPOK
HATE ...
GOH
GOH
POK
POK
POK
GOH
HATE!
GOH
SKRIK
GOH
HATE!
HATE!
LEAVE!
ZWIK
GO!
ZWIK

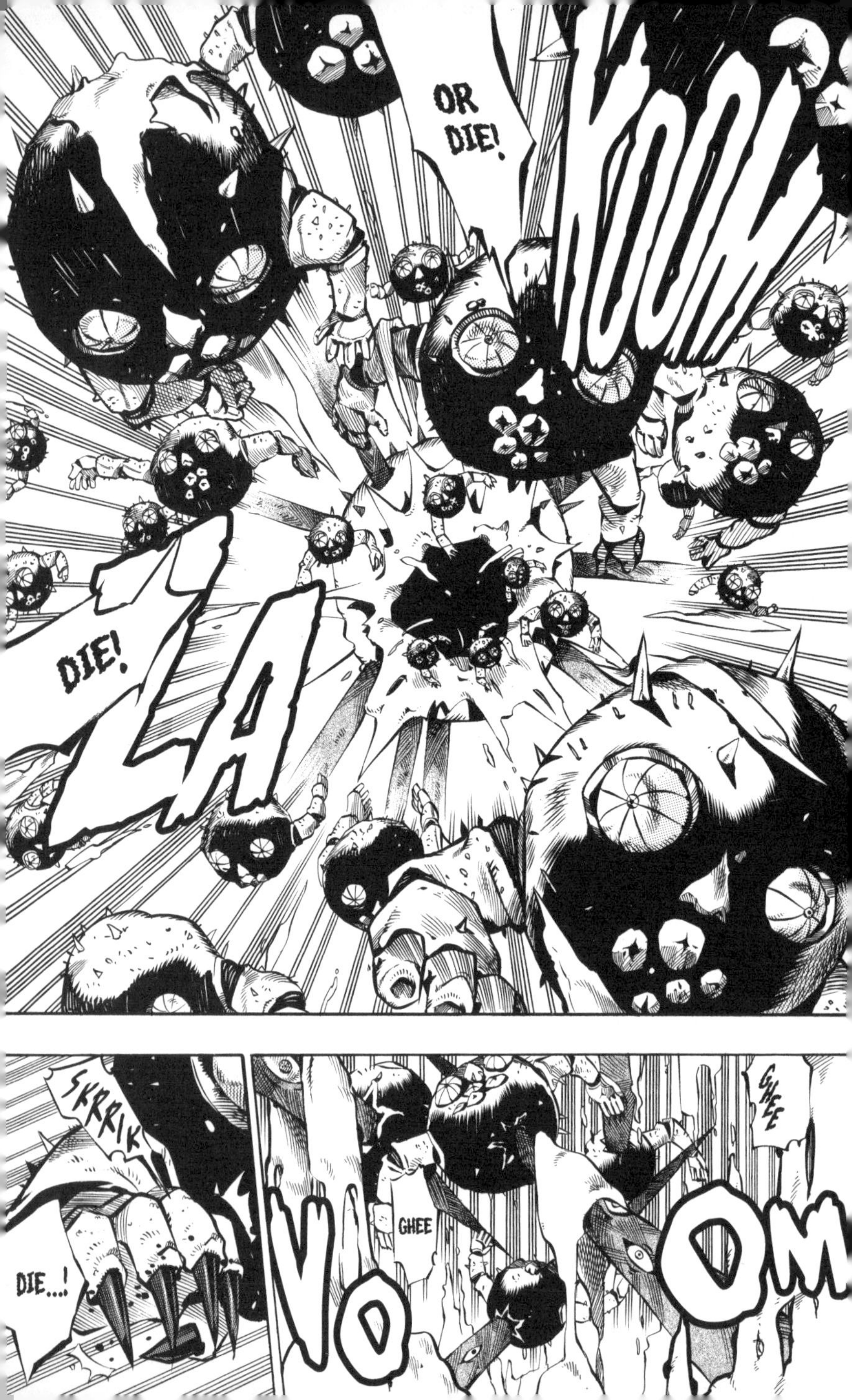
KOOM
OR DIE!
DIE!
ZA
GHEE
GHEE
VOOM
SKRRIK
DIE...!

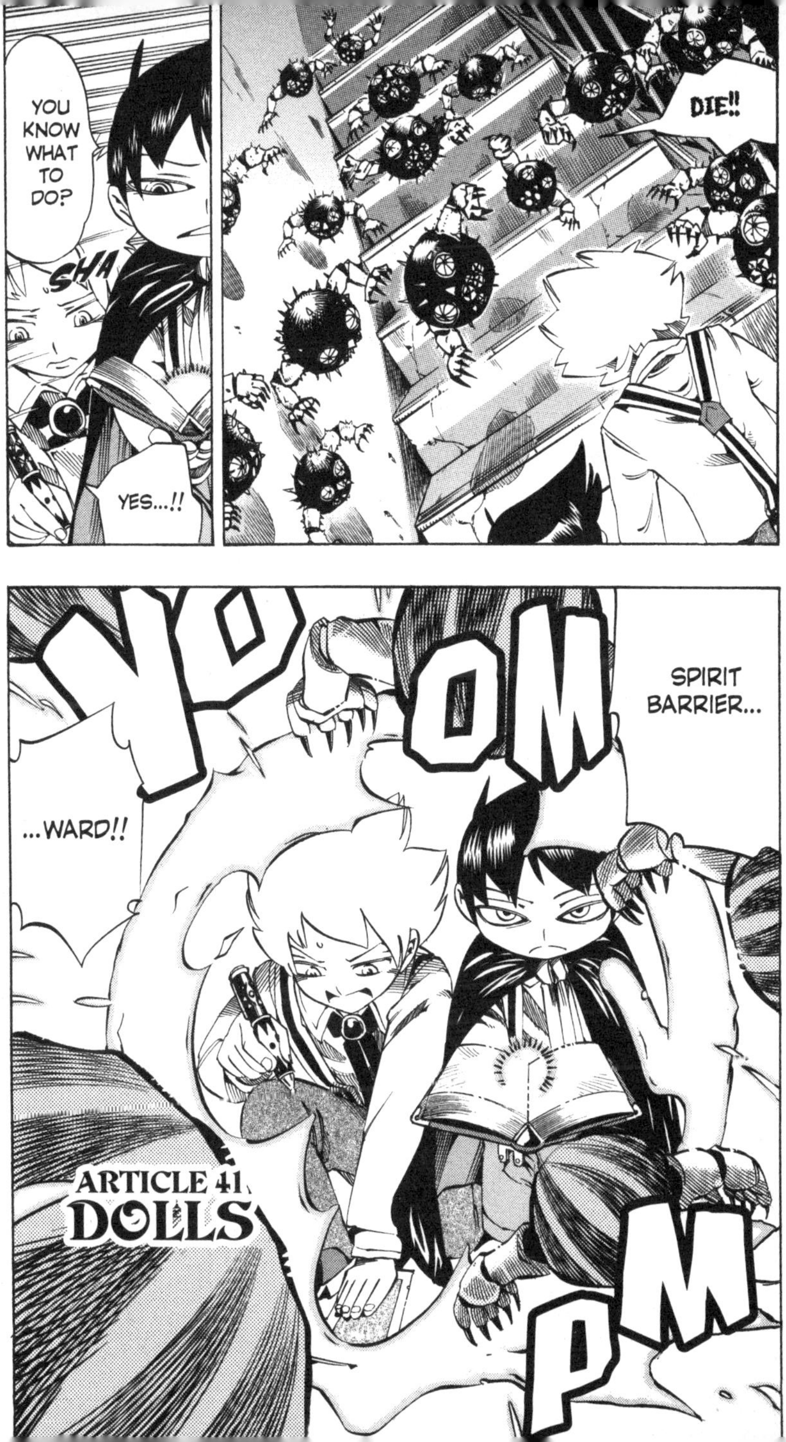
DIE!!
YOU KNOW WHAT TO DO?
SHA
YES...!!
YO OM
SPIRIT BARRIER...
...WARD!!
ARTICLE 41: DOLLS
PM

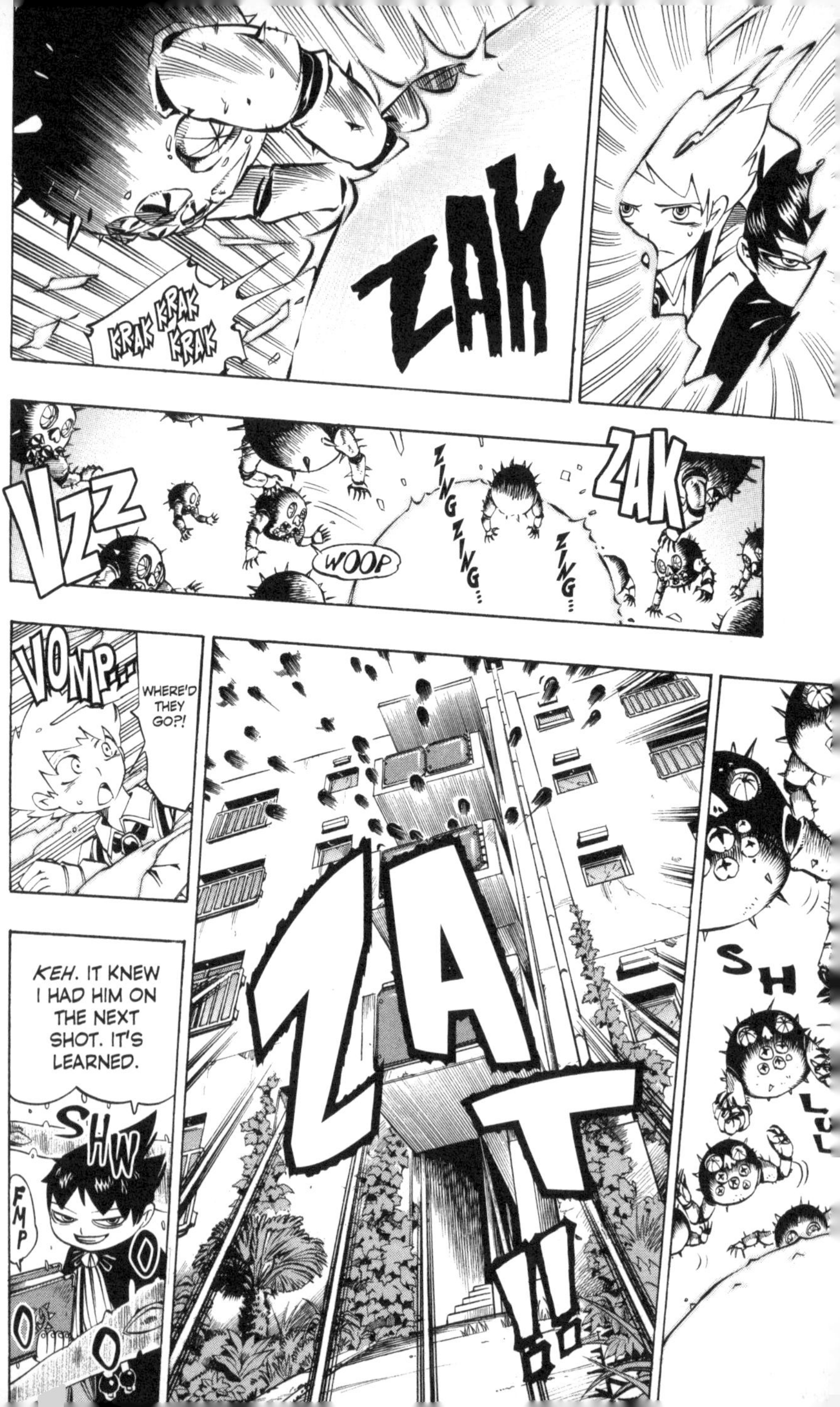
ZAK
KRAK KRAK
KRAK KRAK
ZAK
ZING ZING...
ZING...
WOOP
VZZ
SH
ZAT!!
VOMP...
WHERE'D THEY GO?!
KEH. IT KNEW I HAD HIM ON THE NEXT SHOT. IT'S LEARNED.
SHW
FMP

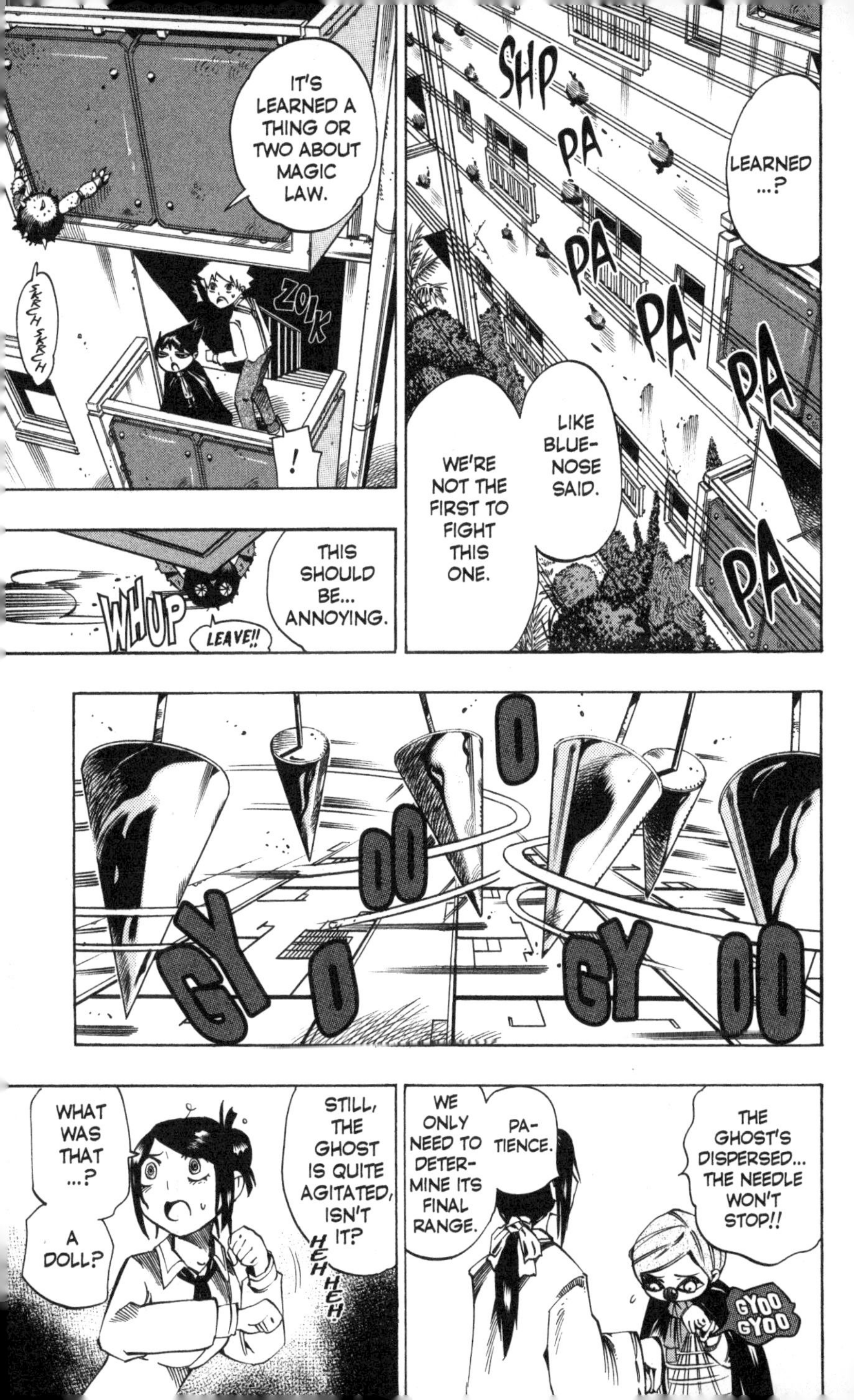
IT'S LEARNED A THING OR TWO ABOUT MAGIC LAW.
SKRCH SKRCH
ZOIK
!
THIS SHOULD BE... ANNOYING.
WHUP
LEAVE!!
SHP
PA PA PA PA PA
LEARNED ...?
LIKE BLUE-NOSE SAID.
WE'RE NOT THE FIRST TO FIGHT THIS ONE.
GYOOOO GYOO
WHAT WAS THAT ...?
A DOLL?
STILL, THE GHOST IS QUITE AGITATED, ISN'T IT?
HEH HEH HEH!
WE ONLY NEED TO DETERMINE ITS FINAL RANGE.
PATIENCE.
THE GHOST'S DISPERSED... THE NEEDLE WON'T STOP!!
GYOO GYOO

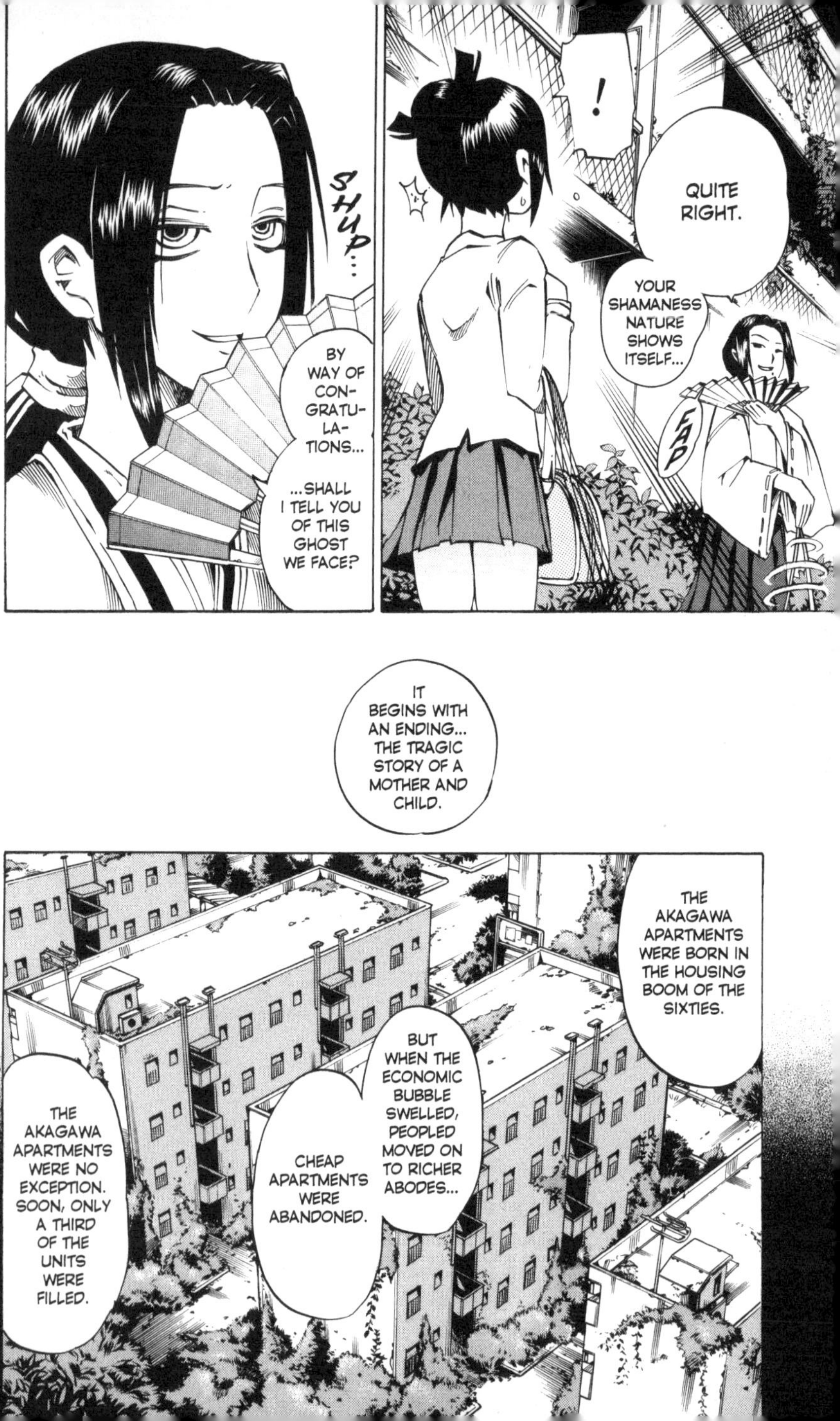
!
QUITE RIGHT.
YOUR SHAMANESS NATURE SHOWS ITSELF...
FAP
SHUP...
BY WAY OF CON-GRATU-LA-TIONS...
...SHALL I TELL YOU OF THIS GHOST WE FACE?
IT BEGINS WITH AN ENDING... THE TRAGIC STORY OF A MOTHER AND CHILD.
THE AKAGAWA APARTMENTS WERE BORN IN THE HOUSING BOOM OF THE SIXTIES.
BUT WHEN THE ECONOMIC BUBBLE SWELLED, PEOPLED MOVED ON TO RICHER ABODES...
CHEAP APARTMENTS WERE ABANDONED.
THE AKAGAWA APARTMENTS WERE NO EXCEPTION. SOON, ONLY A THIRD OF THE UNITS WERE FILLED.

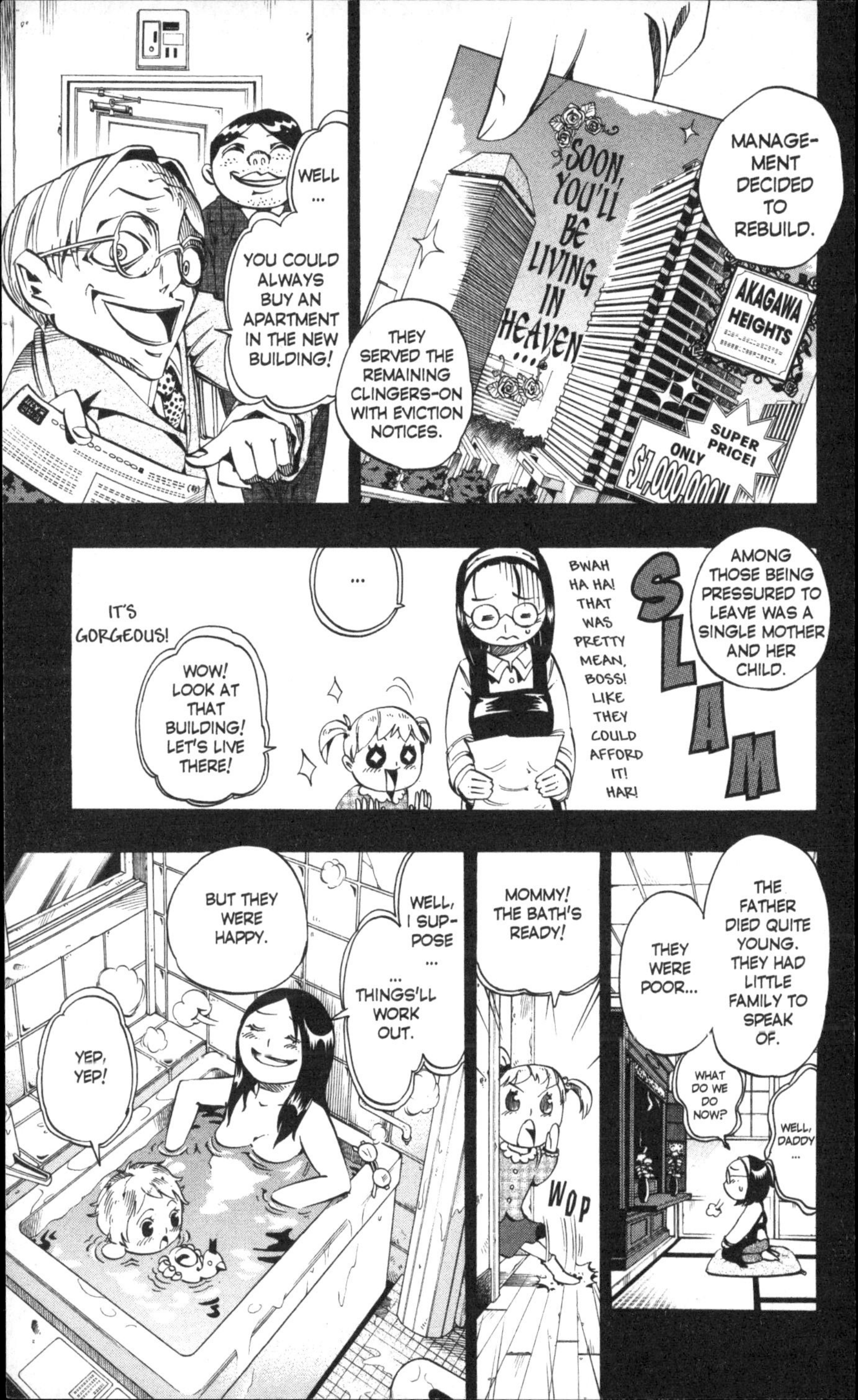
MANAGEMENT DECIDED TO REBUILD.
SOON, YOU'LL BE LIVING IN HEAVEN...
AKAGAWA HEIGHTS
SUPER PRICE!
ONLY $1,000,000!
THEY SERVED THE REMAINING CLINGERS-ON WITH EVICTION NOTICES.
WELL...
YOU COULD ALWAYS BUY AN APARTMENT IN THE NEW BUILDING!
AMONG THOSE BEING PRESSURED TO LEAVE WAS A SINGLE MOTHER AND HER CHILD.
SLAM
BWAH HA HA! THAT WAS PRETTY MEAN, BOSS! LIKE THEY COULD AFFORD IT! HAR!
...
IT'S GORGEOUS!
WOW! LOOK AT THAT BUILDING! LET'S LIVE THERE!
THE FATHER DIED QUITE YOUNG. THEY HAD LITTLE FAMILY TO SPEAK OF.
THEY WERE POOR...
WHAT DO WE DO NOW?
WELL, DADDY...
MOMMY! THE BATH'S READY!
WOP
WELL, I SUPPOSE...
... THINGS'LL WORK OUT.
BUT THEY WERE HAPPY.
YEP, YEP!

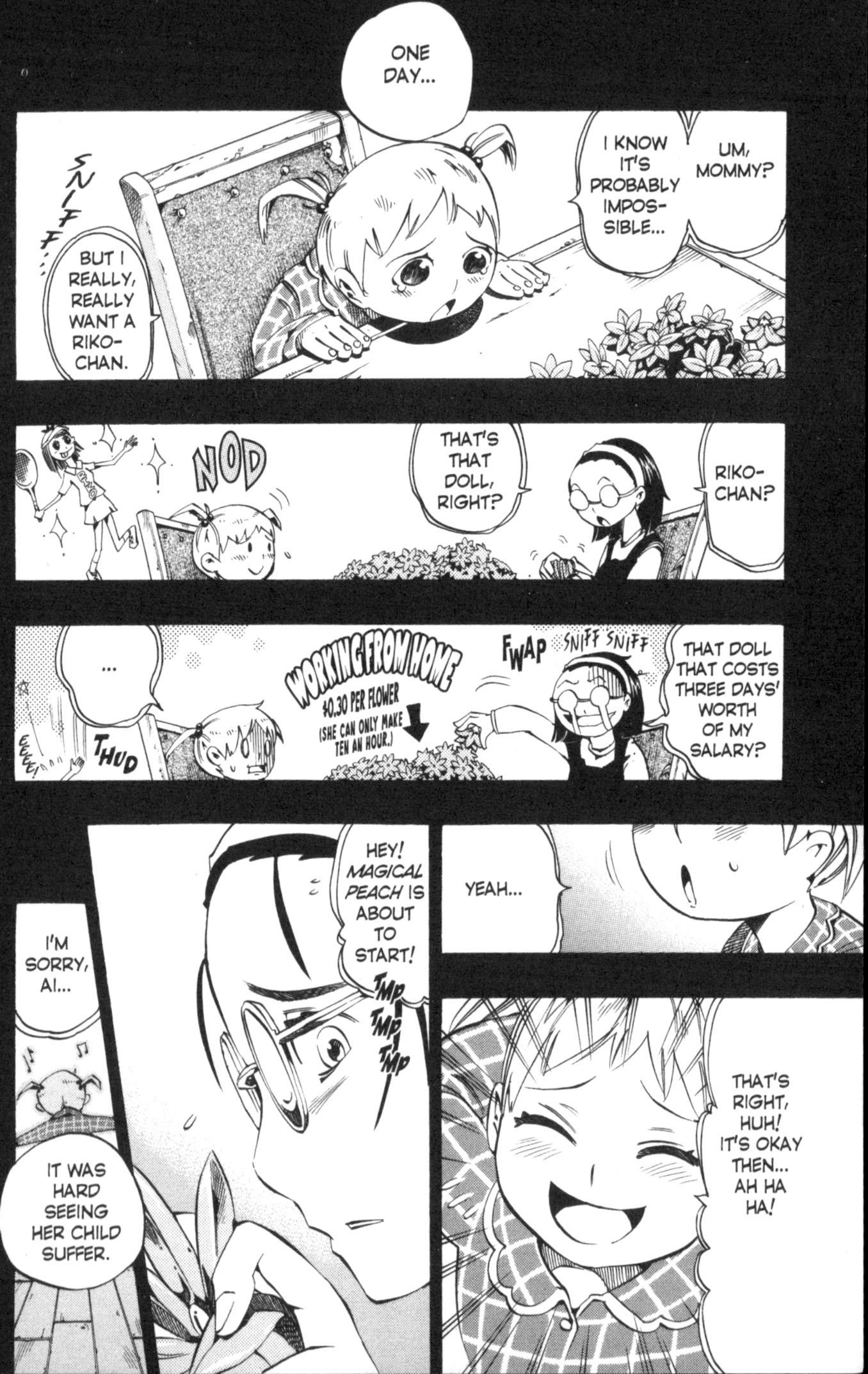
ONE DAY...
UM, MOMMY?
I KNOW IT'S PROBABLY IMPOS-SIBLE...
SNIFF...
BUT I REALLY, REALLY WANT A RIKO-CHAN.
RIKO-CHAN?
THAT'S THAT DOLL, RIGHT?
NOD
THAT DOLL THAT COSTS THREE DAYS' WORTH OF MY SALARY?
SNIFF SNIFF
FWAP
WORKING FROM HOME
$0.30 PER FLOWER
(SHE CAN ONLY MAKE TEN AN HOUR.)
...
THUD
YEAH...
THAT'S RIGHT, HUH! IT'S OKAY THEN... AH HA HA!
HEY! *MAGICAL PEACH* IS ABOUT TO START!
TMP TMP TMP
I'M SORRY, AI...
IT WAS HARD SEEING HER CHILD SUFFER.

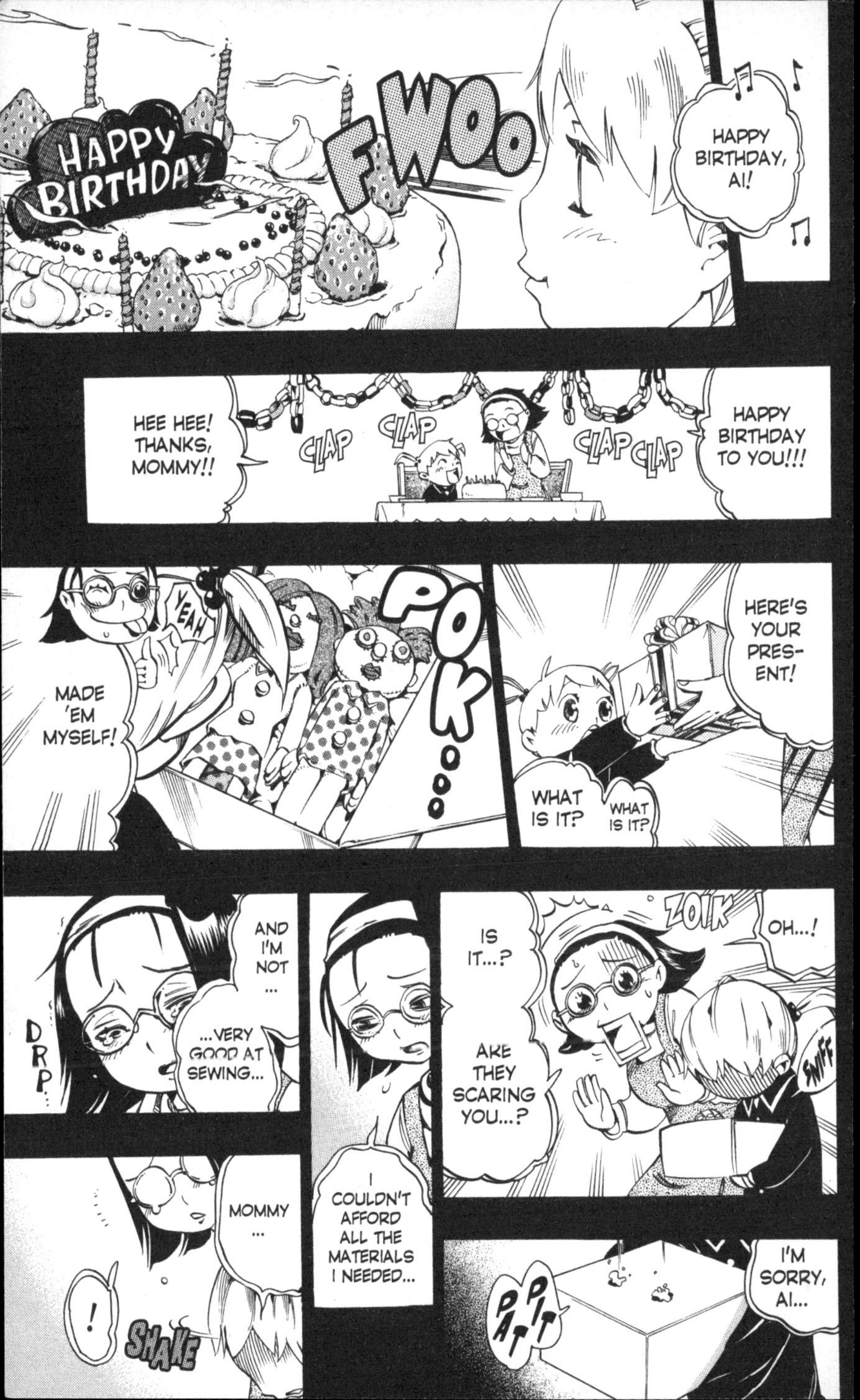
HAPPY BIRTHDAY, AI!
FWOO
HAPPY BIRTHDAY
HAPPY BIRTHDAY TO YOU!!!
CLAP CLAP
CLAP CLAP
HEE HEE! THANKS, MOMMY!!
HERE'S YOUR PRES-ENT!
WHAT IS IT?
WHAT IS IT?
POKOOO
YEAH
MADE 'EM MYSELF!
OH...!
ZOIK
IS IT...?
ARE THEY SCARING YOU...?
SNIFF
I'M SORRY, AI...
PIT PAT
I COULDN'T AFFORD ALL THE MATERIALS I NEEDED...
AND I'M NOT ...
...VERY GOOD AT SEWING...
DRP...
MOMMY ...
!
SHAKE

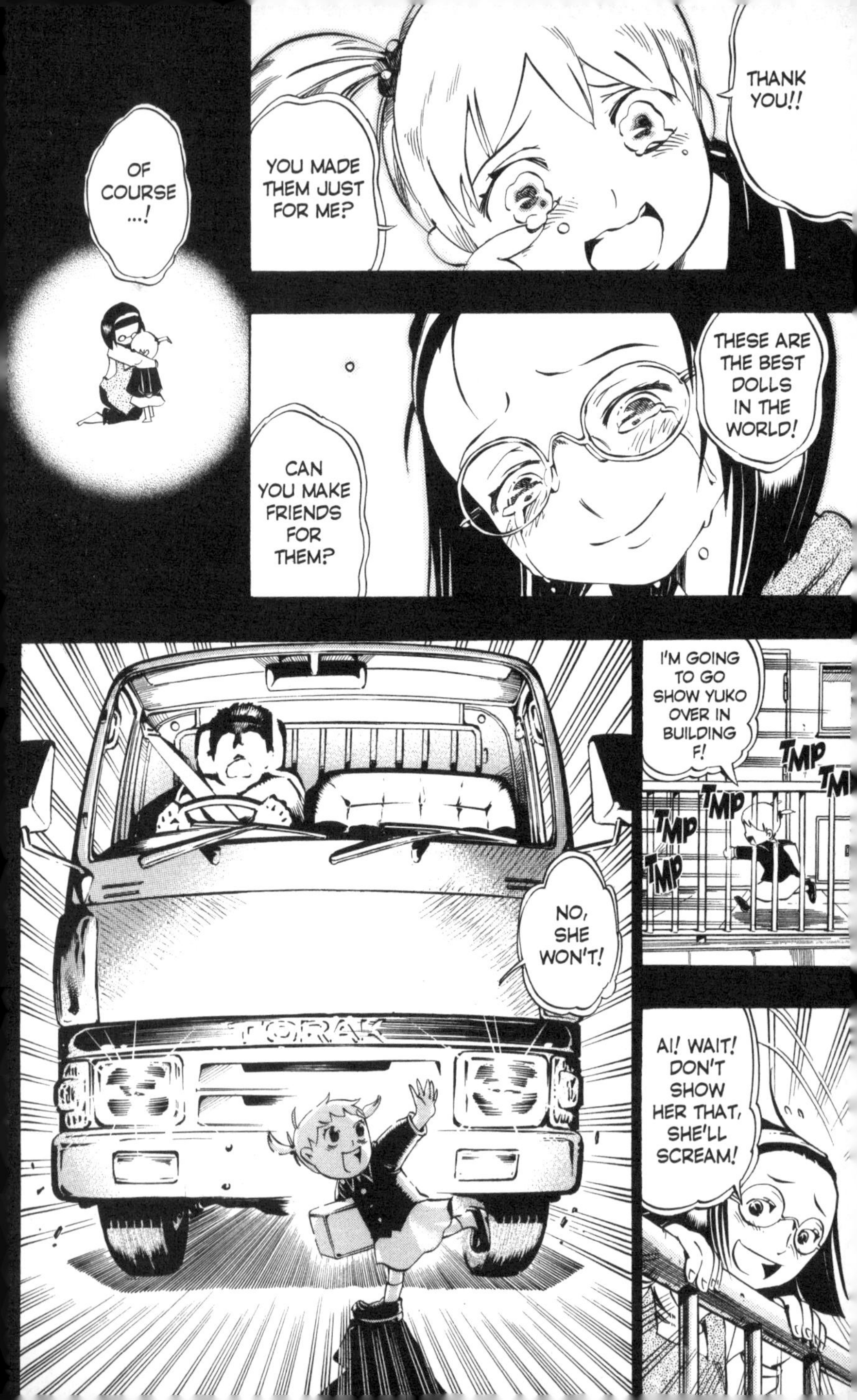
THANK YOU!!
YOU MADE THEM JUST FOR ME?
THESE ARE THE BEST DOLLS IN THE WORLD!
CAN YOU MAKE FRIENDS FOR THEM?
OF COURSE ...!
I'M GOING TO GO SHOW YUKO OVER IN BUILDING F!
TMP
TMP
TMP
TMP
AI! WAIT! DON'T SHOW HER THAT, SHE'LL SCREAM!
NO, SHE WON'T!
TORAK

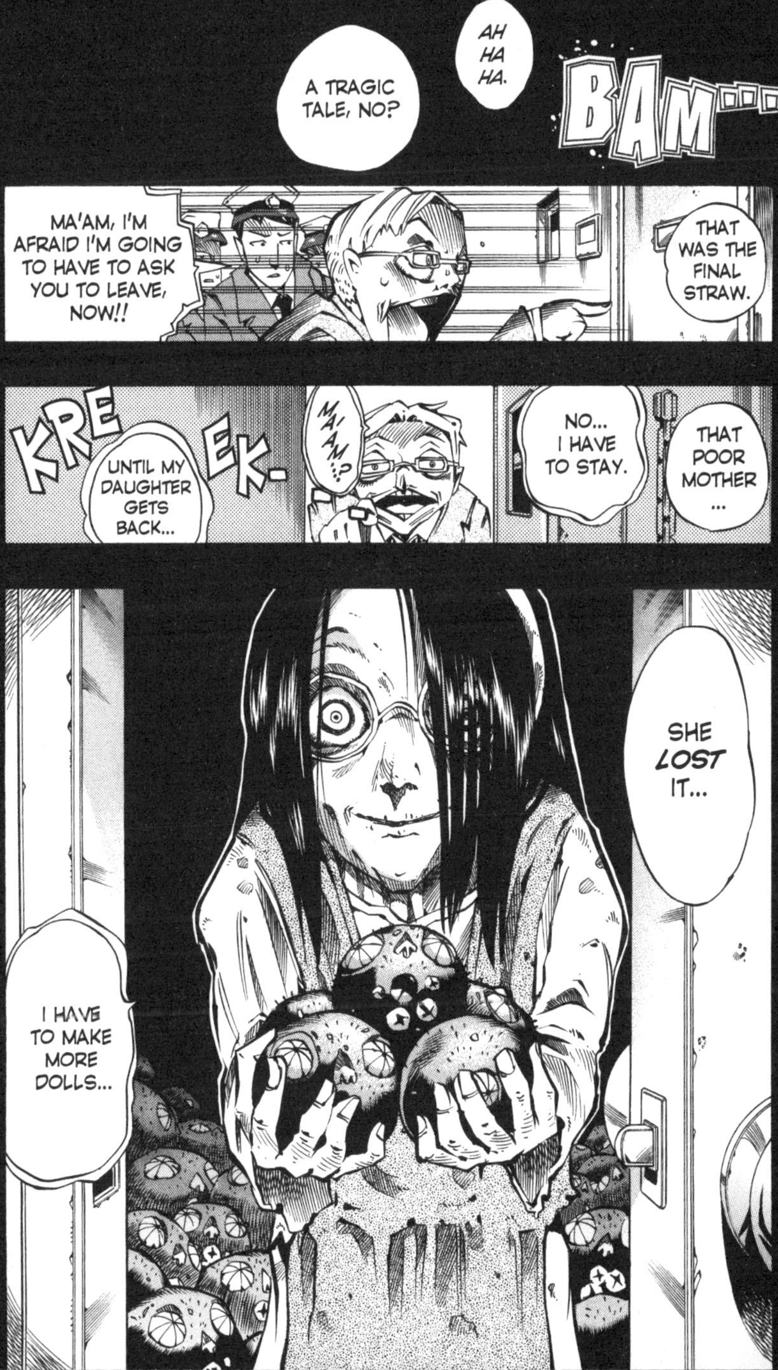
BAM...
AH HA HA.
A TRAGIC TALE, NO?
THAT WAS THE FINAL STRAW.
MA'AM, I'M AFRAID I'M GOING TO HAVE TO ASK YOU TO LEAVE, NOW!!
THAT POOR MOTHER...
NO... I HAVE TO STAY.
MA'AM...!?
KREEK-
UNTIL MY DAUGHTER GETS BACK...
SHE *LOST* IT...
I HAVE TO MAKE MORE DOLLS...

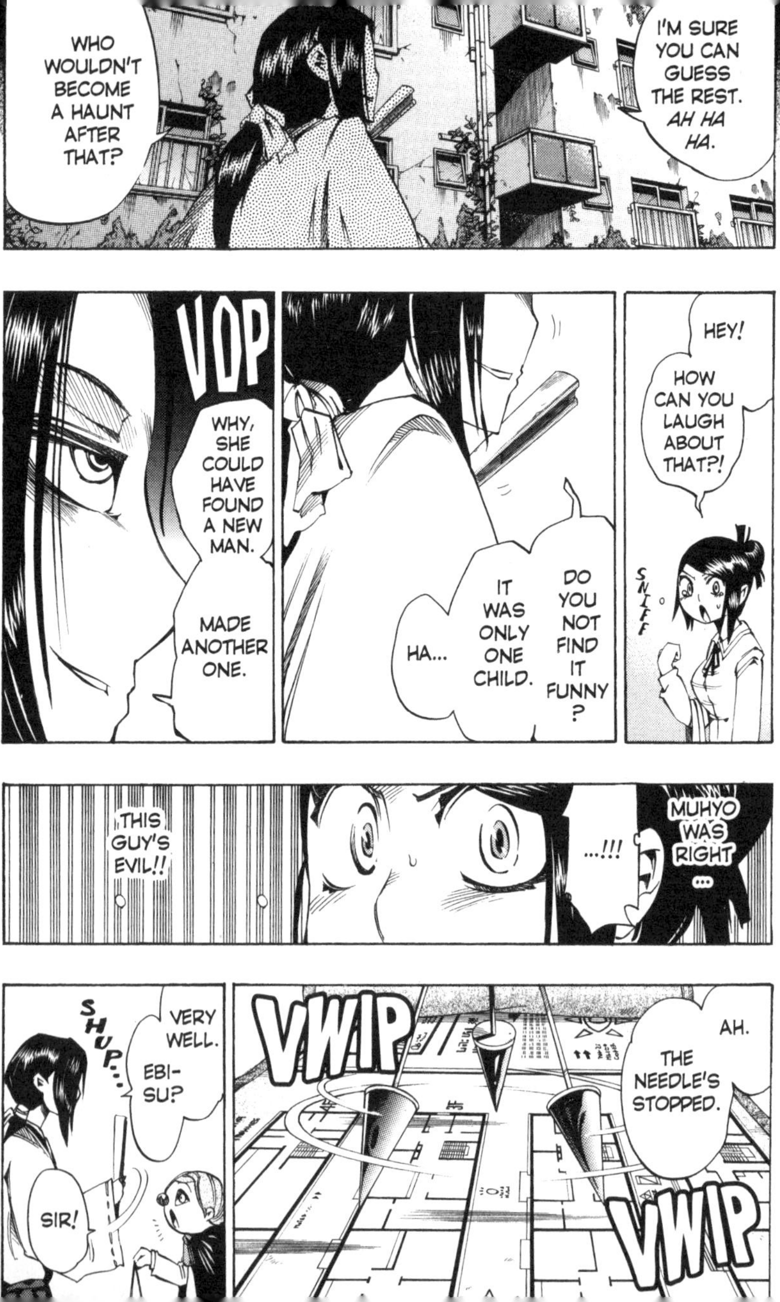
I'M SURE YOU CAN GUESS THE REST. *AH HA HA.*
WHO WOULDN'T BECOME A HAUNT AFTER THAT?
HEY!
HOW CAN YOU LAUGH ABOUT THAT?!
SNIFF
DO YOU NOT FIND IT FUNNY?
IT WAS ONLY ONE CHILD.
HA...
VOP
WHY, SHE COULD HAVE FOUND A NEW MAN.
MADE ANOTHER ONE.
MUHYO WAS RIGHT...
...!!!
THIS GUY'S EVIL!!
AH.
THE NEEDLE'S STOPPED.
VWIP
VWIP
VERY WELL.
EBI-SU?
SHUP...
SIR!

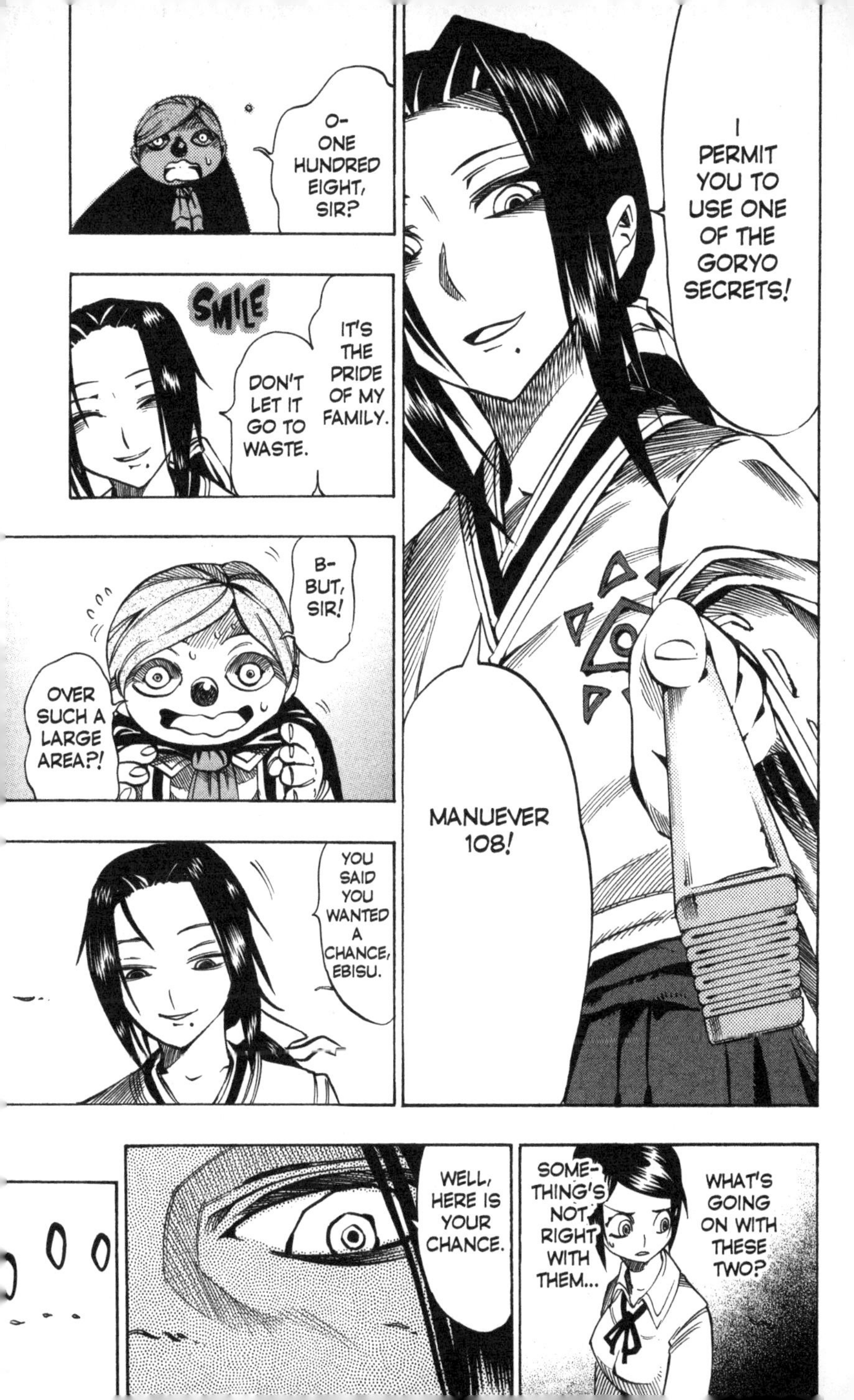
I PERMIT YOU TO USE ONE OF THE GORYO SECRETS!
MANUEVER 108!
O-ONE HUNDRED EIGHT, SIR?
SMILE
IT'S THE PRIDE OF MY FAMILY.
DON'T LET IT GO TO WASTE.
B-BUT, SIR!
OVER SUCH A LARGE AREA?!
YOU SAID YOU WANTED A CHANCE, EBISU.
WHAT'S GOING ON WITH THESE TWO?
SOME-THING'S NOT RIGHT WITH THEM...
WELL, HERE IS YOUR CHANCE.

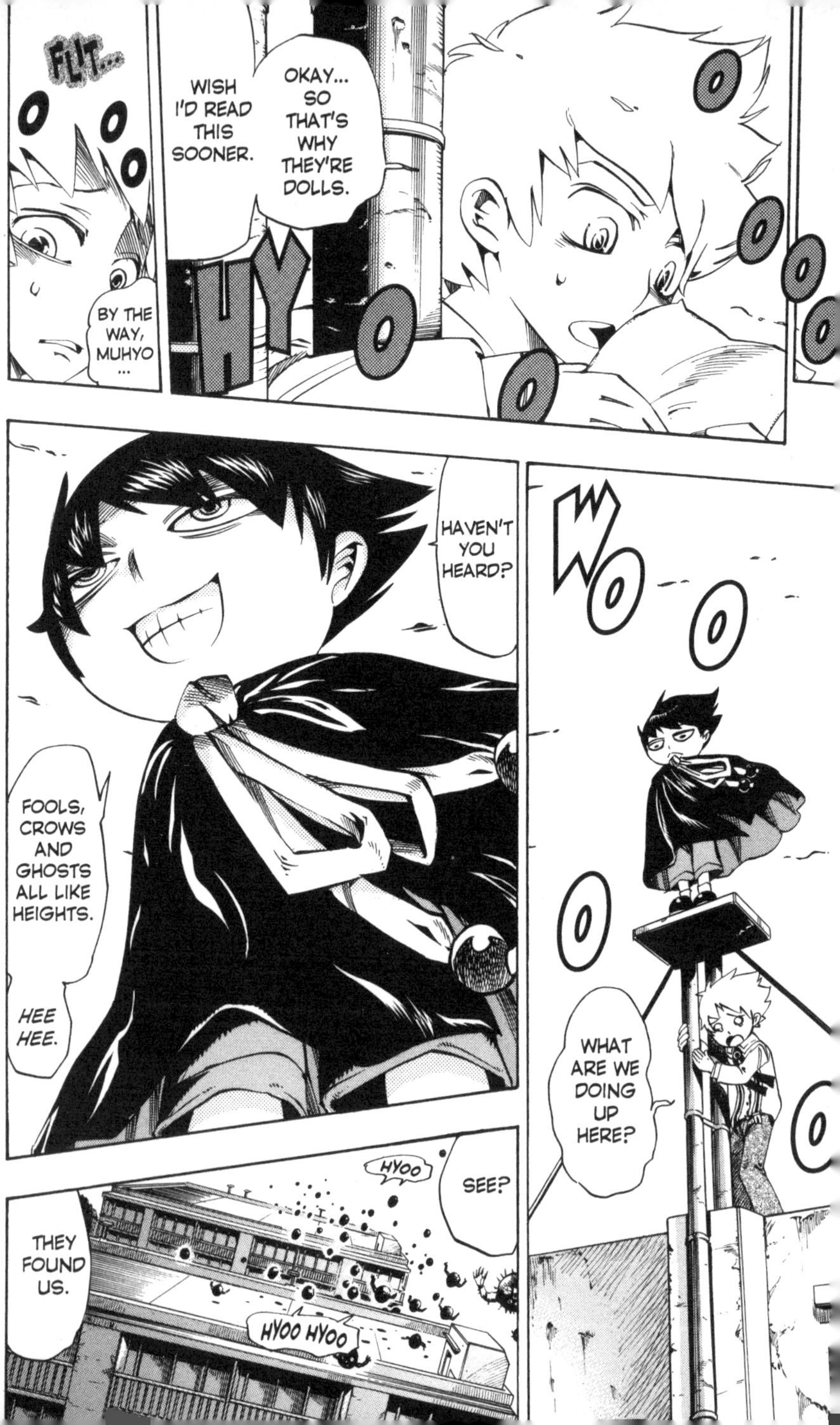
OKAY... SO THAT'S WHY THEY'RE DOLLS.
WISH I'D READ THIS SOONER.
HYOOOOOOOO
FLIT...
OOO
BY THE WAY, MUHYO...
WOOOO
WHAT ARE WE DOING UP HERE?
HAVEN'T YOU HEARD?
FOOLS, CROWS AND GHOSTS ALL LIKE HEIGHTS.
HEE HEE.
SEE?
HYOO
HYOO HYOO
THEY FOUND US.

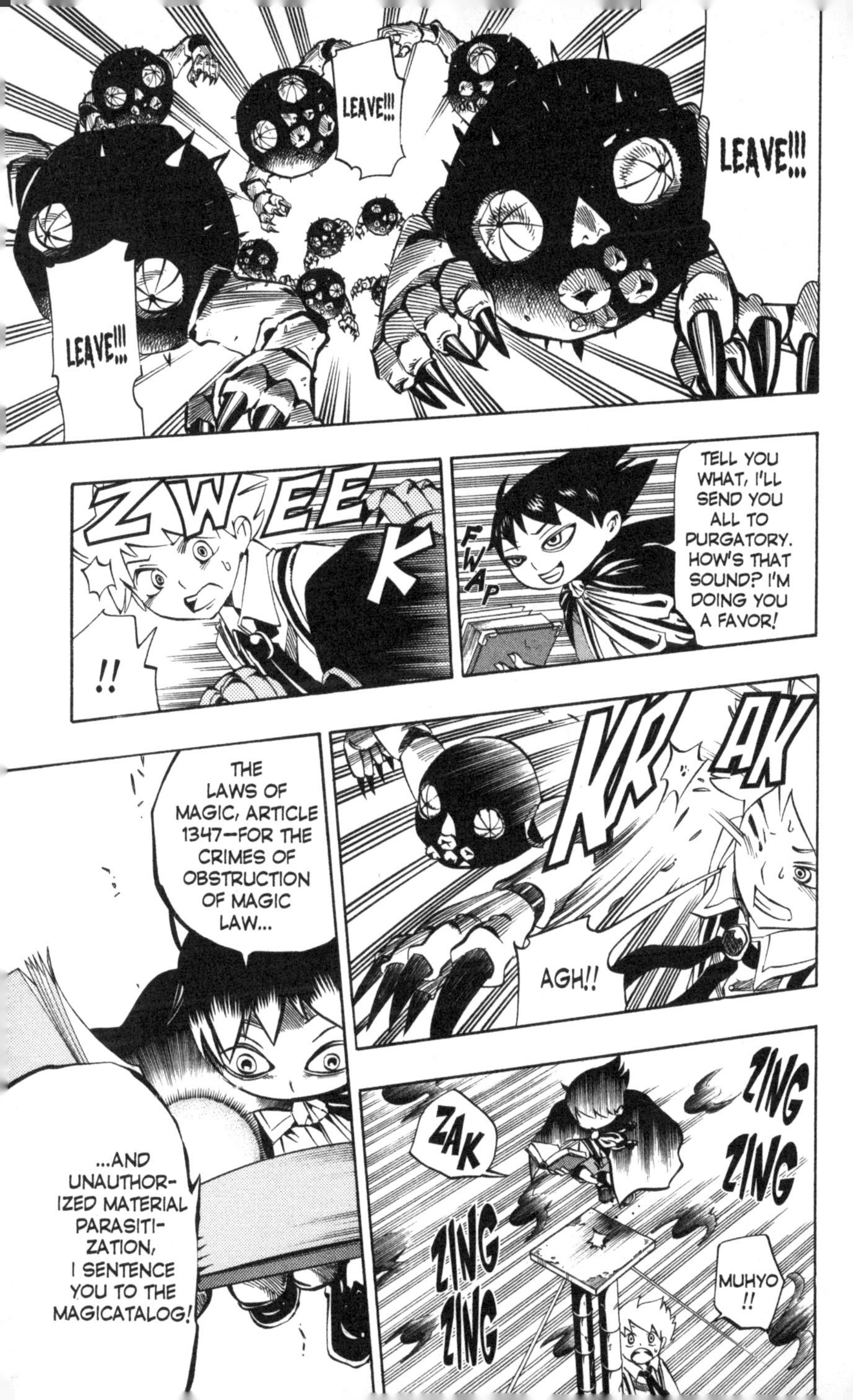
LEAVE!!!
LEAVE!!!
LEAVE!!!
FWAP
TELL YOU WHAT, I'LL SEND YOU ALL TO PURGATORY. HOW'S THAT SOUND? I'M DOING YOU A FAVOR!
ZWEEK
!!
KRAK
AGH!!
ZING ZING
ZAK
ZING ZING
MUHYO!!
THE LAWS OF MAGIC, ARTICLE 1347—FOR THE CRIMES OF OBSTRUCTION OF MAGIC LAW...
...AND UNAUTHORIZED MATERIAL PARASITIZATION, I SENTENCE YOU TO THE MAGICATALOG!

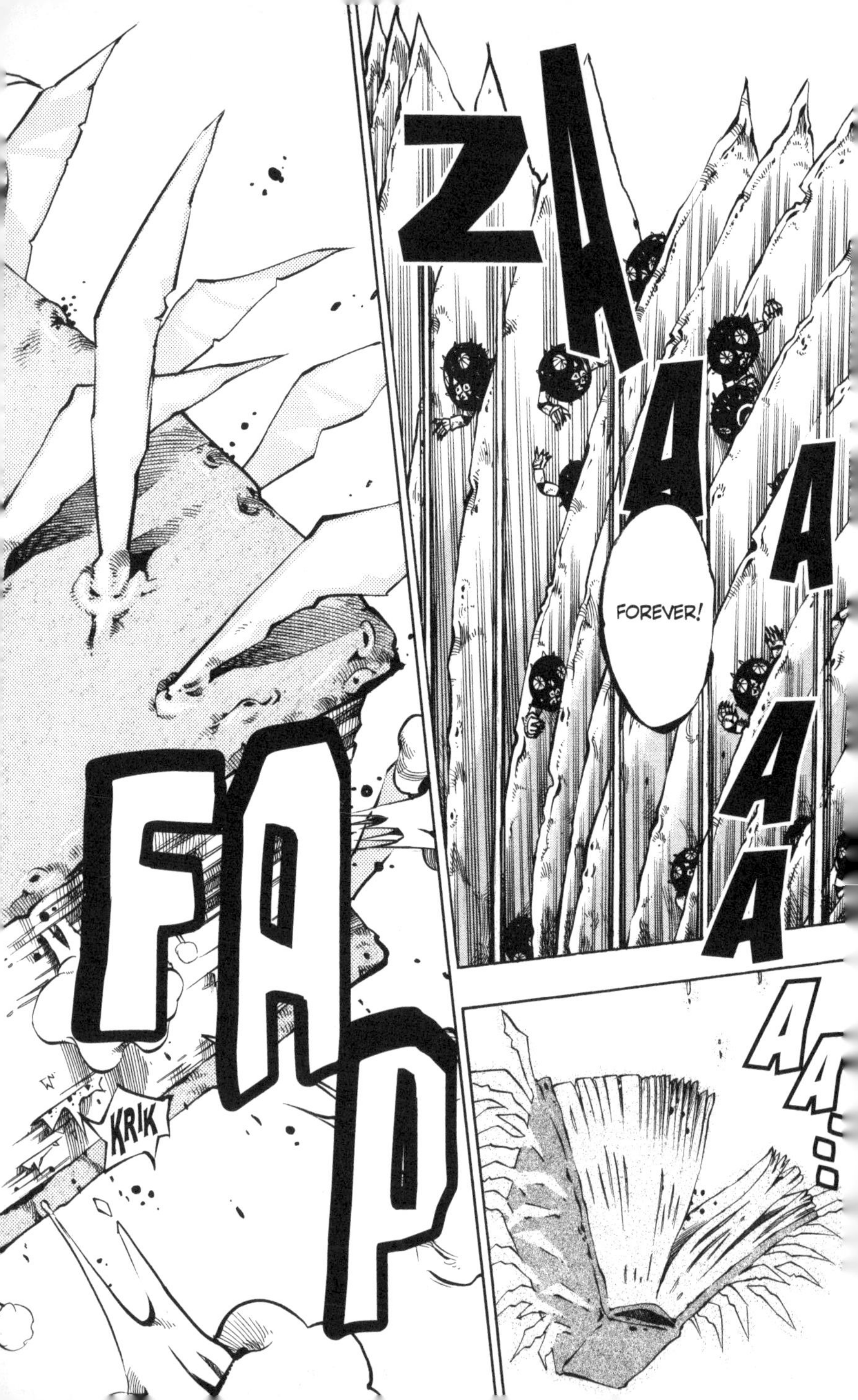
ZAAAAAA
FOREVER!
AAOOO
FAP
KRIK

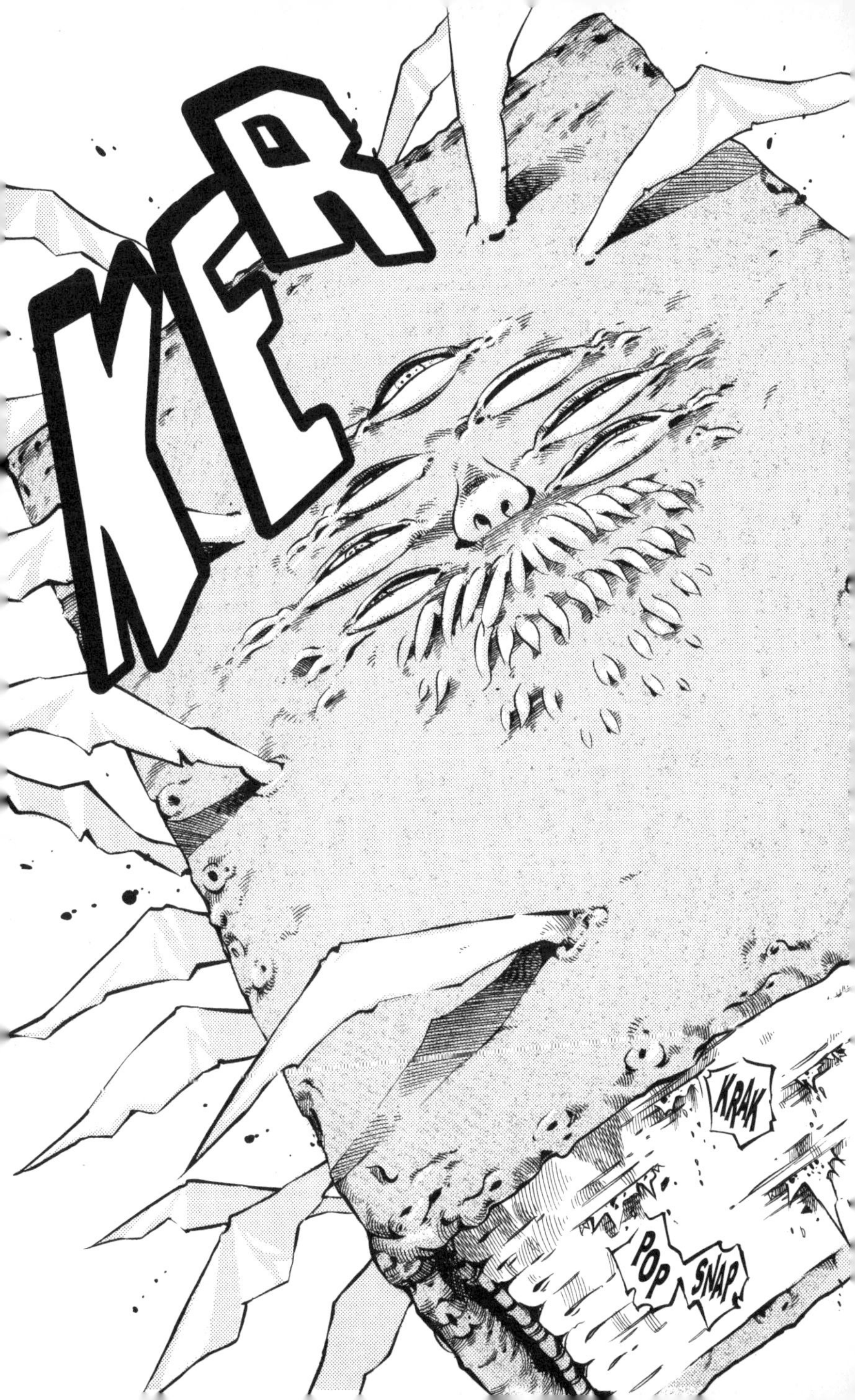
KFR
KRAK
SNAP
POP

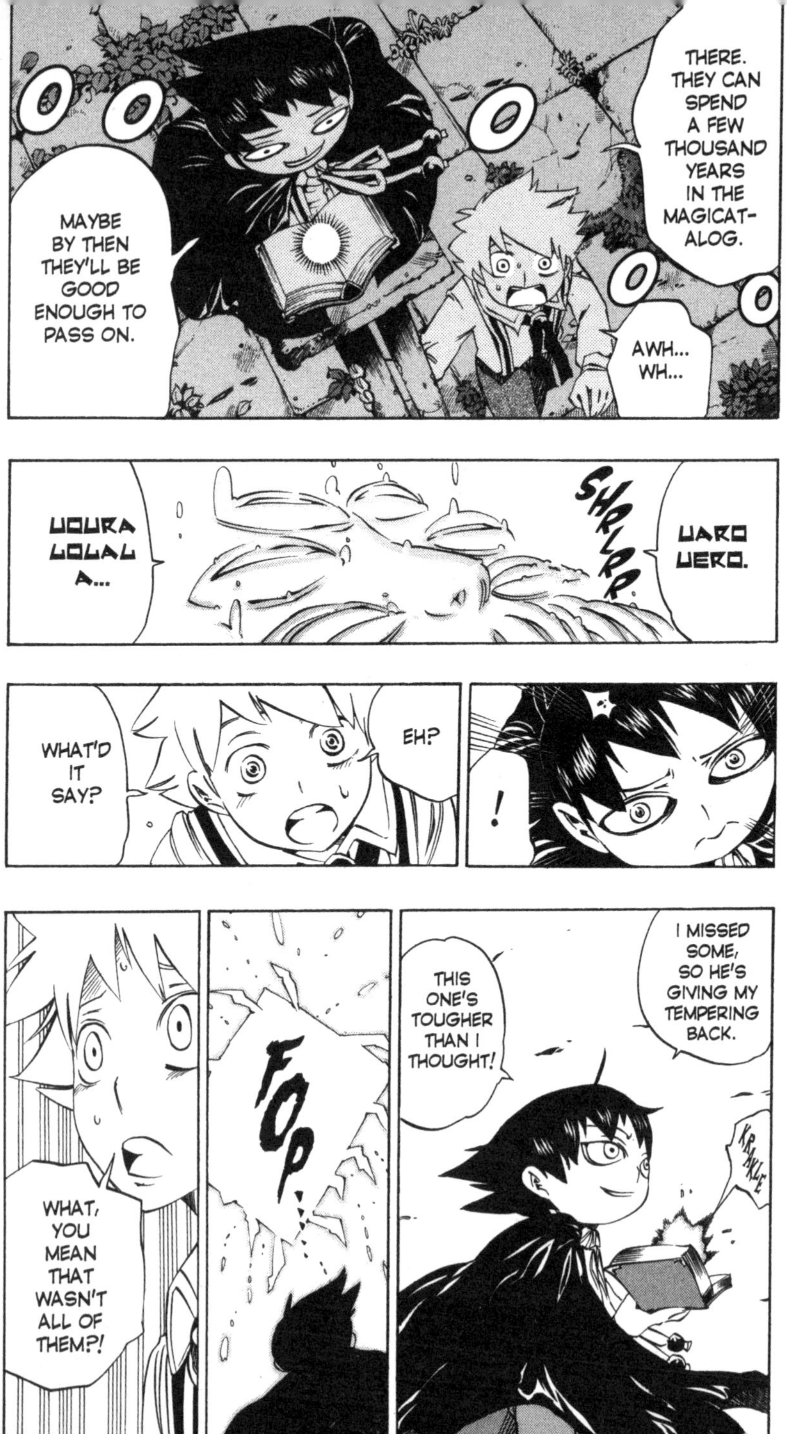
THERE. THEY CAN SPEND A FEW THOUSAND YEARS IN THE MAGICAT-ALOG.
MAYBE BY THEN THEY'LL BE GOOD ENOUGH TO PASS ON.
AWH... WH...
UARO UERO.
SHRLRR
UOURA LOULAL A...
!
EH?
WHAT'D IT SAY?
I MISSED SOME, SO HE'S GIVING MY TEMPERING BACK.
THIS ONE'S TOUGHER THAN I THOUGHT!
KRAKLE
FOP
WHAT, YOU MEAN THAT WASN'T ALL OF THEM?!

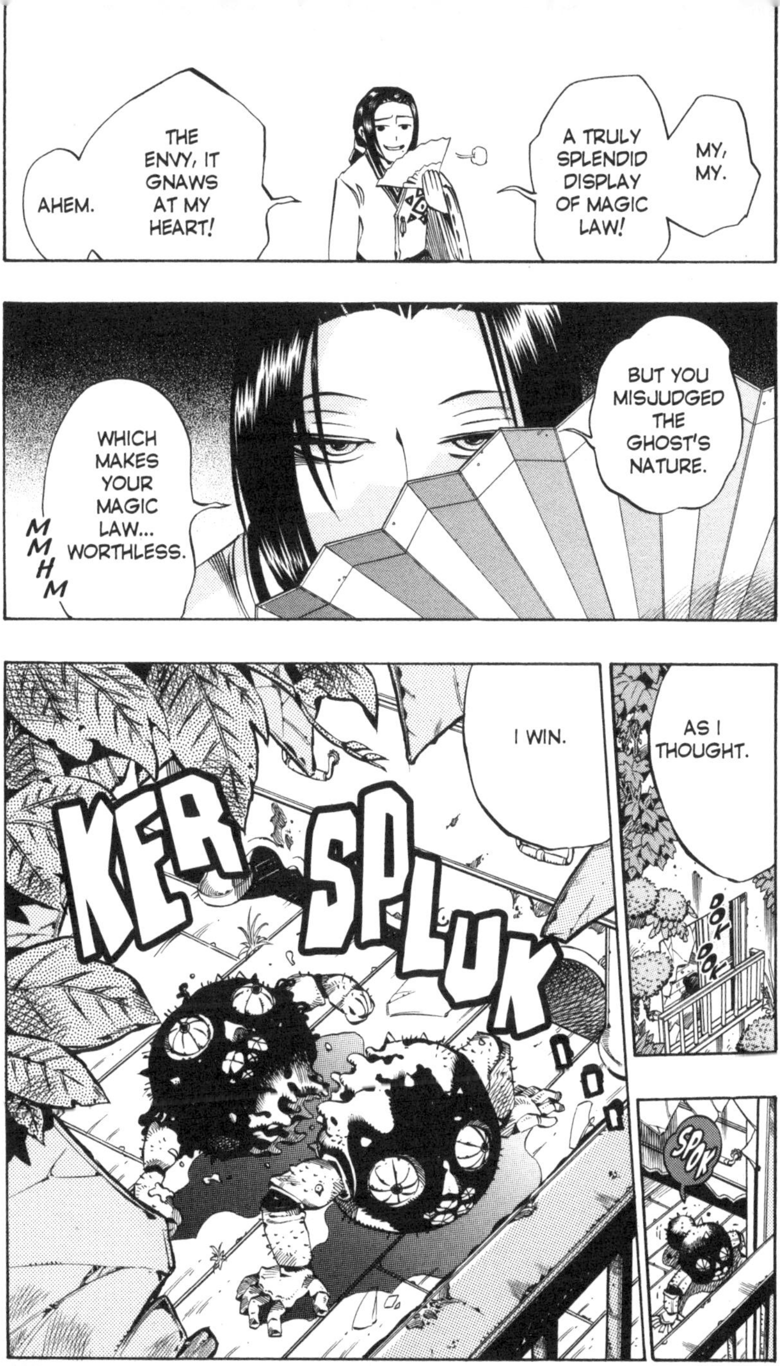

MY, MY.
A TRULY SPLENDID DISPLAY OF MAGIC LAW!
THE ENVY, IT GNAWS AT MY HEART!
AHEM.
BUT YOU MISJUDGED THE GHOST'S NATURE.
WHICH MAKES YOUR MAGIC LAW... WORTHLESS.
MMHM
AS I THOUGHT.
DOK DOK
SPOK
I WIN.
KER SPLUK

VOLUME 5: SWALLOWS IN THE WIND (THE END)

MUHYO & ROJI'S BUREAU OF SUPERNATURAL INVESTIGATION: BONUS STORY

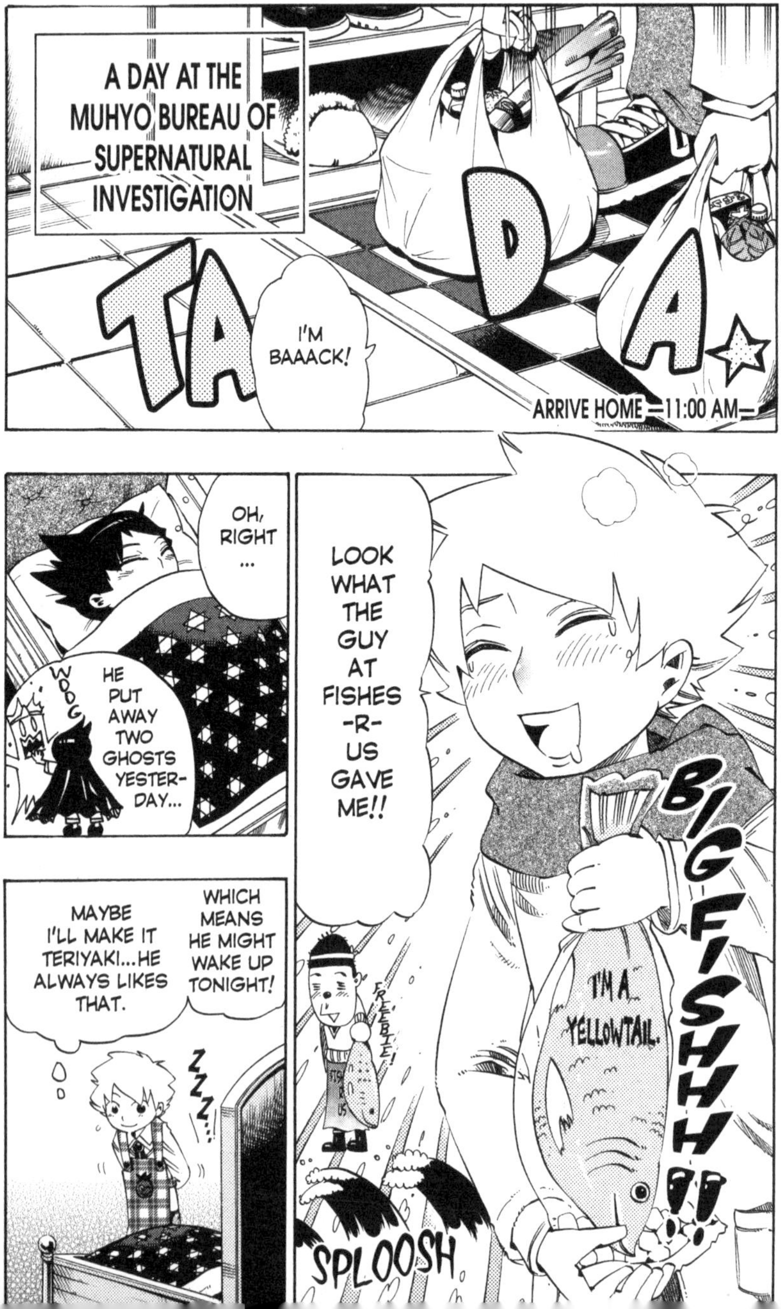
A DAY AT THE MUHYO BUREAU OF SUPERNATURAL INVESTIGATION
TA
D
A
I'M BAAACK!
ARRIVE HOME —11:00 AM—
LOOK WHAT THE GUY AT FISHES-R-US GAVE ME!!
BIG FISHHHH!!
FREEBIE!
FISH R US
I'M A YELLOWTAIL.
SPLOOSH
OH, RIGHT...
HE PUT AWAY TWO GHOSTS YESTERDAY...
WOOG
WHICH MEANS HE MIGHT WAKE UP TONIGHT!
MAYBE I'LL MAKE IT TERIYAKI...HE ALWAYS LIKES THAT.
ZZZ

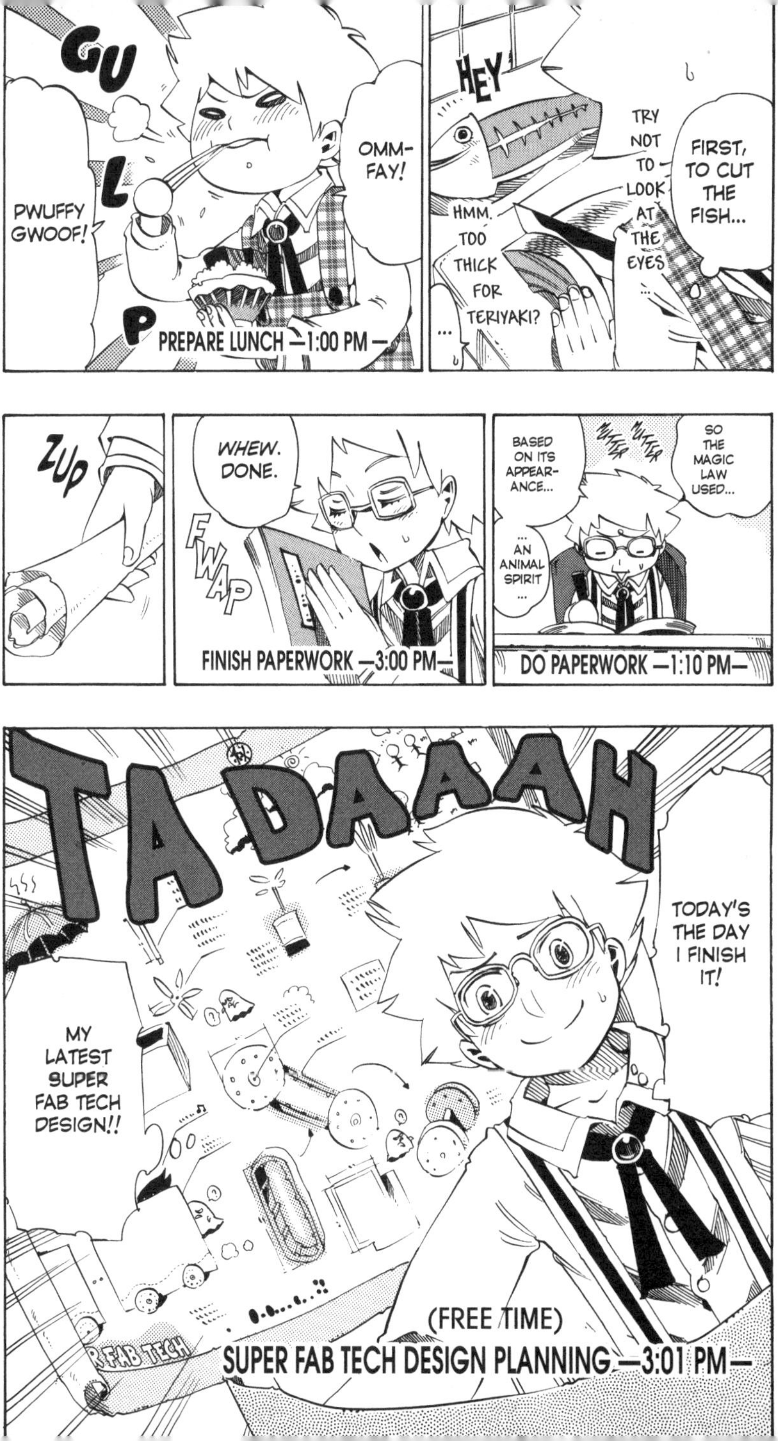
HEY
FIRST, TO CUT THE FISH...
TRY NOT TO LOOK AT THE EYES
HMM. TOO THICK FOR TERIYAKI?
...
GULP
OMM-FAY!
PWUFFY GWOOF!
PREPARE LUNCH —1:00 PM—
DO PAPERWORK —1:10 PM—
MUTTER MUTTER
SO THE MAGIC LAW USED...
BASED ON ITS APPEARANCE...
... AN ANIMAL SPIRIT ...
WHEW. DONE.
FWAP
FINISH PAPERWORK —3:00 PM—
ZUP
TADAAAH
TODAY'S THE DAY I FINISH IT!
MY LATEST SUPER FAB TECH DESIGN!!
R FAB TECH
(FREE TIME)
SUPER FAB TECH DESIGN PLANNING —3:01 PM—

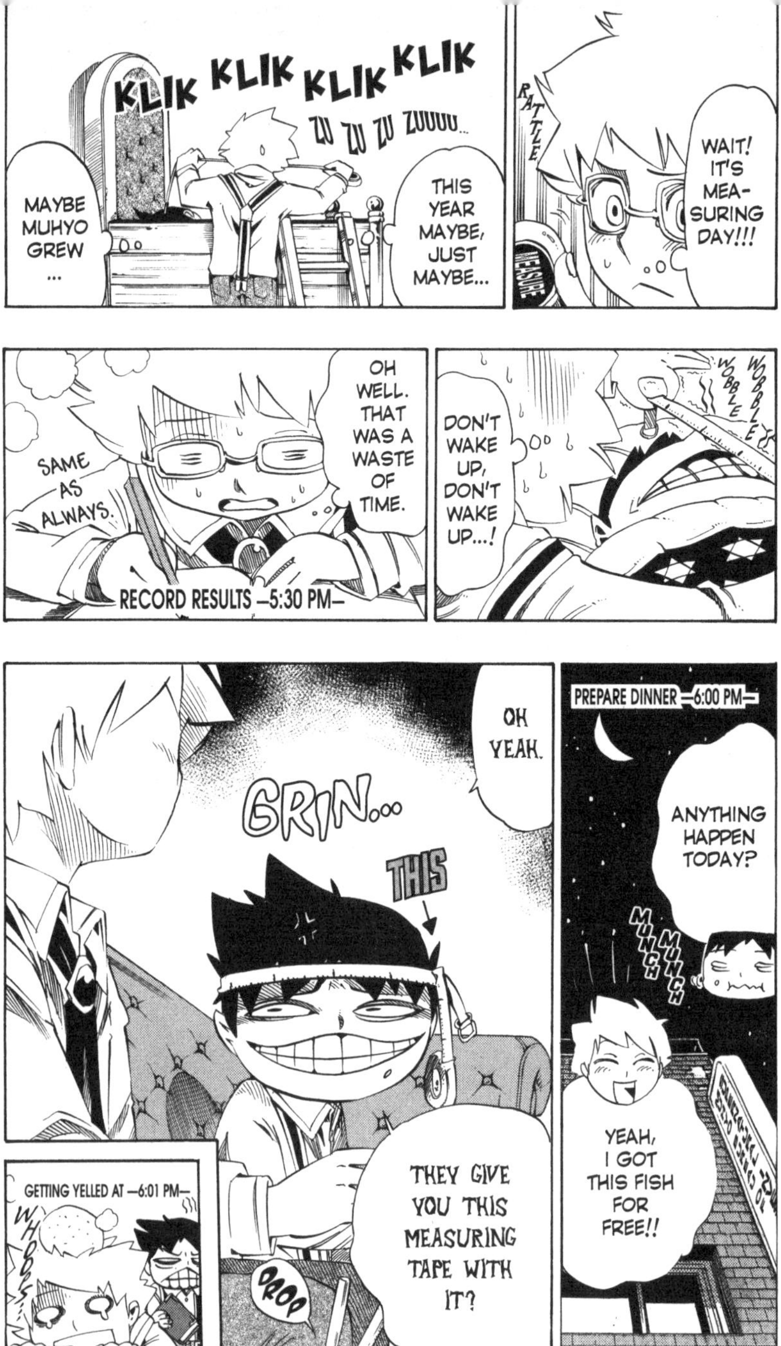
RATTLE
MEASURE
WAIT! IT'S MEA-SURING DAY!!!
KLIK KLIK KLIK KLIK
ZU ZU ZU ZUUUUU...
THIS YEAR MAYBE, JUST MAYBE...
MAYBE MUHYO GREW ...
WOBBLE WOBBLE
DON'T WAKE UP, DON'T WAKE UP...!
OH WELL. THAT WAS A WASTE OF TIME.
SAME AS ALWAYS.
RECORD RESULTS —5:30 PM—
PREPARE DINNER —6:00 PM—
ANYTHING HAPPEN TODAY?
MUNCH MUNCH
YEAH, I GOT THIS FISH FOR FREE!!
OH YEAH.
GRIN...
THIS
THEY GIVE YOU THIS MEASURING TAPE WITH IT?
DROP
GETTING YELLED AT —6:01 PM—

MUHYO & ROJI'S BUREAU OF SUPERNATURAL INVESTIGATION: BONUS STORY (THE END)

(FROM THE PAGES OF AKAMARU)
BONUS MANGA

ROJI'S RECIPE

GETTING SAUCY

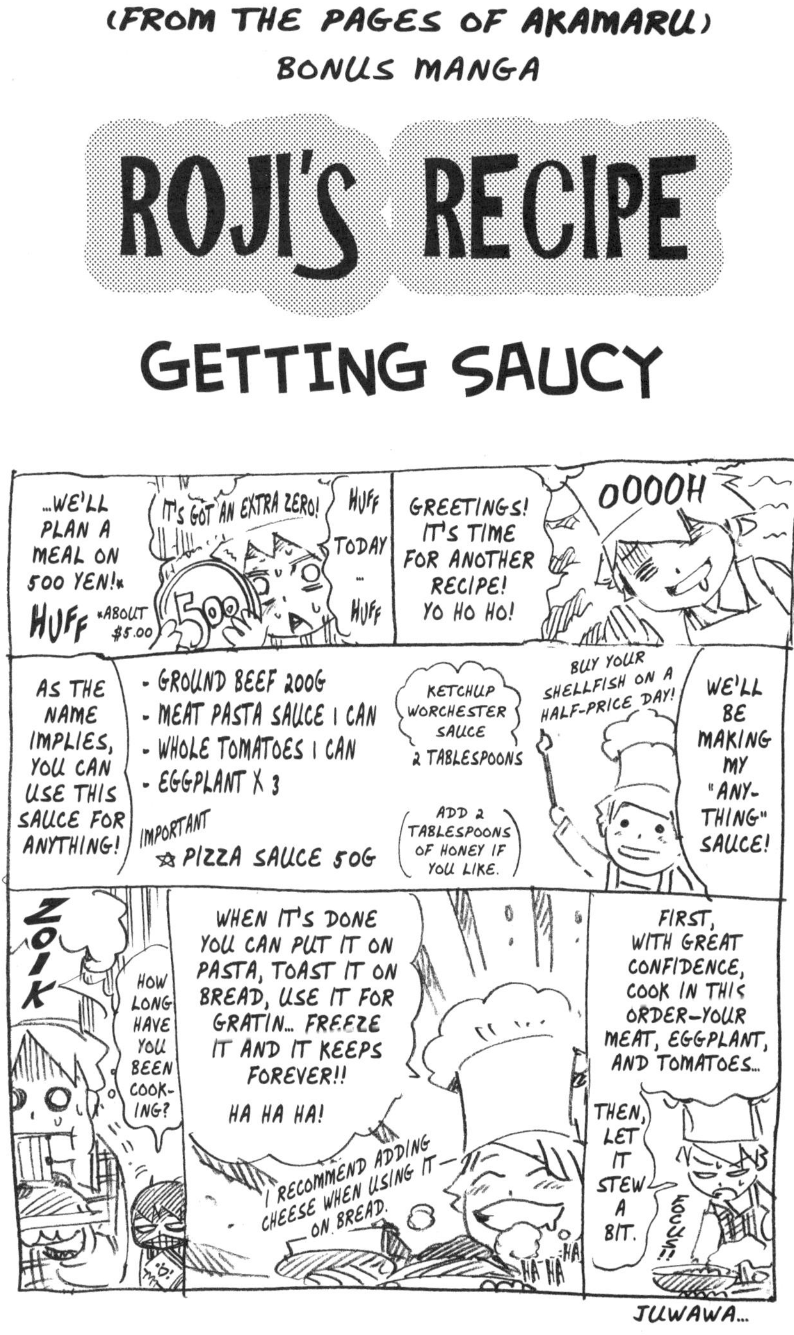
OOOOH
GREETINGS! IT'S TIME FOR ANOTHER RECIPE! YO HO HO!
HUFF
TODAY...
HUFF
...WE'LL PLAN A MEAL ON 500 YEN!*
HUFF
IT'S GOT AN EXTRA ZERO!
500
*ABOUT $5.00
WE'LL BE MAKING MY "ANY-THING" SAUCE!
BUY YOUR SHELLFISH ON A HALF-PRICE DAY!
KETCHUP WORCHESTER SAUCE 2 TABLESPOONS
ADD 2 TABLESPOONS OF HONEY IF YOU LIKE.
- GROUND BEEF 200G
- MEAT PASTA SAUCE 1 CAN
- WHOLE TOMATOES 1 CAN
- EGGPLANT X 3
IMPORTANT
☆ PIZZA SAUCE 50G
AS THE NAME IMPLIES, YOU CAN USE THIS SAUCE FOR ANYTHING!
FIRST, WITH GREAT CONFIDENCE, COOK IN THIS ORDER—YOUR MEAT, EGGPLANT, AND TOMATOES...
THEN, LET IT STEW A BIT.
FOCUS!!
JUWAWA...
WHEN IT'S DONE YOU CAN PUT IT ON PASTA, TOAST IT ON BREAD, USE IT FOR GRATIN... FREEZE IT AND IT KEEPS FOREVER!!
HA HA HA!
I RECOMMEND ADDING CHEESE WHEN USING IT ON BREAD.
HA HA HA
ZOIK
HOW LONG HAVE YOU BEEN COOKING?

In The Next Volume...

Muhyo and Roji face off against rival practitioners Goryo and Ebisu at a haunted apartment! Which magical duo will come out on top?

Available August 2008!

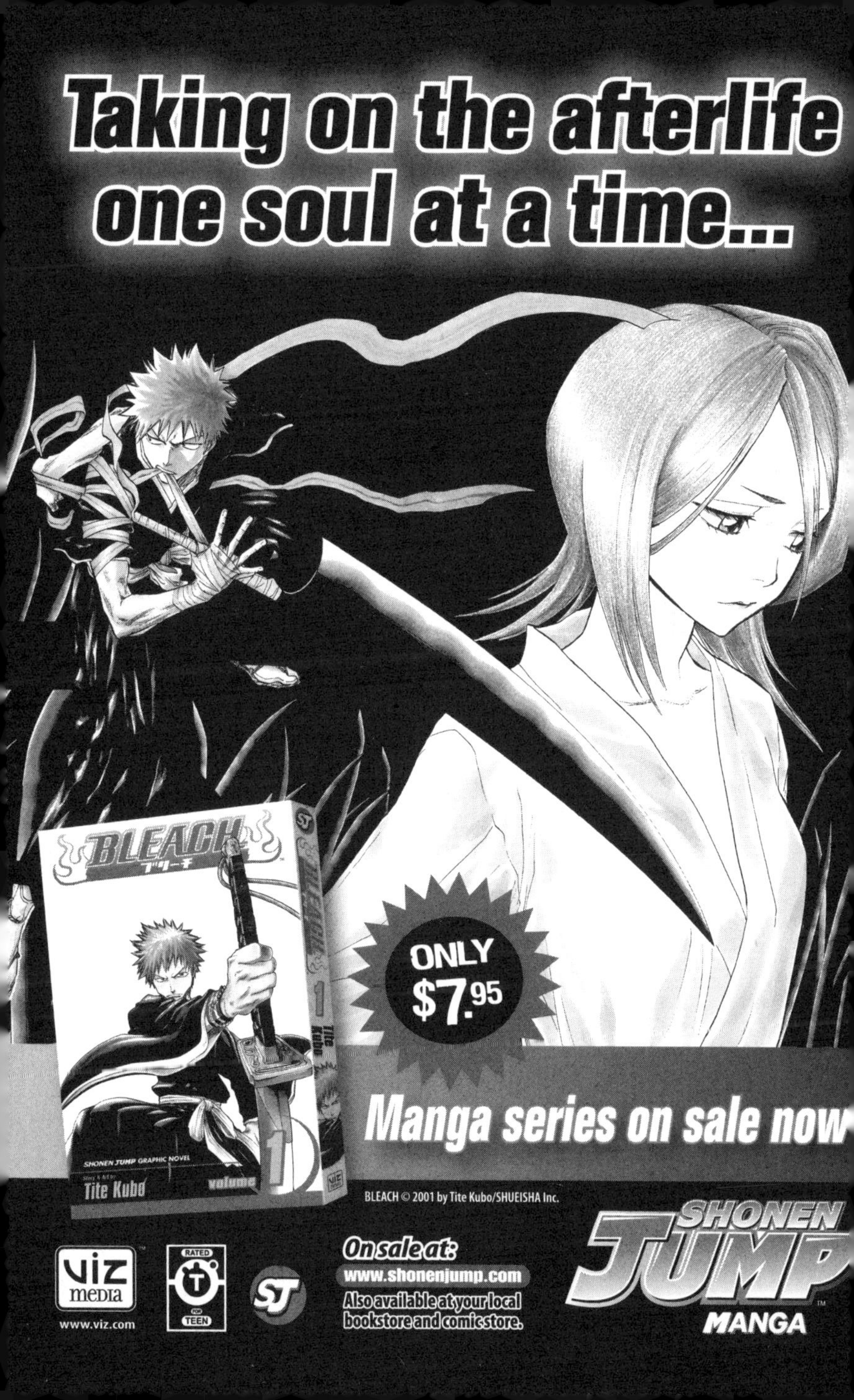
Taking on the afterlife one soul at a time...
BLEACH
ブリーチ
SHONEN JUMP GRAPHIC NOVEL
Story & Art by
Tite Kubo
volume 1
ONLY $7.95
Manga series on sale now
BLEACH © 2001 by Tite Kubo/SHUEISHA Inc.
SHONEN JUMP MANGA
On sale at:
www.shonenjump.com
Also available at your local bookstore and comic store.
viz media
www.viz.com
RATED T FOR TEEN
SJ

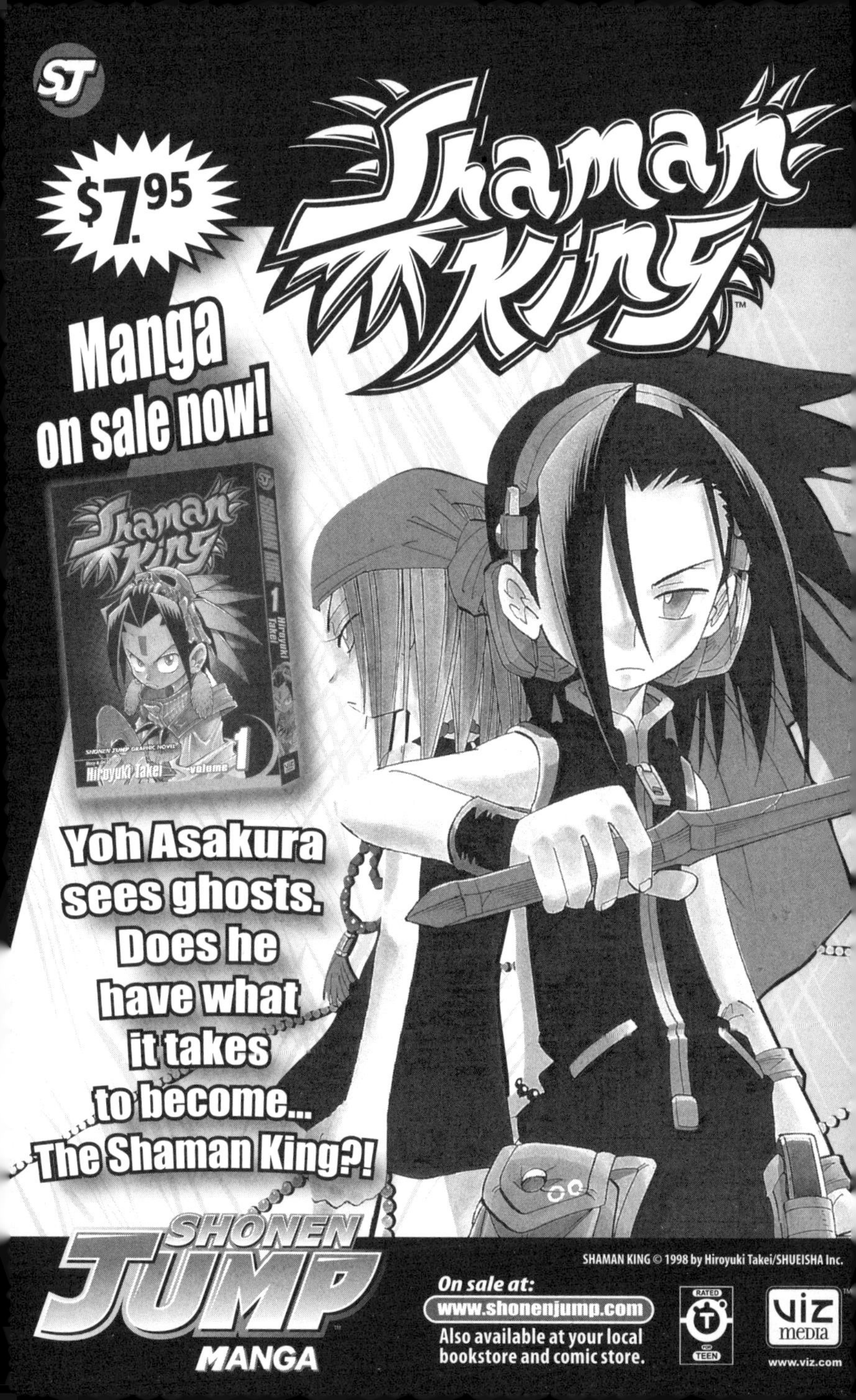
SJ
$7.95
Shaman King™
Manga on sale now!
Shaman King
SHONEN JUMP GRAPHIC NOVEL
Hiroyuki Takei
volume 1
Yoh Asakura sees ghosts. Does he have what it takes to become... The Shaman King?!
SHONEN JUMP™ MANGA
SHAMAN KING © 1998 by Hiroyuki Takei/SHUEISHA Inc.
On sale at:
www.shonenjump.com
Also available at your local bookstore and comic store.
RATED T FOR TEEN
VIZ media
www.viz.com

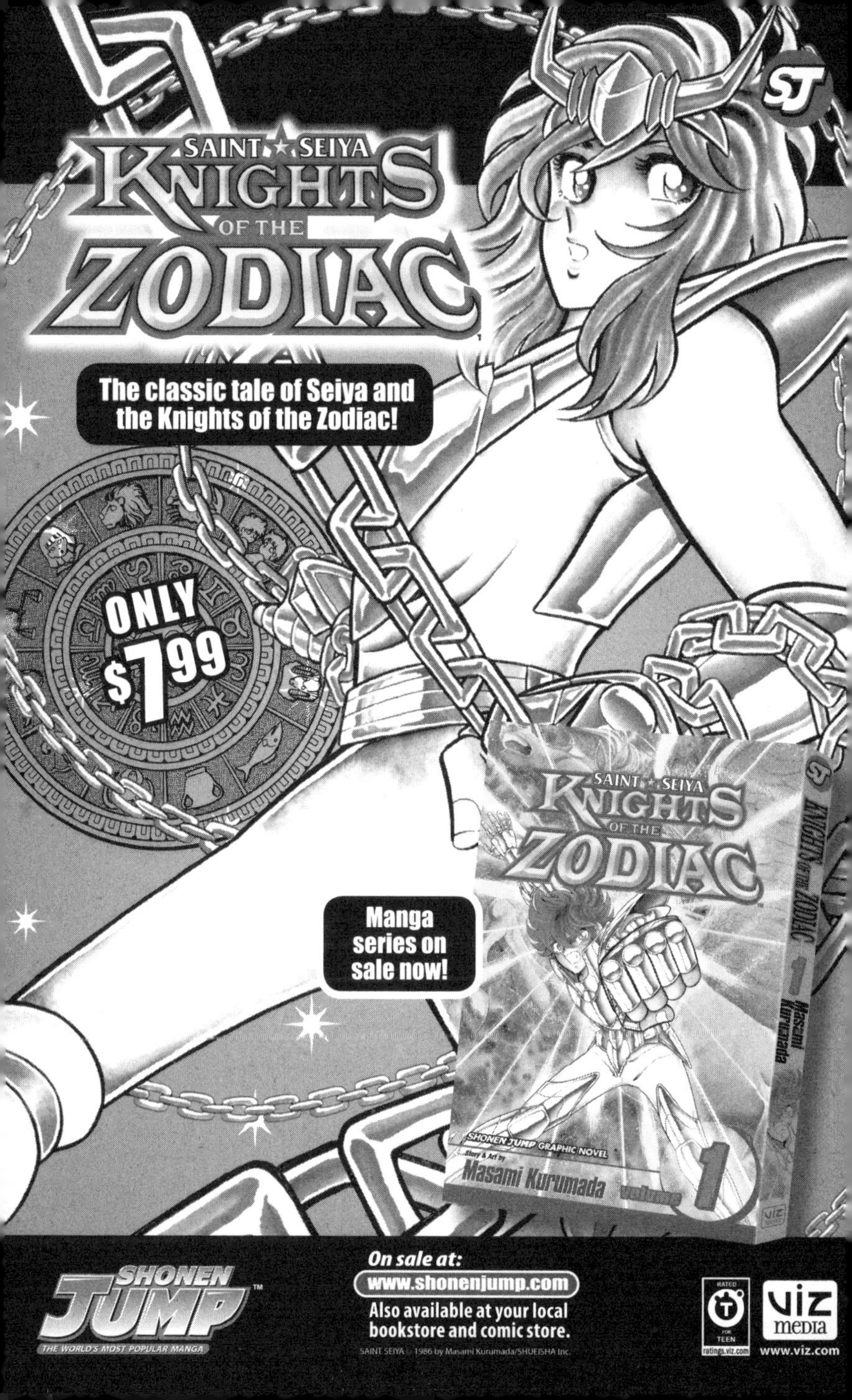
SJ
SAINT ★ SEIYA
KNIGHTS OF THE ZODIAC
The classic tale of Seiya and the Knights of the Zodiac!
ONLY $7.99
SAINT ★ SEIYA
KNIGHTS OF THE ZODIAC
SHONEN JUMP GRAPHIC NOVEL
Story & Art by
Masami Kurumada
volume 1
Manga series on sale now!
SHONEN JUMP
THE WORLD'S MOST POPULAR MANGA
On sale at:
www.shonenjump.com
Also available at your local bookstore and comic store.
SAINT SEIYA © 1986 by Masami Kurumada/SHUEISHA Inc.
RATED T FOR TEEN
ratings.viz.com
VIZ media
www.viz.com

Tell us what you think about SHONEN JUMP manga!

Our survey is now available online.
Go to: www.SHONENJUMP.com/mangasurvey

Help us make our product offering better!

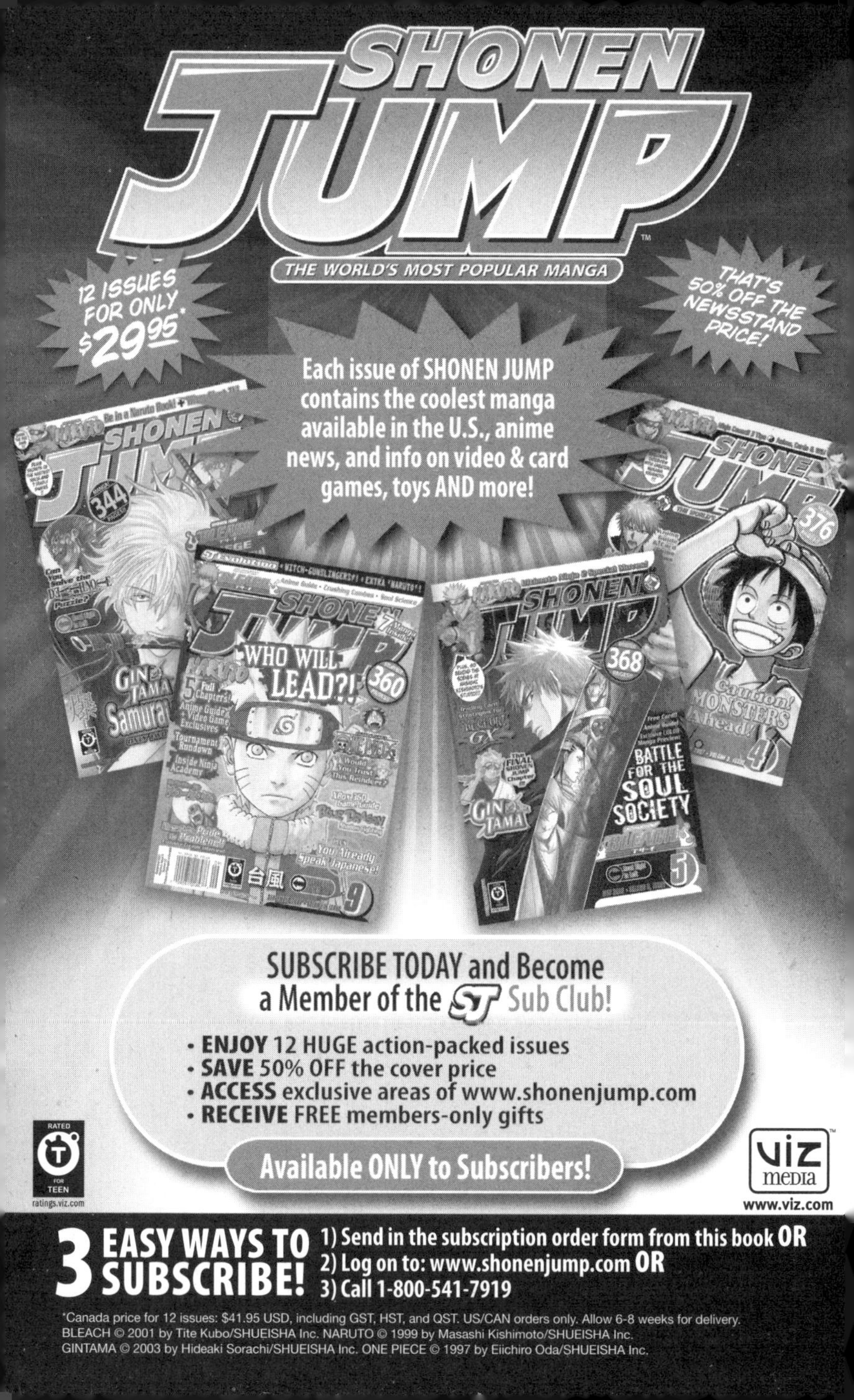
SHONEN JUMP
THE WORLD'S MOST POPULAR MANGA
12 ISSUES FOR ONLY $29.95*
THAT'S 50% OFF THE NEWSSTAND PRICE!
Each issue of SHONEN JUMP contains the coolest manga available in the U.S., anime news, and info on video & card games, toys AND more!
WHO WILL LEAD?!
344
360
368
376
Gin Tama
Samurai
Caution! MONSTERS Ahead!
BATTLE FOR THE SOUL SOCIETY
SUBSCRIBE TODAY and Become a Member of the SJ Sub Club!
• ENJOY 12 HUGE action-packed issues
• SAVE 50% OFF the cover price
• ACCESS exclusive areas of www.shonenjump.com
• RECEIVE FREE members-only gifts
Available ONLY to Subscribers!
RATED T FOR TEEN
ratings.viz.com
VIZ media
www.viz.com
3 EASY WAYS TO SUBSCRIBE!
1) Send in the subscription order form from this book OR
2) Log on to: www.shonenjump.com OR
3) Call 1-800-541-7919
*Canada price for 12 issues: $41.95 USD, including GST, HST, and QST. US/CAN orders only. Allow 6-8 weeks for delivery.
BLEACH © 2001 by Tite Kubo/SHUEISHA Inc. NARUTO © 1999 by Masashi Kishimoto/SHUEISHA Inc.
GINTAMA © 2003 by Hideaki Sorachi/SHUEISHA Inc. ONE PIECE © 1997 by Eiichiro Oda/SHUEISHA Inc.